FINANCIAL POST

GUIDE TO | **INVESTING**
AND PERSONAL FINANCE

Financial Post Guide to Investing and Personal Finance is published
by *Financial Post,* a division of *National Post,* 1450 Don Mills Road,
Don Mills, Ontario, Canada M3B 2X7.

Cover illustration by Nicholas Vitacco.
Inside illustrations by Nicholas Vitacco, Tony Smith
and David Middleton.
Reformatting and production supervision by Zaxis Publishing Inc.
Printed in Canada.

ISBN 1-555-251-020-4

CONTENTS

EDITOR'S NOTE   **5**

1. GETTING STARTED   **7**
How to define your investment goals and get into the stock market.
How to read stock tables and company reports. How to set up an account.
Understanding dividends.

2. UNDERSTANDING EQUITIES   **35**
The basics of buying and selling equities. Block trades. Bid and ask tables.
North American indexes. Foreign market strategies. Technical analysis.

3. BEYOND EQUITIES   **63**
Understanding derivatives. Investment strategies using options,
warrants, shorts and REITs. Commodities markets. Futures and indexes.

4. CURRENCIES, DEBT AND THE ECONOMY   **89**
Short-term securities. The attraction of bonds.
Foreign exchange investments. Bank of Canada.

5. MUTUAL FUNDS   **113**
Mutual funds defined. What they are and how they work.
No loads versus loads. Reading *FP*'s fund tables to track performance and risk.

6. INVESTMENT PLANNING   **147**
The basics of investment strategies and styles. Bonds.
Building a balanced portfolio. GICs. Asset allocation and diversification. Equities.

7. TAX PLANNING   **179**
Tax basics. Measuring after-tax investment returns.
Income splitting. Drawing up a strategy. Trusts.

8. RETIREMENT PLANNING   **209**
Estate planning. Calculate the costs of your retirement. RRSPs.
Maximizing foreign content. Carry-forward options.

9. PERSONAL PLANNING   **241**
Strategy. Protecting your credit rating. Mortgage options.
Buying a home and renting. Financing your family's education. Bankruptcy.

10. INSURANCE PLANNING   **273**
The fundamentals. Home, car and travel insurance. Group plans.
Disability, critical illness and long-term care insurance. ABCs of life insurance.

GLOSSARY OF TERMS   **305**

**HILE MANY OF OUR LONG-TIME READERS** are seasoned investors with considerable knowledge of financial markets, others, including new readers since the launch of the *National Post*, are new to the game. Some may be active equity investors but have no idea of how currencies, for instance, are traded. It is with this thought that we bring you *Financial Post Guide to Investing and Personal Finance*. This book is a pull together of a hugely popular 10-part series that ran in the *FP* in the spring of 1998. It covered how equity, mutual fund, debt and currency markets operate and how they are affected by government policy and the economy. Tables and charts found in the *FP*'s Investing section – now a separate section in the *National Post* – are used to illustrate how the many investment vehicles that now exist work.

We have called on some of our top writers, including William Hanley, Patrick Bloomfield, Sonita Horvitch, David Thomas, Susan Heinrich and Arthur Drache, to provide overviews in their areas of expertise. Former *FP* staffers Peter Galloway and Bud Jorgensen, freelancer Olev Edur and *FP* mutual funds editor Matthew Elder stepped in to do much of the editing and some writing. *FP*'s Thea Partridge and Jeff Wasserman, as well as freelancers Tony Smith and David Middleton, contributed to the layout and art. Thanks also to Peter Vermeltfoort and Chris Watson for their work on the production side. While it is important to make money, it is equally important to preserve it. That is where the personal finance end of the book comes in. Along with a series of overviews from the *FP*'s Jonathan Chevreau, we have dipped into our storehouse of already published articles to provide a full package across the personal finance spectrum, covering tax, retirement, insurance and investment planning.

Whether it is mortgage options, the ABCs of life insurance or income splitting, it is all there. At the back of the book is a helpful glossary, defining many of the hundreds of investment and personal finance terms mentioned. We hope you enjoy the book and find it useful. Happy investing and saving.

DOUG KELLY, *FP* Investing Editor, *National Post*

CHAPTER 1

GETTING | STARTED

- How to define your investment goals and get into the stock market

- How to read stock tables and company reports

- How to set up an account

- Understanding dividends

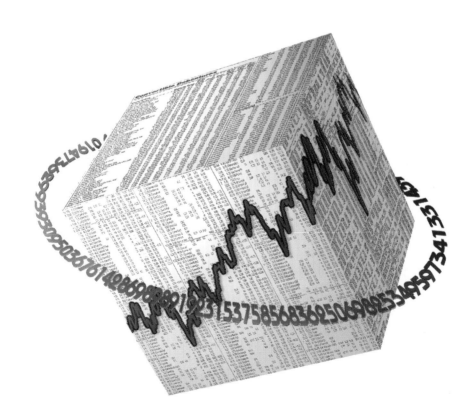

IMPROVING YOUR ODDS

IN THE LOTTERY OF LIFE | BY WILLIAM HANLEY

THE FIRST KNOWN RECORD of the saying "a penny saved is a penny earned" is from 1640. And it pops up regularly in slightly different guises throughout English literature, from Dickens to P.G. Wodehouse to Alison Lurie. It is a compelling theme through the ages and one that is even more compelling today. If you work hard and work smart to earn a living, try to hang on to as much of it as possible. And what you hang on to, put to work. Indeed, as the millennium approaches and as millions of Canadian baby boomers begin to face retirement, saving and investing has become a national pastime, if not an obsession, for many people concerned that state and company pensions may not provide them with the "golden years" lifestyle they expect. But despite a maelstrom of information from every possible source about investment products and plans, studies show that many Canadians start investing too little, too late, with the consequence of facing older age with not enough to show for a lifetime of hard work.

WHEN INVESTING WAS SIMPLER

While the investment universe has exploded in the 1990s, with Canadians forsaking traditional investment vehicles such as GICs for the juicier returns on mutual funds, most people's investing "careers" began when they were children with that first bank account: Your mom or dad took you down to the bank with that birthday cheque from granddad or with the precious proceeds from your piggy bank and you opened a savings account. You added a few dollars here and there, and every time you went to the teller window, the bank book was updated and regularly there was a bit extra added to the total, as if by magic.

Back in the 1950s and '60s, that magic amounted to about 3% per year on a savings account, less on a chequing/savings account. Back then, bank interest and Canada Savings Bonds were basically the known investment universe for two or three generations of Canadians. Many of the ideas on investing held by those generations were forged in

There are two rules of investing. First, don't lose any money.
Second, see rule No.1.

the Dirty '30s of the Great Depression, when deflation made cash king and a penny saved was indeed a penny earned.

In the '60s, for instance, the Canadian stock market seemed a strange hybrid of widows' and orphans' stocks such as Bell Canada and spectacular speculative scams like Windfall Mines. Mutual funds, such as they were, were soon to fall from grace via the IOS scandal.

INFLATION TRIGGERS THE RISE AND FALL OF INTEREST RATES

But that era also brought two watershed personal financial developments for Canadians: the Canada Pension Plan and registered retirement savings plans. The CPP, now undergoing a desperately needed overhaul, was a good idea badly executed. It gave many a false sense of security about retirement and the monies put into it were squandered on general government spending. RRSPs were a fine idea, a tax shelter for everyman and everywoman who could manage to put something aside.

After the relative stability of the '60s, Canadian investors were thrust into the scary new inflationary world of the 1970s, which was marked by a falling stock market and rising interest rates. By the end of the decade the inflation rate was in double digits,

mortgage rates were approaching 20% and some five-year guaranteed investment certificates were paying an astounding 21% a year. Investors didn't quite know how well
they were doing, and whether they were on track.

It took much of the 1980s to unwind the great inflationary spiral. The stock market
recovered, only to crash in October 1987. But the groundwork was painstakingly being
laid for a new era of investing in a relatively inflation-free environment, even though
many retirees yearned for the days of 15%-plus returns on their fixed investments.

The 1990s have felt a lot like the '60s in terms of investing. Interest rates have fallen to
their lowest level in 40 years, slashing returns on GICs and the like to levels last seen about
40 years ago. And tame inflation has provided a vibrant backdrop for the stock market,
which in turn has produced what can only be described as a mutual funds mania.

SOME INVESTORS PREFER TO PLAY IT SAFE WITH GUARANTEED RETURNS

At the time of writing, the stock market was struggling to stay in touch with the record
highs reached in early October 1997 and interest rates were on the rise. Most investors
were saying they were in equity mutual funds for the very long haul, willing to weather
a possible bear market on the belief that financial assets were still the investment of wise
choice for the millennium and beyond.

Warren Buffett, the world's second richest private citizen after Microsoft Corp.'s Bill
Gates, has been a relentless acquisitor of stocks through his Berkshire Hathaway Inc.
holding company, providing investors with returns approaching 25% a year for almost
30 years. While the Wizard of Omaha's investment strategies may seem beyond the
realm of everyman and everywoman, he dispenses much down-to-earth advice in Berkshire's annual report. "There are two rules of investing," Buffett says. "First, don't lose
any money. Second, see rule No. 1."

As glib and folksy as that might sound, keeping what you save is an essential cornerstone of any investment plan. And that's why some people, especially those retired or
approaching retirement, are not comfortable with the risk-reward equation in equities,
preferring to stick with a guaranteed fixed return even if it means missing out on a bull
market in stocks.

PICKING THE RIGHT INVESTMENT CAN SEEM LIKE A GAME OF LOTTERY

Over the long term, studies show that returns on stocks beat returns on all other investments, including bonds, real estate and any number of more exotic instruments. But
that doesn't mean the formula works all the time.

The most prescient and luckiest Canadian investor would have bought stocks in the
'60s, switched into real estate in the '70s, bought gold bullion in 1979, then GICs in
1980, switched back into stocks in 1982, bought some real estate in 1985, sold it in 1989,
and then concentrated on picking and holding stocks since. And all the above as much
as possible in an RRSP.

This, of course, would have been the equivalent of winning the lottery. While Generation X has struggled with rising taxes and falling real incomes, it can be argued that the

generation of Canadians born after the Second World War actually did win in the lottery of life. The baby boomers grew into adulthood in a period of unparalleled prosperity in the world in general and Canada in particular. Most should have been able to save, invest and build assets as a bulwark against any eventuality.

It's ironic that the Xers, immersed in the new investment culture despite tighter times, are far more attuned to the need to save than were their profligate boomer parents.

THE KEY TO SUCCESS IS AN INVESTMENT STRATEGY

Meanwhile, there's still time for laggard boomers to get it right even though, for many people, getting that penny to save and earn is more difficult. There's no excuse for not having a strategy, a plan to live by and with.

Read on. And become your own best investment counsellor.

WHO ISSUES STOCKS AND BONDS, AND WHY

Securities are the fibres that knit together the economy. Stocks represent an ownership stake – literally a share of a company. Bondholders are lenders.

Those who need money – companies and governments – are issuers of securities. Private companies are those in which equity is closely held, either by one or more individuals or by other companies. Going public means giving up some control, in part because the ownership is spread more broadly but also because corporations that sell securities to the public are subject to rules on disclosure of information and other matters.

After a stock is listed on a stock exchange, investors are free to sell their new shares, and trading begins. The company doesn't make money when these shares are traded, although the higher visibility generated through open trading can enhance its profile and credibility.

Companies raise money for a variety of purposes, such as expansion projects or to take over another company, and this can be done with equity or debt.

Governments can't issue stock but they too need funds to finance major public works, such as public buildings and highways. Issuing bonds is a way of spreading the capital cost of these projects over their useful life. Crown corporations, such as electric utilities, are an extension of governments and their debt financings are a guaranteed obligation of taxpayers.

The short-term cash needs of corporations and governments can be covered by borrowing from a financial institution and senior governments can issue treasury bills to meet their short-term requirements. For longer-term borrowing, bonds are the preferred route.

But interest on debt is an unyielding obligation and too much debt can cripple a company. So, a growing company will issue stock to maintain a healthy balance between debt and equity. Common stockholders, even those who hold only a tiny fraction of total shares issued, still have a legal right to a say in a company's business.

Bondholder rights are governed by the terms of the contract under which the bond is issued. Bondholders stand ahead of shareholders if a company is in distress.

MARKET SUMMARY | TABLES AND CHARTS

The summary tables on the front of the FP Investing section of the *National Post* cover the daily highlights of key markets – **stocks, bonds, commodities and foreign exchange.** The information in these tables is available in greater detail within the Investing section, but these tables provide an overview at a glance on general trends in these markets. An important feature of this series are the charts showing trends over the last 12 months and the previous two weeks.

These tables show benchmark indexes (except for the currencies and three high-profile commodities). For all of the entries, the close is for the latest trading day and there is a range of trading values for the last 52 weeks. Other columns track the changes over the last 12 months and the calendar year to date.

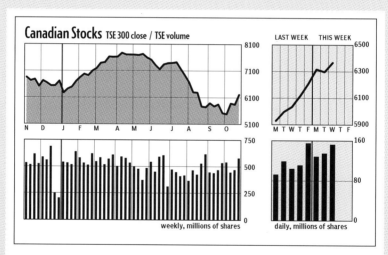

Index	Close	Net chg	% chg	52W high	52W low	—Yr over yr— net chg	% chg	—Yr to date— net chg	% chg
TSE 300	6365.76	+69.25	+1.10	7835.75	5325.79	−561.30	−8.10	−333.68	−4.98
TSE 200	368.01	+4.64	+1.28	473.29	311.44	−78.95	−17.66	−36.86	−9.10
TSE 100	390.01	+4.11	+1.07	477.64	323.63	−23.28	−5.63	−16.26	−4.00
Toronto 35	351.11	+4.84	+1.40	427.10	289.62	−9.26	−2.57	−8.23	−2.29
ME Market Portfolio	3269.23	+44.39	+1.38	3971.66	2719.24	−128.61	−3.79	−135.23	−3.97
VSE Composite	403.64	+1.94	+0.48	769.78	381.97	−366.14	−47.56	−214.84	−34.74
ASE Combined	1738.14	+9.85	+0.57	2498.76	1681.55	−739.39	−29.84	−501.72	−22.40

INVESTORS IN STOCKS HAVE TWO BASIC OBJECTIVES

• Income from dividends provides investors with a portion of a company's earnings. Dividend policies are set by a company's directors and payments are stated in a specific amount for each share. Most blue chip companies pay regular dividends but the board is under no obligation to pay. The boards of many companies prefer to keep most or all of the profits to reinvest in the growth of the firm.

• Buying shares at a lower price and selling high provides investors with a capital gain. Start-up companies provide investors with the opportunity for big gains if growth prospects are realized.

INVESTORS IN BONDS HAVE ESSENTIALLY THE SAME GOALS BUT THE MECHANICS ARE DIFFERENT

• Interest income is fixed with conventional bonds and cannot be changed.

• Buyers of new bonds get the face value returned when the bonds mature but those who buy bonds in the secondary market can have capital gains or losses. Because the interest payment is fixed, the price of a bond will rise or fall as interest rates change. When rates go up, the price falls and when rates decline the price rises.

Tax treatment is among the many factors that go into an investment decision. Capital gains have a different status than dividend or interest income and stocks can be treated differently from bonds. Securities trade in markets that are regulated by tradition and law. Most stocks are traded through recognized exchanges, which are public markets that bring together buyer and seller. Companies must conform to certain listing standards, which vary from exchange to exchange. Thus the reputation of the exchange is an important factor in stock selection by investors. Bonds mainly trade over the counter, which means the market is a network of banks and investment dealers. National government bonds are the benchmark securities in this market and governments are among the direct participants in bond trades. Both governments and corporations rely on the dealer network in raising money but government treasury agencies do more of the work in-house. Distribution of government securities is through a group of "primary dealers," which includes the major banks and brokerage firms. When a company goes to the market for funds, it usually picks one or more of the investment dealers for advice on the size and price of the securities issue. The dealers act as underwriters – buying the new shares and then selling them to the public. The dealers' profit, or underwriting fee, is the difference between their buying price and selling price.

PREPARING A PROSPECTUS IS THE FIRST STEP TO ISSUING NEW SHARES

Once the conditions of the offer are established, the company and the investment dealer must make sure the offer complies with provincial securities regulations. Requirements include preparation of a prospectus – a document that provides potential investors with the information they need to make an informed investment decision. Once the prospectus has been accepted by provincial securities commissions, sale of the new shares can begin.

ECONOMIC SIGNPOSTS TO INVESTMENT

When setting out to invest, the road map is a chart of the economy. Stocks that are good investments in boom times may get marked down more than the average when a slow-down arrives. At a more fundamental level, identifying the stage of the business cycle helps determine whether to emphasize equities or fixed income securities when making changes to a portfolio.

Throughout the industrial era there has been an ebb and flow to economic activity. Central bank management of monetary policy has created a sense of confidence that the modern economy can avoid boom-and-bust excesses but few will maintain the business cycle has been eliminated. Conventional economic analysis divides the business cycle into five stages; they are expansion, peak, contraction, trough and recovery. They can be defined in the following terms:

Expansion: This is a growth period characterized by stable prices, rising corporate prof-its, healthy job creation and a bullish sentiment for stocks. Interest rates begin to creep higher, which means a decline in bond prices

Peak: As an expansion progresses, signs of excess begin to show up in the economy. Business inventories or construction activity get too far ahead of demand and a tight labor market leads to inflationary wage demands. Overstocking leads to price cutting and labor unrest leads to strikes. The result of these developments is falling profits and a weakness in stock prices. Interest rates rise as the economy peaks, so bond prices fall.

Contraction: Too much of a good thing at the peak causes a correction and a severe cor-rection is a recession. Household confidence suffers during this phase and people save more. A higher savings rate means the use of money shifts away from consumption and toward investment.

The practical result of a bigger pool of savings is a decline in interest rates. An ero-sion in corporate profitability affects stock prices. Falling interest rates during this part of the cycle means that bond prices rise.

Trough: The slowdown means business has much less room to raise prices, inventory lev-els are run down and wage demands moderate. But, eventually, deferred spending by consumers and businesses creates pent-up demand and at the bottom of the cycle there is a shift toward greater consumption. Interest rates stabilize and stock prices begin to anticipate a rebound in profits.

Recovery: This is the preamble to a new expansion. Economists define the recovery peri-od to mean the length of time it takes for the total value of goods and services produced by the economy (gross domestic product) to reach its pre-recession peak. Employment grows and inventory is restocked during this period. Interest rates remain stable and stocks start pricing in rising earnings.

Within the business cycle, prices of certain stock groups will behave differently. "Cyclicals" have a special relationship to swings in the economy. For example, resource stocks tend to lead the cycle.

Demand for basic commodities precedes an upturn in economic activity because corporate managers in processing industries will stock up on the raw materials when they see signs of improving demand.

FIRST OF ALL, DO SOME SECURITIES CHECKS

 Making money on the stock market is easy – buy low, sell high. Deciding when to buy or sell is the difficult part and that involves research and experience. Investors can rely on professionals for these attributes but it is always a good idea to know where to find basic information and analyse the significance of that information.

Research on securities is divided into two broad categories – fundamental and technical.

Fundamental analysis involves careful study of an issuer of a security – past records of sales, earnings, assets, markets, management performance and other factors. The issuer can be a company or a government. When looking at provincial government bonds, for example, "sales" could mean revenue from a dominant industry in the province. A study of the fundamentals also includes an analysis of the issuer's performance compared with similar issuers. Another aspect of the fundamentals is how the issuer is affected by economic trends.

TECHNICAL ANALYSIS MEASURES MARKET PERFORMANCE

Technical analysis is the study of the security itself or the indexes that measure market performance – the patterns of past price moves and their predictive ability. In simple terms, it's a study of momentum and how to spot the turning points in price moves. Trading volume is an important element and technicians also make extensive use of averages in price or volume to smooth out day-to-day variations.

QUANTITATIVE ANALYSIS MAKES USE OF SPREADSHEETS AND DATABASES

A third category of research is "quantitative analysis," which is an invention of the computer age. This approach crunches huge volumes of numbers with spreadsheets and databases, using both technical and fundamental factors.

High tech methods of analysing securities tend to be the preserve of those who trade frequently, sometimes in and out of a stock on the same day. But heavy trading is for those with big portfolios because transaction fees eat up the profits from small trades.

For many small investors, the best approach is to buy the shares of good companies for the long term. Basic information is readily available. Financial newspapers are a key resource. They follow major corporate stories as well as routine developments.

Shareholders receive regular financial reports on a company's operations but prospective shareholders are well advised to review recent disclosure documents. They can be obtained from a company's investor relations office, a brokerage firm or a large

COMPANY MEETINGS | TABLE

Annual and special meetings are events that give ordinary shareholders a chance to see senior managers in a public forum and ask questions. The agenda for the meeting is set out in advance in an information circular. Most of these meetings include a report from the chief executive.

COMPANY MEETINGS

Listings supplied by Toronto Stock Exchange, Montreal Exchange

Tues., Oct. 27, 1998

Antoro Resources Inc. (Annual Special)
Marriott Château Champlain, Montreal   10 a.m.
Espalau Mining Corp. (General Special)
Hotel Confortel, Val-d'Or, Que.   10 a.m

COMPANIES IN THE NEWS | INDEX

On the second page of the Financial Post section, a Companies in the News index directs readers to stories that mention companies in that day's Financial Post. Shareholders use this index to monitor news developments affecting companies whose shares they own.

COMPANIES IN THE NEWS

ABC Inc.	C13	Communications	D3	Apple Computer Inc.	C1, D3
AFM Hospitality Corp.	C2	Alliance Pipeline	C6	Austrian Airlines AG	C2
Air Canada	C2, C6	Allican Resources Inc.	C2	Ballard Power Systems	D2
Air India	C2	Amber Energy Inc.	C10	Banro Resource Corp.	C2
Alberta Energy Co.	C10	Amoco Corp.	C10	BelAir Energy Corp.	C2
Allelix Biopharmaceuticals	C4	Anglo American Corp.	C2	Berkshire Hathaway Inc.	C16
Alliance-Atlantis		AngloGold Ltd.	C2	Bezeq Ltd.	C2

Page number

public library. Most corporations have Internet sites. Newswire services on the Web disseminate corporate press releases.

The latest editions of the annual report, the annual information form and the quarterly statement all contain an array of information on the company that is both financial and operational. Other useful documents in doing research on a company are a prospectus, if a company has done a recent financing, and reports from credit rating agencies on the company's securities.

INDEXES MEASURE A MARKET'S PROGRESS

On the question of "How high is high?" the answer in the stock market comes from what is known as an index.

Most equity indexes are designed as a proxy for trends and magnitude of price changes. If an index goes up by 10%, that means stock prices have gone up by roughly 10% and dividends that arrive during a period of rising prices are a bonus.

Bond indexes generally are designed to measure total return, which is a combination of interest income and changes in bond prices. There are a few total return indexes for stocks but most people watch those indexes that track capital gains or losses.

SOME INDEXES ARE MORE INFLUENTIAL THAN OTHERS
AND THERE ARE TWO BASIC REASONS FOR FOLLOWING AN INDEX

• For the average investor, the reason is the index is seen as a broad indicator of market direction in a national market. In Canada, the Toronto Stock Exchange 300 composite index fills that role and in the U.S. it is the Dow Jones average of 30 industrials.

• For professionals in the securities industry, the key indexes are those on which futures and options are traded. For them, these indexes are an investment class as well as market indicators. In North America, the most widely followed index in this category is the Standard & Poor's index of 500 U.S. stocks. The Toronto Stock Exchange 35-stock index also has futures and options but these markets tend to be relatively small and do not attract anything like the investor interest the S&P 500 does.

THE PERFORMANCE OF A STOCK IS TRACKED IN SUBINDEXES

Broad-based indexes like the TSE 300 have subindexes – 14 in the case of the TSE 300 – and these classifications allow investors to track the performance of a stock of one company in relation to the general trend for its sector. Often, those subindexes will also be divided into categories.

THE DOW | IS DIFFERENT

Computers now calculate stock indexes on the run and the high/low points for the day represent real prices at that time. The Dow Jones average is an exception. The Dow is the oldest stock index in use and the reason for the difference is historical. In the early days – long before computers – Dow index values were calculated once a day. From 1884 to 1915, prices of the stocks in the index were stated as a percentage of the par value, and at that time US$50 was a standard par value. Thus, the early index numbers were averages of these percentages. Calculations of highs and lows for the Dow didn't begin until Oct. 1, 1928. Those numbers were calculated by using the average of the high price and the low price for each stock during the trading day. Now the indexes are calculated with computers, the tick-by-tick calculation method adjusts for the highs and lows for component stocks as they are set during the day.

In the U.S., the S&P 500 fills the role of sector benchmark.

The TSE 300 is designed to broadly mirror the composition of the Canadian economy but weightings of the various sectors also reflect the popularity of certain stock groups among investors. For example, the TSE gold subindex accounted for 7% of the composite index when the price of bullion was close to US$300 an ounce but this group made up more than 10% of the index a year earlier when the gold price was above US$400 an ounce.

WATCHING THE PERCENTAGE CHANGES OF AN INDEX ALLOWS FOR COMPARISONS

Changes in the level of an index are measured in points but the significance of a change of, say, 100 points will vary. A move of that size is substantial if the starting point is 500 but negligible if it is 10,000. For that reason, people watch for percentage changes, especially when making comparisons among markets.

The Dow Jones industrial average is the world's most widely watched stock market index, in part because it goes back to 1884. The modern structure of the Dow index dates to 1928, but it still has value as a measure of stock market performance over more than a century and technical analysts follow the Dow for its historical patterns.

The TSE 35 index is roughly comparable with the structure of the Dow because it includes 35 large-capitalization frequently traded Canadian stocks. But the short history of the TSE 35 – it was begun in 1987 – makes it less useful than the TSE 300, which was begun in 1977. The TSE has used old trading records to backdate the 300 to 1956.

Other Canadian exchanges have indexes that reflect general direction. They include the Vancouver Stock Exchange composite index and the Montreal Exchange market portfolio.

In the U.S., the Nasdaq composite index is weighted to technology stocks and regional companies that represent the broad base of U.S. industry.

Among widely followed overseas stock indexes are the Financial Times 100-stock index in London, the Nikkei 225-stock average in Tokyo, the Dax 30-stock index in Frankfurt, the CAC 40-stock index in Paris and the All-Ordinaries 330-stock index in Australia.

WHERE YOUR INFORMATION IS COMING FROM

Pssst! Wanna buy a hot stock?

Lots of people have advice on investing and one piece of good advice is to look carefully at the source of the information.

A famous stock market story is attributed to Joe Kennedy, patriarch of the U.S. political family, who made a fortune on Wall Street in the 1920s. Kennedy started selling after a shoeshine boy offered him a stock tip. He concluded the market was overextended if shoeshine boys were buying.

Stocks often are sold, not bought, and the selling usually is done by promoters. This

North American and international index tables provide a broad overview of trends in markets around the world. Toronto and Montreal index listings also include breakdowns of subindexes and the TSE 300 list shows all the industry categories within the sector subindexes.

THE HIGH AND LOW points for each trading day during the past 52 weeks is the intraday reading. The 52-week high is usually different from the closing high or low for that period. Computers track each change in the combined value of the basket of stocks in each index as it constantly changes throughout the trading day (in the jargon of the investment community, there is a tick-by-tick change in the index).

VOLUME is the number of shares traded in stocks in the index. Volume is stated in board lots, which means units of 100 shares. Most exchanges count a buy or sell of 100 shares as a volume of one board lot. But Nasdaq, the U.S. interdealer network, counts a buy and a sell of 100 shares as a volume of two board lots.

North American indexes

52W high	52W low	Index	% Yield	P/E	Vol 00s	High	Low	Close	Net change	% change
Toronto Stock Exchange										
7835.75	5325.79	**TSE 300**	1.70	25.73	891682	6313.52	6261.30	6296.51	−19.15	−0.3
4423.92	2412.49	**Metals & Minerals**	2.23	31.67	43786	3146.01	3110.14	3146.01	+38.22	+1.2
4593.37	2458.72	Integrated Mines	2.42	20.23	22626	3354.72	3308.92	3339.16	+29.33	+0.9
2609.80	1260.90	Mining	1.34	n.a.	21160	1480.03	1437.60	1480.03	+41.08	+2.9
7951.86	4228.88	**Gold & Precious Mnrl**	0.67	n.a.	64787	6529.02	6461.50	6510.32	−59.83	−0.9
7723.91	4352.47	**Oil & Gas**	0.80	48.38	151515	5512.37	5450.73	5512.37	+48.73	+0.9
9729.68	6488.62	Integrated Oils	1.96	23.32	13864	7754.40	7665.60	7754.40	+8.76	+0.1
6938.94	3827.64	Oil & Gas Producers	0.29	n.a.	133945	4991.32	4907.25	4987.53	+62.41	+1.3

YIELD is the dividend yield for the index or subindex (the weighted average dividend in relation to the weighted average price).

THE CLOSE is the index reading at the end of the trading day.

P/E is the price-to-earnings ratio for the index or sub-index (the weighted average earnings per share in relation to the weighted average price).

INTERNATIONAL INDEXES

— 52 week — high	low		Close	Net chg	% chg
Japan					
17264.34	12879.97	Nikkei	14599.23	186.23	1.29
1300.30	980.11	Topix	1113.42	5.77	0.52
Britain					
3984.00	2806.80	FT Ords	3292.60	-15.30	-0.46
6179.00	4648.70	FTSE 100	5474.00	-28.70	-0.52
5458.80	1647.57	FT 500	2590.71	-13.13	-0.50
2885.17	2166.07	FT All Shr	2517.70	-13.30	-0.53
Germany					
1940.80	1250.50	FAZ	1502.71	-7.05	-0.47

NET CHANGE is in points and % change is that point move expressed as a percentage. For tables published during the week, the change is from the previous day's close. Tables in weekend editions have weekly summaries for the indexes with change from the previous week, a month ago and a year ago.

is a recognized role in the securities business and, in the best light, a promoter raises money for a start-up venture that might otherwise not be able to find financing.

IT IS BUYER BEWARE WHEN SEARCHING STOCK TIPS ON THE INTERNET

Many of Canada's established mining houses started out as penny stock ventures under the guidance of a promoter and the early investors struck paydirt when the company found commercial grades of ore. But prospecting is a high risk business and over the years the majority of the juniors don't strike it rich.

There is a similar failure rate for fledgling high tech firms. A modern forum for stock tips is the Internet. Chat lines are a regular source of investment tips and readers should be aware the format of the Net makes it easy for unscrupulous promoters to conceal their identity to casual readers.

WHO ARE THE BROKERS AND WHAT DO THEY DO?

Broker is a term that covers a lot of ground and investors need to be clear on whose interests are being represented by the various specialists in the investment industry. Traders, corporate finance specialists, fund managers and salespeople all fit into the general category of brokers and their roles in the business are much different.

As well, the roles of the firms can be different. Chartered banks now have a dominant position in the securities industry and some banks have more than one brokerage subsidiary to cover different roles.

TRADITIONALLY, A BROKER ACTS AS AN INTERMEDIARY BETWEEN BUYER AND SELLER

The traditional brokerage function is to serve as an intermediary between buyer and seller. This can be done by discount brokers, firms that simply execute a transaction when an investor makes his or her own decisions.

When research is added to the brokerage function, the investor pays higher commissions because advice is part of the service. Research departments provide recommendations on which stocks to buy or sell and on appropriate weighting in a portfolio among stocks, bonds and other types of investments.

CHINESE WALLS ARE INFORMATION BARRIERS THAT PROTECT CONFLICTS OF INTEREST

Large investment dealers also represent the issuers of securities, which leads to an industry concept called "Chinese walls" in Canada and "firewalls" in the U.S. These are information barriers within a firm that are designed to isolate potential conflicts of interest between, for instance, a firm's corporate finance department, which is representing a company issuing stock, and its investment advisers, who are selling the shares to clients.

PORTFOLIO MANAGERS TAILOR THE PORTFOLIO TO THE CLIENT

Big firms also trade for their own accounts. This is standard practice in bond trading, as trading by the large firms provides liquidity to the market and gives the firm an inventory of bonds from which to fill small orders. Most stock trading is done to fill client orders but specialist traders within a firm can hold inventories from day to day.

Investors who are not comfortable with making decisions themselves can turn to portfolio managers. For small investors, that means mutual funds. A large portfolio can be managed by an investment specialist who tailors the portfolio to the client. Portfolio managers charge fees for their services and their costs include trading fees. Typically, these fund managers are among those who negotiate cut-rate fees for stock trades.

When a client buys or sells a security directly, there is a commission on the transaction. A portion goes to the sales agent and the rest goes to the firm to cover its business costs, which includes salaries and commissions for traders who actually do the share deal for the client.

Fees vary from firm to firm, and clients who do a lot of business often can negotiate commissions. In Canada, brokers must complete the Canadian Securities Course – a comprehensive study course dealing with stocks, bonds, analysis of company financial statements and other securities-related matters.

THE LOWDOWN | ON DIVIDENDS

Dividends are the returns on an equity stake. Dividend announcements may also affect stock prices if there is a change in a regular pattern, if a company that has not paid dividends begins paying, if a dividend-paying company omits a dividend or if there is a change in the rate.

Stock dividends will be announced by companies in advance of payment. **The pay date** indicates when the dividend will be paid. **The record column** indicates that investors who were on record as owners of the companies' shares on that date will receive the dividend.

Stocks will trade ex-dividend (without dividend) from the second business day before the record date. The ex-dividend date is significant if shares are bought or sold around dividend time because the share price normally drops when the dividend is paid (a market adjustment for the payout). The calculation of ex-dividend date has to do with the fact that a stock trade is settled on the third business day after the transaction. Thus, the issue of whether the dividend goes to the new owner or the old owner is based on when the money changes hands in a stock transaction.

DIVIDENDS

Figures supplied by FP DataGroup

Details	Dividend amount	Pay date	Record date
Dividends declared			
Regular			
Caldwell PtrA	.15	Nov 16	Nov 6
General Motor	u.50	Dec 10	Nov 12
Nth Wst Fund	.25	Dec 15	Nov 15
Utility cl C	.1085	Nov 30	Nov 17
Stocks ex-dividend			
Thursday			
Avista RE un	.065	Nov 16	Nov 9
Metro-Rich A	.055	Dec 2	Nov 9
Mobil	u.57	Dec 10	Nov 9
Moffat Comm	.06	Nov 30	Nov 9
Oceanex InmIR	.0937	Nov 16	Nov 9
Power Fin Bpf	.4375	Nov 30	Nov 9
RealFund unit	.115	Nov 16	Nov 9
Royal Host	i.085	Nov 16	Nov 9
Teleglobe	.037	Dec 31	Nov 9

FROM THE BIG FLOOR TO THE SMALL SCREEN

Many people think of stocks and big trading floors when they think of the word exchange, but these days the markets for securities mainly are interlinked networks of computers. Exchanges still exist as intermediaries in the trading of securities and some markets still have large floor operations. More and more, though, the big volume in different markets is being done by trading desks at investment firms and banks.

Computer screens carry offers to buy or sell and the deals are done directly on the screens. Payments are simply electronic transfers and credit lines are regulated by advance authorizations when traders are assigned passwords to sign on to the systems.

Stocks mainly trade through exchanges while bond trading is done over the counter (OTC), which means transactions are among dealers.

DERIVATIVES ENCOMPASS A BROAD RANGE OF FINANCIAL PRODUCTS

Derivatives are a combination of the two. Exchange traded derivatives, such as index and bond futures, tend to serve as pricing guides for their respective markets. Over-the-counter derivatives tend to be specialized hedging arrangements to cover foreign exchange or interest rate risks.

Large financial institutions – generally banks and investment dealers – dominate the over-the-counter market because a large capital base is needed to operate at this level. At the other end of the spectrum, though, are over-the-counter markets in speculative junior stocks. The penny stock market has been a persistent headache for securities regulators because of the potential for abuse or fraud in OTC selling to unsophisticated investors.

A STOCK EXCHANGE HAS REGULATORY POWERS OVER BROKERAGE FIRMS

Part of the value of a stock exchange to investment firms is that an exchange's reputation can give credibility to a broker's services because the exchange has regulatory powers over the conduct of brokerage firms.

Seatholders (the firms that trade on an exchange) must adhere to exchange rules of financial strength, trading practices and business standards.

Typically, a large Canadian brokerage firm will have seats on the Canadian exchanges, the New York Stock Exchange and other major U.S. exchanges. Some have seats on other world exchanges. The Toronto Stock Exchange is by far the largest stock exchange in Canada, accounting for just over four-fifths of the value of all domestic trading.

Bay Street is a nickname for the TSE, just as Wall Street means the New York Stock Exchange to most people. From 1937 to 1983 the TSE was located on Bay Street in Toronto's financial district.

EACH OF CANADA'S FIVE STOCK EXCHANGES SPECIALIZES IN DIFFERENT AREAS

The TSE, founded in 1852, moved to York and Adelaide streets in Toronto in 1983. There is no longer a trading floor for equities, although the TSE has a floor in another building for futures and options trading. The TSE also runs an interdealer market called Canadian Dealing Network, which mainly lists stocks of speculative junior companies.

The Montreal Exchange dates to 1874 and its stock trading operations are mainly in shares of Quebec-based companies. The ME has carved out a specialty in derivatives trading and its futures contract on three-month bankers' acceptance notes has gained wide acceptance as a pricing guideline in the money market. Trading in derivatives is done in pits on the exchange's trading floor.

The Vancouver Stock Exchange is known for its listings of speculative shares of start-up companies in the resource and technology sectors. The VSE began operation in 1907 and since 1990 trading has been conducted through a fully computerized system.

The Alberta Stock Exchange was founded in 1913 as the Calgary Stock Exchange. It deals mainly with Alberta-based companies and many are resource businesses.

The Winnipeg Stock Exchange is Canada's smallest, with trading in shares of a few local companies representing less than 0.1% of the dollar value of business on all Canadian exchanges.

BUILDING A CROWD AND MAKING A MARKET

The "crowd" is an important concept in securities trading. It means having a big enough group of buyers and sellers to ensure the best price is set when a trade is done.

Building a crowd for trading has a long history, from early trading in farm animals through the "curb" market in London, where stock trading was originally done on the street.

Brokerage firms have traders who buy or sell on behalf of their clients but the crowd can be small if a company's shares are not being traded actively.

When there is little trading, a market is illiquid and an investor risks not getting the best price.

Over the years, securities markets have adopted various practices to build liquidity.

The New York Stock Exchange has a group of traders called "$2 brokers." They are independent traders who trade for a fee on behalf of brokerage firms. Their fee used to be US$2 for a board lot (100 shares) and by spreading the business around, a firm could move a large stock order without disrupting the market.

Stock exchanges also have "locals" as traders. They trade for their own accounts and may be managers of pools of investment funds.

MARKET-MAKERS STEP IN TO BUY OR SELL AND MAINTAIN LIQUIDITY

Specialists are a key element in ensuring liquidity on Canadian exchanges. They're also known as registered traders or market-makers and their role is to stand ready to buy or sell up to a pre-set limit.

QUARTERLY SNAPSHOT | TABLES

The Quarterly Snapshot is a series of 10 sets of tables published on the first Saturday after the end of each quarterly period. These tables cover key financial and market developments for leading public companies in Canada.

TOP TSE % WINNERS at *MM.DD.98*

Rk.	Stock	Ticker	Volume 00s	Prev. quarter	Recent close	— 52-week — high	— 52-week — low	Net change
1	Hyal Pharma	HPC	223233	0.31	1.29	5.60	0.17	+316.1
2	Napier Int Tech	NIR	365125	0.88	2.50	4.88	0.10	+184.1
3	Eco Tech Intl	ETI	1574	3.75	8.50	12.75	3.00	+126.7
4	Mytec Tech	MYT	120317	1.20	2.70	4.20	1.06	+125.0

TOP TSE NET WINNERS

Rk.	Stock	Ticker	Volume 00s	Prev. quarter	Recent close	— 52-week — high	— 52-week — low	Net change
1	Fairfax Finl	FFH	7852	487.00	574.00	600.00	253.00	+87.00
2	Fonorola	FON	292500	40.95	67.10	69.75	21.00	+26.15
3	Chrysler	C	1900	59.95	83.00	84.00	44.00	+23.05
4	Power Finl	PWF	72274	54.55	68.75	69.40	32.60	+14.20

TOP TSE % LOSERS

Rk.	Stock	Ticker	Volume 00s	Prev. quarter	Recent close	— 52-week — high	— 52-week — low	Net change
1	Gaming Lottery	GLH	42768	5.55	0.80	7.70	0.50	−85.6
2	Crystallex Int	KRY	152160	6.85	1.15	11.85	0.90	−83.2
3	Gitennes Expl	GIT	35830	2.95	0.91	4.20	0.85	−69.2
4	Adrian Res	ADL	6958	1.05	0.36	2.35	0.35	−65.7

TOP TSE NET LOSERS

Rk.	Stock	Ticker	Volume 00s	Prev. quarter	Recent close	— 52-week — high	— 52-week — low	Net change
1	Biovail	BVF	34810	68.25	46.75	70.20	33.45	−21.50
2	Potash Sask	POT	36181	128.90	110.80	138.20	98.50	−18.10
3	COM Dev Int	CDV	88103	24.10	9.50	40.25	7.75	−14.60
4	Cdn Natl Railwy	CNR	119121	91.15	78.20	96.00	60.25	−12.95

The first four sets of tables in the series are the winners and losers on the Toronto, Montreal, Vancouver and Alberta stock exchanges. This series is much like the daily gainers and losers tables, except that **the quarterly series** highlights the top 25 and the bottom 25 on a quarterly basis. **Quarterly winners and losers** are counted on a net basis and a percentage basis. **Net change** is simply the dollar amount and this list generally includes stocks that start from a price level that is higher than average. **The percentage change table** tends to pick up lower-priced stocks that are more speculative. But this list does provide a valuable guide to the changing fortunes of some industry sectors and companies whose fortunes are rising and falling. Investors should check the volume numbers in these lists because a large price move on small volume may not be significant.

Figures supplied by FP DataGroup

Top 25 dividend yields on the TSE – common

Rank	Stock	Ticker	Recent close	Annual dividend	% yield	Freq.	Most recent rate chg.	Detail	Pymts @ curr.rate
1	Greyvest Cap	GFI	0.39	0.04	10.3	s	July 6, 1998	d	1
2	Fst Aust Prime xc	FAP	9.95	0.96	9.6	m	Jan. 15, 1998	d	10
3	Novicourt	NOV	2.56	0.20	7.8	s	May 29, 1998	s	1
4	Premium Incm A	PIC.A	11.75	0.80	6.8	q	Jan. 31, 1997	s	7

Top 25 dividend yields on the TSE – preferred

Rank	Stock	Ticker	Recent close	Annual dividend	% yield	Redemption price	Redemption date
1	Ivaco pf ser 5	IVA.PR.I	23.00	2.62	11.4	25.00	now
2	Ivaco pf ser 3	IVA.PR.G	20.00	2.25	11.3	25.00	now
3	Mun Bankers pfA	MUN.PR.A	9.10	1.00	11.0	10.00	now
4	Gulf Cda Res pf	GOU.PR.A	2.91	f 0.30	10.3	n.a.	n.a.

The next three sets of tables in this series concentrate on the blue chips listed on the Toronto Stock Exchange. The pair of tables on dividend yield highlight the common and preferred stock issues that paid the return. **Dividend yield** is simply the dividend stated as a percentage of the price. The table on **common share dividends** includes a column showing the date at which the current dividend rate was set. Companies with long-standing, stable dividend policies are prized by investors. **The preferred dividend table** includes columns on redemption price and redemption date, which is the price at which the shares may be bought back by the company and the date on which the buyback rights become effective. (In this table, "now" means the issue can be redeemed at any time.)

Figures supplied by FP DataGroup

Price/earning ratios on the TSE
Lowest   Highest

Stock	Ticker	Recent close	EPS	P/E	Stock	Ticker	Recent close	EPS	P/E
Metals & Minerals				29.0					
Sedna Geotech	SOT	0.26	u 0.12	1.4	Semafo	SMF	0.87	0.01	87.0
Key Anacon	KEY	0.85	0.27	3.0	Novicourt	NOV	2.56	0.10	25.6
Denison Mines	DEN	0.15	0.03	5.0	Rio Algom	ROM	19.00	0.82	23.2

The price earnings table shows the highest and lowest ratios among the industry sectors represented by subindexes in the Toronto Stock Exchange 300 index. The **ratio of price to earnings** is generally considered to be an indicator of whether a stock is over- or undervalued. **P/E** is current market price divided by annual earnings per share.

QUARTERLY SNAPSHOT

Figures supplied by FP DataGroup

Lowest price/book value per share on the TSE

Rank	Stock	Ticker	Recent close	Bookvalue per share	Price per bookvalue
1	Semi-Tech A	SEM.A	0.12	u 2.85	0.03
2	Armada Gold	AAU	0.08	1.28	0.06
3	Petrolex Eng	PXV	0.10	1.30	0.08
4	Cons Enfield	CEZ	0.04	0.46	0.09
5	Merc Intl Pete	MPT.U	u 0.06	1.00	0.09
6	Laminco Res	LMR	0.06	0.61	0.10

Highest price/book value per share on the TSE

Rank	Stock	Ticker	Recent close	Bookvalue per share	Price per bookvalue
1	Zi Corp	ZIC	4.10	0.04	102.50
2	Mond Inds Inc	MII	0.40	0.01	40.00
3	First Silver	FSR	0.90	0.03	31.45
4	CGI Group A	GIB.A	22.85	0.82	27.87
5	Sceptre Inv A	SZ.A	28.00	1.54	18.18

Tables showing the highest and lowest price-to-book ratios measure companies on a break-up value basis. Book value is asset value on the balance sheet that is attributed to the owners, which means shareholders in the case of a public company. **Book value per share** simply divides the total for shareholder equity by the number of shares. **Price per book value** is the share price divided by the book value per share.

QUARTERLY SNAPSHOT

Figures supplied by FP DataGroup

Toronto 35 earnings estimates

Name	Symbol	Quarter end	Report expected	Yr. ago EPS $	No. of analysts	High $	Low $	Mean $
Barrick Gold	ABX	3/31	21/04	0.15	9	0.20	0.17	0.18
Alcan Aluminium	AL	3/31	16/04	0.46	14	0.52	0.32	0.48
Bombardier Cl.b	BBD	1/31	21/04	0.43	2	0.43	0.36	0.40

The final table in this quarterly series is a survey of forecasts by investment house analysts of corporate profits for the companies that make up the Toronto Stock Exchange index of 35 stocks. The **"report expected" column** shows the date on which the company is scheduled to issue financial results for the most recent quarter. Most Canadian companies have a fiscal year that coincides with the calendar year. The **"quarter end" column** shows the different dates. **"Year ago EPS $"** means earnings per share for the year ago quarterly period expressed in C$. **"No. of analysts"** refers to those who contributed to this report and the next three columns give the high, low and average (mean) for the forecasts by this group.

If an order can't be filled by a regular trader because there is an imbalance of orders, the specialist provides a bid or an offer.

Specialists are essentially independent traders who are bankrolled by securities firms and they earn their keep by trading for their own account or a share of the return on a firm's account.

For example, an exchange may stipulate all orders for XYZ Ltd. stock up to 399 shares will be filled; this is known as the minimum guaranteed fill.

If an order is made to sell 300 shares at the market price, and only 200 shares are available, the specialist responsible for XYZ stock will immediately sell the remaining 100 shares.

COMPUTER PROGRAMS AID INVESTMENT DEALERS TO BUY AND SELL STOCK COMBINATIONS

On some exchanges, trading is done by open outcry, whereby traders shout their buy or sell orders. On others, the process is completed through use of computers.

Modern technology not only has made buying and selling stocks a faster, simpler process, but has had an effect on share prices.

One of the most pronounced effects of computerization is program trading. It's a complex strategy whereby investment dealers and their large corporate and institutional clients use computer programs to trigger buy and sell orders in many different stocks at a certain point.

Depending on the levels of stock prices, stock market index options and stock market index futures, computers will automatically trigger these orders. If enough dealers follow the same route, stock prices may soar or plunge in a very short time.

PROOF OF OWNERSHIP NOT NORMALLY REQUIRED

Just as credit cards have reduced demand for paper money, electronic record-keeping has diminished the importance of physical proof of ownership of securities. It's possible to get a certificate but fewer investors see the need to take physical possession of their shares. That's just fine with investment dealers because it's expensive to process and deliver a piece of paper.

The system of securities registration that has evolved has brought about considerable savings for the dealers. It works much like the system used by banks in moving money from one institution to another. It's called "netting" and anonymity of ownership is what makes it work.

ELECTRONIC RECORDS OF TRANSACTIONS ARE KEPT AT THE CDS

When ownership of a security is not registered to the buyer, it is said to be in "street name." That means the record of ownership is in a broker's files.

"The street" is a jargon term for the collection of brokerage houses that make up the dealer community.

QUARTERLY EARNINGS | SURVEY

The quarterly profit survey covers the key financial numbers for the major companies in the Toronto Stock Exchange 300 index. It usually runs the sixth Saturday after the calendar quarter end and eighth Saturday after the calendar yearend. The categories in the table correspond to the subindexes in the TSE 300. The figures are for the most recent quarter compared with a year ago.

Generally, year-to-year comparisons are made with quarter reports in order to account for any seasonal factors in a particular industry.

Revenue is money taken in from operations and does not include special items, such as a sale of assets.

Net income is operating profit after taxes, depreciation and amortization.

EPS is basic earnings per share, which is net income divided by the number of shares outstanding. This calculation does not include shares that may be issued at a future date on exercise of options or other share issue obligations that a company might have.

Cash flow from operations shows the cash kicked off from day-to-day operations of a company, before extraordinary items.

Figures in $millions	Ticker	— Q3 revenues —			— Q3 net income —			—Q3 EPS—		cash flow ops	
		1998	1997	% chg	1998	1997	% chg	1998	1997	1998	%chg
Metals & Minerals											
Alcan Aluminium Ltd.*	AL	2,950.4	2,697.4	+9%	161.9	110.7	+46%	0.70	0.47	443.3	+57%
Aur Resources Inc.	AUR	25.1	23.9	+5%	-0.8	1.3	n.m.	-0.01	0.02	6.9	+9%
Total		6,690.9	8,040.1	-17%	144.6	303.2	-52%	...	...	642.6	-52%
Gold & Precious Minerals											
Aber Resources Ltd. (Jul. 31)	ABZ	nil	nil	n.m.	0.2	-0.2	n.m.	0.01	-0.01	0.7	n.m.
Barrick Gold Corp.*	ABX	490.2	434.6	+13%	115.0	-436.0	n.m.	0.30	-1.16	220.9	+30%
Total		1,363.8	1,291.7	+6%	159.0	-399.2	n.m.	...	...	549.9	+41%

Another component of the street is the Canadian Depository for Securities Ltd. (CDS), which is the organization that maintains electronic records for investment dealers, trust companies and banks.

Before there was central record-keeping, dealers would deliver certificates along the street to settle up for each day's trades.

BROKER, TRUST COMPANY AND BANK HOLDINGS ARE CALCULATED DAILY

Now, they simply report the trades to CDS and CDS adjusts the accounts of each firm. Instead of recording each trade in each security, CDS changes the net holdings at the end of each day.

Stocks held in brokerage house accounts by CDS mainly represent shares held in street name by the brokers. CDS files now hold dealer records for more than $1 trillion worth of stocks and bonds.

Those who actually take delivery of a certificate will find the following information printed on the document:

- **The name of the issuer,** either a company or a government.
- **Par value,** if applicable (otherwise it will say "no par value") and the number of shares (if it's a stock) or value (if it's a bond) represented by the certificate.
- **Conditions,** if any, attached to the security, such as how many votes each common share carries.
- **Details of transfer of ownership.**
- **Reproductions of the signatures of authorized signing officers.**
- **A CUSIP number.** CUSIP stands for Committee on Uniform Securities Identification Procedures and each security issue has a unique number.

CALCULATING THE TSE 300'S MOVES

The moves of the Toronto Stock Exchange index of 300 stocks are calculated by computer at the TSE and the computer program picks up every trade on a running basis during each trading session.

**The formula for calculating the TSE 300 index is
(aggregate float-quoted market value/divisor) X 1,000.**

It sounds complicated but it's actually a straightforward calculation. Aggregate float-quoted market value is a mouthful and it is easier to understand one bite at a time.
Aggregate simply means total.
Float-quoted means the number of free-trading shares listed on the exchange. That's the total number of shares issued minus the number of shares in the control block (when an individual or a group holds a controlling block of shares, that stock is not free-trading).
Market value means the price of the latest trade. Thus, the float-quoted market value is calculated for each listed company and these values are added together to get the aggregate.
The divisor is an invention that adjusts for changes in the composition of the index.

A common reason for change is when a company issues additional shares. Another reason the index changes is substitution, such as when a stock issue disappears because of a takeover and shares of another company are put into the index.

An easier example to follow is a stock split. When a stock is split two-for-one, the price drops in half when the split takes effect. A lower price would bring down the index value but in this case the number of shares in circulation is doubled.

The divisor adjusts for these changes in composition so that the index level is the same immediately before and after each change. The result of dividing market value by the divisor is then multiplied by 1,000 because the TSE 300 index was started at 1,000 in 1975 and this remains the base year for the index.

TRADING SECURITIES OVER THE COUNTER

Securities trading not done on exchanges is said to be done over the counter, a term that goes back to a time when shares could be bought over the counters of banks, investment dealers and even stores. Now, though, it means securities traded between dealers or sold directly by a financial institution to a client.

A general rule for OTC trading is that buyers should be more sophisticated about investing and they should have a keen understanding of risk.

At one end of the OTC scale are custom-made hedges large banks and investment firms create for major clients. A large corporation with extensive foreign operations will

EARNINGS SUMMARY | TABLE

Publicly traded companies report their earnings, or profits, four times a year. These earnings are the gauge of a company's success.

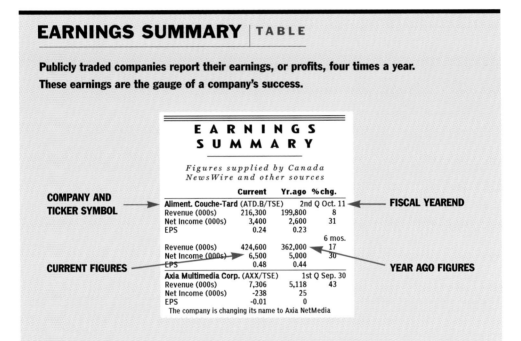

COMPANY AND TICKER SYMBOL

CURRENT FIGURES

FISCAL YEAREND

YEAR AGO FIGURES

EARNINGS SUMMARY

Figures supplied by Canada NewsWire and other sources

	Current	Yr.ago	%chg.
Aliment. Couche-Tard (ATD.B/TSE)		2nd Q Oct. 11	
Revenue (000s)	216,300	199,800	8
Net Income (000s)	3,400	2,600	31
EPS	0.24	0.23	
			6 mos.
Revenue (000s)	424,600	362,000	17
Net Income (000s)	6,500	5,000	30
EPS	0.48	0.44	
Axia Multimedia Corp. (AXX/TSE)		1st Q Sep. 30	
Revenue (000s)	7,306	5,118	43
Net Income (000s)	-238	25	
EPS	-0.01	0	

The company is changing its name to Axia NetMedia

Earnings are what is left after payment of all expenses and are generally stated on the basis of continuing operations. For example, if a company sells a plant because it is dropping a particular line of business, the gain from the sale of the asset and any losses from the operation being sold would be reported separately in the earnings statement.

If a company has no earnings, another reliable measure of its financial record is cash flow, which is net income plus non-cash deductions such as depreciation. That means a company has enough funds to carry on day-to-day operations but is not bringing in enough money to cover future needs, such as buying replacement equipment.

Earnings reports should state the results for the last quarter and for the fiscal year to date. Comparisons are always with the prior year because most companies are affected by seasonal factors and a change from a year earlier will almost always be more significant than from a previous quarter.

need OTC contracts to cover the risks of currency fluctuations or interest rate changes. These OTC contracts are designed for a specific set of circumstances and many are unique to a specific situation.

A core issue for OTC trading is efficient pricing. In auction markets, which is the system at stock exchanges, the steady bid and ask flow for actively traded stocks is designed to ensure each transaction produces the best price at the time.

BONDS, CURRENCIES AND PENNY STOCKS TRADE OVER THE COUNTER

Bond and currency trading is done on interdealer markets and these transactions account for the biggest share of OTC trading. Rules are established by tradition and regulation, which means pricing is efficient for actively traded issues.

On the other side of the OTC spectrum are penny stocks sold by financing houses for high risk startups, mainly in resource and technology sectors.

Sometimes these companies trade over the counter because they are struggling ventures that cannot justify the expense of being listed on an exchange. But sometimes the reason is that the company cannot meet the exchange's listing requirements for capital adequacy and sometimes the promoters of OTC stocks are less than forthright about the company's prospects.

IN CANADA, OVER THE COUNTER TRADING IS MAINLY IN STOCKS OF JUNIOR COMPANIES

Another reason for selling shares over the counter is that trading volume is too low to justify the cost of an exchange listing. Large multinational firms – for example, a British firm with a small number of shareholders in Canada – might be in this category.

A big issue in assessing OTC securities is liquidity. Low trading volume often is the reason a stock is sold on an OTC market, which means the shareholder might not be able to sell quickly. Lack of liquidity also means inefficient pricing.

Over the counter trading of stocks in Canada is mainly in stocks of junior companies. Statistics for the most actively traded can be found in the unlisted stocks tables of financial papers. Unlike other stock tables, no dividends are listed because stocks in this table pay no dividends. In the U.S., the major OTC market is the National Association of Securities Dealers Automated Quotation system, or Nasdaq. This interdealer market has different levels of listing requirements and the Nasdaq senior board includes some of the largest U.S. corporations. Nasdaq listings do include many dividend-paying stocks and the dealer-run computer trading system operates like a stock exchange.

UNDERSTANDING THE REGULATORY NETWORK

Regulation of Canadian financial intermediaries is divided between federal and provincial governments, so investors with a beef need to understand the distinctions when pursuing a complaint.

The basic distinction is that banking is regulated federally and securities trading is

WEEKLY UPCOMING EARNINGS | TABLE

UPCOMING EARNINGS

Figures supplied by First Call 1-800-448-2348

Company	Ticker	Period	Consensus estimate $	Number of estimates	Earnings yr ago $
Monday					
Seagram (US$)	VO	(1Q)	0.26	4	0.37
TransCanada PipeLines	TRP	(3Q)	0.35	3	n.a.
Tuesday					
Newcourt Credit (US$)	NCT	(3Q)	0.36	2	0.26
Novicourt	NOV	(3Q)	0.01	2	0.04

Profits are the most important numbers for mature companies and forecasts are published Mondays in this table. The predictions are the consensus view of investment analysts who follow the companies. The column to the right of the estimate gives the number of analysts who contributed. Usually, these are quarterly forecasts and the period column gives the fiscal period. The outlook for the current quarter is compared with the actual figure from a year earlier because year-to-year comparisons account for seasonal factors that might affect the business.

regulated provincially. But the reality of ownership of financial institutions makes the situation much more complex.

Chartered banks now own securities dealers so Ottawa has a role in overseeing these large financial conglomerates.

Large brokerage firms operate nationally and internationally, so the scope of their operations is beyond the jurisdiction of a single agency.

Credit unions can look much like banks but they are under provincial jurisdiction.

Insurance companies have expanded into certain investment areas and regulation of insurance is split between the two levels of government.

A further wrinkle in the regulatory network is that part of the industry is self-regulating under legislation authorizing "SROs" – self-regulating organizations.

Stock exchanges are SROs and they have rule-making power over the brokerage firms that are the owners of the exchanges. The Investment Dealers Association, which has an industry lobby role, also is an SRO with audit and enforcement authority over the brokerage firms and their employees.

The first question for anyone with a complaint about a securities industry practice or an action by a employee of a financial institution should be: Who is the principal regulator?

HERE IS A QUICK LIST OF REGULATORS

• The Office of the Superintendent of Financial Institutions is the federal regulator for banks, trusts, loan companies and federally registered pension plans.

• In broad terms, provincial securities commissions set policy and subordinate regulators, such as the stock exchanges, do the policing. However, the commissions can pursue disciplinary matters (high-profile cases involving mutual fund managers is an example). Each province has a securities commission but the scope of their activities varies widely. The Ontario Securities Commission is the largest, a recognition of the fact Toronto has the largest concentration of head offices of public corporations. The OSC often provides services to smaller commissions. The Quebec commission is a regional force and the commissions in British Columbia and Alberta have expertise in regulating resource companies. The commissions oversee the SROs in their jurisdiction and act as an appeal body for challenges to decisions made by SROs.

• Stock exchanges used to have extensive audit responsibilities for brokerage firms but that relationship is changing and the primary responsibility of the exchanges is regulation of trading.

• The Investment Dealers Association has primary audit jurisdiction for most brokerage firms and it conducts disciplinary hearings in most cases where a broker is caught in allegations of misconduct.

• The Canadian Investor Protection Fund operates as an insurance fund to cover investor losses, up to a pre-set limit, in the event of a brokerage house failure. Its role is similar to that of the Canada Deposit Insurance Corp., which covers deposit losses in bank failures.

CHAPTER 2

UNDERSTANDING | EQUITIES

- The basics of buying and selling equities
- Block trades
- Bid and ask tables
- North American indexes
- Foreign market strategies
- Technical analysis

CANADA'S INVESTING MOSAIC

THE MARKETPLACE FOR STOCKS IS RELATIVELY SMALL BUT

GEMS CAN BE FOUND | BY PATRICK BLOOMFIELD

THE ART OF INVESTING IN STOCKS can be described as picking a reasonable spread of securities that promise to provide the best return at the lowest relative risk. In that respect, the Canadian marketplace can be a gold mine for a private investor with a talent for uncovering hitherto undiscovered stock values and a somewhat tougher place to dig for value for the money-laden investment professional. To understand the difference, keep in mind the Toronto Stock Exchange, which handles more than 80% of the business done on all four of Canada's stock exchanges, is actually two markets.

The senior market comprises 200 to 300 of the 1,300 to 1,400 companies listed. Pension fund and mutual fund portfolio managers all tend to concentrate their holdings in this relatively narrow stock universe.

As a result, the prices of the stocks within it tend to respond more rapidly to any market rumor or news item and to be more tightly priced than others, particularly as Canadian rules stipulate 80% of the book value of a tax-deferred portfolio must be held in Canadian securities.

INVESTORS SHOULD DO SOME RESEARCH BEFORE ENTERING THE JUNIOR MARKET

The more junior market is made up of 1,000 or more listed companies and can prove a very happy hunting ground for private investors prepared to devote time and money to doing their own research. There's one caveat. The smaller the portion of a company's share capital that is available for public trading, the harder it can be to find ready and willing buyers when you want out. This can be particularly the case when investing in one of the 370 or so companies specifically listed as "junior" stocks, which are subject to special reporting requirements.

For the investor who is seeking a larger selection of smaller, more speculative, companies, there is ample additional choice, coupled with an ample degree of risk, in the stocks listed on both the Vancouver and Alberta stock exchanges. For an investor who

feels comfortable with political uncertainties, there is a selection of Quebec-based companies that are listed solely on the Montreal Exchange.

A good starting point for an investor with an entrepreneurial bent is a look at the spate of new listings in the mid-1990s of entrepreneurially run emerging public corporations. Twenty or 30 years ago, the TSE had half as many companies on its lists as it has today, and its boards were heavily larded with branch plant operations of U.S. majors and with Canadian companies under the control of a relatively small clique of family owners.

MANY JUNIOR STOCK COMPANIES ARE STILL RUN BY THOSE WHO STARTED THEM

Today, this "old" investment money is being replaced steadily with new money invested in younger companies, and the previous entrenchment of voting control of the more senior companies is gradually being eroded.

A late-1997 survey by William Mackenzie of Fairvest Shareholders Corp. of the 300 stocks in the TSE composite index shows the number of companies having a single holder of more than 50% of the voting equity has dropped to 66 (22.5%) from 91 (31%) in 1994. The less happy side of this trend, however, is that 52 of the 300 companies in the index still have "dual-class" capital, with the voting power of outside shareholders either restricted or nonexistent.

Of the more junior stocks, many are still owned significantly by the entrepreneurs who brought them to life (and some have dual voting rights). The benefit of this entrenched control is that managers have their own fortunes at risk. The potential disadvantage is the possibility of being locked in as a minority holder in an enterprise where management is more concerned with its own reward than that of its fellow owners.

An assessment of the integrity and calibre of management, therefore, has to be an investment priority. One excellent yardstick is the extent to which employees are treated as partners in the company. Back in the late 1980s, Linamar Corp.'s majority owner, Frank Hasenfratz, insisted his underwriters restrain the price of the company's initial public offering – just to ensure his employee shareholders had a good ride.

Linamar has since put up by far the best investment returns of all TSE-listed auto-parts makers and ranks as a top TSE performer.

THE CANADIAN MARKET CAN HOLD SOME REAL BARGAINS

There is another characteristic of Canadian markets that should also be kept in mind. They are better suited to those investors who hunt for stocks with a rifle rather than a shotgun. By and large, Canadian juniors tend to be more modestly valued than their U.S. counterparts, being followed by relatively few financial analysts and having a history that is often less well known. So, painstaking individual research can turn up bargains.

On the other hand, Canadian markets are not as well suited to investors who want to spread their holdings right across the economic spectrum. The TSE composite index is made up of only 40 business and industry subsector indexes. Its U.S. equivalent, the Standard & Poor's 500-stock composite, has more than 100 subsectors, reflecting a far greater diversity of listed stocks within a much bigger marketplace.

MECHANISMS THAT MAKE STOCK PRICES MOVE

"More buyers than sellers," or the reverse, is an old stock market cliche that has become a fallback explanation when there is no apparent reason for a price move. It's true prices for securities change when there is an imbalance in supply or demand and looking for reasons behind a price move is part of the process of making investment decisions.

General economic conditions are part of this mix, along with tax rates, political policies and how the domestic situation compares with other national economies.

Among the factors that affect the stock of a single company are assessments of management's competence, the extent to which the company has invested in maintaining its competitive position, the general outlook for its industry sector, the general economic climate and the number of shares outstanding.

Changes in fortune for an individual company occur with stock market cycles – a bull market on the way up and a bear on the way down. A rising tide lifts all boats and a bull market in stocks pulls up share prices for companies that have no news that would affect price. Similarly, a bear market will drag down the share values of companies that are prospering and paying dividends.

The term "bear" is thought to come from the expression "to sell the bear's skin before one has caught the bear," which refers to dealers who would sell bearskins before they caught bears. Eventually the term was applied to investors who were pessimistic about

HOW TO READ | THE STOCK TABLES

Equities on Canadian exchanges are shown in decimals. NYSE, Amex, Nasdaq and Unlisted stocks closing at less than $5 are shown in decimals. Those closing at more than $5 are shown in fractions.

Stocks in bold type closed at least 5% higher or lower than the previous board lot closing price. Stocks must close at a minimum $1 and trade at least 500 shares to qualify.

Underlined stocks traded Friday 500% or more above their 60-day average daily volume. Stocks both bold and underlined closed 5% higher on 500%-plus volumes.

52W high	52W low	Stock	Ticker	Div	Yield %	P/E	Vol 00s	Friday High /ask	Low /bid	$ chg	Interim /fiscal	Earnings data EPS	12 mth EPS	Vol 00s	Week High	Low	Cls/ last	$ chg
↑29.00	21.00	Stockna	MAX	f0.50	1.96	7.4	1234	25.75	25.25	+1.00	Dec98	1.25	3.45	210501	26.75	24.25	25.50	+2.50
n 39.00	31.00	Stockna	MAX	f1.00	2.83	10.3	1234	35.75	35.25	+1.00	Dec98	1.25	3.45	210501	36.75	34.25	35.50	+2.50
↓s49.00	41.00	Stockna	MAX	★f1.50	3.30	13.2	1234	45.75	45.25	+1.00	★Dec98	1.25	3.45	210501	46.75	44.25	45.50	+2.50

1. Up/down arrows indicate a new 52-week high or low in the week's trading
2. 52-week high/low: Highest or lowest inter-day price reached in the previous 52 weeks
3. Stock names have been abbreviated
4. Ticker: Basic trading symbol for primary issues (usually common)
5. Dividend: Indicated annual rate. See footnotes
6. Yield %: Annual dividend rate or amount paid in past 12 months as a percentage of closing price in past 12 months
7. P/E: Price earnings ratio, closing price divided by earnings per share in past 12 months. Figures reported in US$ converted to C$

FRIDAY DATA
8. Volume: Number of shares traded in day in 00s;
nt – no trade;
z – odd lot;
e – exact number of shares
9. High: Highest inter-day trading price or last asking price if no trades. If no asking price . . . shown
10. Low: Lowest inter-day trading price or last bid price if no trades. If no bid price . . . shown
11. Dollar change: Change between board lot closing price and previous board lot closing price

EARNINGS DATA
12. Interim/fiscal: Earnings shown for latest interim or fiscal period, by month and reporting period
13. EPS: Earnings per share for latest reporting period
d – deficit; **u** – US$
14. 12 month EPS: Latest 12 month earnings per share. If earnings are negative, P/E not calculated

WEEK DATA
15. Volume: Number of shares traded in week in 00s
z – odd lot;
e – exact number of shares
16. High: Highest inter-day trading price during week
17. Low: Lowest inter-day trading price during week
18. Cls/last: Closing price or last board lot closing price in the last week
19. Dollar change: Change between board lot closing price and previous week's board lot closing price

If a Canadian listed stock has not traded during the week, its last bid and ask price can be found in the bid/ask table

FOOTNOTES
* – denotes Canadian listed stocks trading in $US
x – stock trades ex-dividend

n – stock is newly listed on exchange in past year
s – stock split in past year
c – stock consolidated in past year
a – spinoff company distributed as shares
◆ – shares carry unusual voting rights
ƒ – denotes companies covered by Financial Post Investor Reports, which may be purchased by calling (416) 350-6500

DIVIDEND/EARNINGS FOOTNOTES
★ – earnings announcement or change in annual dividend during week
r – dividend in arrears
u – US$
p – paid in the past 12 months including extras
y – dividend paid in stock, cash equivalent
f – floating rate, annualized
v – variable rate, annualized based on last payment

The earnings data columns provide the earnings per share for the latest interim period (usually the latest quarter) and the latest 12-month period. The date column in this series shows the month-end for the latest quarter and the stage in the fiscal year for that month.

the outlook for share prices and sold shares they didn't own, gambling the price would later drop so that they could buy them at a lower price.

The origin of "bull" is less certain. It may stem from bull baiting, a sport popular in Europe from the 12th to the 19th century, in which dogs were set loose on bulls chained to a stake. Because there was a similar sport of bear baiting, the stock market interpretation of "bull" may have arisen as a companion term.

Bull and bear markets are largely about expectations. If investors as a group think the economy will improve and corporate profits will grow quickly, they will bid up stock prices in advance. The rule of thumb is that the stock market runs at least six months ahead of the economy.

BULL MARKET OF 1980S AND 1990S WAS DRIVEN BY MICROCHIP REVOLUTION

While the business cycle is the traditional mover of investor expectations, the bull markets in the 1980s and '90s were driven by a supercycle event: the microchip revolution that has put portable computers into offices and homes around the world.

This bull market has created a general aura around stock prices but bull markets don't last forever and investors must be mindful of the other factors that affect stock prices.

There are two basic lists of reasons for movements in the prices of securities – ones that are specific to an issuer of securities and ones that are general.

For example, a gold mining company's stock price is likely to go up if it has a discovery but prices of all gold miners will appreciate if the price of gold is on the rise.

Or, consider what will happen to prices for bonds of a government-owned hydroelectric utility under two sets of circumstances: If it is downgraded by a credit rating agency, its bond prices will fall; but if interest rates fall in industrial economies because of generally easier credit conditions, prices for its bonds are likely to rise.

RESOURCE STOCKS ARE OFTEN FIRST TO PERFORM AS ECONOMY RECOVERS

One of the major influences on pricing of securities is change in returns from different classes of investments.

For example, a rise in interest rates makes bonds and treasury bills a more attractive alternative for investor funds. As money is diverted into fixed income securities, there is downward pressure on stocks. High interest rates also affect company profit, because companies must pay more to borrow for business expansion.

Within the broad flows of investor funds, there are a variety of factors that affect individual sectors. For example, high-tech stocks in the communications industries were star performers in bull markets of the 1980s and '90s.

But the business cycle remains the dominant influence on share prices and various sectors react differently as economic conditions change. When the economy is coming off a low point in the cycle, rising demand first hits the markets for basic industrial commodities. Thus the resource stocks generally are early performers when the economy is coming out of recession, but they tend to suffer badly in a slowdown when orders are cut back.

A recovery period usually means pent-up demand for housing and durable goods bought by consumers and stock prices will anticipate rising profits for companies supplying these markets.

After the economy peaks and a slowdown begins, interest rates will fall and a decline in the cost of money often means higher profits for companies that have high capital financing costs, such as pipeline or electric utilities.

WHERE TO FIND BASIC DISCLOSURE DOCUMENTS

Disclosure of information by an issuer of securities revolves around one basic definition – the meaning of a material fact. Securities laws define a material fact as information that significantly affects, or would reasonably be expected to have a significant effect on, the market price or value of a security.

Deciding what is material to investors and potential investors is mainly a matter of securities regulation and precedent. In most situations, it's obvious what is material and the definition can vary with the size of the company.

Details of a $10-million order for replacement equipment would not be a material fact for General Motors Corp. because the company's annual budget for capital spending would be many times that amount.

GM has ongoing capital costs, and the totals are disclosed in financial statements, but details would only be material if there were a significant change in the pattern or the amount of the capital budget.

However, details of a $10-million capital project would be material to a small mining exploration company that has a mineral discovery but no track record as a producer.

FOR COMPANIES, THE PERTINENT DETAILS USUALLY ARE FOUND IN CERTAIN DOCUMENTS
• Annual and quarterly reports.
• Prospectuses that go out with a new issue of securities.
• Annual information circulars that are sent out to shareholders with a notice for an annual or special meeting.
• Announcement of material corporate developments made through the financial press and professional analysts in the investment business.
• Insider trading reports and other material change reports that are made to securities regulators.

Governments also issue disclosure documents, such as budgets, and information in these documents is material to assessing their bonds.

Investment decisions about bonds, especially corporate bonds, often involve a review of ratings reports from credit rating agencies. These agencies also rate a broad array of corporate securities. The agencies that most widely follow the Canadian marketplace are Canadian Bond Rating Service, Dominion Bond Rating Service, Moody's Investors Service and Standard & Poor's.

Basic disclosure documents often are available through large public libraries. Corporate information usually can be obtained from a company's transfer agent, which maintains an up-to-date list of shareholders and routinely sends these reports to shareholders. Securities commissions provide for reading rooms to view disclosure documents, but there may be a fee for this service. Some corporate information is available through Internet sites maintained by regulators and many companies also post material information on their Web sites.

HOW INVESTORS CAN USE THE ANNUAL REPORT, PROSPECTUS AND AIF

Annual reports of Canadian public companies contain financial statements for the year under review along with a section called "management discussion and analysis," which is a detailed review of the financial results.

Yearend financial statements must be audited and the annual report must include a note from the auditor. If anything in the statements does not conform to generally accepted accounting principles (GAAP), the auditor must flag the discrepancies.

GAAP is a set of accounting standards. Those rules are set by the self-regulatory organization for accountants in consultation with securities regulators.

A prospectus should disclose all the corporate information an investor needs to assess

NEW HIGHS & LOWS | TABLE

This table lists companies whose stock prices reach new 52-week highs and lows. The breakdown is for trades on stock exchanges in Toronto, Montreal, Vancouver and Alberta.

Highs & lows *52-week*

Toronto		Vancouver	
High		**High**	
Cda Brokerlk	CKK	Argentina Gld	ARP
First Maritm	FMM	Green Point	GPT
Genetronics	GEB	Ind Grwth Fdr	IGF
Gennum	GND	**Low**	
Jean Coutu A	PJC.A	Alda Inds	ALD
Key Anacon	KEY	Allegro Ppty	AP
Luscar 10% db	LUS.DB	Amer Copper	ACC
Pac&Wstn nt	PWC.N	Bell Coast	BCP
Parkland Inds	PKI	Carbite Golf	CAB
Petromet Res	PNT	GST Globl db	GGB.DB.U
QuebecorPrint	IQI	GlobalPacifc	GPJ
Scotts Rstrnt	SRG	Global Techs	GBA
ShivaSoft	SOF	Hytec Flow	HYT
TrnsCdaPL pfU	TRP.PR.X	Int Bioremed	ILB
Low		Intl TME Res	ILT
Anadime	AEM	Jersey Pete	JPI
Antares Mng	ANZ	King Georg Dv	KIG

MORE ABOUT | STOCK TABLES

Stock tables provide all the essential information on daily trading activity in markets where most Canadians invest. Weekend editions of The Financial Post carry an expanded summary with details for the previous week. The Canadian markets are the Toronto Stock Exchange, the Montreal Exchange, the Vancouver Stock Exchange, the Alberta Stock Exchange and the over-the-counter market in Toronto called the Canadian Dealing Network (CDN is a subsidiary of the Toronto Stock Exchange).

52W high	52W low	Stock	Ticker	Yield Div	Yield %	P/E	Vol 00s	High	Low	Cls/ last	Net chg
n10.25	7.40	AEC Ppln	ALB	p0.76	8.7		393	8.95	8.75	8.75	–0.20
s28.50	13.25	AGFMgmtB♦	AGF	0.28	1.3	16.5	1292	22.25	20.50	21.00	–0.10
12.60	7.95	AGRA Inc	AGR	0.16	2.0	15.8	1830	8.10	7.95	8.05	+0.05
21.60	6.60	AIM Sfty	AIM			28.9	43	12.25	12.00	12.00	–0.05
2.74	0.20	AIT Advd	AIV				220	0.50	0.47	0.47	–0.01
n25.00	10.00	ALITech	ALT			33.3	2	13.00	13.00	13.00	
3.60	1.40	AMR Tech	AMR			15.3	64	3.00	2.80	3.00	
5.20	1.55	APEX A	AXD			5.7	332	1.65	1.65	1.65	
9.85	8.10	APF Egyun	AY	p1.72	20.6	42.8	31	8.35	8.35	8.35	–0.15
12.50	6.80	ARC Egy un	AET	p1.20	15.2	37.6	207	7.95	7.80	7.90	
n10.50	8.00	ARC Strat	AEF				5	8.90	8.50	8.90	+0.40
13.75	8.00	AT Plstcs	ATP	0.18	2.0	14.8	843	9.25	8.90	9.00	+0.05
38.50	30.00	ATCO I♦	ACO	0.68	1.9	12.7	25	37.00	36.75	36.75	+0.25
38.00	30.25	ATCO II		0.68	1.9	12.7	1	36.75	36.75	36.75	+1.75
s20.20	7.13	ATI Tech	ATY			13.4	38664	11.95	11.20	11.50	–0.45
s27.50	14.50	ATS Auto	ATA			35.2	150	19.45	18.75	19.35	–0.40
4.00	1.10	AZCAR	AZZ			25.5	24	1.30	1.30	1.30	
4.25	0.27	Abacan	ABC				3967	0.44	0.38	0.40	–0.04
19.50	7.25	AberRes	ABZ				224	9.00	8.90	8.90	
23.70	12.00	AbitibCons	A	0.40	2.7	25.1	5054	15.25	14.90	15.05	–0.05

The TSE is the main blue-chip market in Canada. The ME is mainly a regional stock market with a national base in trading in interest-sensitive derivatives. The VSE, ASE and CDN listings are heavily weighted toward speculative junior issues. Vancouver, Alberta and CDN tables do not carry dividend and P/E information because companies on these lists are mainly juniors where the goal is to add value through the stock price.

In the U.S., the main market is the New York Stock Exchange, which lists virtually all of the big blue-chip U.S. companies. After the NYSE, the high-volume market is Nasdaq, which is the acronym from National Association of Securities Dealers Automated Quotation system. Nasdaq is an interdealer market that has different levels of over-the-counter listings. The senior Nasdaq board is heavily weighted toward technology stocks. The American Stock Exchange (Amex) carries listings of second-tier U.S. companies.

High and low prices in the left-hand columns indicate the trading range during the past 52 weeks.

Company names sometimes are abbreviated and are listed alphabetically.

Stocks are common shares unless identified as otherwise. For example, a **pf** after the company name refers to preferred shares.

Warrants are identified as **wts** and rights as **rts.** An **A** beside the name refers to class A shares. Restricted voting shares are identified by a diamond symbol before the company name.

The ticker is the symbol used by exchanges to identify a security.

Dividend rate refers to estimated annual dividends paid to shareholders, based on the dividend rate announced by the company. A **v** indicates variable rate dividends have been estimated at their annual value, based on the latest payment. An **r** means the company is in arrears on its dividend payments.

Yield is a calculation of a stock's dividend as a percentage of its current price. If no dividends are paid, a stock has no yield.

P/E is the price to earnings ratio. This is the price of a stock divided by its annual earnings per share for the latest 12-month period. (Earnings per share are the company's earnings, divided by the number of outstanding shares.)

High, low and close (or latest) indicate the highest and lowest prices for the trading period and the price at the close of trading. Prices of U.S. stocks of less than $5 are listed in cents. Canadian exchanges use decimal pricing for all stocks.

Net change shows the difference between the latest closing price and the price of the last traded board lot on the previous day. If the amount is preceded by a plus sign, the stock is up; if it's preceded by a minus sign, it's down.

Volume shows how many board lots have been traded (for the day in the daily list and for the week in the weekly summary). A board lot is 100 shares, which means actual volume is multiplied by 100. An **e** before the volume indicates exact number of shares; an **nt** means not traded; and a **z** refers to a an odd lot trade (an amount other than a board lot).

Net change is the change in price from the end of the previous week or the last time the stock traded during that week.

a company's securities. However, a prospectus often will refer investors to other corporate documents for a complete picture of the securities.

The annual information form (AIF) covers information not provided in annual reports, such as details of insider shareholdings and executive compensation. These reports may not be sent to shareholders as a matter of routine but must be provided on request. Many companies distribute AIFs with the information circulars that go to shareholders with the notice of annual meetings.

THERE ARE DRAWBACKS TO INVESTING ABROAD

Returns from investments in foreign securities can be attractive, but investors looking beyond the border should consider two factors – taxes and risk. Domestic tax rules give Canadians a break on dividend-paying stocks when investing at home, and buying outside the country involves the prospect of currency fluctuations.

There are other reasons for weighing carefully the returns at home and abroad, but these two factors usually are at the top of the list. There is a solid reason why the tax rules favor investment at home by Canadians. Business needs money to invest in new plant and equipment, so capital formation is essential to the growth and development of the economy.

When Canadian governments were running up big debts, the economic priorities got mixed up and too much of the money invested at home went for the unproductive purpose of paying interest on government debts. But a rediscovered ethic for budgetary restraint is starting to make more room for business in the allocation of investment funds. Dividends paid by Canadian corporations get preferential tax treatment in the

INTERNATIONAL STOCKS | TABLE

INTERNATIONAL 10.27.98

Figures supplied by Reuter

Stock	Close	Chg	Stock	Close	Chg	Stock	Close	Chg	Stock	Close	Chg
London			Eurotunnel	70.50	0.50	Rank	266.00	2.00	Aegon	173.30	2.80
(in British pence)			Flextech	552.00	-5.50	Reckitt&Col	1039.00	-11.50	Ahold	63.80	-0.20
Abbey Natl	1153.00	-22.00	GKN	711.50	-7.00	Rentokil	373.00	-13.00	Bolswess	24.40	0.90
Allied Domc	542.00		Gen Electric	482.00	5.00	Reuters Hld	585.50	-22.00	CSM	94.30	-0.10
Allied Zurich	717.00		Glaxo	1851.00	-10.00	Rexam	213.50	-4.00	DSM	179.50	
Asc Br Food	574.00	-19.00	Granada	888.50	-17.00	Rio Tinto	743.00	5.00	Elsevier	25.60	-0.50
BAA	656.50	-26.50	Gr Universal	683.50	-13.00	Rolls Royce	227.50	3.00	Heineken	97.60	-5.10
			Guardn Ryl	294.75	-5.00	Royal&Sun	510.00	-24.50	Hoogovens	55.30	-1.20

Listings of international stocks show prices in local currencies. See the foreign exchange and major currencies tables to convert C$s. **Close** is the closing price and the **change** is from the previous trading day.

STOCK ACTIVITY | TABLES

Most active stocks 11.03.98

Toronto		Vol. 00s	Cls.	Chg.
Provigo	PGV	107820	14.55	+0.35
TIPS 35	TIP	43384	34.75	-0.20
Pan East Pete	PEC	42194	2.60	+0.02
ATI Technlgys	ATY	38664	11.50	-0.45
Oshawa A	OSH.A	37565	33.35	+1.10
Numac Energy	NMC	30913	3.70	+0.10
Laidlaw	LDM	25404	14.55	-0.05
Loblaw	L	23219	31.80	+1.00
CIBC	CM	20479	31.35	-0.65
TCPL	TRP	17903	23.05	-0.35

Montreal		Vol. 00s	Cls.	Chg.
Uniforet A	UNF.A	6990	1.65	unch
TCPL	TRP	4509	22.95	-0.45
Provigo	PGV	3810	14.55	+0.35
Oshawa A	OSH.A	3521	33.05	+0.80
Imperial Oil	IMO	3273	24.65	-0.05
Premdor	PDI	3003	12.85	unch
Mitel	MLT	2593	11.95	-0.55
Westburne Inc	WBI	2398	14.00	-0.05
BCE	BCE	2376	53.30	+0.20
Air Canada	AC	2093	6.35	+0.15

Vancouver		Vol. 00s	Cls.	Chg.
Argentina Gld	ARP	18935	3.15	-0.16
Botswana	BWD	13010	0.55	+0.10
Donner Mnrls	DML	6302	0.36	-0.05
TM Bioscience	TMC	6260	0.38	-0.09
Winspear Res	WSP	4949	2.05	-0.01
TNR Resources	TRR	3392	0.36	-0.04
Auspex Mnrls	APJ	3088	0.27	-0.01
Infowave Wire	IWM	2656	1.40	+0.11
Vannessa Vents	VVV	2500	0.40	unch
CVL Resources	CVL	2120	0.32	+0.07

MOST ACTIVE STOCKS TABLES

The most active stocks table highlights stocks that have traded most heavily during the day (or the week, in the case of the weekly listing).

Volume is shares traded in board lots (blocks of 100). Most trading arenas count a buy and a sell as one trade, but Nasdaq counts each side of the transaction in reporting volume.

Closing price is the last trade of the day and change is from the previous day (or week in the case of the weekly column). Prices of U.S. stocks of less than US$5 are listed in cents. Canadian exchanges use decimal pricing for all stocks.

Top % gainers

Toronto		Vol. 00s	Cls.	Chg.
Atlantc Coast	ATC	37	6.95	+67.5
Sthn Cross	SXR	50	1.10	+57.1
Clearly Cdn	CLV	583	1.35	+42.1
BatonBrdcstIR	BNB.IR	4313	9.40	+38.2
Cons Rambler	CRR	20	20.35	+37.0
Cdn World Fd	CWF	35	5.00	+26.6
O'Donnell Inv	ODM	391	4.50	+20.0
Club Monaco	CMI	2810	4.00	+19.4
Primetch Elec	PME	10	8.75	+19.0
Rainmakr Ent	RNK	188	2.85	+18.8

Montreal		Vol. 00s	Cls.	Chg.
O'Donnell Inv	ODM	269	4.50	+20.0
Metrowerks	MWK	121	7.00	+18.6
Cominco	CLT	6	18.60	+13.1
Cinram Intl	CRW	91	18.50	+11.8
Domco	DOC	185	10.00	+11.1
Royal Aviatn	ROY	56	3.00	+11.1
Haemacure	HAE	77	5.85	+10.4
Laperriere A	LV.A	237	4.00	+9.6
Saputo Group	SAP	182	36.50	+8.8
Lafarg Cda pf	LCI.PR.E	100	54.00	+8.7

Vancouver		Vol. 00s	Cls.	Chg.
Proginet Corp	PRF.U	65	u0.70	+79.5
Advent Comms	ADV	205	0.65	+71.1
Int Taurus	ITS	176	0.26	+62.5
Green Point	GPT	340	0.37	+48.0
Exito Mnrls	EXM	330	0.40	+33.3
Pachena Inds	PIN	10	0.80	+33.3
Utd Amer Entps	UAE	140	0.40	+33.3
Arrowhead Mnr	AOW	1080	0.37	+32.1
CVL Resources	CVL	2120	0.32	+28.0
AfriOre Ltd	AFO	962	0.52	+26.8

TOP % GAINERS AND LOSERS TABLES

The top gainers and losers tables highlight those stocks with unusual price moves in the latest trading day. A caution in reading this table is that no adjustment is made for volume. An unusual trade of 100 shares can cause a stock to vault to the top of the list on one day if there is little day-to-day trading in that stock. In those situations, that unusual price is often reversed the next day. Prices of U.S. stocks of less than US$5 are listed in cents. Canadian exchanges use decimal pricing for all stocks.

- **Top % gainers** are stocks whose prices gained the most in percentage terms.
- **Top net gainers** are stocks whose shares appreciated most in dollar value.
- **Biggest % losers** indicates stocks with the largest price decline in percentage terms.
- **Biggest net losers** are the stocks that fell the most in dollar value.

SECTORS AND INDEXES | TABLES

DAILY MARKETS TABLE

The daily markets table in weekend editions tracks the day-by-day closing values for the main North American indexes and then compares the close for the week with the previous month and the previous year.

Daily markets

	Monday	Tuesday	Wednesday	Thursday	Friday	Last Friday	Month ago	Year ago
TSE 300	5928.97	5996.78	6033.80	6115.41	6208.28	5841.98	5614.12	6783.68
TSE 200	342.21	345.89	346.53	349.11	353.57	336.85	326.83	443.19
TSE 100	363.37	367.57	370.16	375.62	381.51	358.11	343.47	403.42
Toronto 35	328.11	330.81	331.42	336.85	343.07	322.28	308.75	350.82
DJ Inds	8432.21	8366.04	8371.97	8495.03	8592.10	8452.29	7842.62	7381.67
DJ Trans	2754.34	2765.68	2750.24	2800.52	2891.91	2777.01	2644.67	3091.65
DJ Utils	299.05	298.30	300.28	297.86	301.45	301.45	306.72	241.33
S&P 500	1072.32	1065.34	1068.09	1085.93	1098.67	1070.67	1017.05	903.68
Nasdaq 100	1368.93	1353.34	1379.96	1396.30	1400.52	1340.60	1345.48	1000.70

MARKET DIARIES TABLE

The market diaries table provides a view of the breadth of activity. For example, a sharp move in an index on a day of heavy trading is more significant that a similar change when there is light volume.

Volume is number of shares traded in board lots (blocks of 100). Most trading arenas count a buy and a sell as one trade but Nasdaq counts each side of the transaction in reporting volume. Advances and declines are the numbers of share issues that rose in price or fell.

Advance and decline volume refers to the total for shares that advanced or declined. Unchanged refers to the number of share issues that ended the day with the same price as the previous day. Issues traded is the total for advances, declines and unchanged.

New highs and lows refers to the number of issues that reached new high or low prices in the latest 52-week period.

Market diaries

	Volume 00s	Previous day 00s	Adv.	Adv. vol 00s	Dec.	Dec. vol 00s	Unch.	Issues traded	New highs	New lows
Toronto	1344783	1281826	491	625180	479	591664	292	1262	11	14
Montreal	136082	132010	197	65539	185	53817	68	450	6	5
Vancouver	226826	206794	198	101760	178	88845	171	547	3	13
Alberta	152097	92998	137	67765	111	66062	116	364	3	14
New York	7024746	7584371	1607	3368493	1426	3245012	509	3542	58	15
American	288194	294932	276	105776	293	152972	143	712	9	11
Nasdaq	8905574	8911713	2054	3635818	2049	4841556	841	4944	44	38

HOURLY MARKETS TABLE

Most people look at the closing level of an index for a read on the markets. But activity during the day can be an important indicator. Momentum in a particular direction may show up in the intraday trends. If there is a news development during trading hours that affects the stock price in general, the hourly markets table will provide a snapshot of how that event affected the market. Another measure of market health that can be extracted from this table is volatility, which means unusual swings from high to low. Volatile trading activity often occurs in turning points for markets and this table will show the swings. At one time, index levels were only reported hourly but computer power now allows indexes to be tracked with changes from each stock trade (tick by tick is the street jargon for this instant tracking).

Hourly markets

	Open	10:00	11:00	12:00	1:00	2:00	3:00	Close	Prev day	Wk ago	Mth ago	Yr ago
TSE 300	6289.04	6302.89	6270.51	6267.40	6274.39	6281.41	6307.49	6296.51	6315.66	5996.78	5517.13	6945.83
TSE 200	361.40	361.01	360.28	360.02	360.23	360.48	363.79	363.37	360.35	345.89	326.32	447.12
TSE 100	387.49	386.88	384.65	384.48	384.94	385.41	386.63	385.90	387.96	367.57	336.43	414.66
Toronto 35	347.48	347.11	345.40	345.50	345.90	345.63	347.48	346.27	347.97	330.81	302.65	360.56
DJ Inds	8706.67	8720.57	8697.66	8695.08	8684.78	8718.77	8724.69	8706.15	8706.15	8366.04	7784.69	7674.39
DJ Trans	2953.62	2942.19	2930.74	2924.11	2905.30	2916.39	2918.92	2918.32	2954.85	2765.68	2602.23	3203.25
DJ Utils	304.78	305.53	306.27	306.78	307.23	307.77	307.86	307.77	304.87	298.30	311.19	245.25
S&P 500	1111.60	1112.93	1108.62	1108.15	1107.97	1111.28	1112.63	1110.84	1111.60	1065.34	1002.60	938.99
Nasdaq 100	1418.79	1414.42	1401.99	1399.13	1399.48	1404.18	1409.99	1401.73	1418.79	1353.34	1276.44	1050.72

TSE SECTORS WEEKLY WINNERS AND LOSERS TABLE

The TSE sectors table tracks the gains or losses for sub-indexes during the week and the top moves, up and down, within each sector. Volume is included as well as price because a big move on heavy volume is much more significant than a similar change on low volume. Instead of a dollar change, this table gives a percentage change, which allows for comparisons among stocks in different sectors.

TSE sectors — weekly winners and losers

Sector	Cls	Wk % chg	Best performer		Vol 00s	Cls	Wk % chg	Worst performer		Vol 00s	Cls	Wk% chg
Industrial Products	4317.16	+10.2	Nthn Telecom	NTL	111230	66.15	+27.5	Mitel	MLT	88061	12.45	-12.6
Financial Services	7735.39	+9.3	Kingsway Finl	KFS	7792	12.00	+38.7	Fairfax Finl	FFH	177	460.00	+1.1
Utilities	6733.35	+8.0	BCE	BCE	91079	52.30	+12.6	Maritime Tel	MTT	922	33.20	-6.2
Gold & Precious Mnrl	6716.70	+7.2	Greenstone Rs	GRE	25234	2.21	+29.2	Orvana Mnrl	ORV	2630	0.78	-13.3
Conglomerates	8988.04	+6.6	Power Corp	POW	15153	32.50	+13.4	Onex	OCX	7632	33.00	+3.1
Communs & Media	14235.44	+4.4	Torstar B	TS.B	16068	18.35	+14.7	CHUM B	CHM.B	242	33.00	-5.7
Real Estate	2253.72	+3.9	Brookfld Ppy	BPC	18031	16.50	+8.2	Boardwalk Eqt	BEI	1014	16.30	-3.6
Merchandising	5110.83	+3.2	Provigo	PGV	25344	13.65	+57.8	Loblaw	L	1577	28.75	-7.0
Consumer Products	10531.02	+2.8	Allelix Bio	AXB	5824	4.49	+44.8	Maple Lf Food	MFI	371	13.00	-3.7
Oil & Gas	5433.68	+2.4	Fracmaster	FMA	8985	5.50	+34.1	Glfstrm Res	GUR	3340	4.30	-8.5
Pipelines	6367.61	+2.2	TCPL	TRP	54766	23.30	+3.6	Westcoast Enrg	W	7305	30.25	-0.2
Paper & Forest Prods	3569.36	+2.1	Donohue A	DHC.A	2442	32.00	+10.0	Slocan Forest	SFF	1198	2.80	-20.0
Transn & Envrnmtl	5859.47	+0.9	Cdn Natl Rail	CNR	5179	77.05	+2.5	Air Canada A	AC.A	17743	4.90	-7.5
Metals & Minerals	3095.77	-0.7	Aur Res	AUR	851	3.00	+9.1	Rio Algom	ROM	6840	19.50	-9.3

hands of investors residing in Canada. Companies pay dividends out of after-tax income and this tax arrangement provides a big incentive for Canadians to pick a local company over a foreign one.

This situation tends to favor dividend-paying blue chip companies and the home advantage narrows for companies that do not pay dividends. Usually, a non-dividend paying company is in the development stage and the appeal to investors is the prospect of capital gains if the company is successful and grows. The tax issue takes on a new dimension when the investing is done through a registered retirement savings plan because dividends that accumulate within an RRSP are shielded from tax. There are limits on foreign investment by pension funds. The general limit is 20% of the fund.

FOREIGN SECURITIES IN MUTUAL FUNDS ARE NOT CONSIDERED DIRECT INVESTMENTS

With an RRSP, the foreign limit actually can be higher because the 20% applies to direct investment. If the RRSP holds mutual funds, each fund can hold foreign securities up to a 20% limit and those holdings are not counted as part of the limit on direct investment in foreign securities. With foreign holdings, there is the issue of exchange rate fluctuations. Currencies of the big industrial countries tend to move in long cycles against the currencies of their major trading partners. And those currencies tend not to have sharp adjustments when the trend changes. However, currencies of less developed countries have a history of sudden devaluations that come as a shock to investors.

Thus, the risk of currency surprises tends to be much less when investing in securities in the big industrial economies with large, established markets.

TIMING IS EVERYTHING WHEN SELLING

Often the most important investment decision is not when to buy but when to sell. A legion of investment advisers stands ready with advice on what to buy and when to buy but the decision on selling usually is a lonely one. Often, the reasons for selling are dictated by circumstance. Common reasons are that people need the money or that the securities are held in an estate being liquidated.

STOCKS BOUGHT FOR CAPITAL GAINS SHOULD BE SOLD WHEN TARGET PRICE IS REACHED

The plan for selling should be part of the decision to buy. When buying bonds, for example, a decision should be made on whether to hold to maturity.

Prices will fluctuate during the tradable life of a bond but it returns a fixed amount at maturity and this fact can have a bearing on what is a suitable interest rate for the individual shopping to buy a bond. A similar assessment may be part of the decision to buy a stock if the goal is to have dividend income. With a stock, of course, there is no fixed redemption date, but the timing on when to sell may be affected by the outlook for the business cycle.

In the case of a dividend-paying stock, the fundamental analysis that goes into the

FPX | TABLE

The Financial Post indexes (FPX) appear daily on the front of the Investing sections and Mondays in the same place in an expanded format (see below). They are divided into three basic portfolios: FPX Income index, FPX Balanced index and FPX Growth index. Each is broken down by asset mix, and none holds more than 11 securities. The FPX provides the investor a benchmark to compare how well his or her asset mix is performing.

FPX Growth: 1402.88   Weekly % change: 3.03

	Book* units	price $	value $	% port.	Current units	price $	value $	Wk %chg.	% port.
Cash & equivalents			14,252.91	9.95			16,675.17	0.29	11.89
Cash	...	...	19.98	0.01	...	...	355.94	27.05	0.25
Accrued income	...	...	884.68	0.62	...	...	753.76	-5.15	0.54
Gov't Cda 91-day T-bill	135	98.876	13,348.26	9.32	157	99.143	15,565.46	0.09	11.10
Fixed income			28,690.20	20.03			28,929.60	-0.13	20.62
Gov't Cda 7.25% June 1/07	252	113.850	28,690.20	20.03	252	114.800	28,929.60	-0.13	20.62
Equity			100,313.63	70.02			94,682.90	4.55	67.49
TIPS 100	1,095	45.800	50,151.00	35.01	1,095	38.600	42,267.00	7.67	30.13
S&P 500 Deposit. Rcpts.	137	US110.828	21,525.58	15.03	137	US110.125	23,277.94	2.96	16.59
MS WEBS Germany	49	US20.625	1,432.76	1.00	49	US20.688	1,564.08	3.65	1.11
MS WEBS Japan	813	US9.938	11,454.36	8.00	813	US9.625	12,073.05	-0.76	8.61
MS WEBS U.K.	189	US21.438	5,744.28	4.01	189	US18.938	5,522.39	3.30	3.94
MS WEBS Mexico	131	US15.375	2,855.41	1.99	131	US10.500	2,122.20	0.48	1.51
MS WEBS France	257	US19.625	7,150.25	4.99	257	US19.813	7,856.23	3.82	5.60
Total value			143,256.74	100.00			140,287.67	3.03	100.00

FPX Balanced: 1387.90   Weekly % change: 2.10

	Book* units	price $	value $	% port.	Current units	price $	value $	Wk %chg.	% port.
Cash & equivalents			13,922.42	10.01			17,024.20	0.48	12.27
Cash	...	...	9.39	0.01	...	...	213.61	29.95	0.15
Accrued income	...	...	1,059.15	0.76	...	...	1,145.98	1.62	0.83
Gov't Cda 91-day T-bill	130	98.876	12,853.88	9.24	158	99.143	15,664.61	0.09	11.29
Fixed income			55,577.77	39.95			56,100.87	-0.12	40.42
Gov't Cda 7.0% Sept. 1/01	175	105.862	18,525.85	13.32	175	105.840	18,522.00	0.03	13.35
Gov't Cda 7.25% June 1/07	163	113.850	18,557.55	13.34	163	114.800	18,712.40	-0.13	13.48
Gov't Cda 8.0% June 1/27	139	133.053	18,494.37	13.29	139	135.730	18,866.47	-0.24	13.59
Equity			69,626.19	50.05			65,665.06	4.52	47.31
TIPS 100	759	45.800	34,762.20	24.99	759	38.600	29,297.40	7.67	21.11
S&P 500 Deposit. Rcpts.	89	US110.828	13,983.77	10.05	89	US110.125	15,122.17	2.96	10.90
MS WEBS Germany	36	US20.625	1,052.64	0.76	36	US20.688	1,149.12	3.65	0.83
MS WEBS Japan	592	US9.938	8,340.69	6.00	592	US9.625	8,791.20	-0.76	6.33
MS WEBS U.K.	137	US21.438	4,163.84	2.99	137	US18.938	4,003.00	3.30	2.88
MS WEBS Mexico	96	US15.375	2,092.51	1.50	96	US10.500	1,555.20	0.48	1.12
MS WEBS France	188	US19.625	5,230.54	3.76	188	US19.813	5,746.97	3.82	4.14
Total value			139,126.37	100.00			138,790.14	2.10	100.00

FPX Income: 1350.30   Weekly % change: 1.71

	Book* units	price $	value $	% port.	Current units	price $	value $	Wk %chg.	% port.
Cash & equivalents			27,268.24	20.11			30,811.15	0.35	22.82
Cash	...	...	38.87	0.03	...	...	167.60	16.54	0.12
Accrued income	...	...	1,224.98	0.90	...	...	1,396.34	4.37	1.03
Gov't Cda 91-day T-bill	263	98.876	26,004.39	19.17	295	99.143	29,247.21	0.09	21.66
Fixed income			67,709.92	49.92			68,348.42	-0.12	50.62
Gov't Cda 7.0% Sept. 1/01	213	105.862	22,548.61	16.63	213	105.840	22,543.92	0.03	16.70
Gov't Cda 7.25% June 1/07	198	113.850	22,542.30	16.62	198	114.800	22,730.40	-0.13	16.83
Gov't Cda 8.0% June 1/27	170	133.053	22,619.01	16.68	170	135.730	23,074.10	-0.24	17.09
Equity			40,648.20	29.97			35,870.22	6.68	26.56
TIPS 100	740	45.800	33,892.00	24.99	740	38.600	28,564.00	7.67	21.15
S&P 500 Deposit. Rcpts.	43	US110.828	6,756.20	4.98	43	US110.125	7,306.22	2.96	5.41
Total value			135,626.36	100.00			135,029.79	1.71	100.00

Index base value 1,000 on $100,000 invested April 1, 1996.   * at rebalancing April 1, 1998   Note: Totals may not add up due to rounding.

decision to buy should be kept handy for regular checks on whether the company's performance is living up to expectations. If it isn't, there should be guidelines in place on when to recognize facts and sell. If stocks are being bought on expectations of capital gains, part of the decision should be a target price. Once a stock reaches that target price, there should be fresh reasons for continuing to hold.

THE INSIDE STORY ON COMPANY INSIDERS

Timely information is essential to making investment decisions, and having a head start on that information means having an advantage in the market. That's why special rules apply to insiders – the people inside a company who have access to information that's not available to the general investing public.

One of the rules is that insiders are required to report their trading activity in a timely manner. These trades are reported in securities commission bulletins. News that insiders are buying or selling in big volume usually is an important signal to other investors about the prospects for the company. Insiders are defined in securities legislation and usually they are defined as senior management, the directors and those who hold a share of the voting stock.

INSIDERS HAVE ACCESS TO INFORMATION THAT CAN AFFECT STOCK PRICES

In Canada, the ownership threshold is 10%. The practical reason is that someone who represents 10% or more of the ownership can get through on the phone to the president or the treasurer and chat about the company's operations. But someone who holds a few hundred shares only gets the standard printed information sheets from the investor relations department.

Officers of a company are insiders because they see the financial results first and have the power to affect those results. Employees down the line may have insights not available to the general public, but they don't have the authority to act on those insights. Members of the board of directors are insiders because they get direct reports from management and the board sets the general policy direction for the company.

These definitions can extend to subsidiary companies or affiliated firms because information that is sensitive to the stock price usually is shared by these key people in a corporate structure. When insiders report their stockholdings, they give details on "beneficial" ownership. That extends to shares held by family members or held through personal holding companies.

PROMOTER'S ROLE NOT ALWAYS THE HEAVY

Promoter is a much-maligned term because most companies would never survive the development stage without the services of a promoter. They're the ones who tell the company's story and raise the money. As a group, though, they have a bad reputation because too many oversell the story and divert money away from legitimate corporate expenses.

Still, the securities industry needs promoters, and a working relationship has been established between those who hustle stocks and those who stand on guard against excesses in the investment business.

Securities acts define the role of promoters and this sets the ground rules for regulation of their activities.

THERE ARE TWO BASIC DEFINITIONS OF A PROMOTER

• Someone who "takes the initiative in founding, organizing or substantially reorganizing the business of an issuer [a company]."
• Someone who receives 10% or more of any class of securities issued by a company or who receives 10% or more of the proceeds from the sale of any class of securities.

Securities legislation doesn't distinguish between small and large companies but as a practical matter the role of promoter applies to speculative junior companies.

Typically, promoters are compensated with stock. They often get salaries as well but the big paydays come from getting founders' shares at next to nothing and selling into the market when the company strikes paydirt.

To protect outside investors, securities rules set minimum hold periods for stock held by promoters so as to ensure they cannot cash out while promoting sale of stock to the general public.

TICKERS REVEAL A LOT OF INFORMATION

The word "ticker" is rapidly becoming an archaic market term. In its original meaning, it referred to the ticker tape that transmitted stock trade prices from stock exchanges to brokerage firms. A specialized teletype machine, which made a constant ticking sound, used to print stock price information on long ribbons of paper. Ticker tape parades were possible in New York because Wall Street produced truckloads of ticker tape. They're confetti parades now.

These days, ticker usually means the unique symbol that identifies a stock. Those symbols are important to people who call up stock quotations from electronic databases.

But tickers also are important as a way of identifying the right securities where companies issue more than one class of security and trade on more than one exchange.

Many of the blue chip companies are in that category. For example, a search of Royal Bank of Canada in a securities database turns up about 40 different stock symbols.

There are two or three components to the ticker. Look at "RY/pe.M" as an example. The first is the symbol for the company – RY for Royal Bank. If those two letters appear alone, it is assumed to be a reference to common stock traded on the primary exchange – where the majority of trading takes place – which is the Toronto Stock Exchange in this case. The symbol "RY/pe" refers to the bank's class E preferred stock. The "M" in this example denotes the fact that these shares are listed on the Montreal Exchange.

Stock symbols are a feature of market columns in financial newspapers. Trading information for stocks on major Canadian and U.S. stock exchanges is published in the weekday editions of The Financial Post. The weekend edition also has a weekly trading summary.

All the basic information about trading in stocks is in these tables, including volume and earnings information as well as price activity.

Volume is important because a minimum volume is necessary to ensure liquidity, which means the stock can be bought or sold without a price distortion. A sudden change in volume compared with a longer term average usually means speculation about a corporate development.

Earnings show up in the stock tables as part of the ratio of price to earnings as well as the amount of earnings attributed to each share. Stock tables also show the latest dividend payout rate.

Price details include the high and low over the last 12 months, which provides a hint on how a current stock price fits into any cyclical pattern for that stock.

FUNDAMENTALS APPLY IN ANALYSING STOCKS

Stock picking is the primary job in managing most portfolios and the toolkit for this chore is called fundamental analysis. As the name implies, it involves getting down to basics. The approach is similar for both stocks and bonds. The underlying questions deal with the actual or expected profitability of the issuer.

Can it earn enough to sustain regular dividend payments or continue the flow of interest payments on bonds? And if the issuer is a company, can it expand its market share so that stockholders can share in the growth? As a general rule, there are two components to this line of inquiry – an analysis of different groups of issuers and then an assessment of which are the best performers in the best group. Sector analysis depends partly on broad economic trends. For example, the resource stocks usually lead the market when the economy is coming out of recession.

FUNDAMENTAL ANALYSIS INVOLVES TRENDS AND RATIOS

But the fundamental component of this exercise means looking at whether the resource sector is growing and how it is changing.

For example, what is the impact on mining companies of a trend in the auto industry to replace galvanized metal with plastic? Are the miners finding new customers as demand from the old ones declines?

If prospects for the sector look promising, the job then is to compare the players in that field. This rating often involves looking for the low-cost producers, but investors need to consider their own time horizons.

A company can be a low-cost producer by cutting back on research and development, a strategy that can give a quick boost to profits in the short term but ultimately put the company at a competitive disadvantage.

Fundamental analysis contains large doses of trends and ratios.

HERE ARE SOME OF THE THINGS TO WATCH FOR

• **Revenue, profit and cash flow:** Are these on a rising trend with no serious breaks in the pattern?

• **Profit margin:** Is the company getting a reasonable return on its revenue and invested capital?

• **Interest, asset and dividend coverage:** Is the earnings flow strong enough to ensure that interest and dividends can be paid with no strain and is the asset base big enough in relation to the current debt load.

• **Debt-to-equity ratio:** Is the size of the ownership stake big enough to provide a proper balance against bonds and bank debt? (An acceptable standard for the debt-to-equity ratio will vary from industry to industry.)

• **Product innovation:** Is the company keeping up with its peers in research, or, better, is it out in front?

• **Quality of management:** Is there depth on the bench in key areas – operations, marketing and financial?

THE GOLDEN ALLURE OF BLUE CHIP STOCKS

Perhaps unfortunately, the term blue chip comes from gambling – poker to be exact. Blue chips are the markers worth the most at the card table and in the stock market they refer to blue-blood companies. Another common term for the equity of these firms is widows and orphans stocks – shares that are bought for their income potential over the long haul. Historically, the shares of these senior companies have had earning power and have provided competition for bonds. Investors buy bonds for the interest income, and dividends paid by big companies have had to provide a competitive return.

More recently, rising stock prices have meant that investors have placed less emphasis on dividends. But big companies still retain their appeal because a steady income flow usually means their stock prices are less affected by cyclical turns in the market.

Tax treatment is an important consideration for those who buy dividend-paying stocks. Companies pay dividends with after-tax income. Since the money has already been taxed at the corporate level, shareholders get a tax break on dividend income from equities. Blue chips tend to be the biggest companies in a national economy and the 30 stocks in the Dow Jones industrial average often are seen as the bluest of blue chips. They all are large companies with international divisions and proven dividend records.

The companies in the Toronto Stock Exchange 35-stock index have similar status in the Canadian economy.

PREFERRED SHARES PROMISE HIGH YIELDS

Investors who want the capital gains potential of common stocks but also want high dividends often look at preferred stock. However, the choice is not a simple one because preferred shares – known colloquially as "prefs" – come in several forms.

When research analysts look at a company's capital stock, some prefs are considered equity because they look more like common stock and some are considered debt because they look more like bonds.

GENERALLY, PREFERRED SHARES HAVE THESE COMMON CHARACTERISTICS

• **The dividend payment schedule** is fixed in advance and dividends must be paid. If a company is in financial difficulty, the terms of a preferred issue usually specify that dividends can only be postponed to a future date but back payments must be made when financial conditions improve.

• **Dividends** on most prefs are treated like common stock dividends for tax purposes in that the company pays out of after-tax income and the shareholder gets a tax break.

• **Preferred shareholders** rank ahead of common stockholders but behind bondholders in claims on the assets of a company in any bankruptcy proceeding.

BID/ASK | TABLE

The main stock table lists shares that have traded during the day. If a stock is in a bid/ask table, it means there was no trading activity during the day for which the table is dated. The bid is the best offer to buy and the ask is the best offer to sell. Brokers may have other bid or ask prices on their trading books but only the best prices are listed on lists seen by the public.

VANCOUVER BID/ASK

Quotes for stocks traded in past five days

Stock	Ticker	Bid	Ask	Last	Stock	Ticker	Bid	Ask	Last	Stock	Ticker	Bid	Ask	Last
AGX Res	AXS	0.06	0.12	0.06	BanksVent	BKL	0.18	0.35	0.17	ColumbGld	COB	0.05	0.07	0.05
AIM Grp*	AIG	3.00	3.50	3.00	BardSlv	BDS	0.07	0.12	0.10	ConnDev	CCD	0.03	0.15	0.05
AME Res	AME	0.50	0.70	0.50	Bargold	BGA	0.62	0.90	0.62	ConEarth	CEW	0.13	0.19	0.14
AMI Res	AMU	0.37	0.38	0.38	Barkhor	BHO	0.03	0.04	0.03	ConsEco	CES	0.41	0.50	0.43
AMR Corpt	ARG	0.05	0.07	0.05	BarrierMn	BMI	0.07	0.08	0.05	ConEnviro	CWD	0.55	1.00	0.60
APAC Mnrl	APC	0.49	0.71	0.55	BigBar	BBK	0.04	0.08	0.05	ConEwing	CWG	0.01	0.03	0.03
ASC Inds	ASD	0.20	0.30	0.30	Bitterroot	BTT	0.06	0.09	0.07	ConGnDiam	GDA	0.01	0.03	0.02
AceDev	AE	0.04	0.05	0.04	BlackTusk	BTU	0.35	0.45	0.34	ConGldWin	CGW	0.20	0.24	0.20
Adamas	AMS	0.03	0.06	0.03	Braiden	BZR	0.05	0.10	0.05	ConGulfsd	CGL	0.21	0.24	0.21

CDN UNLISTED | TABLE

The CDN Unlisted table shows stocks that trade on a daily basis on the Canadian Dealing Network. CDN is operated by the TSE as an over-the-counter market in which securities transactions are conducted through a telephone or computer network connecting individual dealers, as opposed to the central auction system as operated by a stock exchange. Over-the-counter stocks are typically smaller cap and tend not to meet the more stringent listing requirements of stock exchanges.

CDN UNLISTED 10.27.98

Figures supplied by Star Data Systems Inc.

Stock	Ticker	Vol 00s	High	Low	Cls	Net chg	Stock	Ticker	Vol 00s	High	Low	Cls	Net chg
AMT Fine	AMTE	118	1.65	1.20	1.65		EWMC	EWMI	310	0.20	0.18	0.19	+0.01
Aavdex	AAEX	50	0.17	0.17	0.17	–0.03	EnginPwr	EPSX	5788	2.25	1.25	2.15	–0.10
AllegEq	ALGN	22	1.05	1.05	1.05		Envtret	ETSI	100	0.005	0.005	0.005	
AlphaGrp	ALFG	50	0.10	0.10	0.10	+0.03	EurNevwt	ERNM	552	23	21½	23	+1½
Ambrex	AMBX	4020	0.08	0.06	0.08	+0.01	FlcnWll	FWSL	80	0.01	0.01	0.01	–0.04
Asian TV	ATNL	10	0.45	0.45	0.45	–0.05	Farini	FRNI	20	0.02	0.02	0.02	
Avenza	AVZA	115	0.10	0.10	0.10	+0.05	Footmax	FTMX	100	0.40	0.40	0.40	
BanroRes	BNRS	50	0.64	0.64	0.64	+0.06	FrNevBwt	FRNV	20	16¾	16¾	16¾	–⅛
BevGlen	BGCC	95	0.30	0.25	0.30		Gemstar	GSTR	20	0.35	0.35	0.35	–0.05
BiogenT	BGTI	400	0.65	0.50	0.50	–0.20	GldCorl	GOCR	135	0.25	0.25	0.25	
BlackMtn	BKMT	408	1.79	1.75	1.79	+0.04	Goldmint	GMEX	z200	0.10	0.10	0.10	
BlkPearl	BLKP	315	0.08	0.06	0.06	–0.02	GolfNth	GFNP	266	2.60	2.00	2.60	

- **Most preferreds** have a "par" or redemption value, which is the price a company pays for each share if it buys back a preferred stock issue.
- **Preferred stock** usually is non-voting stock.

Dividends on conventional preferreds are a fixed amount but some preferreds have variable rate dividends pegged to a benchmark, such as the prime loan rate. And some preferreds have provisions that allow a company to skip dividends under specified distress situations.

PREFERRED SHARES GENERALLY HAVE BUYBACK TERMS SET OUT AT ISSUE

A conventional, or straight, preferred share issue looks somewhat like a common stock, except that the prefs pay dividends and usually have a par value. But straight prefs usually are considered part of the permanent equity of a company. The distinction is that these preferred shares do not have a redemption date and the company is under no obligation to buy back the shares on a fixed future date.

Most preferred shares are callable (or redeemable), which means the company can buy back the stock at its convenience. The redemption price will be part of the terms of issue. If a pref share is retractable, the holder can force the company to buy back the stock. Again, the terms of a buyback will be set out in the terms of the issue, usually at a fixed price and on a certain future date or after a certain future date.

Convertible preferred shares can, as the name implies, be swapped for another class of security at a preset conversion rate. Usually, they're convertible to common stock and features will vary on when and how the conversion clauses are triggered.

Whether a preferred issue is more like a stock or a bond will affect the market price.

For example, a convertible preferred issue that can be exchanged for common shares will react to changes in the market price of the common. But a simple preferred issue with a fixed dividend amount, a par value and a pre-set redemption date looks much like a bond and the price of this preferred will react to changes in the general level of interest rates, just as bonds do.

A POUND OF ADVICE ON PENNY STOCKS

 Canadian markets have a long history of financing junior companies and some of these penny resource stocks have gone on to become blue chips. High-tech and biotechnology companies are a significant component of the penny stock universe and they share many of the features associated with stocks of junior mining exploration companies.

Like any small business, the failure rate is high among start-up companies with stock exchange listings. A further complication is that markets for these juniors have been a natural magnet for unethical operators and, in a few cases, outright crooks.

Dealing with shares of these companies means recognizing some of their inherent characteristics. They need promoters to raise money and the job is to sell a dream, whether it be a gold mine or the next breakthrough in medical science.

A concept driven by intellectual analysis always is at the core of an honest penny stock. With a resource exploration company, it is the geology of the area and likelihood of underground riches. With a technology company, it is a research project that the promoters believe can be turned into a commercial venture.

THUS, THERE ARE THREE COMPONENTS TO A PENNY STOCK
• **The concept:** Is it an idea that stands up to rigorous analysis? If it is an exploration project, have others found commercial grades in similar geology? If it is a technology concept, is it based on sound science? Obviously, research will be necessary to answer these questions – either direct research on the concept or a search for opinions from people who understand the concept.

• **The promoter:** Does the promoter have a track record for straightforward dealings and for backing winning projects?

• **The commercial application:** If a discovery or breakthrough is made, can it be brought to market? There are plenty of examples of exploration properties with real discoveries but grades that are too low or so far away from refining operations that transportation costs eat up the profits. With technology projects, there are plenty of examples where the breakthrough produces a product that no one needs or that too many others can imitate cheaply.

If a junior company does hit the jackpot, the historical lesson is that the company is not likely to survive as the operator. In most cases, the junior becomes a takeover target for two reasons. The first is that it will need development funds, which usually means a lot more money than is spent on the discovery process and it is the mature companies that have better access to big pools of capital. The second reason a successful junior is likely to be bought out is that the promotion skills in the junior are no longer needed and the junior is not likely to have the depth of management skills that are required to turn a concept into a profitable commercial venture.

When a junior company does strike it rich, the shareholders usually have two choices. They can sell into the market for cash when the company is shopping for a well-heeled partner to manage the project. If they wait, they likely will end up with stock in the senior company because most big companies prefer to pay with stock and not cash when taking over a junior with a valuable property.

NAVIGATING THE MUCH-CHARTED WATERS
By Roman Franko

Equity investors place their hard-earned savings in the market to make a return higher than they could earn in risk-free investments such as money market funds.

To profit successfully and consistently, they must identify stocks that offer favorable risk-reward odds. A close examination of a stock's past price and volume behavior over time can be a valuable, sometimes indispensable, form of analysis in ongoing efforts to reduce risk and maximize return. Here we will introduce the basic tools of technical analysis, as well as the mindset required to apply them successfully.

USING PRICE-BASED TECHNIQUES, ANALYSTS CAN IDENTIFY TRENDS
The technical analyst today typically first examines price in its raw chart form to identify trends and patterns that have forecasting value and then uses a computer to calculate indicators to reveal price relationships not readily apparent. We'll first examine three price-based techniques and then apply them to that quintessential Canadian stock, Canadian Pacific Ltd.

Once a trend, either up or down, is established, it cannot be expected to proceed in an absolutely straight line. Rather, price typically moves higher in a two steps forward, one step back fashion. One technique of tracking whether a trend remains in place is seeing whether today's price remains above, or below, its average price over a selected period of time. Typically, two time frames are chosen: a shorter one such as 13 periods and a longer one such as 40 periods.

In a strong trend, the price will remain above/below its shorter term **moving average** (MA). On occasion, it will move temporarily through its shorter MA but as long as the price does not penetrate the longer one, it remains in its trend. A penetration by the price and the short term MA of the longer one is a sign the trend is ending, and a sideways consolidation or reversal can be expected.

Many trading systems, which generate buy or sell signals to be mechanically taken without second guessing, are based on some variations of price and/or the shorter term MA crossing the longer one.

INVESTORS KEEP AN EYE ON A STOCK'S UP AND DOWN TREND

 The next step is to establish the boundaries of an up or down trend. Once a couple of **wave tops** or **bottoms** are established, one line can be drawn, with another initially unconfirmed line drawn parallel to it. These lines delineate the outer limits of the stock's value range. At the upper line, bearish investors think price is overvalued and will sell and drive the price down. At the lower line, bullish investors feel the price is undervalued and will buy and bid it back into the range. A decisive break out of this range indicates the former consensus has broken down and a new one is being formed.

There are many price-derived indicators other than moving averages, some particularly helpful in trending markets, while others are of greater utility in markets that are

TECHNICAL ANALYSIS | BY ROMAN FRANKO

THE MONEY FLOW INDEX peaked early 1996 and by 1997 was hitting noticeably lower highs.

THE LOWER MACD HIGHS during late 1997 were an important sign of weakness before the November 1997 sell signal.

CP nicely illustrates the saying that a trend will stay in motion until some factor disrupts it. Between March 1995 and December 1997, CP created a very clean and reliable channel, indicating a certain rate of advance by bulls and of retreat by the bears. This rate of rise abruptly came to an end December 1996, when the bears staged a strong counter-attack. Bear trends tends to much less predictable than their bullish counterparts, and thus it is normally very difficult to establish clear channels during a price drop.

MOVING AVERAGES are another frequently used method of following a trend. Once an up trend was clearly established by early 1996, trading in the direction of the 40-week moving average would have kept investors on side. The only breakdown through this MA occurred April 1997, but here use of channel lines should have kept the investor in the trade, albeit not without some anxious days!

* The Moving Average Convergence Divergence indicator consists of two moving averages revolving above and below a zero line. A buy signal occurs when the faster (solid) line crosses above the slower (broken) line; a sell is signalled when the converse occurs. Data supplied by Reuters trading sideways. **Moving average convergence divergence,** or MACD, is a popular one as it is useful in confirming trends in both kinds of markets. Its principal utility, however, is in signalling a change in trend by diverging, or not confirming, a price trend.

MONEY FLOW IS ONE INDICATOR OF A STOCK'S STRENGTH

Before we apply these techniques to Canadian Pacific, let's note that CP made a series of higher highs and lows between March and November 1995 – a basic confirmation of an up trend. The November 1995 move up took the price above its moving averages, and the MACD gave a buy signal, triggered when the faster solid line crossed above the broken slower line. These tools were important interim ones, as the upper trend line could not be drawn until the price reversed from a major wave top in December 1996. At that point, a line parallel to the upper one could be drawn from the November 1995 bottom, and this lower channel line indeed proved its forecasting utility when the price reversed from it in May 1997. More recently, the MACD hit a lower high in August 1997, even as the price hit a new high, a negative divergence subsequently confirmed by the price fall below its moving averages.

Volume similarly provides a host of clues to the technical position of a stock. Very simply, rising volume provides a solid underpinning and confirms a price rise, while falling

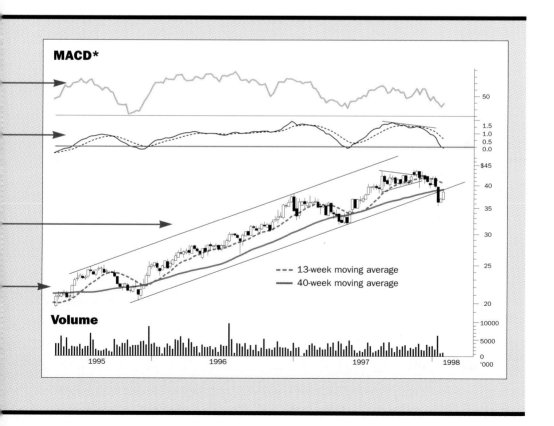

BLOCK TRADES | TABLE

Block transactions – 100,000 shares or a value of more than $1 million – usually are trades for institutions, such as pension or mutual funds.

Ticker is the stock symbol; price is the trade price; volume is the number of shares. Buyer and seller are the brokerage firms on each side of the transaction.

A single name indicates it is a "cross," where the broker represents both sides.

A cross may mean that both buyer and seller are clients of the firm or that the brokerage house is buying or selling shares out of inventory in house accounts.

BLOCK TRADES

Stocks trading minimum 100,000 shares or $1 million

Ticker	Price	Vol. 00s	Buyer/ Seller	Ticker	Price	Vol. 00s	Buyer/ Seller	Ticker	Price	Vol. 00s	Buyer/ Seller
Toronto				BarrickGld IR	ABX.IR	21.30	570	Bunting	Franco-Nevada	FN	29.75	3000	Griffith
AGRA Inc	AGR	7.95	1170	CT Secs	Baton Brdcst	BNB	18.00	4000	TD Secs	Geac Computer	GAC	34.75	300	Research
ATI Technlgys	ATY	11.80	1000	Yorkton	BatonBrdcstIR	BNB.IR	7.70	4000	TD Secs	Geac Computer		34.75	500	Gordon
ATI Technlgys		11.70	1250	Gordon	Beau Cda Expl	BAU	2.00	2000	Gordon	Gldn Knight	GKR	0.66	7000	Fairvest
ATI Technlgys		11.70	1000	LevBeau	Beau Cda Expl		2.00	1000	Nesbitt	Gulf Cda Res	GOU	6.00	2000	TD Secs
ATI Technlgys		11.50	6250	Gordon	Beau Cda Expl		2.00	1272	Nwcrst	Harrowston A	HRW.A	5.10	1478	Sprott
ATI Technlgys		11.25	1000	Gordon	Bid.Com Intl	BII	1.10	1294	Yorkton	Hudson's Bay	HBC	19.40	1000	Merrill
ATI Technlgys		11.25	1000	Research	Bombard B	BBD.B	18.60	2200	CIBC	Hurricane A	HHL.A	3.00	1000	Griffith
ATI Technlgys		11.35	1100	HSBC	Bowater Cda	BWX	62.15	250	Gordon	Hurricane A		2.99	7892	Instnet
ATI Technlgys		11.45	1000	Gordon	Bowater Cda		62.50	1000	TD Secs	Husky Injctn	HKY.W	13.20	4000	Scotia
ATI Technlgys		11.50	1000	Research	Brookfld Ppy	BPC	16.50	1000	Scotia	Husky Injctn		13.00	1500	Scotia
ATI Technlgys		11.50	2000	Research	Brookfld Ppy		16.50	610	CIBC	Husky Injctn		12.65	1000	Nesbitt
Abitibi-Cons	A	15.05	1100	CIBC	CAE	CAE	9.40	1000	Yorkton	IPSCO	IPS	30.90	1075	Nesbitt
Air Canada	AC	6.30	1000	Nwcrst	CAE		9.30	1000	Merrill	Imasco	IMS	28.95	500	Scotia
Air Canada A	AC.A	5.20	1000	Nwcrst	CE Franklin	CFT	4.50	2000	Peters	Imasco		28.75	1540	CIBC
Alberta Enrg	AEC	36.20	480	Peters	Cadillac Frvw	CDF	28.75	681	CIBC	Imperial Oil	IMO	24.65	500	Peters
Alcan	AL	38.35	1000	RBCDS	Cadillac Frvw		28.75	500	CIBC	Inco	N	15.95	1000	RBCDS
Alcan		38.35	825	CIBC	Canada Bread	CBY	21.50	500	CIBC	Inco pf E	N.PR.U	38.00	9250	Scotia
Alcan		38.50	300	LevBeau	CIBC	CM	31.70	500	Scotia	Inmet Mining	IMN	3.10	1300	RBCDS
Alcan		38.50	297	LevBeau	CIBC		31.70	500	CIBC	Inmet Mining		3.10	2000	Griffith
Astral Comm B	ACM.B	17.75	968	Griffith	CIBC		31.70	500	CIBC	Intrawest	ITW	24.00	1000	Research
BC Gas	BCG	31.90	500	Merrill	CIBC		31.05	372	CSFB	JDS FITEL	JDS	23.25	500	Nesbitt
BCE	BCE	52.80	250	Nesbitt	CIBC		31.25	1375	CIBC	JDS FITEL		23.00	2090	Nesbitt

volume after a price rise has been in progress for some time is a sign of incipient weakness. In a bear market, the situation is somewhat different, for while a volume surge as a stock falls is a sign of urgent selling, the price can and often does fall on thin volume.

Volume-derived indicators have also been developed, all of which attempt to identify accumulation or distribution of stock. One helpful indicator is money flow, which measures the strength of money flowing in or out of a stock. In the case of CP, money flow strength peaked in the first half of 1996, and the lower highs of late 1996 and July 1997 indicate the buying power that underpins a bullish campaign was dissipating.

TIME PLAYS KEY ROLE IN THE RESOLUTION OF PATTERNS

The time factor can play an important role in at least two different ways. Most stocks cycle up and down with a greater or lesser regularity, generally in concert with others in their group. These cycles may be longer term and related to, for example, the oft referred to four-year business cycle, or shorter term and dependent on, for example, seasonal fluctuations in supply and demand. CP's current bull market will be three years old in March 1998, and thus the odds increasingly favor a correction over the next 15 months.

Time also becomes important in the resolution of patterns. For example, CP formed a narrowing symmetrical triangle pattern between late July and mid October of 1997. The rule of thumb is that if the price breaks out before it reaches two-thirds of the way to the apex of that triangle, the subsequent move will typically be strong. If, however, the breakout does not come in this time period, the price displays a strong tendency, even if it does breakout, to drift sideways to down. Thus, another sign of upcoming CP weakness was given when its price broke out of its triangle late and in a weak fashion.

TECHNICAL ANALYSTS DRAW ON YEARS OF EXPERIENCE

In short, technical analysis can minimize risk by identifying stocks that are: at the lower edge of their price channels, at or above their moving averages, have rising momentum, are supported by favorable volume trends, and are early on in their longer term cycles.

Conversely, these tools can identify stocks that are high risk if they are: at an upper channel line, at or below their moving averages, have falling momentum and unfavorable volume trends, and are late in their longer term cycles.

To be done well, technical analysis has to be done thoroughly, looking at all relevant aspects of a stock's behavior in as objective a manner as possible. Like other forms of analysis, a partial or superficial treatment to justify an opinion previously arrived at, or seizing on one aspect while ignoring contradictory evidence, will undermine its utility.

Finally, the good technical analyst needs to strike a balance between taking a position and holding to it, and changing a position when the preponderance of evolving evidence requires it. At what point this change in evaluation takes place can only be decided in specific cases by drawing on years of intensive experience in assessing the many combinations and variations that arise.

CHAPTER 3

BEYOND | EQUITIES

- Understanding derivatives
- Investment strategies using options, warrants, shorts and REITs
- Commodities markets
- Futures and indexes

HOW THE TOP GUNS PICK

THEIR STOCK MARKET TARGETS | BY SONITA HORVITCH

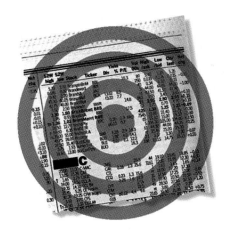

THE HALLMARK OF PROFESSIONAL money managers is that they apply a consistent, disciplined approach to selecting stocks and constructing equity portfolios. The two principal styles employed by equity managers are value investing and growth investing. These two broad categories encompass a wide variety of practices as managers develop their own variations on the basic theme. In a nutshell, a value manager tries to identify stocks that are fundamentally cheap based on such standard valuation ratios as stock price to earnings, stock price to cash flow, stock price to book value and stock price to revenue. In a value portfolio, the standard valuations of stocks would typically be below those for the market as a whole.

Growth managers look for companies that are generating very high revenue, earnings and cash flow growth. They are hoping to find the next Microsoft Corp., Procter & Gamble Inc. or Coca-Cola Co. A growth manager's portfolio would typically trade at valuation ratios above those for the market as a whole.

Investing professionals say neither the value nor the growth style alone will result in peak performance at all times. Pension fund consultant and money manager Frank Russell Canada Ltd. recommends a mix of styles in a portfolio to reduce fluctuations in returns over the long haul.

The concept of value investing is very much associated with Benjamin Graham who, in his magnum opus *Security Analysis*, published in 1934, suggested investors should be able to detect undervalued or bargain stocks by looking at key financial ratios.

Howson Tattersall Investment Counsel Ltd. of Toronto is a value manager in the strictest sense of the discipline. It assesses a stock based on existing financials and not on potential. A test Howson Tattersall employs compares a company's total market capitalization (market price multiplied by the number of shares outstanding) against its private market value. The private value is what a knowledgeable investor would pay for the whole company.

VALUE-ORIENTED INVESTORS LOOK AT TRACK RECORD TO PREDICT EARNINGS

Often, companies in the portfolios of value managers become takeover targets of other companies because their market capitalizations are below their private market values.

Another leading proponent of value-oriented investing is the Templeton group. It starts with the traditional approach, looking at historical valuation ratio benchmarks such as price/earnings, price/cash flow and price/book value.

Templeton then takes this assessment further by estimating the company's likely earnings growth or asset growth over the next five years.

Its mission is to find stocks worldwide that it believes to be selling at the greatest discount to calculated value five years hence. Included in the exercise is a detailed analysis of the factors that may cause earnings and/or assets to increase over the next five years.

VALUE MANAGERS TARGET BARGAIN STOCKS

Templeton's analysts and portfolio managers worldwide generate a global list of bargains. Each stock on that list has an established buy and sell target.

Although value managers are essentially stock pickers, on occasion an entire industry or sector may present bargain opportunities. For example, the Canadian retail industry in the mid-1990s was seen to be under siege from foreign competition and was suffering from a general reluctance by consumers to spend. The stock prices of retailers were beaten down and canny value managers started to buy the shares of some of Canada's largest listed retailers.

Generally, the value style of investing is viewed as conservative. Value managers say inexpensive stocks are likely to be less vulnerable to a market downturn. Their values are already depressed.

If the market as a whole is overvalued, and therefore vulnerable to correction, the value manager might have a tougher time identifying cheap candidates and is likely to have a high cash component that will serve as a cushion in a downturn.

GROWTH INVESTORS LOOK FOR STOCKS WITH CONSISTENTLY HIGH RETURNS

The focus of the growth investor is decidedly on the future. This type of investor looks for companies or sectors able to produce the highest and most consistent growth in revenue, earnings or cash flow. The discipline is not to pay too much for this growth, says

Laura Wallace, who is one of Canada's leading growth managers. She is vice-president and portfolio manager at AGF Management Ltd. of Toronto.

There are some sectors that are viewed as the traditional hunting ground for growth stocks. These include technology, both hardware and software, biotechnology, telecommunications, health care and consumer staples such as beverages, cigarettes and household products. A company may be generating earnings and cash flow growth both internally or through acquisition.

Because the prospects of these companies are generally seen to be excellent, the stocks trade at multiples that can be very high relative to the market average.

For example, in July 1997, Coca-Cola shares were trading at 40 times the consensus analyst forecast for earnings per share for the following 12 months.

This P/E multiple was roughly double that of the company's prospective annual earnings growth rate and at least twice that of the comparative price/earnings multiple for the U.S. equity market as a whole

GROWTH STOCKS CAN WEATHER MARKET DOWNTURN

Such high multiples make stocks vulnerable to any disappointing results. The stock of a company reporting earnings or cash flow below analysts' expectations can take a severe beating – even in a bull market. High technology companies are a prime example.

In a market downturn, growth stocks may initially take a beating as investors take profits in their top performing stocks. But growth managers argue such stocks are likely to recover more quickly than the market as a whole – provided their growth potential is unscathed. This is because their earnings power will stand out relative to the rest of the market.

Growth businesses are, by definition, less sensitive to the economic climate than are, say, retailers or real estate developers.

Wallace notes the U.S. equity market has a far wider range of growth companies than the Canadian market does. The Canadian market has a heavier weighting in resource and economically sensitive stocks. This is why a Canadian growth portfolio will feature stocks – mining, forest products and oil stocks, for instance – that might not appear in a U.S. growth portfolio.

FORMULA HELPS GROWTH MANAGERS PREDICT EARNINGS PROSPECTS

Wallace adopts a two-step approach to stock selection. First, she identifies companies that are expected to produce superior revenue, cash flow and earnings growth over the next two to three years. Then she assesses how much to pay for that growth.

One measure of the attractiveness of a growth stock is when its price earnings ratio is less than the expected earnings growth rate.

Another measure relates the relative price/earnings ratio and growth rate to that of the overall market.

Growth managers will sell a stock when there has been a deterioration in the fundamentals or when the stock price is too high relative to its earnings prospects.

THE SAFE HARBOR THAT'S KNOWN AS DIVERSITY

Jay Gould, the 19th-century railroad baron, provides an insight into the potential perils of staking a portfolio on a single stock. Clifton Fadiman, in a book of anecdotes, tells a story of the rector at Gould's church who went to the financier for advice on how to invest his life savings. Buy Missouri Pacific, Gould said, but keep it confidential. The share price for Missouri Pacific did rise for a while, but then it plunged.

DIVERSIFYING IS KEY TO A BALANCED PORTFOLIO

The distraught minister complained to Gould, who promptly wrote a cheque to cover the loss.

This act of apparent generosity left the minister feeling guilty and he admitted to Gould that he had told several members of the congregation about the stock tip. "I know that," Gould said. "They were the ones I was after."

Diversification would have given the last laugh to Gould's enemies.

The goal in balancing a portfolio is to ensure that losses in a single security don't sink the investment fund.

Professional managers usually have limits imposed by their boards or investment committees. Typically, no more than 5% can go to one security and with a large fund the big holdings are in top quality investments.

For individual portfolios, a 10% limit usually is recommended for investment in a single stock.

A DIVERSIFIED PORTFOLIO HAS INVESTMENTS IN DIFFERENT ASSET CLASSES

In addition to limits on a single security, most portfolios also have guidelines on how much to invest in different asset classes – common stocks, preferred stocks, bonds, money market notes, cash, commodities and derivatives. For small portfolios, the mix usually is limited to the major categories of stocks, fixed income and cash. (The cash category generally includes term deposits.)

Diversification also can include a mix of types of securities within a class. For example, a portfolio can include foreign and domestic stocks and a collection of stocks from different industry sectors.

The mix of security classes and types in a portfolio will vary with the risk profile of an individual. Younger investors often will include more stocks that are considered speculative while seniors usually want a mix that emphasizes safety and a steady flow of interest and dividends.

All portfolios should be reviewed on a regular schedule to reassess the appropriate mix of investments.

HOW MUCH RISK ARE YOU WILLING TO TAKE?

Good fences make good neighbors and a financial hedge is aptly named – a proper hedge is designed to put a fence around risk.

Everyone wants a big return from their investments but too often the risk part of the equation doesn't get enough attention. In the jargon of the street, it's the reach for yield. Attitudes of many of today's investors were conditioned by the inflationary bubble of the late 1970s and early '80s. A high inflation rate brought with it a high return on term deposits at financial institutions. When those certificates came due, the holders looked around to reinvest at similar rates.

INVESTORS SHOULD FOLLOW BASIC TECHNIQUES WHEN DEALING WITH RISK

The stock market provided similar dazzling returns through the first two-thirds of the 1990s, with little inflation, and many investors now see double-digit returns as normal.

But the lessons of history are that double-digit returns are extraordinary and high yields usually come with high risk.

The further lesson is that risk should be hedged.

Managers of large pools of funds use a variety of sophisticated hedging techniques but small investors also can follow basic techniques in dealing with risk.

A primary rule is to decide in advance the amount you can afford to lose. If the answer is zero, then stick to investments that will preserve the principle, such as good quality bonds that are held to maturity.

Once risk comes into the picture, some commonsense tools can be used. The basic approach is to assess the odds that something will go wrong.

The first thing to look at is "market" risk, the odds that prices in general will fall dramatically. This involves an assessment of the state of the business cycle and of the general level of prices in relation to long-term averages.

MEASURING VOLATILITY GIVES A GUIDE TO DEGREE OF RISK

In focusing on specific securities, a risk assessment can be done in relation to the market – is this particular security more or less volatile than the general market?

This measure of volatility is known as "beta" – which is a measure based on a scale that starts at one. A stock with a beta higher than 1.0 is more volatile than the general market and a beta below 1.0 means less volatility.

Betas are routinely calculated and brokers can provide this information on individual securities. Using betas can provide a rough guide to the degree of risk in a portfolio.

If there is high risk in a portfolio, derivative securities can hedge that risk. Stock options can fix a floor price for someone who owns the shares.

Options have a pre-set strike price and a put option can set a limit to loss. Options on market indexes can be used as a hedge against declines in the price of a basket of stocks. There is a cost to buying an option and that becomes a charge for protection against risk.

THERE ARE SOME BENEFITS TO BEING SHORT

Not everybody waits for a bull market to make money. Some people profit when stock prices fall. It's known as selling short, which is the reverse order from a normal stock purchase. Shorting a stock means selling first and buying later. If successful, the short seller buys back at a lower price in order to make a profit. A short seller is selling something he or she doesn't own. Doing so involves borrowing certificates from someone who does own the stock.

Those who lend out certificates are known as short banks and usually it is a brokerage firm or a large institution that has a big inventory of stocks held for the long term. Short

THE SHORT POSITIONS | TABLE

Short positions is a tally of shares sold by people who think the price will fall. Short sales are done with borrowed share certificates and the sellers hope to buy in later at cheaper prices to replace the borrowed certificates. Short sales are reported to the stock exchanges, which produce a twice-monthly summary of short sale activity that covers all trading on Canadian-listed issues.

The table reports the latest total for each stock sold short compared with the previous reporting period and the net change between the two. Average daily trading volume also is listed because trading activity is important in assessing the significance of a short position. The measure is how many days of buying would be required to buy back all the shares sold short. A large short position in relation to volume means a lot of people are betting the stock will take a big drop. If they are wrong, the stock price could rise sharply when they are forced to cover their short positions. This table appears on the second and fourth Saturday of each month.

SHORT POSITIONS 10.27.98

Figures supplied by TSE and FP Datagroup. Includes short interest positions for Canadian listed issues (except warrants and preferred shares), where current position is greater than 50,000 shares or the change is above 25,000 shares. Average volume excludes short sales.

Stock	Ticker	Xxx	Yyy	Net change	Avg. daily volume
ARC Enrg Tr un	AET.UN	62,216	34,500	27,716	23,473
ATCO I	ACO.X	167,025	126,206	40,819	17,135
ATI Technlgys	ATY	178,900	51,027	127,873	990,067
ATS Auto Tool	ATA	189,229	209,803	-20,574	53,716
Abitibi-Cons	A	981,044	2,079,307	-1,098,263	452,794
Absolut Res	ALR	59,800	...	59,800	15,759
AEterna Labs	AEL	123,900	145,500	-21,600	25,415
Agrium Inc	AGU	153,983	155,430	-1,447	77,333
Air Canada A	AC.A	217,961	72,561	145,400	472,165
Air Canada	AC	373,663	792,663	-419,000	1,471,667
Airboss of Amer	BOS	34,726	7,725	27,001	63,205
Alberta Enrg	AEC	457,070	278,165	178,905	202,602
Alcan	AL	1,303,666	1,045,099	258,567	677,427
AlimentCouche B	ATD.B	253,465	254,965	-1,500	3,500
Allnce Atlant B	AAC.B	446,142	716,500	-270,358	70,587
AlphaNet Tel	FAX	158,700	158,965	-265	18,789

banks charge a fee for lending certificates and this is part of the cost of short selling. Typically, short selling is done on margin – in other words, with borrowed money. The need for cash arises if the stock price rises after a short sale. The margin account will cover that price difference up to a pre-set limit

Beyond that limit, the seller must cover, either by putting up cash to bring the margin account back into line or by buying the stock to replace the borrowed certificates.

PLACE YOUR BET ON FUTURE OF COMMODITIES

Businesses buy commodities in the cash market but the real action is in the futures market, which provides the pricing mechanism for raw materials from aluminum to zinc.

The cash market, also known as the spot market, doesn't exist in the formal sense. It's not a single formal trading arena. Instead, it's a broad trading network that includes specialized dealer firms, places like public stockyards where producers sell, and single-purpose agencies such as the Canadian Wheat Board.

Most futures trading takes place in organized exchanges and this is where commodity price trends are set.

The system is similar for futures in major currencies, bonds and stock market indexes. Futures markets for financial assets play a lead role in setting cash market values for underlying securities.

There is a fundamental reason for the importance of futures trading in commodities – producers are spending money long before they go to market and their products are subject to influences beyond their control.

When a farmer plants in the spring, the weather during the growing season is an unknown. When a mining company breaks ground for a new smelter, it can't be sure of industrial demand on the date that freshly minted ingots start rolling out the door.

COMMODITIES PRODUCERS FIND PROTECTION IN FUTURES

Producers can, and do, hedge against those uncertainties with futures – either with a contract for future delivery or with a forward sale. In the former technique, they are buying a specified amount of a commodity at a fixed price so they can cover delivery commitments if there is a production problem. In the latter, they are selling their product for future delivery and thus locking in an assured price.

In the case above of the contract for future delivery, the producer will deliver its goods if things work out as planned and the futures contract would simply expire with no action taken. The practical fact is that most futures contracts are not completed, which is what allows the system to work. The underwriter of futures contracts knows most contracts will expire unexercised and this allows the issue price of a single contract to be set at a price that is only a fraction of the value of the underlying commodity.

FINANCIAL FUTURES ARE AFFECTED BY BUSINESS CYCLE

Once a contract is issued, its price is affected by factors that will move the price of the underlying commodity. Wheat futures drop if there is a bumper crop. Copper futures rise if there is a labor dispute at a major producer. Natural gas futures fall if it is a mild winter. Oil futures spike higher if there is a threat of war in the Middle East, which still has the world's biggest, lowest-cost oilfields.

In each of these situations, the futures price is anticipating a change in the cash market when producers go to market with their products.

Financial futures work much the same way. Price moves for bond futures are reacting to the outlook for changes in interest rates. Swings in a stock index futures contract reflect expectations about general market trends. Currency futures respond to expected shifts in foreign exchange rates.

WHAT ARE CANADA'S COMMODITIES?

Chicago, London and New York are the world's major centres for trading in commodities and financial derivatives but markets in many other cities have staked out specialty roles in this business.

In Canada, the key derivative markets are in Winnipeg, for farm commodities, and in Montreal, for contracts on financial products. Montreal and Toronto share the market for stock options.

CANADIAN EXCHANGES SPECIALIZE IN FUTURES MARKET NICHES

Winnipeg's position comes naturally from its historic role as a supply centre for the Prairie farming industry. Montreal's hold on financial derivatives is based on a calculated policy to develop a distinct market because of Toronto's dominant position in equity trading.

The Winnipeg Commodity Exchange has contracts on five Prairies crops – barley, canola, flax, oats and wheat – but the big volume item is canola.

There are two reasons for Winnipeg's pre-eminence in trading futures and options on canola – it is a major crop for the region and canola is not a big contract in the huge commodity trading pits in Chicago.

In Montreal, the key contracts are in interest rate futures and options on three-month bankers' acceptance (BA) notes and government of Canada bonds. The most active market in Montreal is for BA futures and this contract is becoming an important pricing mechanism in the Canadian money market.

These exchanges have carved out market niches. A successful derivatives market needs a big volume of trading to be efficient and it can take years to build a dominant position. The C$ futures market provides an example of the significance of an established trading environment.

Chicago markets have active futures and options contracts on all the major currencies, including the C$. At one time the Toronto Stock Exchange, through its futures subsidiary, set up a competing market for C$ futures but the TSE never attracted enough volume and ultimately scrapped the contract.

COMPANIES TRADING IN FUTURES HAVE CONTRACTS IN KEY MARKET CITIES

Futures and options are bought and sold through investment dealers and specialized commodities brokers.

Large Canadian companies that rely on futures markets will have trading desks in those key market cities, the banks in Chicago and London for currencies and the big resource firms in London and New York.

CASH PRICES | TABLE

Cash commodity prices are for wholesale volumes of common grades. While industrial use in any commodity may span dozens of grades, certain key grades provide benchmark pricing. Futures and options contracts will be based on those benchmark grades. The definition of benchmark may vary around the globe. In crude oil markets, for example, the main benchmark grade in North America is West Texas intermediate while in Europe it is Brent (from North Sea wells).

Delivery point is an issue that enters into the pricing of many commodities. Canadian grains, for example, usually are priced at shipping terminals in Thunder Bay, where grains are loaded on to ships. (Sea transport is the cheapest way to move bulk cargo.)

Cash prices
Supplied by Reuters

	Latest	Prev	Wk ago		Latest	Prev	Wk ago
Gold				Gallium ingot	420.00	420.00	420.00
(US$ per troy oz)				Germanium (kg)	1200.00	1200.00	1250.00
London a.m. fix	288.60	292.75	293.00	Indium (kg)	200.00	200.00	200.00
London p.m. fix	288.60	292.70	293.00	Mangan. (tne)	1090.00	1090.00	1090.00
Zurich a.m. fix	288.00	291.50	292.00	Mercury flask	140.00	140.00	140.00
Zurich p.m. fix	291.50	291.50	291.00	Molybd. Ferr. (kg)	6.30	6.30	6.50
Silver				Ruthenium (oz)	37.00	37.00	38.00
(US$ per troy oz)				Selenium	1.20	1.20	1.20
London a.m. fix	4.97	5.04	5.03	Tantalite	26.00	26.00	26.00
N.Y. Handy&Har	4.91	5.06	5.02	Titanium (kilo)	6.60	6.60	6.60
Palladium (tr oz)	270.75	271.00	279.00	**Tropicals**			
Platinum (tr oz)	339.00	336.40	341.70	(US cents per lb unless stated)			
Industrial metals (London fix)				Arabica coffee	120.83	110.92	111.25
(US$ per tonne)				Robusta coffee	80.00	78.00	80.75
Aluminum std	1292.00	1295.00	1262.00	Cocoa (US$)	1733.00	1742.00	1729.00
Copper gr A	1582.00	1590.00	1554.00	Sugar World 11	8.34	8.18	8.18

The London Metal Exchange and the New York Mercantile Exchange perform key pricing functions for basic industrial commodities. Each commodity futures contract has a specific trading unit. For canola on the Winnipeg Commodity Exchange, it is 20 tonnes.

Prices are quoted in points and the size of a point can vary. For canola, it is 1/20th of the value of the contract, or, more simply, the price for one tonne.

Prices move up or down in ticks. A tick is the minimum amount by which a price can move, and varies, depending on the commodity.

SEVERAL FACTORS WILL AFFECT THE PRICE OF A CONTRACT

- **The price of the underlying commodity.** Seasonal and business cycles can influence the supply and demand of some commodities, thus influencing their prices.
- **Supply and demand for the contracts themselves,** created largely by speculators.
- **The time until the delivery date.** This reflects the carrying costs for the commodity.

Commodities exchanges often impose daily price limits to avoid panic selling and put a lid on frenzied buying. These limits govern price moves in a pre-set time period, often the trading day.

Futures contracts vary in length, depending on the commodity. Gold contracts, for example, can expire in anywhere from a few months to a number of years. Active grain contracts rarely go beyond a year.

OBLIGATION THE KEY TO HEDGING FUTURES RISK

A futures contract is a deal that won't actually take place for months – and sometimes years – down the road. It's an obligation to buy or sell a large amount of a commodity at a specific time in the future.

The price is set in advance, when the contract is made.

The key word here is obligation. Unlike options – where buyers have the right to not exercise their contracts – futures contracts are done deals.

That means the holder of a futures contract to buy 10 tonnes of cocoa must take delivery if the contract is held on the day it expires.

Similarly, the holder of a futures contract to sell 10 tonnes of cocoa must produce a truckload of cocoa on the delivery date.

COMMODITIES COMPANIES ARE MAJOR PLAYERS IN FUTURES MARKET

It may sound as though there's a whole lot of cocoa – or coffee, wheat, orange juice, lumber and other commodities – trading hands. But in reality, there isn't – only about 2% of all futures contracts involve physical delivery.

Most positions are closed out before the delivery date.

Closing out a contract is simply a matter of buying or selling an offsetting position.

For example, that holder of a contract to buy 10 tonnes of cocoa would buy a futures contract to sell the same amount and the two contracts would cancel each other.

Why don't holders of futures contracts take delivery instead of buying goods on the cash market?

Futures contracts are based on standard grades and most producers have highly specialized requirements. Substitutions of one grade for another may not be suitable. By buying on the cash market, producers get exactly what they need.

Major participants in futures markets are companies that deal in the commodities involved.

For example, growers of cacao and makers of chocolate bars are big players in the cocoa futures market.

Similarly, banks are big players in fixed income and currency futures because their product is money.

MOST FUTURES CONTRACTS ARE CLOSED OUT BEFORE DELIVERY

The traditional purpose of a futures market is to hedge risk. Commodity producers use futures to cover the risk of a price fall from oversupply and consumers cover the risk of high prices in cases of shortage.

Considering the amounts involved in commodities markets, the costs associated with buying futures contracts are negligible – mainly commissions paid to brokers.

Buyers and sellers of futures contracts must put up a margin deposit but this will be a fraction of the full cost of the contract, usually less than 5%.

The real cost of the contract for a buyer would be the money due upon delivery.

For the seller, it would be the commodity to be delivered. But, as has already been noted, delivery seldom takes place.

FUTURES MARKETS: HEDGER MEETS SPECULATOR

Futures markets are where you'll find an odd combination of players – from the high rollers of the investment world to conservative investors looking to hedge their bets.

It's easier to understand the ins and outs of these complicated securities by knowing something about the main players and how they use futures.

Speculators take on the risks that hedgers attempt to avoid. Their role in the market is not unlike that of an insurance underwriter, who assumes risk in exchange for a premium (in this case, the speculator's profit).

A hedger uses the futures market for insurance against fluctuating prices of commodities that are bought or sold. A hedger can be anyone, from a farmer selling grain to a big construction firm buying large amounts of lumber. Whoever they are, the goal of hedgers usually is not to make money, but to make sure they don't lose money.

Leverage is what makes futures so attractive to speculators. Using borrowed money magnifies profits far beyond what they would be if a speculator put up the full cost of

FUTURES PRICES | TABLE

The futures prices table lists futures under commodity groups: market indexes, currencies, interest-sensitive securities, grains, livestock and meat, foods, precious metals, industrial metals, petroleum and woods and fibres. The commodity is listed at the top of each series of prices. The abbreviations in brackets refer to the exchange where the futures are traded. For example, WPG refers to the Winnipeg Commodity Exchange. When contracts for the same commodity are traded on more than one exchange, separated listings are included for each exchange. Exchange specifications will list the size of the contract in relation to the underlying commodity.

Next to the contract size is the definition of a price tick. That is the unit of quotation stated in relation to the value of the contract. In the example of a gold contract traded on the Commodity Exchange, a US10¢ change in the price of the future represents a US$10 change in the value of the underlying contract for 100 troy ounces of gold.

The tables give price ranges between high and low for the latest trading day and for the life of the contract to date. **Month** is the month in which the contract expires, usually on the third Friday.

Open, in the price columns, refers to the price at which each contract opened when it began trading on the exchange. **Settle** is settlement price as determined by the closing range of prices. This is used to calculate trading gains and losses (setting an end-of-day market value for a portfolio). This notional settlement price also will be used for margin calls and is not necessarily the same as the closing trade price on the exchange

Previous open interest is the open interest – the total number of contracts that have not yet been offset by an opposite transaction or fulfilled by delivery – for the previous day. Previous open interest in the last column indicates the open interest for each contract on the previous day.

Estimated volume and previous volume are the trading volume estimates for the day of the listings and the previous day. Figures are the total for all the contracts on each commodity.

FUTURES PRICES 10.27.98

Figures supplied by Star Data Systems Inc.

—Lifetime—			——Daily——					Prev
High	Low	Mth	Open	High	Low	Settle	Chg	op.int

Currency

Australian Dollar (IMM)
A$100,000, US$ per A$; 0.0001 = $10 per contract

| 0.6690 | 0.5470 | Dec98 | 0.6247 | 0.6290 | 0.6225 | 0.6240 | –0.0014 | 19,651 |

Est. vol. 769   Prev. vol. 790   Prev. open int. 19,684

British Pound (IMM)
62,500 pounds, US$ per pound; 0.0002 = $12.50 per contract

1.7300	1.5630	Dec98	1.6602	1.6618	1.6490	1.6532	–0.0072	49,601
1.7150	1.5950	Mar99	1.6440	1.6500	1.6420	1.6468	–0.0072	1,500
1.7060	1.5880	June99	...	...	1.6370	1.6404	–0.0072	1,202

Est. vol. 6,983   Prev. vol. 9,211   Prev. open int. 52,304

Canadian Dollar (IMM)
C$100,000, US$ per C$; 0.0001 = $10 per contract

0.7400	0.6300	Dec98	0.6522	0.6570	0.6520	0.6564	+0.0040	49,605
0.7247	0.6290	Mar99	0.6544	0.6571	0.6544	0.6566	+0.0040	3,124
0.7170	0.6300	June99	0.6570	0.6570	0.6555	0.6568	+0.0040	1,391

Est. vol. 10,297   Prev. vol. 7,986   Prev. open int. 55,003

European Currency (CME)
125,000 ECUs, US$ per unit; 0.0001 = $12.50 per contract

Est. vol. 0   Prev. vol. 0   Prev. open int. 1

French Franc (IMM)
500,000 francs, US$ per franc; 0.00002 = $10 per contract

| 0.1868 | 0.1656 | Dec98 | 0.1796 | 0.1800 | 0.1796 | 0.1799 | –0.0008 | 2,001 |

Est. vol. 45   Prev. vol. 18   Prev. open int. 2,001

German Mark (IMM)

| 74.10 | 67.80 | Dec99 | 68.20 | 68.30 | 68.15 | 68.25 | –0.15 | 9,875 |

Prev. vol. 7,226   Prev. open int. 95,928

Flaxseed (WPG)
20 metric tons, C$ per metric ton; 10 cents = $2 per contract

332.00	294.00	Nov98	...	...	...	324.60	+1.10	2,192
332.00	303.00	Jan99	325.00	326.00	323.00	326.00	+0.90	2,658
335.50	308.10	Mar99	327.00	328.00	326.80	328.00	+1.00	1,644

Prev. vol. 309   Prev. open int. 7,256

Hogs (CME)
40,000 lbs., US cents per lb.; 2.5 cents per cwt. = $10 per contract

58.500	34.550	Dec98	34.900	35.650	34.550	35.525	+0.125	17,142
59.400	40.600	Feb99	41.400	42.700	41.300	42.625	+0.625	9,888
58.200	42.650	Apr99	44.800	46.000	44.400	45.900	+1.050	4,159
65.500	51.500	June99	53.800	55.000	53.600	54.950	+0.550	2,918
64.500	51.625	July99	53.800	55.000	53.800	54.600	+0.450	1,287
63.300	51.250	Aug99	53.900	53.900	53.100	54.625	+0.600	1,393

Est. vol. 12,289   Prev. vol. 13,661   Prev. open int. 37,307

Lumber (CME)
80,000 bd. ft., US$ per 1,000 bd. ft.; 10 cents = $8 per contract

| 332.00 | 253.00 | Nov98 | 262.50 | 268.20 | 262.50 | 267.90 | +6.70 | 2,095 |
| 332.00 | 264.20 | Jan99 | 272.10 | 278.50 | 272.10 | 276.90 | +5.90 | 1,922 |

Est. vol. 1,335   Prev. vol. 629   Prev. open int. 4,405

Oriented Strand Board (CME)
100,000 sq. ft., US$ per 1,000 sq. ft.; 10 cents = $10 per contract

Est. vol. 0   Prev. vol. 3   Prev. open int. 22

Oats (CBOT)

the commodity. But it's also the reason a great deal of money can be lost on futures.

When futures just involved basic commodities, the market was easier to understand. Hedgers were mainly producers. Speculators were mainly investment houses that specialized in commodities.

With the creation of financial futures – on stock indexes, bonds and currencies – the mosaic of players in this market has changed.

HEDGE FUNDS REQUIRE LARGE MINIMUM INVESTMENTS

The basic division between speculators and hedgers remains, but it's no longer as easy to classify the participants. For example, any large financial institution will be a hedger when operating in a traditional banking role but also may have a division or subsidiary that takes a speculative position in these markets.

The investment community now includes a group called "hedge funds." This has become a catch-all name for a broad range of money managers, but the original meaning of hedge fund was a variation on the traditional hedger.

The original hedge fund technique was to structure offsetting investments so that the fund made money whether the price of a security went up or down. As the hedge fund category has grown, it has come to include funds that take speculative positions in the derivatives markets.

One thing these funds have in common is that they only deal with sophisticated investors, which means there are large minimum investments for single units in the funds.

A sophisticated investor is a term that has a special meaning in securities law. Anyone who spends a lot of money on a single security – generally more than $100,000 – is considered to be exempt from the usual rules that govern the issuance of securities. These are people who, in the view of regulators, can look after themselves financially.

However, many of the traditional participants in the futures markets are not heavy hitters. Farmers still constitute a core group and the farm example still is the best way of following the essential elements of the futures market.

THE FUTURES MARKET CAN BE EXPLAINED IN SIMPLE TERMS

Imagine a farmer who has planted his barley crop, but is worried that by the time it is harvested and ready to be sold, the going price for barley will have declined because of a bumper crop flooding the market.

To protect himself from that possibility, the farmer can enter a series of futures contracts to sell the amount of barley he expects to grow at a price that will cover his expenses. Those contracts become an insurance premium – if there is a bumper crop and prices drop, the farmer can deliver his own barley at the contract price.

But the contract will come into effect only if delivery takes place and most contracts are not completed.

For this example, assume the cash market price of barley is $100 a tonne and the farmer expects the crop to come in at 200 tonnes. To protect his crop, he sells futures contracts with a face value of $20,000, which the farmer calculates to be his break-even price on the crop.

By the time his barley is ready to take to market, the price has dropped to $90 a tonne. As expected, the farmer's crop totals 200 tonnes. He sells the barley to a brewery and gets $18,000 for his crop at current market prices – which is $2,000 under his break-even price. In other words, he's selling his crop at a loss.

During the same period, the price of barley futures on the commodities exchange has dropped proportionately – down to $90 a tonne. (The price of a commodity and the price of futures contracts usually move in the same direction, although the price differential may narrow or widen, owing to market forces.)

PROFITS BALANCE OUT LOSSES

So the farmer buys futures contracts that give him the right to $18,000 worth of barley. By doing this, he is closing out his position – buying as many contracts as he originally sold, so the offsetting contracts cancel each other. The difference between the earlier selling price of $20,000 and the buying price of $18,000 represents a profit of $2,000 – which covers the farmer's $2,000 loss from his barley crop. All without any barley changing hands on the futures market.

If the price moves in the other direction, the farmer will have extra profits from sale of the crop to cover a loss on the futures transactions.

THE GREEKS FIRST TO HAVE OPTIONS MARKET

Credit for inventing the options market goes to Thales, the earliest of the ancient Greek philosophers He made a fortune speculating in olive presses in a year when there was a bumper crop – sometime around 600 B.C. The story, as told by Aristotle, is that Thales became an investor after being stung by criticism that he was just an ivory tower theorist with no useful skills in the real world.

Thales was one of the first to predict an eclipse and he studied meteorology, which led to his forecast of a big harvest in the olive groves. Early in the season, Thales bought what amounted to options on all the olive presses in Miletus.

University of Toronto Greek scholar Lloyd Gerson says the translation from Aristotle's account suggests Thales leased the olive presses and then rented them to farmers at harvest time. "He made a killing," Gerson says.

Thales' strategy is essentially how the options market works. The leases tied up assets at a fixed price at a time when the future value was unknown. Then he collected a profit from the market rate when the value of the asset rose. An essential element in this strategy is that Thales' risk was limited to the cost of the leases. It's likely that the lease rate for one season was relatively low but the return soared when farmers needed every available press in the region.

Options often are seen as a sophisticated speculative strategy, and they sometimes are. But they can also be used as part of a conservative investment strategy.

The purchase of an option contract gives the holder the right to buy or sell a specific quantity of something at a stipulated price within a certain period of time.

Options can be bought on stocks, bonds, stock market indexes, commodities futures and other investments.

FUTURE OPTIONS | TABLE

Options on futures are a high-leverage way of taking a position on the direction of a particular market. The advantage of options is that the potential loss is limited to the price of the option. Futures options on commodities, currencies, stock indexes and interest-sensitive securities are mainly based on exchange-traded futures. Contracts are listed under the names of the commodities exchanges on which they trade. The **strike price** is the price at which the underlying futures contract can be bought or sold when the option is exercised.

A call is an option to buy.

A put is an option to sell.

Options have a limited lifespan, often only three months. Usually the settlement date is the third Friday in the month. **Settle** in the column heading refers to the month in which the contract will be settled.

Volumes is the number of contracts traded and **open interest** is the number of outstanding contracts.

The price is the last trade price. An **s** in the price column means no options were offered for trading; an **r** means no trades took place.

FUTURES OPTIONS 10.27.98

Figures supplied by Star Data Systems Inc.

Currency
British Pound (CME)
62,500 pounds, US cents per Pound

Strike	Calls-Settle Nov	Dec	Jan	Puts-Settle Nov	Dec	Jan
1520	s	13.36	s	s	0.08	s
1560	s	s	s	s	0.16	0.38
1580	s	s	s	s	0.22	0.62
1600	s	5.64	s	0.02	0.34	1.02
1620	s	3.98	s	0.08	0.68	1.62
1630	s	r	s	0.14	0.96	2.00
1640	r	2.62	r	0.28	1.30	2.44
1650	0.94	2.06	r	0.62	1.74	r
1660	0.42	1.56	r	1.10	2.24	r
1670	0.20	1.16	r	1.88	2.84	4.06
1680	0.10	0.88	1.42	2.78	3.56	s
1690	0.05	0.62	r	3.74	4.28	s
1700	0.03	0.46	0.92	4.72	5.12	s
1710	0.02	0.34	r	5.70	6.00	s

Strike	Calls-Settle			Puts-Settle		
73	14.170	14.170	s	r 0.035		s
73.500	s	13.670	s	r 0.035		s
74	13.170	13.180	s	r 0.040		r
74.500	12.670	12.680	s	r 0.045		s
75	12.170	12.190	s	r 0.050		s
75.500	11.670	11.700	s	r 0.060		s
76	11.170	11.210	s	r 0.070		s
76.500	10.670	10.720	s	r 0.080		s
77	10.170	10.230	11.450	r 0.090		s
77.500	9.670	9.740	s	s 0.100		s
78	9.170	9.250	10.500	r 0.110	0.210	
78.500	s	8.760	s	s 0.120		s
79	8.170	8.280	9.570	r 0.140	0.280	
80	7.170	7.330	8.650	r 0.190	0.360	
80.500	6.670	s	s	r 0.230		s
81	6.180	6.410	s	0.010	0.270	s
81.500	5.680	5.970	s	0.015	0.320	0.560
82	5.190	5.530	6.930	0.020	0.380	0.630
82.500	4.700	s	s	0.035	s	s

Strike	Calls-Settle			Puts-Settle		
76.500	0.040	0.220	s	2.690	s	s
77	0.030	0.180	r	3.180	3.320	s
78	0.020	0.130	s	s	4.260	s
79	0.010	0.100	0.270	s	s	s

Est. call vol. 236 — Est. put vol. 347
Prev. open int. 14,249 — Prev. open int. 10,193

Food and Fibre
Barley (WPG)
20 metric tons, C$ per metric ton

Strike	Dec	Mar	May	Dec	Mar	May
105	21.50	24.40	s	r	0.10	s
110	16.60	19.70	s	r	0.40	s
115	11.60	15.30	17.50	r	0.90	1.50
120	6.70	11.40	13.70	0.20	1.90	2.60
125	2.80	8.00	10.50	1.20	3.50	4.20
130	0.70	5.40	7.70	4.10	5.80	6.40
135	0.10	3.40	5.50	8.50	8.70	9.00
140	r	2.00	3.80	13.40	12.30	12.30

OPTIONS | TABLE

Prices for options traded on Canadian stock exchanges can be found in the Options table. Canadian Derivatives Clearing Corp. (CDCC), jointly owned by the Toronto and Montreal stock exchanges, is the clearing organization for Canadian stock, bond and stock index options.

Equity options in Canada are American-style options, which means that they can be exercised at any time during their lifetime. European-style options, which includes many of the index options, can only be exercised at expiry.

The 10 most active options for the trading day are shown at the top of the table.

Each series is for options on a single security and the name of the issuer is at the top of the series. Names beginning with **Cda** are government of Canada bonds.

The name includes the expiry year and the coupon for the bond issue. After the name for each security is the symbol and an abbreviation for the exchange where options are traded.

The closing price for the underlying security is listed on the same line as the name.

EXP is the expiry month. Options expire on the third Friday of the expiry month.

P/C refers to whether the option is a call (an option to buy the underlying security) or a put (an option to sell).

VOL is the volume of option contracts traded and total volume for the series appears at the bottom on the section for each issue.

BID AND ASK PRICES are in C$s unless otherwise marked.

STK refers to strike price, which is the price at which the underlying security can be bought or sold when the option is exercised.

OPINT means open interest, which is the number of open positions at the end of trading. These are contracts that have not been exercised, closed out or allowed to expire.

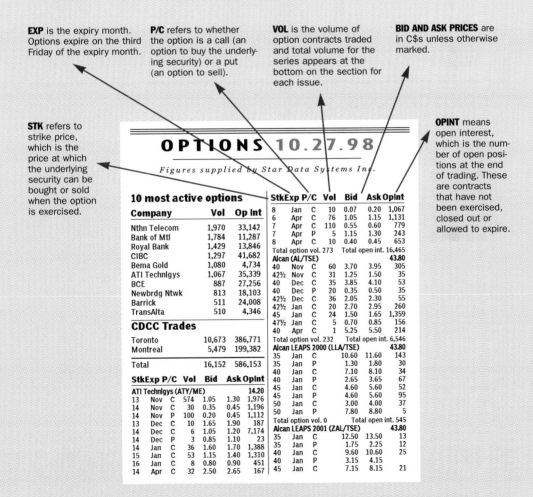

OPTIONS 10.27.98

Figures supplied by Star Data Systems Inc.

10 most active options

Company	Vol	Op Int
Nthn Telecom	1,970	33,142
Bank of Mtl	1,784	11,287
Royal Bank	1,429	13,846
CIBC	1,297	41,682
Bema Gold	1,080	4,734
ATI Technlgys	1,067	35,339
BCE	887	27,256
Newbrdg Ntwk	813	18,103
Barrick	511	24,008
TransAlta	510	4,346

CDCC Trades

	Vol	Op Int
Toronto	10,673	386,771
Montreal	5,479	199,382
Total	16,152	586,153

Stk	Exp	P/C	Vol	Bid	Ask	Opint
ATI Technlgys (ATY/ME)						14.20
13	Nov	C	574	1.05	1.30	1,976
14	Nov	C	30	0.35	0.45	1,196
14	Nov	P	100	0.20	0.45	1,112
13	Dec	C	10	1.65	1.90	187
14	Dec	C	6	1.05	1.20	7,174
14	Dec	P	3	0.85	1.10	23
14	Jan	C	36	1.60	1.70	1,388
15	Jan	C	53	1.15	1.40	1,310
16	Jan	C	8	0.80	0.90	451
14	Apr	C	32	2.50	2.65	167

Stk	Exp	P/C	Vol	Bid	Ask	Opint
8	Jan	C	10	0.07	0.20	1,067
6	Apr	C	76	1.05	1.15	1,131
7	Apr	C	110	0.55	0.60	779
7	Apr	P	5	1.15	1.30	243
8	Apr	C	10	0.40	0.45	653
Total option vol. 273				Total open int. 16,465		
Alcan (AL/TSE)						43.80
40	Nov	C	60	3.70	3.95	305
42½	Nov	C	31	1.25	1.50	35
40	Dec	C	35	3.85	4.10	53
40	Dec	P	20	0.35	0.50	35
42½	Dec	C	36	2.05	2.30	55
42½	Jan	C	20	2.70	2.95	260
45	Jan	C	24	1.50	1.65	1,359
47½	Jan	C	5	0.70	0.85	156
40	Apr	C	1	5.25	5.50	214
Total option vol. 232				Total open int. 6,546		
Alcan LEAPS 2000 (LLA/TSE)						43.80
35	Jan	C		10.60	11.60	143
35	Jan	P		1.30	1.80	30
40	Jan	C		7.10	8.10	34
40	Jan	P		2.65	3.65	67
45	Jan	C		4.60	5.60	52
45	Jan	P		4.60	5.60	95
50	Jan	C		3.00	4.00	37
50	Jan	P		7.80	8.80	5
Total option vol. 0				Total open int. 545		
Alcan LEAPS 2001 (ZAL/TSE)						43.80
35	Jan	C		12.50	13.50	13
35	Jan	P		1.75	2.25	12
40	Jan	C		9.60	10.60	25
40	Jan	P		3.15	4.15	
45	Jan	C		7.15	8.15	21

Options differ from futures in that the holder of an option contract isn't obligated to exercise the right to buy or sell the underlying security. That means option buyers will normally exercise their options only when it is to their financial advantage.

However, the underwriter of an option contract is obligated to carry out the other side of the transaction if an option is exercised.

Like stocks and bonds, options can be traded. Most options sold in North America can be exercised at any time. European-style options can be exercised on only one day.

The key to following the workings of modern options is understanding the strike price. An option gives the holder the right to buy or sell a security at a specific price.

For example, options can be used to limit losses if stock prices fall. If an investor holds stock with a current value of $100, an option could be purchased to sell at a strike price of $90. In that situation, the holder has a guaranteed price of $90 for the stock.

VOLATILITY AND OVERALL MARKET TREND PLAY ROLES IN OPTIONS MARKET

The cost of an option rises as the strike price get closer to the market price. If it is option to sell, the option is cheaper as the strike price falls further and further below the current market price. With an option to buy, the pricing is reversed. The option gets cheap-

INDEX OPTIONS | TABLE

Index options represent a way of taking a position on the direction of a market. They are widely used by institutions as hedges against adverse moves in large stock holdings. The heading on each section is for the underlying index and the letters in brackets indicate the exchange where the options trade (for example, CBOE means Chicago Board Options Exchange).

The strike price is the price at which the underlying futures contract can be bought or sold when the option is exercised.

A call is an option to buy.

A put is an option to sell. Options have a limited lifespan, often only three months, and the month in the listings is the month in which the contract will be settled. Usually the settlement date is the third Friday in the month.

Volumes represent the number of contracts traded and **open interest** is the number of outstanding contracts.

The price is the last trade price.

An **s** in the price column means no options were offered for trading; an **r** means no trades took place.

INDEX OPTIONS 10.27.98

Figures supplied by Star Data Systems Inc.

	Calls			Puts		
DJ Inds Avg (CBOE)				Index close 8879.68		
Strike	Dec	Jan	Feb	Dec	Jan	Feb
68	r	r	r	r	r	i
75	r	15⅞	s	r	r	s
76	13¼	r	r	⅜	r	r
79	10⅛	r	s	½	r	s
80	r	10	r	¼	⅝	r
81	r	r	s	¼	r	s
82	r	r	r	⅛	1	2¾
84	5⅝	r	r	½	1¼	r
85	r	r	s	⅝	r	s
86	4	r	r	⅞	2	2⅞
87	3½	r	s	1⅛	r	s
88	2⅜	r	r	1½	2⅝	2⅞
89	1¾	3⅜	s	1¾	2⅞	s
90	1⅜	2⅝	r	2¼	3½	3⅝
91	¾	2⅜	s	2¾	4	s
92	½	1⅞	r	3⅝	4½	r
93	¼	1¾	s	4½	4½	s
94	¼	1	s	5¼	4⅝	s
95	⅞	¾	s	6	r	s
96	r	⅝	1½	r	6⅞	r
100	r	⅞	r	r	10⅛	r
Total call vol. 3,507				Total put vol. 4,862		
Prev. open int. 85,806				Prev. open int. 210,256		
Japan Index (AMEX)				Index close 151.88		
Strike	Dec	Jan	Feb	Dec	Jan	Feb
125	r	r	r	¾	r	r
140	11⅞	12	r	r	2⅜	r

er as the strike price rises higher and higher above the current market price.

Options prices also vary according to the length of time to the expiry date. A short-dated option means less risk of price surprises.

But the price of the option rises as the term gets longer because there is a rising risk of price changes for the underlying security.

Two factors that come into play in the pricing of options are volatility and the trend of the overall market.

If the underlying security is volatile (fluctuates widely in price), the option price will be higher because of the increased possibility that investors will profit from their options.

If prices in general are rising, an option to buy will be more expensive because of the greater odds that market momentum will increase the price of the underlying security. Similarly, an option to sell will be costlier in a falling market.

INVESTING WITH OTHER PEOPLE'S MONEY

Buying on margin means using borrowed money.

Financial leverage is called gearing in Britain, which leads to a London variation on an old saying – "gear today, gone tomorrow." The meaning, of course, is that there is risk in leverage, as well as opportunity.

Margin simply involves getting a loan from a broker. In effect, it is a line of credit from an investment dealer that allows a portion of a securities purchase to be financed.

Returns to the investor can multiply when using someone else's money.

Typically, a purchase on margin involves putting up half the money. Rules on margin buying vary and speculative stocks often can be bought with less money down.

For an example of how margin works, assume there is a 50% limit. If a block of stock costs $2,000, buying on margin means borrowing $1,000. Thus, if the market value of the security goes up by 10% to $2,200, the investor's gain of $200 is a 20% return on the cash investment of $1,000. The fees associated with margin financing must be deducted from the return to the investor.

These calculations work the same way in reverse, so losses mount quickly if a stock price declines and the investor still must pay financing costs.

When the price declines, there will be a "margin call" requiring the investor to put up additional cash to maintain the 50% margin in the account.

This type of buying involves having a separate brokerage account called, logically, a margin account.

HAVING A MARGIN ACCOUNT MEANS GETTING A DOUBLE CLEARANCE FROM A BROKER

• The broker needs to ensure that the investor has sufficient tolerance for the risk involved in margin buying.

• And the broker will want to do a credit check to ensure that the investor has sufficient financial resources to cover potential losses.

INDEX CONTRACTS GIVE PIECE OF THE PIE

Basket trading, which means holding a bundle of related securities, is part of the standard strategy for managers of big pools of money, but new investment products have substantially broadened the possibilities of the technique.

Futures and options on indexes allow investors to take a position on the general direction of a particular market and now there are specialized funds that hold only indexes.

THERE ARE TWO BASIC REASONS FOR THIS APPROACH

- One is to go with the momentum of a particular market or market sector.
- The other is to improve the odds of picking the best performers with a bundle.

Large institutions can afford to buy baskets of stocks that mirror an index or an index category, but futures and options allow reasonably small investors to participate in this type of investing. High-volume markets for index products are those based on the world's biggest stock markets – in New York, London and Tokyo. The spectrum of index futures is much broader but investors should check the liquidity of those products before plunging into smaller markets. The Toronto Stock Exchange has a futures market on its 35-stock index but this has never been a big-volume market. (The index is traded on the Toronto Futures Exchange, which is a TSE subsidiary.) A much more popular way of investing in a basket of Toronto stocks is through TIPs – which stands for Toronto 35 Index Participation units. TIPS is a weighted basket of stocks that mirrors the index and it is sold in units that make it accessible to the average retail investor.

The TSE also has developed a basket of 100 stocks that includes the top tier in its 300-stock index. This basket is called HIPS – Hundred Index Participation units. It is possi-

INDEX FUTURES | TABLE

Index futures, allowing investors to hold a bundle of related securities, go with the momentum of a particular market or market sector and improve the odds of picking the best performers.

Indexes

Commodity Research Bureau (NYFE)
500 x index points; 0.05 pt. = $25 per contract
234.75 199.60 Nov98   204.00 205.60 203.50 205.50 +1.65   1,021
Est. vol. 600   Prev. vol. 210   Prev. open int. 2,334

Dow Jones Indl Avg Index (CBOT)
10 x index points; 1 pt. = $10 per contract
9515.00 7415.00 Dec98 8770.00 8779.00 8695.00 8730.00 −46.00 14,063
9586.00 7550.00 Mar99 8810.00 8840.00 8770.00 8801.00 −46.00   1,507
9395.00 7670.00 June99 8880.00 8900.00 8845.00 8870.00 −45.00   1,344
                    Prev. vol. 12,482   Prev. open int. 17,073

Goldman Sachs Cmmdty Index (CME)
250 x index points; 0.10 pt. = $25 per contract
169.90   142.70 Nov98   147.70 148.50 147.10 148.20 +0.20 26,362
Est. vol. 331   Prev. vol. 227   Prev. open int. 26,659

Municipal Bond Index (CBOT)
US$1,000 x index points; 1/32 pt. = $31.25 per contract
130-07 123-14 Dec98 124-29 125-14 124-28 125-04 +0-11 21,711
                    Prev. vol. 2,773   Prev. open int. 21,885

NIKKEI 225 Index (CME)
$5 x index points; 5 pts. = $25 per contract
17330   12690 Dec98   14325   14435   14325   14365   +135 20,877
Est. vol. 1,091   Prev. vol. 1,466   Prev. open int. 21,041

WARRANTS | TABLE

Warrants are, in effect, options to purchase shares. The difference is that warrants are issued by the company as a way of raising funds and warrants often are included as an incentive extra to a stock issue. They trade on stock exchanges just like common shares.

The WT attached to the stock symbol identifies the warrant and the table shows where the warrants are listed.

Generally, warrants are issued for periods of up to three years and the expiry date is listed in the table. **Years left** is the time to the expiry date in decimal format.

The exercise price is fixed at the time of issue, which means that prices for warrants can be volatile when the price of the underlying security changes. Intrinsic value is the market price of the share minus the exercise price of the warrant. This can be a negative number when the market price is below the exercise price.

Time value is the market price of the warrant minus the intrinsic value. In effect, time value represents the opportunity for a warrant to appreciate in value.

Leverage is the reason investors buy warrants because a small investment provides a call on the underlying security. In the table, leverage is a ratio derived from dividing the market price of the stock by the market price of the warrant.

WARRANTS 10.27.98

Figures supplied by TSE and FP DataGroup

Company	Stock close	Bid/ ask	Ticker	Stock exch.	Exercise price	Recent close	Bid/ ask	Intrinsic value	Time value	Lev'ge	Years left	Expiry date
Amblin Resources Inc	0.250	Bid	AX.WT	ASE	1.100	0.040	Bid	-0.850	0.040	6.25	0.8	Aug. 6, 1999
Appalaches Res inc	0.280	Bid	APP.WT.A	ME	0.650	0.050	Bid	-0.370	0.050	5.60	0.6	June 8, 1999
Arctic Group Inc	2.000		AGP.WT	ASE	1.250	0.550	Bid	0.750	-0.200	3.64	0.4	Feb. 24, 1999
Arlington Res Inc	0.100	Bid	ARLL.WT.B	CDN	0.250	...		-0.150	n.a.	n.a.	0.2	Jan. 14, 1999
Asia Pac Concrete	0.190		AFI.WT	ASE	1.000	0.030	Ask	-0.810	0.030	6.33	0.5	Apr. 30, 1999
Aurado Expl Ltd	0.075	Bid	AEO.WT	TSE	0.250	0.020	Ask	-0.175	0.020	3.75	0.1	Dec. 9, 1998
BGR Precious Metals	10.900	Bid	BPT.WT.A	TSE,ME	25.000	2.000	Bid	-14.100	2.000	5.45	5.4	Feb. 20, 2004
Baltic Resources Inc	0.350		BLR.WT	ASE	1.000	0.010	Bid	-0.650	0.010	35.00	0.3	Feb. 10, 1999
Barrington Petroleum	3.750		BPL.WT	TSE	4.100	0.070	Ask	-0.350	0.070	53.57	0.1	Nov. 27, 1998
Bearcat Explorations	0.380		BEA.WT.B	ASE	3.000	0.100 2	Ask	-2.620	0.100	3.80	0.1	Nov. 30, 1998
Bid.Com Intl Inc	0.660		BIII.WT	CDN	1.650	0.020	Bid	-0.990	0.020	33.00	0.2	Jan. 3, 1999
Boreal Expl Inc	0.160		BOR.WT	ME	0.500	0.005	Bid	-0.340	0.005	32.00	0.6	May 6, 1999
Bridge-It Corp	...		BRIC.WT.A	CDN	1.000	...		n.a.	n.a.	n.a.	0.2	Dec. 31, 1998
CME Telemetrix Inc	2.500		CMET.WT	CDN	5.000	0.010	Bid	-2.500	0.010	250.00	0.5	Mar. 31, 1999
CVL Resources Ltd	0.160		CVL.WT.A	VSE	1.100	0.020		-0.940	0.020	8.00	0.2	Dec. 15, 1998
Campbell Res Inc	0.630		CCH.WT	TSE,ME	U 1.500	0.005	Bid	-1.676	0.005	126.00	0.4	Feb. 26, 1999
Canadian Airlines	2.260		CA.WT.R	TSE	16.000	0.100 2	Ask	-13.740	0.100	22.60	0.5	Apr. 27, 1999
or cl A	2.150	Bid	CA.WT.R	TSE	16.000	0.100 2	Ask	-13.850	0.100	21.50	0.5	Apr. 27, 1999
Cdn Gen Investments 4	11.750		CGI.WT	TSE	10.060	4.250		1.690	2.560	2.76	8.7	June 30, 2007
Cdn Medical Labs Ltd	5.800		CLC.WT	TSE	6.000	0.100		-0.200	0.100	58.00	0.1	Nov. 30, 1998
Canop Worldwide Corp	0.510		CWC.WT	ASE	1.250	0.020	Bid	-0.740	0.020	25.50	0.7	June 30, 1999
Cascade Metals Inc	0.040	Bid	CEM.WT	ASE	0.500	0.040 2	Ask	-0.460	0.040	1.00	1.0	Oct. 30, 1999
Cell-Loc Inc	1.400		CLQ.WT	ASE	2.000	0.350	Bid	-0.600	0.350	4.00	1.0	Oct. 21, 1999
Christopher James	0.270	Bid	CJG.WT.A	VSE	0.600	0.020	Ask	-0.330	0.020	13.50	0.1	Nov. 10, 1998
Citadel Diversified	6.700		CTD.WT	TSE	8.500	0.040		-1.800	0.040	167.50	0.9	Sept. 16, 1999
Conor Pacific	0.700		CPAA.WT	CDN	1.000	0.050	Bid	-0.300	0.050	14.00	0.1	Dec. 1, 1998
Coromandel Res Ltd	0.050	Bid	CND.WT	VSE	0.500	0.010	Bid	-0.450	0.010	5.00	0.4	Mar. 19, 1999
CrownJoule Expl Ltd	1.100	Bid	CJE.WT	TSE	2.250	0.010	Bid	-1.150	0.010	110.00	0.4	Mar. 16, 1999
Cypress Mnrls Corp	0.120		CYP.WT.A	VSE	0.550	0.190	Ask	-0.430	0.190	0.63	0.1	Nov. 19, 1998
DDJ Cdn High Yield	15.000		HYB.WT	TSE	22.500	0.075		-7.500	0.075	200.00	1.9	Aug. 31, 2000
Darnley Bay Res Ltd	0.500		DBL.WT.C	VSE	0.850	0.070	Bid	-0.350	0.070	7.14	0.5	Mar. 31, 1999
Datalex Corp	2.700		DXK.WT	ME	3.600	0.870		-0.900	0.870	3.10	1.7	June 30, 2000
Domco Inc	10.250		DOC.WT	TSE,ME	11.000	0.020	Bid	-0.750	0.020	512.50	0.1	Nov. 6, 1998
Eldorado Gold Corp	0.510		ELD.WT	TSE,VSE	8.000	0.050 2	Ask	-7.490	0.050	10.20	0.1	Nov. 19, 1998
Euro-Nevada Mng Corp	102.600 1		ERNM.WT.B	CDN	100.000	12.500		2.600	9.900	8.21	0.1	Nov. 12, 1998
First Asia Income Fd	5.200		FAI.WT	TSE	8.500	0.050		-3.300	0.050	104.00	1.6	May 15, 2000
Foreign Currency	2.300	Bid	FCEC.WT	CDN	2.750	0.030	Bid	-0.450	0.030	76.67	0.6	May 26, 1999
Franco-Nevada Mining	127.400 1		FRNV.WT.B	CDN	200.000	18.500	Bid	-72.600	18.500	6.89	4.9	Sept. 15, 2003
Geomaque Expls Ltd	1.500		GMQE.WT	CDN	4.000	0.010	Bid	-2.500	0.010	150.00	0.4	Mar. 18, 1999
Georgian Bancorp Inc	1.000	Ask	GRB.WT.B	VSE	2.000	0.100	Bid	-1.000	0.100	10.00	1.0	Oct. 8, 1999
Global Equity Corp	1.800	Bid	GEQQ.WT	CDN	3.250	0.030	Bid	-1.450	0.030	60.00	0.0	Oct. 21, 1998

CONVERTIBLE DEBENTURES | TABLE

Convertible debentures are bonds that may be converted to equity, usually common stock. Many of these are exchange trade securities, unlike conventional bonds.

The list of issuer names also shows the security symbol and the exchange. Those that do not trade on an exchange are shown as OTC (over the counter).

This listing has both bond and stock information for a conventional pricing of each security – maturity, coupon, bond price, yield to maturity and share price.

The conversion price is the pre-set price at which the bonds may be converted to stock. The conversion ratio states the conversion price in relation to a $100 unit of the bond. For example, a conversion ratio of 5 means the stock price is $20 (5 x $20 = $100).

The premium is a percentage and is the amount paid for the debenture in excess of the market value of the underlying share. The formula is the ((bond price – (share price x conversion ratio))/(share price x conversion ratio)) x 100.

Convertible debentures

*Supplied by RBC Dominion Securities Inc. Selected quotations on actively traded debentures. Premium is stated as a percentage and is the amount paid in excess of the market value of the bond's underlying shares. Yields are calculated to maturity. *US$*

Bond Issuer/listing	Maturity	% Coup.	price	Prem.	Yld	Share price	Conv. ratio	Conv. Price
Agnico* AEGGF	27-Jan-04	3.50	62.75	139.85	13.70	4.69	5.58	17.93
Bowater BWA.DB	8-Feb-04	7.50	150.25	9.77	0.00	62.50	2.19	45.66
Brookfield BPC.DB	14-Feb-07	6.00	122.72	10.84	2.89	16.60	6.67	15.00
Cad. Fairview CDF.DB	30-Sep-08	5.70	98.00	33.64	5.97	28.60	2.56	39.00
Cambridge CBG.DB	1-Mar-03	8.00	100.38	116.83	7.89	12.05	3.84	26.03
Cambridge CBG.DB.A	1-Jun-04	7.50	97.75	188.06	8.01	12.05	2.82	35.51

ble to invest in a single security that represents a diversified portfolio of Canadian companies and tracks the general performance of the stock market.

Index contracts, like all futures, can be used as part of a hedging strategy. An investor who holds a portfolio of Canadian stocks and feels the stock market is about to decline can sell a TSE 35 futures contract. That way, if the market declines, the investor's loss will be offset by the profits from buying back the contract at a lower price. Likewise, someone who believes the stock market is about to rise may buy a TSE 35 contract and resell it at a profit when the market rises.

A DEEPER POOL OF ASSET-BACKED SECURITIES

Asset-backed securities (ABS) represent a relatively new investment class in Canada and the field is still evolving. Mortgage pools in the U.S. were the first big market in this area and this has been the market to develop first in Canada. The U.S. now has a broad range of ABSs – including pools of credit card receivables and car loans – and Canadian financial institutions are heading in the same direction. A variation of the ABS market that has developed in Canada is the investment trust. Two sub-categories are real estate investment trusts (REITs) and royalty trusts. REITs, as the name implies, are pools of funds that invest in real estate assets. Royalty trust are pools that buy the cash flow from resource operations, natural gas wells and coal mines, for instance.

INVESTORS IN AN ABS HOLD UNITS THAT REPRESENT A PORTION OF THE POOL. CHARACTERISTICS OF ABSs CAN BE DIVIDED INTO THREE BROAD CATEGORIES

• **Pass through:** Units represent a pro rata share of the pool. Income generated by the pooled funds is "passed through" to the investors after management fees are deducted. These pools will be set up by large financial institutions, often banks. Assets in the pool, such as mortgages or credit card receivables, are removed from the balance sheet of the institution that created the pool and put on the books of the pool itself.

• **Pay through:** These pools are, in effect, bonds that are backed by a pool of assets.

THE MORTGAGE-BACKED SECURITIES | TABLE

Mortgage-backed securities are asset pools of mortgages insured under the National Housing Act (NHA). There are two basic types of pools – those that include mortgages that can be paid off early (prepayable) and those that do not.

Units in these pools return to investors portions of the interest and principal payments made each month by homeowners. If the pool receives extra funds from mortgage pre-payments, the investors may get an additional distribution.

These pools act much like bonds. Coupon and maturity date are fixed. The yield varies with the general level of interest rates and that affects the price of a unit. The issuer will be a financial institution that has assembled the pool.

NHA Mortgage backed securities

Supplied by RBC Dominion Securities Inc. Bid side levels on minimum $1 million. Indicated yields assume no prepayments. All MBS are priced to their weighted average maturity date.

Non-prepayable

Pool #	Issuer	Coupon	Maturity	Price	Yield
99005779	TD Bank	6.375	Nov 01/98	-0.10	5.11
99007213	National Bnk	5.500	Mar 01/99	99.92	5.11
99007122	CIBC Mort	6.000	Mar 01/99	100.08	5.11
96600465	Equit Trust	6.625	Jan 01/01	102.81	5.02
99007205	Peoples Trst	6.375	Mar 01/01	102.62	5.02
99007411	TD Bank	5.125	Jan 01/02	99.72	5.15
99007585	Manufac Trst	5.000	Dec 01/02	99.12	5.19
99006355	Sun Life	9.250	Sep 01/04	118.99	5.22
96600895	Pafco Ins	5.875	Nov 01/07	102.85	5.40
96600945	Maritime Lfe	5.000	Dec 01/07	96.43	5.55

Prepayable

Pool #	Issuer	Coupon	Maturity	Price	Yield
96409099	CIBC Mort	6.625	Nov 01/98	-0.11	5.41
96407911	Firstline	7.750	Mar 01/00	102.31	5.14
97000038	Canada Trust	6.500	Jan 01/01	101.79	5.16
97000004	Canada Trust	5.750	Sep 01/01	100.88	5.20

Income from the assets is paid through to the investors but the assets remain on the books of the institution that created the pool.

- **Investment trusts:** These pools operate much like a pass-through pool, except that the trust nature provides certain tax advantages. The investor, who puts in money, also is a beneficiary of the trust (unlike a conventional trust, where the beneficiary is not a contributor). Creators of these trusts generally retain a hold on the assets in the trust. Many of these trust structures have the ability to borrow, which leverages the investors' funds. Borrowed funds will be put to work to buy additional assets and this gives investors the prospect of capital gain.

With pass-through and pay-through pools, the return generally is a combination of payments of principal and interest. A grey area with ABSs is the issue of liability to both issuers and investors in the event of financial problems in the pool. Issuers who move assets off their balance sheets may continue to have obligation for those assets. Investors in REITs that take on debts may have an obligation to cover those debts.

CURRENCY AND INTEREST RATE PROTECTION

Currency and interest rate risks are among the constants of modern investing and financial institutions have responded with a broad array of securities designed to hedge these risks.

Most of these financial instruments are aimed at big institutional investors, but some are accessible to small investors. For large institutions, these markets provide an opportunity to hedge. Generally, though, any retail investor would be a speculator because it takes a large portfolio to justify the costs of sophisticated hedge products.

Financial futures provide for hedging and work much the same way as conventional futures on commodities.

Futures or options on fixed-income securities such as government bonds, treasury bills and bankers' acceptances provide ways to hedge against unexpected shifts in interest rates.

For example, an insurance company may sell bond futures when it feels rising interest rates are threatening the value of its bond portfolio. If interest rates go up, the value of bonds will fall. So will the price of futures contracts on bonds. That means the company will have sold its bond futures contracts at higher prices and bought them back at lower prices.

The difference represents a profit that will offset the declining value of bonds in the insurance company's portfolio.

Currency futures operate in a similar way and corporations with large business dealings in foreign countries can lock in an exchange rate at a future date with a variety of hedge products.

As with commodities futures, the other side of a hedge is taken by speculators who are willing to assume the risk.

In Canada, futures contracts on government of Canada bonds and bankers' acceptances notes – short-term debt issued by bankers – trade on the Montreal Exchange.

Contracts on 10-year government bonds can be used to hedge long-term interest rates, while bankers' acceptances can be used to hedge short-term rates.

The world's most actively traded futures contracts are U.S. treasury bond futures, which were introduced in 1977, and are traded on the Chicago Board of Trade.

U.S. and other commodities exchanges around the world offer a host of other financial futures, including treasury bills and bonds issued by the large industrial nations and all the major currencies.

THE REIT TABLE

The REIT report is a monthly feature on real estate investment trusts and the accompanying table carries unit information on Canadian REITs, which are structured somewhat like a mutual fund.

Unit pricing is similar to the pricing for mutual funds, except that many of the REITs were issued as instalment receipts. With this type of financing, the investor gets a temporary security (the instalment receipt) with a downpayment and the underlying security is delivered when the final payment is made at a later date. The typical arrangement for REITs was $6 down and a further payment of $4 for each unit.

The distribution is estimated annual payment and the forward yield is the estimated distribution as a percentage of current market price. (In the case of instalment receipts, the forward yield includes a factor for the future payment.)

Market capitalization is number of units times current price on a fully paid basis, which means it includes the future payments on instalment receipts.

REIT REPORT 10.27.98

Figures supplied by CIBC Wood Gundy Securities Inc.

	10/30/98 close $	Monthly % chg.	YTD % chg.	52-wk. high $	52-wk. low $	1998E $ distr.	Current % yield	1999E $ distr.	Forward % yield	Units O/S (mil.)	Market cap ($mil.)
Avista REIT (AVS.UN)	7.85	12.1	(24.5)	8.95	6.00	0.89	11.4	0.97	12.3	20.0	157
CAP REIT (CAR.UN)	9.50	(1.0)	(9.5)	10.50	7.70	0.95	10.0	1.00	10.5	12.0	114
CHIP REIT (HOT.UN)	8.15	(10.4)	(40.1)	14.00	8.00	1.25	15.3	1.41	17.3	33.9	276
Cominar (CUF.IR)	9.50	4.4	(5.0)	10.35	8.10	0.77	8.1	1.03	10.8	14.5	138
CPL REIT (CPL.UN)	19.50	(4.4)	0.5	24.10	18.25	1.43	7.3	1.70	8.7	16.0	312
CREIT (REF.UN)	10.85	4.3	(14.6)	14.15	9.25	1.13	10.4	1.23	11.3	33.2	360
H&R REIT (HR.UN)	9.75	(2.0)	(10.1)	12.30	9.00	1.02	10.4	1.10	11.3	34.4	335
Legacy Hotels (LGY.UN)	6.40	12.3	(34.0)	10.15	5.00	0.76	11.9	0.90	14.1	28.7	184
Legacy Hotels (LGY.IR)	6.35	11.4	(36.5)	10.25	4.92	0.76	12.0	0.90	14.2	30.5	194
Morguard (MRT.UN)	8.20	3.8	(17.2)	8.25	7.00	0.86	10.5	0.94	11.4	25.2	207
RealFund (RFN.UN)	12.40	7.8	(20.5)	16.10	10.75	1.36	11.0	1.48	11.9	26.6	330
RESREIT (REE.IR)	8.95	1.1	(10.5)	10.75	7.85	0.83	9.3	0.90	10.1	21.6	193
RioCan (REI.UN)	9.65	7.2	(9.2)	11.35	7.25	0.95	9.8	1.08	11.2	70.5	680
Royal Host (RYL.IR)	6.85	5.4	(39.9)	11.50	5.75	1.06	15.5	1.19	17.4	20.4	140
Summit REIT (SMU.UN)	12.60	11.0	(19.5)	17.20	10.20	1.50	11.9	1.63	12.9	16.4	207
CIBC Wood Gundy Cdn. REIT Index	169.37	4.7	(14.2)	204.40	152.53						

Note: CIBC Wood Gundy REIT Index based 12/31/93= 100. All REITs and corresponding calculations are represented on a fully paid basis. Distributions are I/B/E/S Inc. where CIBC Wood Gundy has no forecast.

The REIT Report appears the first Saturday of each month.

CHAPTER 4

CURRENCIES, | DEBT AND THE ECONOMY

- Short-term securities
- The attraction of bonds
- Foreign exchange investments
- Bank of Canada

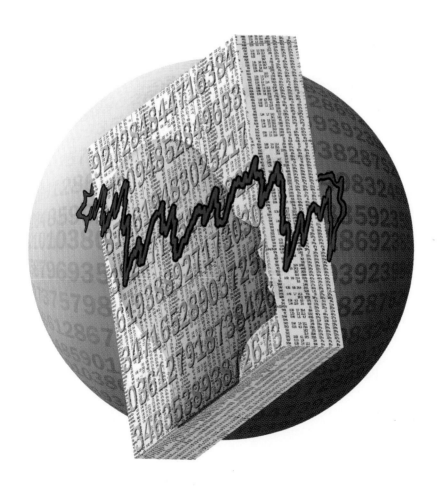

WINDS OF ECONOMIC CHANGE

CAN BUFFET INVESTMENTS | BY DAVID THOMAS

THE VALUE OF ANY INVESTMENT you choose is influenced by broad economic trends. This is true whether you are taking a position in one currency versus another or buying Canada Savings Bonds, gold bullion or shares in a public company. The big economic picture is especially important to the bond market, whose value is eight times larger than the stock market, and to the currency market, which is five times the size of the bond market.

With rapid growth in global capital flows, events in other markets have a strong impact on local markets. National fiscal and monetary policies are more than ever influenced by global events.

Interest rate policy is especially important to fixed income markets. In Canada, the key cost of borrowing is the bank rate, which is the rate the Bank of Canada charges on short-term loans it makes to the big commercial banks. The banks build on that rate in their lending. The rate is also a base for calculating the interest on government treasury bills and corporate bonds.

Bonds are negotiated initially to pay a fixed amount of interest regularly over a set period. When that time is up, the principal is due to be repaid as well. Simply put, bonds are a tradable loan. The terms are negotiated based on rate conditions at the time. Then, when bonds begin to trade in the secondary market, their value varies in relation to prevailing interest rates, anticipated future rates and competing returns from other investments such as stocks.

CENTRAL BANKS USE INTEREST RATES TO CONTROL INFLATION

The direction of interest rates has a dramatic effect on bond markets. Central banks use interest rates as a tool to keep inflation in check. When inflation is rising, central banks will hike their key interest rates, which will increase the cost of borrowing throughout the economy, thereby cooling off economic expansion. When inflation is at a low level, rates can be lowered, which will encourage growth. Rate manipulation is a key part of monetary policy.

ECONOMIC INDICATORS INFLUENCE BOND AND STOCK MARKETS

Rising interest rates push bond prices down and vice versa. The reason for this inverse relationship is that when rates rise, investors will find new bonds, with higher interest payments, more desirable than existing bonds that were priced at lower interest rates. Bond and stock markets pay a lot of attention to the indicators that chart the economy's progress. The broadest economic measure is gross domestic product, or GDP, which is the value of all goods and services.

Monthly updates on GDP growth, adjusted for inflation, enable economists to take the pulse of the economy. Other indicators such as manufacturing shipments, retail sales, the rate of unemployment and housing starts offer pieces of a puzzle that put together point to the direction of the economy and how fast it is moving.

NO TWO BUSINESS CYCLES ARE THE SAME, BUT THEY ALL GO THROUGH SIMILAR STAGES

- Economic recovery facilitated by low interest rates.
- Rising momentum as new investment feeds growth.
- Overheating as the economy hits capacity, costs and inflation rise and interest rates are raised to cool things off.
- Contraction and rising unemployment.
- Recession, with falling interest rates.

Signs of steady growth may bode well for continued low interest rates, while signs of overheating and growing inflation signal interest rate rises are coming.

The consumer price index (CPI) charts the price of a fixed basket of goods, providing the best way of tracking inflation. Investors subtract inflation rates from the return on their investments to determine the real rate of return. Economists often try to predict the level of natural or full employment beyond which inflationary pressures begin to kick in and business cycles shift gear.

As technology continues to increase productivity, it has changed the labor market and altered conceptions of the business cycle. As the new millennium approaches, some economists argue technology has altered the "natural" limits of healthy economic expansion. The business cycle as we know it may actually be dead, they say.

While economic pressures at home and abroad may sometimes limit its choices, the Bank of Canada has the ultimate word on interest rates. The central bank has a fine-tuning role in the economic cycle. Its job is to act to smooth out the bumps and to encourage or slow down growth as needed. The central bank monitors closely the amount of stimulus in the economy created by money supply, the value of the currency and interest rates. It has direct control over interest rates and money supply and can step in to intervene in currency markets during periods of volatility.

A CHANGE IN THE VALUE OF CURRENCY AFFECTS BONDS FOR FOREIGN INVESTORS

The value of a currency depends on a host of factors, including GDP, balance of trade and fiscal debt or deficits. Here, government spending and policies can have a major impact on fixed-income markets. The strength of the currency is especially important for bond markets because any change in the currency affects the value of bonds for foreign investors.

WHAT'S FOR SALE ON THE MONEY MARKET?

The money market is the part of the capital market in which short-term debt securities are bought and sold. Most of these securities mature in one year or less. In Canada, treasury bills are the main component of the money market. Like regular bonds, T-bills are tools used chiefly by governments for borrowing. They are short-term instruments, usually maturing in 91, 182 or 364 days. The federal government and several provinces issue T-bills. Instead of paying interest, T-bills are sold at a discount to their par value. The difference between the price paid and the maturity value represents the investor's return (which is then converted to a percentage figure). Federal government T-bills are auctioned biweekly by the Bank of Canada.

OTHER MONEY MARKET INSTRUMENTS

• Bankers' acceptances: Short-term debt securities issued by a corporation and guaranteed by its bank.

• Commercial paper: Short-term debt securities issued by companies. Their terms range from a few days to a year. Normally this paper is not secured by assets, although it may be backed by bank lines of credit.

• Finance company paper: Short-term debt issued by finance companies.

The money market now provides Canadians with the main alternative to bank or credit union savings accounts. Money market accounts are set up as a type of mutual fund but their investments include only top-quality short-term notes – T-bills or commercial paper from senior issuers.

PRESERVATION OF CAPITAL THROUGH BONDS

In times of high inflation, such as the late 1970s and early '80s, investors look for securities that will keep pace with price increases. These periods generate expectations that have come to be called "the reach for yield." Between 1978 and 1982, ordinary bank term deposits paid more than 10% and for a while these no-worry investments returned almost 20%. It took a long time to squeeze out the inflationary excesses of that period, with the result that double-digit returns seemed normal.

That high-rate period was followed by an extraordinary bull market in stocks and a continuation of expectations of double-digit returns on investing. But stock prices have great exposure to market forces – they can go down as well as up and there is no guarantee of principal at some future date. When a bull market for stocks ends and a bear market sets in, investors rediscover the merits of bonds. Simply stated, stocks start at one end of the risk spectrum and bonds at the other.

THERE ARE THREE ESSENTIAL ELEMENTS TO THIS EQUATION

• **Total return:** This is the combination of earned income and capital gains. Earned income is interest from bonds and dividends from stocks. A capital gain is the increase in value of the security itself. Interest payments are fixed for conventional bonds, which means the price will vary with changes in the general level of interest rates in the economy. The price of a bond is fixed if an investor buys when the bond is first issued and

BENCHMARK YIELDS | TABLE

Benchmark treasury bills and bonds are those issues, mostly government, that provide a pricing point for other fixed income securities. The yield changes with market conditions and price is reached with a calculation that factors in the fixed interest payment and the variable market rate.

Latest % is the market close in North America. These issues can be traded on the interbank network around the world, so the close is a matter of convention based on local time zones.

Previous close is the prior trading session. Bond market close on weekends and bank holidays. Bond trades settle on a same-day basis, so banks must be open.

The spread is the difference in basis points (1/100ths of a percentage point) between one issue and a comparable Canadian issue.

BENCHMARK YIELDS

Bond or bill	Latest %	Prev. close %	Spd off Canada
Canada 3-mo. T-bill	4.55	4.65	
U.S. 3-mo. T-bill	3.94	4.03	61
Canada 2-yr bond	4.37	4.58	
U.S. 2-yr bond	3.83	4.10	54
Canada 10-yr bond	4.86	4.97	
U.S. 10-yr bond	4.41	4.61	45
Australia 10-yr bond	4.88	5.04	-2
Britain 10-yr bond	5.05	5.07	-20
France 10-yr bond	4.22	4.27	64
Germany 10-yr bond	4.11	4.11	74
Japan 10-yr bond	0.89	0.91	397
Canada 30-yr bond	5.30	5.36	
U.S. 30-yr bond	4.97	5.03	33

For other yields see page xx

BONDS TABLE

Bond tables list prices and yields of federal, provincial and corporate issues. The provincial category includes bonds issued by provincial agencies such as utilities. The name of the issuer often is abbreviated. The key information in identifying a bond is the coupon (interest rate) and the maturity date. A dealer may refer to "Canada nines of 25," which means a government of Canada bond that pays a 9% interest rate and matures on June 1, 2025.

COUPON is the interest rate that is fixed as part of the terms of the issue.

YIELD usually refers to yield to maturity. But if the bond can be called in at an earlier date, the yield will be yield to the call date. A callable will have a three-character notation after the name – c06, for example. This example means that the bond may be called in 2006. Other special notations may be used. **CV** refers to convertible bonds, **EXT** is extendible, **RET** is retractable.

Bonds

Supplied by RBC Dominion Securities Inc./International from Reuters

DS Barra Index	Index level	Total ret	Price ret	MTD tot.ret
Market	316.95	0.32	0.30	-0.18
Short	269.12	0.15	0.13	-0.13
Intermed	322.61	0.36	0.34	-0.23
Long	390.20	0.53	0.51	-0.19
Govts	315.97	0.30	0.28	-0.20
Canadas	308.55	0.29	0.27	-0.21
Provs	335.08	0.35	0.33	-0.17
Munis	115.83	0.32	0.30	-0.24

	Coupon	Mat. date	Bid $	Yld%
Canada	9.250	Dec 01/99	104.56	4.82
Canada	5.500	Feb 01/00	100.87	4.77
Canada	8.500	Mar 01/00	104.71	4.77
Canada	5.000	Mar 15/00	100.32	4.75
Canada	10.500	Jul 01/00	108.94	4.81
Canada	7.500	Sep 01/00	104.67	4.79
Canada	5.000	Dec 01/00	100.69	4.65
Canada	10.500	Mar 01/01	112.22	4.86
Canada	7.500	Mar 01/01	105.81	4.82
Canada	9.750	Jun 01/01	111.62	4.88
Canada	7.000	Sep 01/01	105.61	4.84
Canada	9.750	Dec 01/01	113.66	4.90
Canada	8.500	Apr 01/02	111.12	4.91
Canada	5.500	Sep 01/02	102.17	4.87
Canada	11.750	Feb 01/03	125.54	4.98
Canada	7.250	Jun 01/03	109.33	4.94

	Coupon	Mat. date	Bid $	Yld%
Canada	5.250	Sep 01/03	107.66	4.86
Canada	7.500	Dec 01/03	111.27	4.96
Canada	10.250	Feb 01/04	123.80	5.02
Canada	6.500	Jun 01/04	107.33	4.98
Canada	9.000	Dec 01/04	120.55	5.03
Canada	8.750	Dec 01/05	121.57	5.08
Canada	14.000	Oct 01/06	156.49	5.19
Canada	7.000	Dec 01/06	112.10	5.15
Canada	7.250	Jun 01/07	114.38	5.15
Canada	6.000	Jun 01/08	106.41	5.14
Canada	10.000	Jun 01/08	135.74	5.21
Canada	5.500	Jun 01/09	102.72	5.16
Canada	9.500	Jun 01/10	136.26	5.27

Provincial

	Coupon	Mat. date	Bid $	Yld%
Alberta	6.250	Mar 01/01	102.87	4.92
Alberta	6.375	Jun 01/04	105.69	5.19
B C	9.000	Jan 09/02	111.00	5.19
B C	7.750	Jun 16/03	110.01	5.27
B C	9.000	Jun 21/04	117.70	5.32
B C	6.000	Jun 09/08	103.06	5.58
B C	8.500	Aug 23/13	125.78	5.87
B C	6.150	Nov 19/27	100.77	6.09
B C MF	7.750	Dec 01/05	112.73	5.55
B C MF	5.500	Mar 24/08	98.39	5.72
HydQue	10.875	Jul 25/01	114.41	5.12

MATURITY DATE is when investors will be paid their principal. Only the last two digits of the year are used, so 05, for example, means 2005.

THE BID COLUMN lists the price at which investment dealers are willing to buy the bond. These prices are always quoted in relation to 100, no matter what the par value of the bond. Think of the bond price as a percentage. A price of 95 means that the bond traded at 95% of the face value, regardless of the size of the transaction. (Prices here are institutional prices, which usually means a minimum $100,000 trade.)

holds the bond until it matures. Anytime in between, the price will be subject to market forces and the investor has the prospect of a capital gain or loss but the bond buyer still is assured of getting the face value at maturity.

• **Relative return:** This is the question of whether a particular asset class is likely to pay better than another asset class – bonds versus stocks, or hard assets (such as real estate) versus financial assets (such as stocks).

• **The sleep factor:** As potential return rises, the potential risk rises and investors need to have a portfolio that allows them to rest comfortably at night. The big advantage of high-quality bonds is the investors can count on getting the principal back when the bond matures.

Risks associated with bonds vary from issuer to issuer. Few investors do the time-consuming research needed to ascertain that risk, so they rely on rating agencies. The likelihood of a bond investment turning sour generally can be divined from ratings established by agencies that measure the financial stability of businesses and governments.

In Canada, the major bond rating services are Dominion Bond Rating Service and Canadian Bond Rating Service. The major U.S. rating services are Standard & Poor's Corp. and Moody's Investors Service. U.S. agencies also rate many Canadian bonds. Bond ratings not only give investors an idea of how likely it is that their interest and principal will be paid, but also have an impact on the level of interest paid by new bond issues. High risk borrowers have to pay higher interest to attract investors. Issuers with good credit ratings pay less.

THE ATTRACTION OF BONDS IS THEIR SAFETY

Bondholders are lenders, and therefore creditors, and part of the appeal of bonds is that creditors are second in line to get their money back if a company has problems. First in line is the tax collector. That potential claim on assets is why investment grade corporate bonds are considered safer investments than stocks. But government bonds are considered the safest of all because of the tax collector's preferred status.

Most Canadians probably think of Canada Savings Bonds when government bonds are mentioned, but CSBs are a tiny element in the fixed income universe. In fact, CSBs are not real bonds – instead they are term deposits issued by Ottawa with a feature that allows the holder to cash them in at any time. Bonds are tradable securities and the market in bonds is huge, much bigger than the stock market. Estimates of the value of average daily turnover in the bond market are about 14 times the value of stocks traded on a typical day. The total of outstanding bond issues numbers in the thousands.

The anomaly in this situation is that most of the trading volume in bonds is confined to a small number of issues – perhaps 30 or 40 in the Canadian market. Federal government bonds are at the top of the active list and there is a good reason for having big volumes in a few issues. Bonds issued by the sovereign – in Canada, the federal government – carry the highest credit rating in any national market. Those bonds then become benchmarks for the pricing of other bonds, both when they are first issued and when they trade in the secondary market.

BONDS COME IN TWO BASIC FORMS: BEARER BONDS AND REGISTERED BONDS

The Bank of Canada, which is the fiscal agent for the national government, identifies key bond issues as benchmarks. These are bonds with at least $6 billion in circulation in maturities of two, three, five, 10 and 30 years. Investment dealers will pick certain other issues as benchmarks to fill out the range of maturities and to expand the benchmark category so that it includes some provincial issues and a few top-quality corporates. These benchmarks then become the standard when pricing other issues. For example, a lower quality 10-year corporate bond might be sold at 100 basis points over benchmark, which means the yield would be one percentage point higher than the yield on the 10-year Canada benchmark.

The price of a bond is set from the yield, which represents the prevailing rate of interest in wholesale markets for funds. Take the example of a 10-year bond that pays interest at 6.125%. But market conditions have changed slightly and on the issue day market yield has to be set at 6.176% to attract investors. In this example the price would be 99.624 instead of par at 100.

Bonds come in two basic forms – bearer bonds and registered bonds. Bearer bonds feature detachable coupons, which are clipped and cashed when scheduled interest payments are due. That's why the interest rate of a bond is referred to as its coupon rate. Bearer bonds are assumed to belong to whoever holds them. A registered bond shows the name of the owner and usually interest payments are sent to the registered owner by cheque from the borrower's trustee or paying agent. In Canada, a debenture is similar to a bond, but no assets or property are pledged as security for the loan. Instead, the debenture is backed by the general credit of the borrower and is an unsecured promise to repay the amount of the loan.

The line between bonds and debentures often is blurred. Technically, government bonds are debentures because no assets are pledged for the loan. But the power to tax means the government is highly unlikely to go broke. When bond traders and other investment professionals refer to yields, they are usually talking about the yield to maturity. But some bonds can be called in before the maturity date and the quoted yield on these issues usually will be based on the call date.

BONDS OFFER A PREDICTABLE RATE OF RETURN

When preparing to sell new bonds to the public, corporate issuers and some government issuers will consult with investment dealers and other distributors on the size of the bond issue, interest rate to be offered and any other attributes or conditions attached to the bond. This involves researching the current bond market carefully, including prevailing interest rates for other bonds and similar interest-bearing investments. Dealers will act either as principals – buying the issue and reselling it to investors

– or as agents collecting commissions on sales. Large institutions, such as pension funds, represent the major market for bonds.

Pension funds like bonds because a predictable rate of return can be factored into the fund's actuarial requirements for future pension payments. Individuals can buy bonds in relatively small denominations and bond mutual funds are an important part of the buyer base for bonds. The popularity of bonds with institutions has led to the development of the "medium-term note" market. Essentially, these are bonds issued through a shelf prospectus, which means the issuer has all the required documents ready so that a bond can be sold on short notice, as short as a few hours.

If an investment dealer has a client with spare funds, the dealer will shop around for a corporate issuer with a need for funds and the two sides to the deal will be matched quickly. Actually, the name "medium-term note" is misleading. Originally, these bond issue programs were for shorter term securities but now they can be issued for long terms. The size of a note issue can be as little as $1 million – a small amount compared with a standard prospectus bond issue, which usually is at least $75 million.

THE DIFFERENCE BETWEEN THE BID PRICE AND THE ASK PRICE IS BOND DEALER'S PROFIT

Most federal government bonds are sold by auction with the Bank of Canada acting as the government's adviser on terms and conditions.

After new bond issues are sold to investors, they begin trading on the secondary market. As investors buy and sell bonds among themselves, the bonds begin trading at prices other than their face value. In Canada, most bonds are sold over the counter, although some fixed income securities are traded on stock exchanges. The bond trading network is an interdealer community made up of large financial intermediaries. On the secondary market, bond dealers act as principals. Instead of collecting commissions on sales, as they would in the stock market, they purchase bonds and resell them. They list prices at which they are willing to buy a specific bond – the bid price – and a price at which they are willing to sell – the ask price. The difference between the two prices is the dealer's profit.

CANADA SAVINGS BONDS STILL HOLD APPEAL

Victory Bonds proved popular during the Second World War, and the government of the day in Ottawa, knowing a good thing when it saw it, followed up with Canada Savings Bonds. At times, CSBs have been a mainstay of the federal government's financing program. More recently, Ottawa has relied mainly on conventional bonds. Canada Savings Bonds differ from the rest of Ottawa's bonds in that they are not marketable. They are sold in the fall through banks, investment dealers and other financial institutions.

A core element in the government's distribution system is the payroll deduction plan and sales through this method are stable year after year. One of the appeals of CSBs is that they can be cashed at any time at any bank in Canada and the holder receives interest up to the latest full month. This liquidity has been an advantage over conventional bank term deposits. There are two types of CSBs – regular interest bonds and compound interest. Regular interest bonds allow bondholders to collect annual interest by cheque or by direct deposit to a bank account. With compound interest bonds, a bondholder collects no annual interest. Instead, the interest accumulates (with interest on the interest) until the bond is cashed.

CAUGHT IN CURRENCY CROSS-CURRENTS

Currency risk and the opportunity to make gains from foreign exchange used to be issues that only concerned bankers and the treasurers of big companies in Canada. But the increasing globalization of markets means ordinary investors must pay much more attention to shifting rates for currencies. Individual portfolios may not contain direct investments in foreign securities, but almost every portfolio will have some exposure to currency risk.

THERE ARE TWO COMMON REASONS WHY FOREIGN CURRENCIES CAN AFFECT INVESTMENTS

• Investors who buy stocks indirectly through mutual funds are likely to have a foreign currency component because these institutions will have non-Canadian stocks within many of their portfolios.

• Canadian public companies are increasingly global and their foreign currency expo-

CROSS RATES | TABLE

A cross is simply a trade between two currencies. Generally, currency values are set in relation to the reserve currency – C$ vs US$, German mark vs US$, and so on. Cross rates then recalculate those currency values to produce exchange rates for the C$ vs the mark and so on. This table shows the currencies on which there is an active C$ market. These also are currencies that can be hedged through the futures market. Gold is included in this list because of its historic role as an alternative currency. These rates are wholesale market rates, which means trades of at least $100,000.

Currency cross rates
Supplied by Royal Bank of Canada – indicative wholesale late afternoon rates

	C$	US$	DM	Yen	£	Fr. fr.	Sw. fr.	A$
Canada $	...	1.5235	0.9180	0.0132	2.5267	0.2737	1.1215	0.9504
U.S.$	0.6564	...	0.6026	0.0087	1.6585	0.1797	0.7361	0.6239
DMark	1.0893	1.6595	...	0.0144	2.7523	0.2982	1.2216	1.0353
Japan yen	75.66	115.28	69.46	...	191.18	20.71	84.85	71.91
British pnd.	0.3958	0.6030	0.3633	0.0052	...	0.1083	0.4438	0.3762
French franc	3.6530	5.5654	3.3537	0.0483	9.2302	...	4.0967	3.4720
Swiss franc	0.8917	1.3585	0.8186	0.0118	2.2531	0.2441	...	0.8475
Australian $	1.0521	1.6029	0.9659	0.0139	2.6585	0.2880	1.1799	...
Gold	440.22	288.95	479.51	33308.71	174.22	1608.12	392.54	463.17

REAL RETURN BOND | TABLE

Real return bonds are government bonds that are indexed to inflation as measured by the consumer price index. They pay a base rate of 4.25% (the real return). Then there is an adjustment, called the index ratio, based on changes in CPI. The real yield is a combination of real return and the indexing for inflation. In addition to the inflation adjustment on the coupon, there is an inflation adjustment to the payment of principal at maturity. These bonds were first issued in 1991 with a 30-year maturity and the federal government now issues additional real return bonds on a quarterly schedule.

Real return bond
Supplied by RBC Dominion Securities Inc.

Bid side levels

Coupon	Maturity	Real price	Real yield	Index ratio
Issuer: Government of Canada				
4.250	Dec 01/21	104.00	3.98	1.10053
Issuer: Government of Canada				
4.250	Dec 01/21	104.00	3.98	1.10053

sure in trade will have a bearing on their earnings outlook, which in turn affects stock prices and the ability to cover bond interest payments. A related factor is that many industries are global and prices charged by foreign competitors can have an impact on the pricing power and profitability of Canadian companies.

One way of looking at currency value is to think of it as the stock price for a country. A strong currency represents solid national earning power. A weak currency represents a weak economy and any signs of improvement will be reflected in a rise in the currency value. There are several reasons why a currency value fluctuates. When interest rates change more in one country than in others, foreign investors take notice. Higher rates in Canada compared with the U.S. represent a Canada premium to offshore investors looking to place money in North America. High rates attract money into the country, creating a demand for C$s.

That demand pushes up the value of the currency. Strength in the currency allows interest rates to fall, which means swings in currency values will be corrected by the market if there are no other factors in the equation. But there may be political risks that force interest rates higher and those risks can depress a currency value. The Quebec referendum on separation is one of the best examples of how political risk can drive down a currency.

TOO MUCH DEBT PUTS DOWNWARD PRESSURE ON CURRENCY

Inflation is another significant factor in the mix of influences on currency values. A rapid rise in prices represents an artificial increase in the value of assets within the domestic economy and the international marketplace will correct that situation by devaluing the currency. Too much debt within the domestic economy – either through government or private sector borrowing – can put downward pressure on the currency. In this situation, the borrowers must rely on foreign lenders and the currency will suffer if the economy is seen to be dangerously exposed to external creditors.

An important concept in the study of money is the reserve currency, which is the anchor of the international monetary system. The reserve currency is now the US$. As that name implies, the US$ is the unit of measure for official reserves held by central banks around the world. Those reserves are kept for the defence of the local currency during times of instability. For example, the Bank of Canada intervened in currency markets – selling US$s to buy C$s to support the C$'s price – when there were turbulent trading periods at the time of the last Quebec referendum.

INTRODUCTION OF EURO MAY RIVAL US$ AS MAJOR RESERVE CURRENCY

Another feature of the reserve currency is that it is the unit for pricing major commodities. It's also the currency used for the accounts of such international agencies as the World Bank and the International Monetary Fund. While the US$ is the world's most important currency, the German mark has developed into a regional reserve currency in Europe. That situation is scheduled to change in 1999 with the introduction of the euro. This is a pan-European currency that will replace national units. If the euro is introduced as planned, it will become a rival to the US$ as a major reserve currency.

There is no comparable currency in Asia and until 1997 many Asian currencies were

MAJOR CURRENCIES | TABLE

Trading desks at financial institutions measure currency values against the reserve currency, which is the US$. But the exchange rates that matter for Canadians are with the C$. The Major Currencies table gives both in relation to those currencies that represent Canada's major trading partners. Changes are given over the past four weeks and the % change columns allow comparisons of trends for different currencies.

Major currencies

*Supplied by Royal Bank of Canada – indicative wholesale late afternoon rates. * inverted*

Per US$	Latest	Prev day	Week ago	4 wks ago	% chg on day	% chg in wk	% chg 4 wk
Canada $	1.5235	1.5330	1.5429	1.5475	-0.62	-1.26	-1.55
DMark	1.6595	1.6530	1.6532	1.6305	0.39	0.38	1.78
Japan yen	115.28	114.73	117.88	130.63	0.48	-2.21	*****
UK pound *	1.6585	1.6637	1.6765	1.6815	-0.31	-1.07	-1.37
France franc	5.5654	5.5430	5.5428	5.4670	0.40	0.41	1.80
Swiss franc	1.3585	1.3507	1.3450	1.3400	0.58	1.00	1.38
Australia $ *	0.6239	0.6249	0.6179	0.5922	-0.16	0.97	5.34
Mexico peso	9.9650	10.0000	10.1200	10.1875	-0.35	-1.53	-2.18
Hong Kong $	7.7440	7.7435	7.7493	7.7483	0.01	-0.07	-0.06
Singapore $	1.6190	1.6240	1.6255	1.6723	-0.31	-0.40	-3.18
China renminbi	8.28	8.28	8.28	8.28	0.00	0.00	0.00
Per C$							
U.S. $	0.6564	0.6523	0.6481	0.6462	0.62	1.27	1.58
DMark	1.0893	1.0783	1.0715	1.0536	1.02	1.66	3.39
Japan yen	75.66	74.84	76.40	84.41	1.10	-0.96	*****
UK pound *	2.5267	2.5505	2.5867	2.6021	-0.93	-2.32	-2.90
France franc	3.6530	3.6158	3.5925	3.5328	1.03	1.69	3.40

FOREIGN EXCHANGE | TABLE

This foreign exchange list is a handy guide for business travellers or vacationers. A cautionary note, though: These are wholesale market rates and foreign exchange dealers will add a commission when buying or selling. The tables gives exchange values in both C$s and US$s, and these two exchange rates can be valuable to investors. If a Canadian company in an investor's portfolio is expanding into a foreign country, the C$ exchange rate is a guide to the company's local costs in that country and the US$ exchange rate is a guide to costs for commodities that are priced in world markets.

Foreign exchange by country
Supplied by Bank of Montreal Treasury Group – noon rate

Currency	in C$	in US$	Daily % chg	Currency	in C$	in US$	Daily % chg
Antigua,Gr. EC $	0.5644	0.3704	nil	Lebanon (Pound)	0.001015	0.000666	0.07
Argentina (Peso)	1.52410	1.00020	0.01	Luxemb. Franc	0.04451	0.02921	-0.47
Austria (Schill)	0.13051	0.08565	-0.47	Malaysia (Ringgit)	0.4021	0.2639	0.26
Bahamas (Dollar)	1.5238	1.0000	nil	Malta (Lira)	4.0270	2.6427	-0.42
Bahrain (Dinar)	4.0419	2.6525	nil	Netherlands Guild.	0.8144	0.5345	-0.43
Barbados (Dollar)	0.7576	0.4972	nil	Neth. Ant. Guilder	0.8513	0.5587	nil
Belgium (Franc)	0.04451	0.02921	-0.47	New Zealand $	0.8091	0.5310	-0.11
Bermuda (Dollar)	1.5238	1.0000	nil	Norway (Krone)	0.2066	0.1356	-0.63

formally pegged to the US$. The notable exception has been the Japanese yen and financial reform in Asia may involve the emergence of the yen as a regional reserve currency. The relationships between the currencies of different countries are established on foreign exchange markets in much the same way as the values of other investments are determined – through supply and demand. Currencies are traded through a computer and telephone network, much as bonds are bought and sold. Banks and investment dealers that operate internationally form the core of this market and London is the main centre for trading. New York is also a large currency trading location and Chicago has the leading markets for currency futures.

THE SHINE HAS GONE OFF INVESTING IN GOLD

In the span of a generation, gold has moved from the centre of the monetary system to become the ultimate contrarian symbol. Until 1971, gold had an official role as a reserve currency. In that year, the U.S. dropped the gold standard (by then, it was only a partial gold standard). Central banks still hold gold but the mystique is gone and in recent years there have been steady reductions in official holdings.

The Bank of Canada, at the direction of the minister of finance, has sold off most of its gold over time. At the end of 1979, the Bank of Canada's gold store was worth more than its holdings of US$s. By late 1997, the central bank held US$120 in US$ assets for

INTERNATIONAL RATES | TABLE

Euro-deposit rates and London interbank offer rates (Libor) are the international equivalent of commercial paper. These are short-term rates in an interbank market that operates outside the regulatory environment of national economies. Participants in this market are mainly financial institutions and multinational corporations. These rates are financing costs in the major currencies when a borrower goes abroad. The euro and Libor markets provide benchmark pricing in the international marketplace for funds. The table shows changes over the past four weeks. These trends reflect shifts in credit conditions or in currency values, or both.

International

Supplied by Royal Bank of Canada.

Euro-deposit rates (bid)

		Latest	Prev day	Wk ago	4 wks ago
US$	Overnight	5.31	5.50	4.93	5.37
	1-month	5.18	5.12	5.15	5.31
	3-month	5.29	5.15	5.15	5.22
	6-month	5.03	4.93	4.90	5.10
C$	3-month	5.17	5.09	5.06	5.28
DM	3-month	3.51	3.52	3.51	3.49
YEN	3-month	0.62	0.68	0.71	0.56
GBP	3-month	6.96	6.94	6.98	7.21

London interbank offer rate US$

	Latest	Prev day	Wk ago	4 wks ago
1-month	5.25	5.25	5.21	5.37
3-month	5.31	5.28	5.21	5.28
6-month	5.09	5.06	5.00	5.12

every US$1 worth of gold. Only the hardiest of gold bugs still believed in the traditional safe haven status of gold in the latter part of the 1990s. The gold standard meant that governments backed their currencies with gold. In theory, someone could go to the central bank with paper money and swap it for gold at the official exchange rate.

Full convertibility to gold ended in Canada in the 1920s. Following the Second World War, a modified international gold standard, in which only national governments could convert their foreign currency holdings into gold, was instituted. But that system fell away in the 1970s. Now, gold trades like any other commodity and there are no official rates. Annual mine production has been less than market demand for several years, but central bank selling has steadily depressed the price. Gold is important as an industrial metal and the electronics industry is among the big consumers. Gold is a good conductor of electricity and it can be spun into fine wires – these features make it ideal for tiny computer chips. (Copper is far less useful for these miniature applications.)

GOLD MAY NEVER REGAIN ITS MONETARY APPEAL

Gold also retains its appeal for jewelry and this demand is consistent from year to year. But hoarding – the term used for buying gold as a currency – has gone out of style. The historical reason that people hoarded gold was its reputation as a store of value. It was an international currency that could be cashed anywhere during times of war. Gold also was seen as a protection against inflation. When paper money was devalued, gold held its purchasing power. The rule of thumb used to be that an ounce of gold was roughly equal to the price of a good men's suit.

Silver has had a role similar to gold's in many parts of the world, notably Latin America and Asia. Silver still has monetary appeal in parts of Asia and gold still has its fans, but the monetary power of gold has been weakened considerably. Central banking has changed the popular notion of gold's value. Now, faith is placed in the ability of central banks to protect the value of money. Many people question whether gold will ever regain its monetary appeal.

Gold can still be bought as bullion by those who have kept the faith. Wafers begin at an ounce and gold still can be bought in bars. Those who do buy often do not take physical delivery. Instead, they have a certificate from the seller, usually a bank, and they pay a storage fee. People who buy gold and hold it themselves usually go to coins. Several countries have gold coin series and the Canadian Maple Leaf program is among the most popular in the world. The most common way to invest in gold is through the com-

CANADIAN/U.S. YIELDS | TABLE

Yields in this table represent the basic financing costs in the domestic market for business. They are for large value transactions by those companies or institutions that have top credit ratings. Those with lesser credit ratings would pay a premium over these yields. The significance of this table is that it shows the trend over the latest four weeks for interest rates at different terms (from one month to 30 years).

Treasury bills and bonds are benchmark issues of federal government securities. Bankers' acceptance notes are the highest quality commercial paper. They are notes issued by a corporation and guaranteed as to principal and interest by a bank.

Forward rate agreements (FRAs) are contracts for delivery of a specific amount at a rate for a future term. In effect, an FRA is a forward contract for funds.

Canadian yields   U.S. yields

Supplied by Royal Bank of Canada. Indicative wholesale late afternoon rates.

Canadian	Latest	Prev day	Week ago	4 wks ago	U.S.	Latest	Prev day	Week ago	4 wks ago
T-Bills					**T-Bills**				
1-month	4.61	4.69	4.75	4.37	1-month	4.65	N.A.	N.A.	N.A.
3-month	4.75	4.76	4.68	4.61	3-month	4.36	4.29	4.05	4.05
6-month	4.77	4.77	4.72	4.90	6-month	4.32	4.36	4.03	4.18
1-year	4.76	4.77	4.68	4.83	1-year	4.14	4.15	3.85	4.05
Bonds					**Bonds**				
2-year	4.64	4.67	4.53	4.51	2-year	4.25	4.28	4.11	4.10
5-year	4.87	4.89	4.71	4.50	5-year	4.36	4.38	4.21	4.05
7-year	4.97	5.01	4.83	4.59	7-year	4.62	4.63	4.55	4.19
10-year	5.15	5.18	4.99	4.69	10-year	4.74	4.76	4.61	4.23
30-year	5.53	5.55	5.43	5.17	30-year	5.21	5.23	5.10	4.75
Banker's acceptances					**Commercial paper**				
1-month	5.25	5.27	5.29	5.43	1-month	5.03	5.03	5.00	5.19
3-month	5.14	5.17	5.19	5.30	3-month	4.95	4.95	4.95	5.05
6-month	4.99	5.02	4.93	5.13	6-month	4.82	4.82	4.81	4.93
3-mth forward rate agreement					**3-mth forward rate agreement**				
3 months	4.84	4.88	4.69	4.94	3-month	5.76	5.76	5.76	5.76
6 months	4.59	4.61	4.41	4.57	6-month	5.72	5.72	5.72	5.72
9 months	4.53	4.54	4.36	4.47	9-month	n.a.	n.a.	n.a.	n.a.

FORWARD EXCHANGE RATES | TABLE

Currencies can be bought or sold for delivery at a future date at a current price. You buy a contract (a sort of down payment) to lock in the exchange rate. The spot price is the current price, stated as an exchange rate in relation to US$s (the reserve currency). The forward rates are the exchange rates that will apply in the future when the delivery takes place. The changes over time represent the present market sentiment on exchange rate trends, plus factors for the time value of money and the risk of surprises during that time. These rates are wholesale rates for large transactions and there will be fees or commissions to the bank or investment dealer that underwrites the transaction.

Forward exchange rates

*Supplied by Royal Bank of Canada. Indicative wholesale late afternoon rates. * inverted*

Per US$	Spot	1-mo	3-mo	6-mo	1-yr	2-yr	3-yr	4-yr	5-yr
Canada $	1.5235	1.5235	1.5231	1.5230	1.5228	n.a.	1.5235	1.5255	1.5285
Japan yen	115.28	114.78	113.66	112.33	109.83	104.53	100.17	95.31	91.01
DMark	1.6595	1.6568	1.6523	1.6470	1.6370	1.6145	1.5990	1.5874	1.5751
UK pound*	1.6585	1.6560	1.6516	1.6459	1.6355	1.7040	n.a.	n.a.	n.a.
Per C$									
U.S.$	0.6564	0.6564	0.6566	0.6566	0.6567	n.a.	0.6564	0.6555	0.6542
Japan yen	75.66	75.34	74.62	73.75	72.12	n.a.	65.75	62.47	59.54
DMark	1.0893	1.0875	1.0848	1.0814	1.0750	n.a.	1.0496	1.0406	1.0305
UK pound*	2.5267	2.5229	2.5156	2.5067	2.4905	n.a.	n.a.	n.a.	n.a.

mon stocks of producers or promising exploration companies. As well, there are several mutual funds that specialize in precious metals and these funds may hold bullion as well as stocks. More adventurous investors can buy gold futures or options on gold. These options and futures are traded on major exchanges.

CENTRAL BANKS GUARD MONEY'S VALUE

A cornerstone of modern central banking is that the bank should be independent of political decisions made by the government of the day. In Canada, the finance minister holds all the shares of the central bank. The finance minister and the governor of the Bank of Canada meet regularly and there is broad agreement on policy.

As the owner of the bank, the finance minister appoints the deputy finance minister to represent the government on the board of the Bank of Canada. This is a non-voting position and by tradition the government treads carefully when giving the Bank of Canada its views on monetary policy. The government has the power to issue a policy directive to the central bank, but this unusual step would only be taken in the event of a crisis of confidence in central bank management.

Successive finance ministers and bank governors have been mindful of the fact that the perception of independence is important. The German central bank, the Bundesbank, is widely considered to be the model for modern central banks. It came into being after a period of runaway inflation caused social breakdown in Germany during the 1920s. That experience instilled a deep faith in the need for a credible monetary authority to protect the value of money.

North American central banks have followed that pattern and in the U.S. the Federal Reserve Board has unequivocal power to set monetary policy. The Fed, as it is known, has not worried much about currency value because the US$ is the world's reserve currency. But that fact also means the Fed has a de facto influence on the monetary policy of other industrial countries. When the Fed changes monetary gears, the Bank of Canada usually has to make a shift as well.

INTERNATIONAL STANDARDS FOR BANKING ARE SET IN SWITZERLAND

Globalization of markets has brought with it a globalization of policy. It now is almost impossible for one country to maintain for long a policy stance that is at odds with general trends elsewhere in the world. The usual reason for one central bank being out of step is that the government of the day wants easier credit conditions to stimulate local business. But when interest rates are artificially depressed, the usual result is a devaluation of the currency and the local economy pays a bigger price in the end.

Within the industrial world, the monetary authorities are connected through the Bank for International Settlements (BIS), based in Basel, Switzerland. This is the central bankers' bank and its main role has been in the setting of international standards for commercial banking. BIS has a role complementary to that of the International Monetary Fund (IMF), which is the lender of last resort when national financial systems get into trouble. When the IMF provides funds for a bailout, the terms will include negotiated agreements to implement financial reforms. IMF funds come from the industrial countries and the workouts are done in less developed countries. The other major international financial institution is the World Bank, which provides development financing to poorer countries.

BANK RATES | TABLE

These are benchmark rates that are subject to change without notice. The prime rate is generally considered to be the rate charged the most creditworthy customers and adjustable rate commercial loans will be set at a rate pegged to prime but at a fixed number of basis points above prime.

Bank rates			
Canada		U.S.	
Bank of Can.	5.50	Discount	4.75
Prev. o/n comp.	5.40	Prime	8.00
Prime	7.00	Fed Funds	5.25
Call Loan Ave	5.00		

The Bank of Canada rate is the rate charged by the central bank in its role as lender of last resort to the financial system. In the U.S., the discount rate and the fed funds rate are like the bank rate.

The call loan rate is the market rate for overnight loans between financial institutions.

BANK OF CANADA EXERCISES ITS POWER

Ottawa's banker – the governor of the Bank of Canada – is the most powerful unelected official in the country. Looking after the federal government's finances is just part of the job. The bigger chore for the central bank is in finding the right balance for the C$ and the interest rate structure. As the name implies, the central bank is the banker to the financial system. It's the lender of last resort when a commercial bank is short of cash.

The Bank of Canada is the only bank in the country that can print paper money, although that was not always the case. After Confederation in 1867, the government allowed chartered banks to issue money. The stock market crash of 1929 and the depression that followed created a crisis for the world's banking system and governments looked for ways to prevent a recurrence of that devastating experience. Creation of the Bank of Canada in 1935 was part of the policy prescription. It was a public stock company at first but political pressure for more government control resulted in the federal government buying back all the shares by 1938. The bank's role has been revised and expanded over the years but the essential job is still managing monetary policy.

• Most of the day-to-day work at the Bank of Canada is in overseeing the smooth functioning of the financial system. It conducts a daily balancing of accounts for the banks as a group. This is called the payments settlement process, which means making sure that Bank A gets money owed from Bank B and so on.

• In its policy role, the bank controls the money supply and exercises a direct influence on the level of interest rates. These actions are carried out within the broader goal of sustaining non-inflationary growth in the economy. Price stability – which means low inflation – is the essential element in the bank's master plan.

• As fiscal agent for the government, the Bank of Canada advises the Finance Department on how to best to manage taxpayers' money. It conducts the government's banking. When Ottawa needs extra cash, the bank is the underwriter for the sale of bonds, treasury bills, Canada Savings Bonds and other securities.

• The bank is the designated crisis manager when there are problems in Canada's economy or when this country's financial system is exposed to problems elsewhere in the world. That can include intervention in the currency market or loans to financial institutions.

The central bank does not set a target rate for the foreign exchange value of the C$. When it does intervene in the currency market, the purpose is to smooth the trading patterns. However, the bank does influence the value of Canadian currency through its hold on the interest rate structure. The general policy stance is that by keeping a lid on inflation, the central bank provides a stable environment and that in turn allows the economy to give strength to the C$.

The Bank of Canada is governed by a board of directors, which is appointed by the finance minister. The board appoints the senior officers of the bank and sets broad corporate objectives. By tradition, there is a regional balance to the board. Monetary poli-

WHAT YOUR SAVINGS EARN | TABLE

Money in the bank is a loan to the bank and in a normal market the cost of money rises as the length of the loan increases. To a point, there is a premium as well for larger loans. For that reason, most financial institutions have minimum levels for posted rates on term deposits. This table gives those posted rates. In certain circumstances, lenders may be able to negotiate for a better return.

The lowest rates are for demand deposits, which means money in the bank can be withdrawn on demand. Rates may vary among institutions because of the situation of the borrower. Financial institutions try to balance their deposit and loan business and this can be a factor in setting rates. For example, if a financial institution has had a big demand for five-year mortgages, it may pay a premium to attract five-year term deposits.

Financial institutions listed in this table may vary from week to week.

Rates are "annualized" – the rate for a full year, not the return for the period specified. Institutions may offer variations on the certificates of deposit listed here and these rates provide benchmarks to assess the value of returns from other combinations.

Minimum amounts generally apply to deposits for fixed terms and these minimums are indicated in the various categories below – up to six months, one to five years, monthly interest and compound interest.

Most fixed-term deposits pay interest at the end of a term if less than a year and annually if more than a year.

The table also shows rates for five-year deposits that pay interest monthly and that pay compound interest. (Compounding means the payments are held by the financial institution and reinvested, so the lenders get a lump sum payment at the end of the term.)

WHAT YOUR SAVINGS EARN 10.27.98

Rates are quoted on Thursday and subject to change. Selection of financial institutions may vary weekly. Figures supplied by Fiscal Agents.

	Savings monthly	Accts daily	Term Deposits min inv	30-59 days	60-89 days	90-119 days	120-179 days	min inv	Certificates/Debentures 1 yr	2 yr	3 yr	4 yr	5 yr	5 yr Term Int paid monthly min inv	%rate	Comp base int	Cert $ value aftr 5 yrs
Banks																	
Amex Bank of Canada	-	0.25	-	-	-	-	-	1,000	4.05	4.55	4.65	4.70	5.00	-	-	-	-
BCI Bank	0.75	0.50	5,000	3.75	3.75	3.75	3.75	1,000	3.75	3.85	3.95	4.00	4.25	5,000	3.65	4.000	1,216
Bank of Montreal	-	0.35	5,000	3.75	3.75	3.75	3.75	1,000	3.75	3.85	3.95	4.00	4.25	5,000	4.00	4.250	1,231
Bank of Nova Scotia	-	0.35	5,000	3.75	3.75	3.75	3.75	500	3.75	3.85	3.95	4.00	4.25	5,000	4.00	4.250	1,231
CIBC	-	0.25	5,000	3.75	3.75	3.75	3.75	1,000	3.75	3.85	3.95	4.00	4.25	5,000	4.00	4.250	1,231
Citibank Canada	-	0.35	5,000	3.75	3.75	3.75	3.75	5,000	3.75	3.85	3.95	4.00	4.25	5,000	4.00	4.250	1,231
Citizens Bank	-	0.50	5,000	4.00	4.00	4.25	4.25	500	4.50	4.50	4.50	4.50	4.75	500	4.25	4.500	1,246
Hongkong Bank	-	0.25	5,000	3.75	3.75	3.75	3.75	1,000	4.15	4.25	4.35	4.00	4.25	5,000	4.00	4.250	1,231
ING Direct	-	4.75	-	-	-	-	-	0	4.60	4.65	4.80	4.85	5.00	-	-	5.000	1,276
Laurentian Bank	-	0.05	5,000	3.55	3.55	3.55	3.75	1,000	3.75	3.85	3.95	4.00	4.25	10,000	3.87	4.250	1,231
Manulife Bank	-	-	25,000	4.90	4.95	4.70	4.70	500	4.10	4.30	4.40	4.45	4.50	10,000	4.25	4.500	1,246
National Bank	-	0.02	5,000	3.50	3.50	3.50	3.75	1,000	3.85	4.10	4.32	4.37	4.62	10,000	4.12	4.625	1,253
National Bank of Greece	0.75	1.00	5,000	3.75	3.75	3.75	3.75	1,000	3.80	3.85	3.95	4.00	4.50	5,000	4.00	4.500	1,246
Republic National Bank	-	3.25	50,000	4.15	4.10	4.00	3.80	50,000	3.90	4.15	4.25	4.35	4.45	-	-	-	-
Royal Bank	-	0.15	5,000	3.75	3.75	3.75	3.75	500	3.75	3.85	3.95	4.00	4.25	5,000	4.12	4.250	1,231
State Bank of India(Can)	1.50	1.50	5,000	4.75	4.75	4.75	4.75	5,000	4.50	4.75	5.25	5.25	5.25	-	-	-	-
Toronto Dominion Bank	-	0.35	5,000	3.75	3.75	3.75	3.75	1,000	3.75	3.85	3.95	4.00	4.25	5,000	4.00	4.250	1,231

cy is formulated by a governing council that consists of the governor, senior deputy governor and four deputy governors. The governor is appointed for a seven-year term and senior officers usually are career employees at the bank.

The monetary tool that attracts the most public attention is the bank rate. This interest rate has two roles, as a policy signal and as a backstop to the banking system. The policy role is easier to understand by knowing the basics of the practical application of the bank rate. The Bank of Canada will lend overnight funds to a financial institution at the bank rate. The central bank will borrow from a financial institution at a rate that is 50 basis points lower. This 50-point spread – one half of a percentage point – is called the central bank's "operating band."

THE BANK OF CANADA SETS THE BANK RATE – THE BASIS FOR INTEREST RATE STRUCTURE

Commercial banks need overnight money to meet obligations when they settle accounts at the end of the day. Usually, another bank will have spare cash to lend and most of the time the overnight rate in commercial markets is close to the middle of the Bank of Canada's operating band. Only if there are distortions will a bank be forced to rely on the central bank.

But when the Bank of Canada sets the bank rate, it is fixing the starting point for the interest rate structure. When the bank rate goes up or down, commercial interest rates and bond yields generally follow. In this way, the bank has a direct influence on an easing or tightening of credit conditions. It has two essential enforcement options to back up its view of the appropriate level for interest rates. In effect, this involves making the financial system an offer it can't refuse.

If the bank wants to push commercial rates down, it uses "special purchase and resale agreements," a financial tool known colloquially as "specials." These are overnight loans offered at a rate that is below the prevailing market rate. By making cheap money available, the bank takes the steam out of upward pressure on rates. The opposite tactic is a "sale and repurchase agreement," generally referred to as an SRA. With this instrument, the bank can nudge commercial rates higher by, in effect, borrowing at a rate that is above the prevailing commercial rate. In this situation, the bank is paying a premium in the market.

INVESTMENTS DON'T EXIST IN A WORLD APART

Any portfolio strategy is incomplete without an assessment of how security values are affected by political policy, natural events and social trends. One of the most widely talked about examples is the impact of baby boom demographics on asset values. When the boomers started having children, there was a building boom and home prices soared. Now, the boomers are looking ahead to retirement and their savings patterns have been credited with powering a bull market in stocks. The influence of that demographic bulge will continue as they sell down their equity portfolios to finance retirement.

MORTGAGE RATES | TABLE

The Mortgage Rates table provides rates for standard terms at selected financial institutions. This is the largest class of consumer loans and the spread between mortgages and wholesale funds for similar terms is an indicator of credit conditions. When there is easy credit, the spread, or difference, will be narrow between wholesale and retail rates of the same term.

For shorter terms, lenders offer both closed and open mortgages. **Open** means the loan can be paid off early. Rates for open mortgages are indicated by the **op** symbol.

Variable rate mortgages are those with rates that fluctuate according to general interest rate trends. Often, these mortgages are pegged to the prime rate. If this type of mortgage is not offered, it is indicated by an **n.a.** in this column.

MORTGAGE RATES 10.27.98

Rates are subject to change. Selection of financial institutions may vary weekly. Figures supplied by Fiscal Agents.

	Variable rate	6 months	1 yr	2 yr	3 yr	4 yr	5 yr
Banks							
BCI Bank	n/a	6.85 - 7.15op	6.40 - 7.00op	6.65	6.85	7.00	7.15
Bank of Montreal	6.50 - 7.00op	6.85 - 7.15op	6.40 - 7.00op	6.65	6.85	7.00	7.15
Bank of Nova Scotia	7.00	6.85 - 7.15op	6.40 - 7.00op	6.65	6.85	7.00	7.15
CIBC	6.75	6.85 - 7.15op	6.40 - 7.00op	6.65	6.85	7.00	7.15
Citizens Bank	n/a	6.35 - 6.90op	5.85 - 6.65op	5.85	6.05	6.20	6.35
Hongkong Bank	6.75	6.85 - 7.15op	6.40 - 7.00op	6.65	6.85	7.00	7.15
Laurentian Bank	n/a	6.85 - 7.30op	6.40 - 7.00op	6.65	6.85	7.00	7.15
Manulife Bank	n/a	6.85	6.40 - 7.00op	6.65	6.85	7.00	7.15
National Bank	n/a	6.85 - 7.15op	6.40 - 7.00op	6.65	6.85	7.00	7.15
National Bank of Greece	n/a	6.85 - 7.15op	6.40 - 7.10op	6.65	6.85	7.00	7.15
Royal Bank	6.75	6.85 - 7.15op	6.40 - 7.00p	6.65	6.85	7.00	7.15
Toronto Dominion Bank	6.75	6.85	6.40 - 7.00p	6.65	6.85	7.00	7.15
Trust & Loan							
Canada Trust	6.75	6.85 - 7.15op	6.40	6.65	6.85	7.00	7.15
Canadian Western Trust	n/a	6.85 - 7.15op	6.40	6.65	6.85	7.00	7.15
Co-operative Trust	n/a	6.85 - 7.15op	6.40 - 7.00op	6.65	6.85	7.00	7.15
Desjardins Trust	n/a	6.85 - 7.15op	6.40 - 7.00op	6.65	6.85	7.00	7.15
Effort Trust	n/a	6.85 - 7.15op	6.40 - 7.00op	6.65	6.85	7.00	7.15

A broad range of government actions affects securities values and the most common examples are tax measures. Tariff policies are another high profile valuation issue, but many other government regulations have an impact. Some of these rules, such as environmental standards, affect the cost section of corporate income statements. A government policy issue that is more significant to Canadian companies than to those in the U.S. is one that comes under the general heading of sovereignty.

Several domestic industries have been protected over the years by the Canadian government. Energy, financial services, transportation and cultural sectors are prominent examples of industries that have been protected because of the view that Canadian ownership was a national priority.

ECONOWATCH TABLE

FP Econowatch appears in Monday editions and provides a snapshot of the Canadian economy. Key statistics on the U.S. economy also are included. These statistics on business activity, banking, prices and the labor market in Canada are the key numbers that define the state of the economy. Generally, these numbers are adjusted to account for seasonal factors and the table gives the latest figures compared with the previous period. The year-to-year % column provides percentage change and these figures are guides to annual growth rates in the economy.

The top numbers in the list are for gross domestic product, which is the total value of goods and services produced by the economy.

The quarter figures are all-inclusive counts of domestic activity. The monthly GDP figures are less inclusive in that they do not account for indirect taxes. But the monthly figures provide a valuable interim assessment of the pace of economic activity. **Business activity** statistics take stock of the economy at various stages, from new orders at factories through to retail sales. **Banking** statistics measure the base costs of money (treasury bill yields and bank rate) as well as volume (money supply and loan activity).

Price indexes (not shown below) are measures of inflation and also are commonly used in contracts to regulate price changes.

Labor market figures (not shown below) provide a rough measure of prosperity but they are also a guide to business activity. Month-to-month changes in employment are, essentially, a count of jobs created in the economy.

FP ECONOWATCH 10.27.98

Figures supplied by Bank of Canada, Canada Mortgage & Housing Corp., U.S. Federal Interagency Council on Statistical Policy, Statistics Canada.

Business activity

	Term	Latest period	Previous period	% chg. year/year
GDP $bil.†	2Q98	876.12	870.04	2.9
GDP 1992=100, $bil.†	2Q98	819.04	815.42	2.8
GDP price deflater 1992=100†	2Q98	107.0	106.7	0.1
GDP 1992=100, $bil.†	Aug.	710.17	705.56	1.9
Composite Leading Indicator 1981=100	Oct.	207.3	207.1	3.2
Pretax profits $bil.†	2Q98	74.31	76.10	-1.4
Manufacturers shipments $bil.♦	Sept.	37.41	37.39	2.8
New orders $bil.♦	Sept.	37.92	38.85	2.3
Inventories $bil.♦	Sept.	50.30	49.91	6.1
Unfilled orders $bil.♦	Sept.	47.81	47.30	16.4
Manufacturing capacity usage %♦	2Q98	86.2	86.2	84.3*
Retail sales $bil.♦	Sept.	20.96	20.74	4.7
Housing starts 000s†	Oct.	139.6	134.7	-6.0
Motor vehicle sales 000s♦	Sept.	127.22	120.80	7.0

Banking

	Term	Latest period	Previous period	% chg. year/year
Money supply, M1 $bil.♦	Oct.	85.76	88.85	7.4
Money supply, M2 $bil.♦	Oct.	408.39	410.26	0.9
Treasury bills, 3-mo. biwkly auction, %	Nov. 24	4.82	4.86	3.63*
Treasury bills, 6-mo. biwkly auction, %	Nov. 24	4.93	4.96	3.93*

Almost by definition, those protected industries are less competitive than their foreign counterparts. Usually, the goal of protection is to give local firms time to develop to the stage where they can stand toe-to-toe against outside competition. Sometimes this works and sometimes it doesn't. A recent example is in the brewing industry, where Canadian beer companies have had difficulty adjusting as tariff and non-tariff barriers have tumbled.

THESE ARE KEY ISSUES FOR AN INVESTOR
• To what extent is the issuer of a security dependent on special circumstances?
• What is the likelihood that those circumstances will change?

These two questions can apply to governments, as well as corporations. For example, how would the ratings of Newfoundland bonds be affected by a prolonged ban on cod fishing that resulted in continued high social assistance costs? Many of these non-financial influences on securities values can be anticipated by a careful reading of the daily news. But sometimes there are genuine shocks – fires, train wrecks, chemical spills and so on.

The issue here for investors is to check on the extent to which an issuer of securities protects against the unexpected. Often, this involves relying on professional analysts who visit the companies and quiz financial managers about insurance coverage and disaster plans. But if the investment is in a company that has facilities open to the public, a visit will give an impression of how well the company is run. If the facilities are well maintained and the staff appears knowledgeable and courteous, it's likely that the same standards apply in back-office operations.

CHAPTER 5

MUTUAL | FUNDS

- Mutual funds defined

- What they are and how they work

- No loads versus loads

- Reading *FP*'s fund tables to track performance and risk

A TOOLKIT FOR TUNING UP

YOUR MUTUAL FUND INVESTMENTS | BY SUSAN HEINRICH

THIS INVESTMENT GUIDE IS DESIGNED to better acquaint mutual fund investors with the information available in the *Financial Post*'s various fund reports and show how it can help them understand their fund investments. The reports offer more than performance information. The statistics in the monthly and quarterly reports and the 15-year review, as well as the weekly packages, are designed to be a comprehensive and accessible resource for fund investors of all types. Whether for a quick glance at the latest returns or more in-depth analysis of holdings and asset allocation, they are organized to provide fast answers.

All investors would be wise, no matter how trustworthy their advisers, to try to understand their investments and follow their performance and costs. Although a mutual fund investment may be appropriate when it is made, markets and circumstances change. A fund's performance can lag, a portfolio manager departs, new products become available or the investor's objectives change. Monitoring is important and the *FP*'s mutual fund tables are monitoring tools.

MUTUAL FUNDS MONTHLY REPORT TRACKS PERFORMANCE OVER THE SHORT AND LONG TERM

Most experts agree longer terms of historical performance data provide a better indication of how a fund will perform in the future. *FP*'s *Mutual Funds Monthly Report,* for example, allows readers to look at a fund's performance over the short or long term. Returns are calculated based on the latest available data but extend as far back as 10 years (15 years in the case of the Mutual Funds 15 Year Review).

In using the tables to interpret performance, readers should remember that rates of return for periods of more than one year are expressed as "average annual compound returns." These figures do not show fund volatility – a particular fund may have achieved 16% in the first year, -3% in the second year and 5% in the third, but the table would show a 6% three-year return. The three-year standard deviation numbers provide an indication of fund volatility. For example, the Oct. 31, 1997, Monthly Report

Average figures for each mutual fund tell you whether the performance is above or below average

shows fixed income (bond) funds as having a three-year standard deviation of 1.3. Compare that with Canadian equity funds that have an average three-year deviation of 3.9 or equity funds that invest in emerging equity markets, such as Latin America, for which the figure is 6.6.

Average figures for each fund category can tell you whether a particular fund's performance is in line with the rest of the group or above or below average. *FP*'s fund reports also include a list of benchmarks – stock and special indexes created and tracked by investment firms – such as the Scotia Capital Markets bond indexes.

MANAGEMENT EXPENSE FEES CAN IMPACT THE BOTTOM LINE

Many investors do not realize they pay management expense fees on every fund. Those fees can have a major impact on the bottom line. Based on the *FP* report of Oct. 31, 1997, the average MER for a money market fund was 1%. But the management expense ratios (MERs) of individual money market funds varied from as high as 2.55% to as low as 0.12%. When you're earning a 5% yield or lower, this spread can be a pretty significant factor. Full-service investment dealers invariably look at MERs along with performance.

"We want good value," says John Platt, vice-president of mutual fund research at Nesbitt Burns Inc. in Toronto. "We don't mind paying for advice, we preach that at Nesbitt Burns. If there's a good manager who is perhaps a little more expensive than the average, that will show through in the return numbers, which will be above average, net of fees. [But] all things being equal, we will choose a fund with a lower MER."

MONTHLY AND QUARTERLY REPORTS LOOK AT WORLD PERFORMANCES

For those investors who are keen market watchers, both the monthly and quarterly reports analyse what has gone on in the markets around the world and how that has affected fund returns. The *Quarterly Report* is designed to help investors better understand how money managers react to changing market conditions by providing an in-depth analysis of portfolio holdings. An investor might learn, for example, that his or her balanced fund – which usually holds a combination of bonds and equities – is no longer balanced at all. Bullish on equity markets, the manager of the fund may have moved out of fixed income entirely and placed all bets on the stock market.

Some investors like this sort of strategy, but others buy balanced funds in the expectation they'll remain diversified. *FP*'s fund reports can help them make sure their investments are on the right course.

INVESTING IN MUTUAL FUNDS

A mutual fund is a pool of money contributed by many individuals and invested by professional investment managers. There are many types of mutual funds. Some invest in stocks, some in bonds, some in specialty investments such as real estate. Some are high-risk funds where investors hope to make big gains. Some are extremely conservative, investing in low-risk money market instruments that produce moderate returns.

Yet they all work on the same principle: a pool of capital contributed by mutual fund investors is used to buy and sell securities and other investments held by funds. Just what is bought and sold is controlled by investment managers who aim to do what every investor wants to do – make money. Most of the profits go back to the individuals who invested in the fund. There are a number of ways this can occur, depending on the nature of the fund and its investment.

OPEN-END FUNDS

Almost all Canadian mutual funds are known as open-end funds. That means you can invest money or cash in your investment at any time. When you invest in a fund, you buy units (also known as shares) of that fund. As with stocks, the value of these units fluctuates, so you pay the current price when you buy into the fund.

HOW UNITS ARE PRICED

Unlike stocks, mutual fund unit prices don't fluctuate because of supply and demand. They fluctuate according to the value of the investments and other assets held by the

MUTUAL FUNDS 10.27.98

Close or latest for NOV 03, 1998 supplied by Fundata Canada Inc. Prices reported are for information purposes only. Confirmation of price should be obtained from fund. Date following fund name denotes last valuation. The codes mean: X - ex-dividend; U - US$; ... - change less than 1¢; * - RRSP eligible (funds without * may generally be held in RRSPs as foreign property); Z - not available to the general public; N - No load fund; F - Front end acquisition fee (generally negotiable); D - deferred declining redemption fee based on original capital invested; R - deferred declining redemption fee based on market value; FD - F or D at buyer's option; FR - F or R at buyer's option; B - both front end and back end fee. (n) - not a member of IFIC.

Fund	Specifics	NAVPS	$ chg
ABAX			
ABAX Brady 10/29	UF	10.60	
ABC Funds			
Amer-Value 10/30	N	5.44	+.11

Fund	Specifics	NAVPS	$chg
AGF Glo R/E Equ	FD	5.98	-.01
AGF Grth & Inc	*FD	17.11	-.02
AGF Grth Equity	*FD	24.23	+.07
AGF High Income	X*FD	10.24	unch
AGF Intl ST Inc	FD	11.24	-.06
AGF Intl Stock	FD	7.08	-.02
AGF Intl Value	FD	38.38	-.15
AGF Japan	FD	4.95	-.05
AGF RSP Gbl Bnd	X*FD	5.41	-.02
AGF RSPIntlEqAl	*FD	5.45	-.03
AGF Special US	FD	10.50	-.06
AGF US Income	XFD	12.47	-.06
AGF US ST HiYld	XFD	4.06	-.01
AGF World Bal	FD	15.31	-.06
AGF World Equ	FD	8.51	-.02
AGF Group of Funds US$			
20/20 Aggr Gbl	UFD	4.04	-.02
20/20 Aggr Gth	UFD	10.67	-.07
20/20 Emerg Mkt	UFD	1.92	+.03
20/20 India	UFD	1.27	-.01
20/20 Latin Am	UFD	2.58	+.12
AGF Amer Grth	UFD	18.08	-.19
AGF Amer TAA	UFD	14.74	unch
AGF Asian Grth	UFD	5.87	+.15
AGF Cda Class	UFD	3.17	unch
AGF China Focus	UFD	3.79	+.10

Fund	Specifics	NAVPS	$chg
Amer Aggr Grth	FR	8.75	-.06
Amer Premier	FR	8.97	-.07
Cdn Balanced	*FR	13.85	-.02
Cdn Premier	*FR	7.73	+.01
Europa	FR	20.35	-.22
Glo Hlth	FR	16.94	-.20
Glo RSP Income	X*FR	12.88	-.09
Glo RSP Index	*ZFR	10.32	+.07
Glo Tech	FR	14.80	-.27
Intl	FR	8.72	-.08
Korea	FR	3.94	-.01
Nippon	FR	7.29	-.10
Tiger	FR	6.68	...
AIM Family of Funds US$			
Amer Agg Gr U$	UFR	5.74	+.01
Amer Premier U$	UFR	5.88	+.01
Europa U$	UFR	13.34	-.02
Glo Hlth Sci U$	UFR	11.11	-.03
Glo RSP Inc U$	XU*FR	8.44	+.02
Glo Tech U$	UFR	9.70	-.09
Intl U$	UFR	5.72	...
Korea U$	UFR	2.58	+.01
Nippon U$	UFR	4.78	-.02
Tiger U$	UFR	4.38	+.04
AIM GT Family of Funds C$			
Amer Gth	FD	7.36	-.08

Daily listings permit constant monitoring of fund performance. For those mutual fund investors who like to stay on top of their investments, the *Financial Post* publishes daily mutual fund performance listings. Unlike the other listings, these are organized by fund management company rather than investment category. Separate listings are provided for segregated life insurance company funds venture capital funds, and a general "other" category. The first column after the fund name shows a number of fund specifics as follows:

X – ex-dividend

U – US$

••• – change is less than 1¢

* – fund is RRSP/RRIF eligible as 100% Canadian content

Z – unavailable to the general public

N – no load

F – front-end load

D – deferred declining back-end load (redemption fee) based on original acquisition cost

R – deferred declining redemption fee based on market value

FD – F or D at buyer's option

FR – F or R at buyer's option

B – both front-end and back-end loads

n – not a member of the Investment Funds Institute of Canada (IFIC)

Money Market

Fund	Specifics	Curr yield	Eff yield	%pt chg
Acadia Investment Funds				
MMF 11/02	*N	2.67	2.71	+.44
AGF Funds Inc.				
MMF	X*F	3.68	3.75	unch
US MMF	XUF	4.07	4.15	-.03
AIC Income Fund Series				
MMF	*FD	4.93	5.05	unch
AIM Family of Funds C$				
Cash Prf	*FR	3.80	3.87	-.04

The next column of the listings shows the fund's NAVPS (net asset value per share) as at the previous day's or latest closing, and the final column shows the dollar change from the previous day's/latest closing. The daily listings provide a separate section for money market funds (segregated as well as regular), with different performance figures than for other funds. In this case, after fund names and specifics, the tables show the fund's current annualized yield, the effective yield over the past 12 months and the dollar-change figure over the preceding day's/latest close. The daily listings also provide a table of dividend distributions made that day or recently, showing type, amount and distribution date.

fund. The unit value is calculated by taking the total assets of the fund, subtracting the fund's liabilities, and dividing that amount by the number of units outstanding. For example, if the net value of assets is $100 million and there are 10 million units, each will be worth $10. This is known as the net asset value per share (NAVPS).

Let's say you buy 100 units for a total of $1,000. And thanks to some wise decisions on the part of the fund manager, the fund's investments double to $200 million over a few years while the number of shareholders remains the same. Each unit is then worth $20, and your investment has doubled to $2,000. At that point, any new investors in the fund have to pay $20 a unit. Of course, the number of unitholders isn't likely to remain the same. More units will be bought, and some will be cashed in. But if the fund is doing well, it is likely to attract more investors than it loses.

There is no set number of units. That's because every time new units are sold, the proceeds increase the fund's assets and the net asset value per share, or unit price, remains unchanged. To return to our example, if 10 million new units were added to the fund at $20 a unit, it would increase total assets by another $200 million. The fund would then be worth $400 million, and each of the units, now totalling 20 million, would be still worth $20.

The NAVPS remains the same when units are redeemed, or sold back, to the fund. If 10 million units were bought back by the fund, its assets would be reduced to $200 million, and the number of units would be back to 10 million. The NAVPS would still be $20.

Many funds calculate their net asset value daily. That's easy to do for an equity fund, for instance, because the value is based on the price of stocks. So you may see the price of your units change from day to day. Some funds calculate their assets weekly; real estate funds do so even less frequently, as they have to have properties appraised to determine their value.

WHO OPERATES MUTUAL FUNDS?

Many mutual funds are part of groups, or families, of funds operated under the auspices of a central company. They may be sold directly by the company's sales force or through investment dealers and other independent agencies. Some funds are managed and sold by banks, trust companies, credit unions, caisses populaires and life insurance companies.

WHY FUNDS CHARGE FEES

Mutual funds are in the business of making money for investors. But they also charge investors fees for managing their money. Those fees can take a number of forms.

• **Sales charges:** Some funds charge commissions when you buy units. These are known as front-end loads, and the charge can be as much as 9% of your purchase price. But the percentage is often lower and may decline as the number of units purchased increases. These fees aren't added to the cost of your investment. Instead, they are deducted from your total contribution to the fund, with the remainder used to buy units. So if you invest $10,000 with a fund that has a 5% front-end load, $500 will go toward commis-

WEEKLY MUTUAL FUNDS | TABLES

Weekly tables allow closer monitoring of investment performance. In addition to the monthly and quarterly mutual fund reports, the *Financial Post* publishes complete fund listings every weekend, providing detailed daily as well as historical weekly NAVPS (net asset value per share).

As with the weekday listings, the funds are grouped by fund company and, if applicable, fund family.

Money market funds, segregated funds and venture capital funds are listed separately from the mainstream mutual funds.

How to read the mutual fund tables

Mutual fund rate of return figures appear in the Financial Post Mutual Funds Monthly Report, which runs the third Saturday of each month.

1. 52-week high/low: Highest and lowest price reached in the previous 52 weeks

2. Fund: name

3. Specifics: footnotes: ✦ – denotes segregated fund **Y** – delayed NAVPS or yield **U** – US$ ✱ – RRSP eligible (funds without * may generally be held in RRSPs as foreign property) **X** – trading ex-dividend **Z** – not available to general public **N** – no load fund **F** – front-end load or fee **D** – deferred declining redemption fee based on original capital invested **R** – deferred declining redemption fee based on market value **FD** – For D at buyer's option **FR** – For R at buyer's option **B** – both front- and back-end fee ... – data not available

Friday NAVPS data:

4. Dollar change: from previous day

52W high	52W low	Fund	Spec.	Fri. NAVPS $chg	%chg	Wkly NAVPS high	low	cls	$chg	%chg
9.51	6.63	Global Equity	FR	0.10	1.31	7.75	7.31	7.75	0.76	10.87

5. % Change: from previous day
Friday NAVPS data:
6. High on week
7. Low on week
8. Close on week
9. % Change from previous week
Money Market Funds
Data for money market funds and segregated

money market funds reflect current yields, not NAVPS. For example, under "dollar change" the figures would indicate the change in a fund's current yield in terms of percentage points. Pricing and yield data supplied by Fundata Canada Inc. is for information purposes only. Confirmation of price should be obtained from the fund sponsor.

sions and $9,500 will be used to buy units.

Back-end loads, or deferred sales charges, are levied by some funds when you redeem units. These loads may be based on the initial cost of your units or on the redemption value. In most cases, the percentage declines over time, and can be reduced to zero after a number of years.

No-load funds charge no fees when you buy or sell units. This practice, spearheaded by banks and trust companies that offer funds, is becoming more popular in the competitive mutual funds marketplace.

• **Management fees:** All mutual funds charge management fees. These are calculated as a percentage of assets managed by the fund and typically range up to 2% a year. Sometimes the percentage will decline as the value of assets under management grows. These fees are not levied directly on investors. Instead, they are charged to the fund. So if your fund's investments generate a 10% annual return, a 2% management fee would reduce the return to 8%. This is the return that is published in *The Financial Post.*

• **Other fees:** Some funds charge distribution fees, or sales administration fees. They are used to provide commissions paid to sales personnel and are also charged directly to the fund.

TYPES OF MUTUAL FUNDS AND WHAT THEY INVEST IN

Mutual funds cover a variety of investments. There are many types of funds, but they fall into three main groups:

Growth funds invest mainly in stocks, with the aim of providing a significant increase in the value of your investment. They may include Canadian equity funds, funds that invest in U.S. equities, international funds, real estate funds and specialty funds.

Fixed-income funds invest in bonds, preferred shares and mortgages and other fixed-income vehicles. They aim to provide security for your investment, plus a high level of income from that investment.

Money-market funds provide a level of income based on general interest rates, along with high security of capital. As the name suggests, they invest in various money-market instruments.

CLOSED-END FUNDS

There are a handful of closed-end investment funds in Canada. These funds operate differently from conventional open-end funds. When they start out, closed-end funds offer shares to the public in much the same way as a new stock offering. They then use the money to make investments.

After the initial offering, shares of closed-end funds trade on stock exchanges or over the counter. Instead of redeeming your shares to the fund, you sell them on an exchange, just like stocks. New investors in the fund must buy shares on exchanges, not directly from the company.

The market price for shares in closed-end funds is generally less than their net asset value per share. This reflects the fact that it may be more difficult to sell closed-end shares, tax liabilities and other factors.

CHOOSING A FUND

Before you invest in a mutual fund, you should decide on your investment objectives. For example, do you want growth, income or low risk? Only then should you begin the task of finding suitable funds for your investment. Fortunately, there is plenty of information and advice available.

Stockbrokers, financial planners, bank mutual fund representatives and independent mutual funds salespeople are all excellent sources of advice. Keep in mind, however, that their advice is not always objective – some have a vested interest in selling you certain funds.

There are many sources of mutual funds. No load funds – those that don't levy sales charges – are usually sold directly by the fund organization. These no load funds include those sold by banks, trust companies and credit unions.

Some are sold by independent fund organizations, the largest of which are Philips Hager & North Ltd. and Altamira Investor Services Inc. Funds that charge loads usually are sold through sales representatives such as stockbrokers, financial planners and independent mutual fund brokers.

MONTHLY PERFORMANCE TABLES

The *Financial Post*'s monthly fund performance survey is the primary source of performance-related statistical information on more than 1,600 mutual funds, grouped in 34 categories, available in Canada. It is published in the *Mutual Funds Monthly Report* on the third Saturday of each month and provides data covering various periods up to the end of the preceding month.

The monthly fund listings are broken into 34 categories and subcategories, generally reflecting the nature of each fund's underlying investments. Some funds may hold those types of investments exclusively, while others may invest in other types of assets as well. For example, certain bond/fixed-income funds might also invest in mortgages; equity funds typically keep a small portion of assets in cash or equivalents such as treasury bills. Following are the categories and subcategories in *FP*'s monthly fund listings:

CANADIAN EQUITY FUNDS

This general category consists of funds that invest primarily in stocks and other equitized securities of Canadian corporations. All of these funds are RRSP/RRIF eligible, meaning they qualify as Canadian content for RRSP/RRIF purposes. The category is broken down into the following subcategories:

• **Canadian large-cap equity funds.** These funds invest in a diversified portfolio of common stocks and other equitized securities of Canadian companies with large market capitalizations. The subcategory includes funds investing primarily in the stocks of companies with market capitalization of $500 million or greater.

• **Canadian diversified equity funds.** Generally no market capitalization restrictions.

• **Canadian small/mid-cap equity funds.** Invest primarily in common stocks and other equitized securities of Canadian companies with market capitalization below $500 million. They tend to be more volatile than general equities, although there are exceptions.

• **Canadian sector equity funds.** They invest specifically in Canadian industry sectors, such as financial services, technology or consumer products.

• **Canadian resource equity funds.** Invest in stocks and equitized securities of companies in the Canadian resource sector, e.g. mining, oil and gas or forestry. They tend to be more volatile than small/mid-cap and general equities.

• **Canadian gold/precious metals equity funds.** Invest in gold and other precious metals through stocks and/or equitized securities of Canadian precious metal mining companies. These funds may also invest directly in precious metal bullion certificates. Like resource equities, these funds have fairly high volatility.

• **Canadian labor-sponsored equity funds.** Invest in businesses that are just starting up or are expanding. Purchases of these venture-capital funds are eligible for federal and, in some jurisdictions, provincial tax credits.

U.S. EQUITY FUNDS

This general category includes about 150 funds that invest primarily in common stocks

WEEKLY MUTUAL FUND | HIGHLIGHTS

Fund snapshot offers a package of information on a noteworthy fund. The weekly mutual fund highlights page is built around a Fund Snapshot package featuring a fund that has been chosen for its exceptional performance or for a recent development. The snapshot includes a brief statement of why the fund was chosen, then provides detailed information on the fund and its operations.

Fund information: The list of information includes fund category, legal status, fund managers, inception date, total net asset and NAVPS figures as at the indicated date, RRSP eligibility as Canadian content, loads, minimum investment requirements, MER and category average MER, valuation frequency, dividend distributions and their frequency.

Comparative performance: The second component of the snapshot is a series of tables depicting the annual percentage performance of the fund, the category average and related indexes and/or subindexes over each of the preceding five years. For example, a precious metals fund might be compared with the TSE 300 as well as the TSE gold and precious metals subindex. This shows at a glance how well the fund performed against the averages.

Asset allocation: This section of the snapshot includes two pie charts showing the asset allocation of the highlighted fund and the corresponding category average.

Top holdings: This listing shows the top holdings of the fund as a percentage of total assets (as at the specified date).

Fund comparison: The featured fund is included in a listing of several similar funds, ranked according to the percentage of their assets invested in the featured fund's primary area of focus. For example, a Far East fund specializing in Hong Kong would be compared, in terms of percentages invested in Hong Kong, with several other Far East or Pacific Rim funds.

P/E ratios or volatility: The snapshot also provides a chart of the featured fund's price-earnings ratio (in the case of Canadian equity funds) or three-year standard deviation (for other funds) compared with other similar funds and two market indexes.

Fund Snapshot: Trimark Select Canadian Growth

This is the biggest of Trimark's Canadian funds, which all rebounded strongly last month and since have benefitted from corporate takeover bids, including Torstar-Sun Media.

Fund category: Cdn. divers. equity (value)
Legal status: unit trust
Managers: Phillip Taller, Vito Maida, Ian Hardacre, Carmen Veloso (since Jan. 1, 1995)
Inception date: Nov. 23, 1992
Asset value: $4.13 billion
RRSP eligibility: yes
Load: front or back-end
Min. investment: $500
Fund MER: 2.35%
Category average MER: 2.17%
Distribution (past year): 81.4¢
One-month return: 5.9%

Data at Sept. 30, 1998

P/E ratios

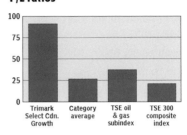

Performance % annual return

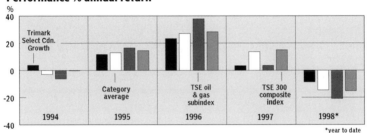

*year to date

Asset allocations

Trimark Select Cdn. Growth

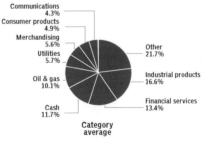

Category average

Top holdings at Sept. 30, 1998	
Holding	**% assets**
Renaissance Energy	3.8
Alberta Energy	3.0
Shell Canada A	2.9
Inco	2.4
Fletcher Chlg Cda Lt A	2.4
Alcan Aluminium	2.2
Anderson Exploration	2.2
Dofasco	2.1
Teck B	1.9
King World Productions	1.8
Franco-Nevada	1.8
Kinross Gold	1.8

Funds with largest oil & gas positions		
Fund	**% assets**	**as of**
Altafund Investment	35.7	8/98
Mackenzie Sentinel Canada Eq.	27.7	9/98
Global Strategy Cdn. Opportunities	25.2	6/98
Goodwood Fund	23.3	4/98
20/20 RSP Aggr. Smaller Cos.	21.4	9/98
CUMIS Life Cdn.n Growth Equity	19.7	9/98
Power Canadian	19.5	9/98
Trans-Canada Value	19.0	6/98
Standard Life Growth Equity	18.1	9/98
AGF Growth Equity	16.5	9/98
Guardian Growth Equity Classic	15.9	6/98
Mutual Alpine Equity	15.5	9/98

and other equitized securities of U.S. companies. Although most of these funds are considered foreign content for RRSP/RRIF purposes, some qualify as Canadian because of the nature of the investments they make. For example, they may primarily contain stocks of U.S. companies listed on Canadian exchanges or U.S. stock-related derivative products. Volatility is generally comparable to Canadian equity funds. There are three subcategories:

- **U.S. diversified equity funds.** Generally no market capitalization restrictions.
- **U.S. large-cap equity funds.** Invest mostly in stocks of companies with market capitalization of US$1 billion or more.
- **U.S. small-cap equity funds.** Invest mostly in stocks of companies with market capitalization of less than US$1 billion.

NORTH AMERICAN EQUITY FUNDS

These funds invest mainly in the common stocks and equitized securities of Canadian and U.S. companies but may also hold stocks/securities of Mexican companies. Although these funds are generally considered foreign holdings for RRSP/RRIF purposes.

FOREIGN EQUITY FUNDS

These funds invest in the common stocks and equitized securities of companies around the world, or in specific geographic areas outside North America. This category is com-

CLOSED-END FUND | PERFORMANCE FIGURES

As part of its weekly mutual fund performance listings, the *Financial Post* provides performance figures for "closed end" funds. Once a predetermined number of units/shares have been purchased, the fund is closed to further investment – although, like stocks, shares already issued can be traded on the open market. The fund cannot issue any more shares. The listings provide the fund name as well as its stock ticker identification. This is followed by:

Closed end funds

Fund	Ticker	NAVPS	Mkt. val. per sh.	Prm.(+) or disc. (-) %
ARC STRATEGIC	AEF.UN/TSE	9.75	8.50	-12.82
BGR Precious Mtls	BPT.A/TSE	14.49	10.75	-25.81
BioCapital Invstmts	BCK.IR/TSE	7.33	3.25	-55.66
Cda Trust Incm (Sep)	CNN.UN/TSE	9.95	10.00	0.50
Cdn General Invstmts	CGI/TSE	14.63	13.15	-10.12
Canadian World Fund	CWF/TSE	5.74	5.00	-12.89
Central Fund of Cda	CEF.A/TSE	5.87	6.30	7.33
China Opportunities	CHF.UN/TSE	12.01	10.10	-15.90
Citadel Diversified Inv	CTD.UN/TSE	7.86	7.00	-10.94
DDJ Cdn Hgh Yld Fd	HYB.UN/TSE	22.94	18.35	-20.01
Diversified Mthly Incm	XMI/TSE	25.62	23.25	-9.25
Economic Invstmt Tr	EVT/TSE	144.54	97.00	-32.89
First Asia Income Fd	FAI.UN/TSE	7.38	5.30	-28.18
First Australia Prime	FAP/TSE	12.60	10.35	-17.86
First Mercantile Curr	FMF.UN/TSE	15.48	14.00	-9.56
Health Care & Biotch	HCB.UN/TSE	6.49	4.75	-26.81
MINT	MID.UN/TSE	7.27	7.00	-3.71
NCE Diversified	NCD.UN/TSE	4.13	3.30	-20.10
New Altamira Value	NVL.UN/TSE	11.63	9.30	-20.03
Newcastle Mkt (Sep)	NMN.UN/TSE	16.08	11.25	-30.04

stock ticker identification. This is followed by:

NAVPS: the net asset value per share (see monthly listings for definition).

Market value per sh.: This is the closing market price of the shares as of the date specified at the bottom of the table. The price at which the shares would change hands.

Prem.(+) or disc.(-)%: The final column of this table indicates the premium (+) or discount (-) between NAVPS and market value, expressed as a percentage of NAVPS. When the market value is lower than NAVPS, it is said to be discounted, and vice versa.

MUTUAL FUND | AND OTHER INDEXES

Mutual fund / other indexes at month end

	— Rate of return —					— Rate of return —			
	1mo.	1yr.	3yr.	5yr.		1mo.	1yr.	3yr.	5yr.
TSE Top 100	1.5	-18.1	7.7	7.4	Mex IPC (Bolsa)	19.3	-32.9	14.3	14.2
TSE Top 200	1.8	-28.6	6.1	5.5	Nasdaq Comp	13.0	0.5	17.5	17.3
TSE 300 Comp	1.5	-20.3	7.4	7.1	NB Sm Cap Index	4.3	-34.1	1.7	2.3
30 Day T-Bill	-10.0	74.3	-7.9	2.0	NYSE Composite	5.0	1.5	17.2	14.6
TSE 35	3.3	-15.1	9.1	9.3	MSCI Pac ex Jap	8.5	-35.5	-9.8	...
91 Day	0.4	3.9	4.3	4.9	TSE Real Estate	0.6	-25.0	5.3	-5.0
Amex Comp Index	9.9	-11.2	...	...	Russell 3000	6.6	3.0	17.7	15.5
JPM Brady Bond	9.7	-19.9	13.4	...	Russell 1000	6.5	5.7	19.1	16.4
CAN/US Exchange	-2.3	10.7	4.5	2.8	Russell 2000	7.6	-19.9	5.4	7.5
Prime Rate	-3.3	52.6	-3.2	4.7	SM Universe Bnd	3.8	8.8	11.7	9.9
Cdn $ Exchange	-0.2	0.7	1.3	1.3	S&P 600 Ind $Cd	6.0	-19.3	7.7	...

Each weekly mutual fund report includes a brief summary of performance figures for mutual fund and other indexes.

This table provides each index's rate of return over one month and one year (simple rates of return), as well as three and five years (compounded average annual returns). For definitions of these indexes, refer to the "benchmark" information on page 131.

prised of seven subcategories, based on the geographic scope of their investment activities. Volatility is generally on a par with Canadian, U.S. or North American equity funds. Most are considered foreign content for RRSP/RRIF purposes, but some qualify as Canadian either because foreign content is limited to 20% (or less) of total assets or because of the nature of their foreign investments. The eight subcategories are:

• **Global equity funds.** As their name implies, these funds invest in common stocks and other equitized securities from around the world, including Canada and the U.S. The majority are relatively new, in operation for three years or less.

• **International equity funds.** Much the same as global funds, except they tend not to invest in the common stocks and other equitized securities of Canadian and U.S. companies.

• **Global sector equity.** Invest primarily in common stocks and other equity securities of Canadian, U.S. and foreign companies that are focussed on specific industries such as health sciences, telecommunications and precious metals.

• **Emerging markets equity funds.** These funds invest in common stocks and other equitized securities of companies with principal business activities in countries with emerging economies, excluding those funds that focus on Asia-Pacific and Latin American markets. All these funds are relatively new and only two have track records of five years or more. Volatility tends to be a bit higher than general Canadian or U.S. equity funds.

• **Asia-Pacific equity funds.** Invest primarily in common stocks and equitized securities of companies with principal business activities in one or more of the countries in the Asia-Pacific Rim region, excluding Japan.

• **Japanese equity funds.** Invest primarily in common stocks and equitized securities of Japan-based companies.

This section of the weekly mutual fund report involves the selection of a newsworthy stock that soared or plummeted during the week. The stock's weekly performance is charted, and a brief explanation is provided of why the stock performed as it did.

Finally, mutual funds are ranked according to their holdings of each stock; the eight biggest holders are listed beneath the chart and explanation. This top eight list shows the number of shares held by each fund, the percentage that this represents of the fund's total assets, and the date upon which the fund information is based.

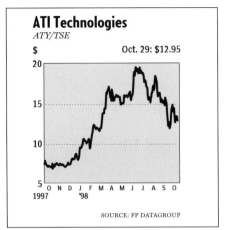

Where the funds are

ATI Technologies
ATY/TSE

Oct. 29: $12.95

SOURCE: FP DATAGROUP

Strong earnings failed to boost the computer chip maker's shares as investors worried a recent acquistion.

Top holders

Fund	No. shares	% total assets	as of date
Acuity Pooled Global Equity	1,800	9.7	9/30
Acuity Pooled Environ.Sci.& Tech.	2,200	9.7	9/30
Hartford Canadian Advan.Tech.	8,600	9.6	9/30
Clean Environment Equity	1,666,100	8.8	9/30
20/20 RSP Aggr. Sm. Cos.	2,214,108	8.6	9/30
Acuity Pooled Cdn. Balan.	8,800	8.5	9/30
20/20 RSP Aggressive Equity	1,590,692	8.3	9/30
Acuity Pooled Conservative Asset Alloc	81500	7.8	9/30

• **European equity funds.** Invest mostly in common stocks and equity securities of companies with principal business activities in European countries.

• **Latin American equity funds.** Invest primarily in common stocks and equitized securities of companies with principal business activities in Central and/or South America.

DIVIDEND FUNDS

These funds invest in dividend-paying preferred and sometimes common shares of Canadian and, occasionally, foreign companies. Almost all are RRSP/RRIF-eligible because they hold little or no foreign content. Volatility tends to be considerably lower than that of equity funds because of the relatively steady dividend income stream. Dividends from Canadian corporate shares held by these funds are generally eligible for the dividend tax credit on your income tax return.

CANADIAN FIXED INCOME FUNDS

This category of fund invests primarily in interest-generating securities such as bonds, but may also invest in mortgages or occasionally in preferred shares providing high dividend yields. Volatility tends to be lower than for dividend funds and much lower than for equities. All the funds in the three subcategories are RRSP/RRIF eligible as Canadian content.

• **Canadian long/mid-term bond funds.** They invest primarily in fixed-income securities with maturities of five years or longer issued by Canadian governments and corporations.

• **Canadian short-term bond funds.** These funds invest in fixed-income securities with maturities of less than five years issued by Canadian governments and corporations. Volatility tends to be slightly lower than for longer-term bond funds.

• **Canadian mortgage funds.** These funds invest in Canadian residential and commercial mortgages. Volatility is about on a par with short-term bond funds.

U.S./INTERNATIONAL FIXED INCOME FUNDS

• **U.S. bond funds.** These fixed income funds invest primarily in U.S. government and corporate bonds and other fixed-income securities or in Canadian government or corporate securities denominated in U.S. currency. In part because of currency fluctua-

---

WEEKLY PERFORMANCE | THE BEST AND THE WORST

As part of the weekly fund report, all the funds in several broad categories (e.g. Canadian equities) are ranked according to their performance over the past one-week period. The eight best and eight worst-performing funds in terms of percentage growth (or decline) in NAVPS are then listed on this table. The listings show the fund name, its most recent Friday closing price and the dollar and percentage changes between this figure and the preceding Friday closing price. The listings also provide the weekly performance average for each fund category.

Weekly performance *Data supplied by Fundata Canada Inc.*

Best %	$ Close	% chg	chg	Worst %	$ Close	% chg	chg
Canadian equity average			**+4.83**	**International equity average**			**+3.56**
High Yield Debt Tr (SAGE)	12.86	+6.82	+112.91	Clarington Asia Pacific	9.53	+1.15	+13.70
First Tr Wealth Mgmt 1997	11.37	+1.41	+14.16	Glo Mgr German Geared	31.87	+3.83	+13.66
CIBC Financial Companies	11.17	+1.14	+11.34	Trimark Discovery Fund U$	3.94	+.37	+10.36
YMG Enterprise Fund	5.46	+.55	+11.20	Glo Mgr U.K. Geared Fund	28.39	+2.62	+10.17
O.I.Q. FERIQUE Growth	9.22	+.91	+10.92	Trimark Discovery Fund	6.04	+.53	+9.62
Perigee Cdn Agg Gro Equ	7.32	+.71	+10.80	Trimark Discovery Seg	5.16	+.45	+9.55
AIC Advantage	67.14	+5.91	+9.65	Cambridge China U$	1.4	+.12	+9.38
CTI Canadian Equity Fund	9.43	+.83	+9.63	Cambridge Pacific	1.29	+.11	+9.32
U.S equity average			**+3.60**				
Navigator American Growth	12.82	+1.05	+8.87	**Special equity and real estate average**			**+3.20**
First Tr NA Tech 1997 C$	19.15	+1.53	+8.68	GtcInfinity Wealth Mgmt	8.4	+.87	+11.55
First Tr NA Tech 1997 U$	12.38	+.96	+8.41	Infinity Wealth Mgmt	8.4	+.87	+11.51
First Tr NA Tech 1998 C$	15.31	+1.05	+7.36	Navigator Cdn Technology	8.73	+.75	+9.36
McDonald New America Fund	14.27	+.97	+7.27	Altamira Science & Tech	9.64	+.74	+8.31
Co-operators U.S. Equity	230.06	+15.09	+7.02	Royal Life Science & Tech	14.95	+1.03	+7.42
First Tr NA Tech 1998 U$	9.89	+.64	+6.92	C.I. Sector Glo Fin SerU$	11.73	+.74	+6.73
Royal US Gro Strat Index	8.44	+.54	+6.78	Green Line Science & Tech	24.01	+1.48	+6.57

tions, the volatility of these funds tends to be somewhat higher than for their Canadian counterparts. Some are RRSP-eligible as Canadian content.

• **International bond funds.** Same as U.S. bond funds, except that their investments are primarily foreign rather than U.S.-based or denominated.

CANADIAN BALANCED FUNDS

This category includes funds that invest in a blend of Canadian stocks, bonds and cash. Because of the stabilizing effect of the income from their bond holdings, these funds have volatility ratings that are generally lower than for equities but higher than for pure

BEST/WORST PERFORMERS | OVERALL

As part of the *Mutual Funds Monthly Report,* the *Financial Post* provides a table listing the best and worst-performing funds overall for the six periods used in the main listings – one month, six months, one year, three years, five years and 10 years – as of the end of the preceding month. The table ignores fund categories and simply looks at the bottom line. For the most part, the best performers tend to be equity funds, foreign or domestic, plus the occasional bond fund. The worst performers tend to be equities as well, particularly foreign or specialty funds. This table underscores the vast divergence in performance that these types of funds can generate.

WINNERS AND LOSERS
OCTOBER

Best performers		Worst performers	
One month	**%**	**One month**	**%**
Global Mgr HK Geared	58.61	Glo Mgr H–Kong Bear	−25.94
Clarington Asia Pac	38.92	Friedberg Currency	−12.93
Fidelity Far East	35.99	Friedberg Futures	−11.91
AIM Korea	29.72	Cambridge Growth (US$)	−10.77
Glo Mgr H–Kong Index	28.84	Cambridge Balanced (US$)	−10.19
CI Glo Fin Serv Sect	25.36	Friedberg Diver	−10.18
Talvest/Hyp China Pl	23.59	Friedberg Tor Intl	−9.79
GWL Asian Gth (A) B	22.74	Cambridge Global (US$)	−8.38
GWL Asian Gth (A) A	22.71	Friedberg Tor Eq–H	−7.68
Allstar AIG Asian	22.54	AGF US S–T H–Yield	−7.35
Six month	**%**	**Six month**	**%**
Pharmaceutical Tr 97	25.16	Cambridge Resource (US$)	−50.70
Pharmaceutical Trust	24.50	Cambridge China	−50.45
Opt Strat Glo Fix	20.17	Caratax LP – 1997	−50.28
First Cdn Intl Bond	20.15	20/20 Mgd Future Val	−50.09
G–Line Glo Gov't Bd	20.11	Cambridge Pacific (US$)	−48.62
CIBC Glo Bond Index	19.44	Cambridge Balanced (US$)	−48.35
Transam GS US 21st C	19.34	Cambridge Prec Metal	−47.76
Royal Global Bond	18.62	Strategic Value	−47.24
Univer World Tact Bd	18.18	Cambridge Growth (US$)	−45.39
F–Cdn Glo Sci & Tech	17.93	20/20 Latin America	−42.40

bond funds. All are RRSP/RRIF eligible as Canadian content. The category is divided into two subcategories:

- **Canadian strategic balanced funds.** Asset-type weightings remain relatively stable over time, and funds generally must maintain minimum holdings in each asset class.
- **Canadian tactical balanced funds.** These funds also invest across the three broad asset classes but are different from strategic funds in that the portfolio manager attempts to enhance performance by switching between the classes as anticipated returns change. Normally, there are no minimum asset-class holding requirements.

GLOBAL BALANCED FUNDS

These funds invest in a blend of U.S. and/or international stocks and bonds or Canadian issues in U.S. or other foreign currencies. Volatility is slightly higher than that of Canadian balanced funds because of the effect of currency fluctuations. Some are RRSP/RRIF eligible as Canadian content. The category is divided into two subcategories:

- **Global strategic balanced funds**. See Canadian strategic balanced funds.
- **Global tactical balanced funds.** See Canadian tactical balanced funds.

ASSET ALLOCATION SERVICES

These are services that combine a range of portfolios into funds that invest in various asset types within Canada as well as the U.S. and abroad. Some services use existing mutual funds while others have their own portfolios. Asset-class weightings are adjusted by the service's adviser according to market conditions.

CANADIAN MONEY MARKET FUNDS

These funds invest almost all their assets in short-term money market instruments such as treasury bills, certificates of deposit, short-term government bonds and commercial paper. As such, these funds are highly liquid (some even offer limited chequing privileges) and are generally used to constitute the "cash equivalent" portion of an investor's overall portfolio. Volatility is extremely low.

U.S./INTERNATIONAL MONEY MARKET FUNDS

Same as Canadian money market funds except they invest in U.S. and/or international money market instruments or in Canadian money market instruments denominated in U.S. and/or other foreign currencies.

REAL ESTATE FUNDS

These funds invest in commercial and industrial real estate, primarily in Canada. Most are RRSP/RRIF eligible as Canadian content.

SPECIALTY FUNDS

These funds invest in specific markets not covered by other categories, such as commodities or derivatives. Volatility is relatively high.

The monthly performance tables provide a broad range of statistical information for investors, but the two monthly "snapshots" that accompany the tables provide some key data in a handy encapsulated format.

The first snapshot table shows the average one-year simple returns and average five-year compound returns for each of the 27 categories in the main listings, again as of the end of the preceding month. This enables investors to quickly determine how their own fund(s) fared against the category averages.

The second snapshot table provides the average one-year returns for the 20 largest mutual funds in terms of total assets. The first column shows the fund, the second column shows the fund's net assets in millions of dollars, and the third column shows each fund's one-year return as of the end of the preceding month.

PERFORMANCE SNAPSHOTS
OCTOBER

The asset groups

The following table lists the average one-year rates of return at Oct. 31 for the principal fund categories.

Fund category	1-yr. % return	5-yr. % return
European equity	21.38	15.98
U.S. large-cap equity	18.60	17.89
U.S. diversified equity	15.79	15.44
Global tactical balanced	15.42	11.40
U.S. bond	12.98	5.67
Global sector equity	10.59	5.65
International bond	10.50	7.10
International equity	10.50	9.01

The giant funds

Average one-year returns at Oct. 31 for the largest individual funds (in terms of total assets in $millions).

Fund	Assets $mil.	1-yr. % return
Templeton Growth	9,960.3	2.80
Royal Balanced	7,169.1	0.55
Templeton Intl Stock	5,413.3	5.46
Ivy Canadian	5,378.7	3.91
Trimark Select Gth	5,092.8	-2.45
Investors Dividend	4,743.3	3.35
Trimark Sel Cdn Gth	4,335.6	-9.01
Trimark Select Bal	4,269.9	-3.04

SURVEY OF MANAGEMENT EXPENSE RATIOS

A fund's management expense ratio (MER) can have a significant impact on the yields investors end up receiving. Although loads tend to be higher in percentage terms, they're a one-shot cost; management expenses are deducted annually, and over several years they can far outstrip the dollar cost of any one-time load. The survey of MERs published in the *Mutual Funds Monthly Report* is calculated using PAL Trak software by Portfolio Analytics Ltd. It shows these expenses can range from a fraction of a percentage point of fund assets up to 4% or even more in a few cases (excluding any sales loads or redemption charges).

The first part of the table provides the unweighted average MER figures for each of the 27 fund categories. The expense ratio figures are expressed as a percentage of assets. The listings also provide the one-year total returns for each fund category. The survey goes on to list those funds with the highest and lowest MERs in their respective general groupings (for example, all Canadian equities are treated as a single group in this table). Where available, the one-year total return for each fund is provided as well.

As can be seen from the category figures, MERs tend to be lowest with money market funds (which also tend to have the lowest yields). Equity funds generally tend to have the highest MERs and bond funds fall between these two categories. But the individual fund listings display many exceptions to this general rule – some equity fund MERs are lower than for many money market funds, and some bond funds have MERs higher than many equities. These listings enable investors to gauge how their own fund(s) fare compared with other funds of the same type, as well as with their respective categories.

MARKET BENCHMARKS MEASURE PERFORMANCE

The *Financial Post* monthly performance survey includes a list of market "benchmark" indexes that can be useful in evaluating the performance of mutual funds. These indexes are meant to reflect the performance of a particular market or markets during each of the years listed. Non-Canadian index figures have been adjusted to reflect exchange rate fluctuations during the period in question (as have returns for funds investing outside Canada). All indexes used by *FP* are total return indexes, meaning any dividends or interest payments made by the underlying securities are assumed to be re-invested. This is important since the same methodology is used in calculating the annual performance of mutual funds.

An important distinction must be made between indexes and mutual funds. Because they are not actively managed, indexes do not have to account for management expenses. Mutual funds do. For example, if a fund reports a one-year return of 8% and expense ratio (MER) of 2%, the manager actually had to achieve a 10% gross return, because performance is reported net of expenses. Managers of mutual funds are often evaluated by how much or how often they are able to outperform an appropriate index, often referred to as "beating the market." The key is to select the index(es) that most closely reflect the fund type. But keep in mind that comparing a fund's performance with an index is only one way to measure performance – one should compare other "like" funds as well.

Following are brief descriptions of the indexes used as benchmarks:

CANADIAN EQUITY
- **Toronto Stock Exchange 300 composite index:** A collection of 300 of Canada's largest, most liquid stocks, representing 14 broad industry groups. The TSE 300, like many indexes, is said to be capitalization-based (or capitalization-weighted), meaning larger stocks are weighted more than smaller stocks. (Size is measured by market float, or the number of shares outstanding times the current price of the stock.) Price changes for larger companies therefore have a more dramatic effect on the overall index than do price changes for smaller companies.

How to read the performance tables

Fund name	notes	R fgn	%	Net assets $mil.	NAV per sh.$	YTD distr. $	% simple rate of return 1 mo.	6 mo.	YTD	1 yr.	% avg annual compound return 3 yr.	5 yr.	10 yr.	Std dev 3 yr.	Exp rat %	L
PerformFund	i	R	8	623.9	34.86		−0.3	−25.3	−18.0	−22.6	+8.7	+9.5	+8.7	5.1	1.09	N
PerformFund Plus		R	16	181.8	18.56	0.29	+0.5	−24.5	−15.9	−21.8	+8.5	+9.3	+9.1	5.0	1.18	F
PerformFund Eq Pen	e		16	1060.3	54.95		−0.6	−23.2	−14.8	−18.4	+11.6	+10.9	+9.6	5.0	0.54	C

This instalment of the Financial Post's monthly mutual funds report compares funds at 10.31.98. **Performance returns shown in boldface** type are those outperforming the group average in the given period. All footnotes are shown in the first column after the fund name. Here's a guide to each column:

1. Fund name provides the fund name (sometimes abbreviated). Some funds are split into series or classes, depending on when sales fees are levied. Refer to the Load column.

2. Notes **a** - fund entry is restricted to certain groups or professions, **b** - the minimum initial purchase is more than $5,000, **c** - sold by offering memorandum (not by prospectus), **d** - total assets and NAVPS are shown in US$, **e** - the fund is not available for direct purchase, **f** - the fund's portfolio may include some precious metals, leases or other non-equity investments, **g** - unit values are stated before management fees, **h** - returns do not take into account performance fee charged to individual unitholders, **i** - insurance fund, **j** - there is a restricted redemption policy; see fund's prospectus for details, **k** - NAVPS and total assets are shown in German marks, **l** - labor sponsored fund, **m** - management fee in lieu of an expense ratio, **n** - a new fund launched in the past year, **o** - offshore fund, **p** - NAVPS and total assets are shown in British pounds, **r** - NAVPS and total assets are shown in Italian lire, **s** - not a mutual fund: funad-company asset-allocation service, **t** - NAVPS are shown in US$, total assets shown in C$, **u** - NAVPS are shown in C$, total assets shown in US$

3. RRSP and RRIF eligible 'R' indicates eligibility for registered retirement savings plans (RRSPs) and registered retirement income funds (RRIFs).

4. Percentage foreign ownership shows the amount each fund has invested outside Canada.

5. Net assets is total assets minus current liabilities—the fund's size at month end.

6. Net asset value per share is total assets minus current liabilities, divided by the number of shares outstanding. Investors buy at this value, plus sales charge (if any), and sell at this value, minus redemption charge (if any).

7. Year to date distribution indicates the total value of distributions (dividends paid in the form of interest, stock dividends, or capital gains) by the fund to its unitholders from Jan. 1 to the end of the month surveyed.

8. Simple rate of return over one month, six months, year-to-date, and one year is the change in net asset value over the period, including reinvestment of dividends and capital gains, and excluding sales or redemption charges. An ellipsis (**...**) indicates no data for this period. A zero value (**0.0**) indicates return is not meaningful, rounding to less than 0.1%.

9. Average annual compound rate of return three, five and 10 years measures the average annual change in NAVPS, assuming all dividends and capital gains are reinvested on the date of distribution or realization. This measurement excludes any sales or redemption fees. An ellipsis (**...**) indicates no data for this period. A zero value (**0.0**) indicates return is not meaningful, rounding to less than 0.1%.

10. Three-year standard deviation shows variability in the fund's rate of return. It provides a measure of volatility, and therefore a measure of risk.

11. Expense ratio is total operating costs per $100 of assets (exclusive of any sales or redemption charge) as a percentage of the assets.

12. Load is sales fee charged to investors for purchasing fund. Five load methods are denoted: **N** - no load, **F** - front-end load, **D** - deferred sales charge (or back-end load), **C** - combination of front- and back-end loads, **O** - optional front- or back-end load. Some no-load funds may charge early redemption fees.

Data supplied by Financial Post DataGroup

- **TSE 100 index:** The top 100 (by capitalization) stocks found in the TSE 300. This index is useful for comparisons with funds that focus primarily on "large-cap" stocks.
- **TSE 200 index:** The bottom 200 stocks of the TSE 300. Used in evaluating small to mid-cap Canadian equity funds.
- **Toronto 35 index:** This index is a collection of 35 large stocks that are maintained by a TSE committee and is meant to include very liquid issues that closely track the performance of the TSE 300 index. Useful in evaluating diversified Canadian equity funds.
- **Russell 300 growth index:** This index consists of a number of TSE 300 stocks that have a greater-than-average growth orientation. Stocks in this index tend to exhibit higher price-to-book and price-earnings ratios, lower dividend yields and higher forecast growth values than those found in the Russell 300 value index. Because higher earnings levels have yet to be realized, these stocks typically have less earnings to distribute in the form of dividends, hence the typically lower dividend yields. This is a useful index when evaluating the performance of growth-oriented, Canadian equity funds.
- **Russell 300 value index:** Contains those TSE 300 stocks with a lower-than-average growth orientation. Stocks in this index generally have low price-to-book and price-earnings ratios, higher dividend yields and lower forecast earnings growth than more growth-oriented stocks. This is a useful index for comparing Canadian equity funds oriented toward value investing.
- **Russell 100 growth index:** Contains those Russell 300 growth stocks that are also in the TSE 100 index. Useful in comparing Canadian mutual funds that invest in large-cap, growth-oriented stocks.
- **Russell 100 value index:** Contains those Russell 300 value stocks that are also TSE 100 members. Useful for evaluating mutual funds that invest in relatively large, value-oriented Canadian stocks.
- **Midland Walwyn Canadian equity fund index:** This index is made up of 30 of Canada's largest Canadian equity funds and is "dollar-weighted," meaning that larger (by total assets) mutual funds have more influence than smaller ones. It is intended to track the general performance of Canadian equity mutual funds. As at March 31, 1995, this index reflected 67.25% of Canadian equity funds as reported by FundData Canada.
- **Nesbitt Burns Canadian small-cap index:** This index is composed of 400 stocks with a market capitalization of less than 0.1% of the TSE 300. Useful for evaluating Canadian small-cap mutual funds.
- **C.M. Oliver Canadian REIT index:** A market weighted total return index allowing investors to measure the return of all Canadian real estate investment trusts in terms of price appreciation and distributions.

U.S. EQUITY
- **Standard & Poor's 500 composite index:** A basket of 500 U.S. stocks, selected primarily from the New York Stock Exchange, designed to reflect the broad U.S. equity market. Because the S&P 500 is constructed to reflect as many industry groups as possible, it does not take just the largest stocks, although it is normally representative of 75% to

80% of the total value of stocks traded on the NYSE. This is a useful index for evaluating diversified U.S. equity funds.

- **Dow Jones industrial average:** One of the most quoted U.S. indexes and also the oldest, this is a basket of 30 of the New York Stock Exchange's largest and best-known industrial stocks. The DJIA is price-weighted, meaning that higher-priced stocks affect index performance more than lower-priced ones. Although popular, the usefulness of this index has been criticized in recent years. Because it is price weighted, it does not properly reflect the relative size of the companies listed and it does not accurately reflect the more diverse (both by size and industry) nature of the broader U.S. equity market.

- **Nasdaq composite index:** The most broadly based U.S. equity index, it includes more than 5,000 stocks traded over-the-counter. These stocks are not listed on the New York Stock Exchange or other major U.S. exchanges.

- **Russell 2000 index:** This index comprises the 2,000 smallest U.S. securities found in the Russell 3000 index (which consists of the 3,000 largest U.S. securities as determined by market capitalization). Representing 11% of the Russell 3000's total market capitalization, the 2000 is a widely used small-cap index, useful for evaluating funds that specialize in small U.S. companies.

- **Midland Walwyn U.S. equity index:** Composed of 26 of Canada's largest U.S. equity funds, this index is "dollar-weighted," meaning that larger mutual funds (by total asset size) have more influence than smaller ones over the overall value of the index. It is intended to track the general performance of U.S. equity mutual funds in Canada.

FOREIGN EQUITY

- **Morgan Stanley world index:** All MS indexes are constructed to ensure that all industry groups are proportionally represented and are also capitalization-based. In each case they are designed to represent at least 60% of the market capitalization of each country, across all industry groups. The world index is made up of more than 2,700 stocks from 22 countries with developed markets. This is a useful index for evaluating global mutual funds.

- **Morgan Stanley EAFE index:** Comprised of about 1,500 stocks (representative samplings of small, medium and large caps) from 20 developed European, Australasian and Far East countries. Useful for evaluating funds in *FP*'s international equity category.

- **Morgan Stanley emerging markets index:** Includes 1,400 stocks from 23 "emerging market" countries.

The average GDP per capita of the countries in this index is $3,100, in contrast to the $20,535 for the Morgan Stanley world index.

- **Morgan Stanley Europe index:** Comprised of stocks from European countries.

- **Morgan Stanley Far East index:** Comprised of stocks from Far East countries.

- **Morgan Stanley Pacific ex-Japan index:** Comprised of stocks from the Pacific Rim countries, excluding Japan.

- **London Financial Times FT-SE 100 index:** The principal measure of the British equity market, the "footsie" includes 100 blue-chip stocks traded on the London Stock Exchange.

As part of the Mutual Funds Monthly Report, the *Financial Post* publishes a table of "winners and losers" from each of the 34 mutual fund categories in the main listings. At left in bold type is the fund category, accompanied by the unweighted average total percentage yield for the month for that category. Reading across, the middle column shows the fund with the best performance for the month in that category, along with its total return. The right-hand column shows the fund with the worst performance, along with its total monthly return. This table provides a frame of reference for evaluating the monthly performance of any fund(s) you may own: Is your fund's performance near the top or the bottom of these two extremes? The table also provides a snapshot of relative performance between different fund categories during the month.

Monthly winners & losers 10.27.98

Category	Average return on month	Best performer	Return on month	Worst performer	Return on month
Cdn gold/precious metals	+34.4	NCE Prec Metals Gth	+52.0	Cambridge Prec Metal	+20.2
Cdn. resource equity	+15.9	Lion Natural Res	+27.5	Hirsch Natural Res	+5.7
Global sector equity	+8.9	O'Donnell World Prec	+31.1	AIM GT Glo Telecom	−3.8
Asia-Pacific equity	+4.2	Clarington Asia Pac	+26.8	India Excel	−7.8
Dividend	+3.8	Guardian Mthly H–I M	+11.3	Altamira Dividend	−1.3
Cdn long/mid bond	+3.6	G–Line Mthly Income	+5.7	Tal/Hyp Hi Yield Bd	−6.4
U.S. small-cap eq.	+3.6	Univer US Emerg Gth	+11.7	Cambridge Amer Gth	−1.2
U.S. diversified eq.	+3.1	NN Can–Daq 100	+19.4	Cote 100 US US$	−7.4
North American eq.	+2.5	North Amer Tech Tr	+16.7	Marathon Perf NA L–S	−7.2
U.S. large-cap eq.	+2.4	McDonald New America	+8.6	Co–operators US Eq	−17.9
Cdn. strategic balan.	+2.4	ABC Fully–Managed	+5.4	Cambridge Balanced	−3.4
Cdn. short bond	+2.3	Acadia Bond	+4.9	Synergy Cdn S–T Inc	+0.2
Cdn. tactical balan.	+2.3	London Life Bal (BG)	+10.6	Protected American	−5.1
Cdn. large-cap eq.	+2.2	Westbury Cdn Life A	+5.3	Marathon Per L–C Cdn	−5.4
Cdn. divers. eq.	+2.2	Industrial Growth	+21.5	Goodwood Fund	−9.5
International bond	+1.9	Fidelity Emer Mkt Bd	+7.3	Univer World H–Yield	−4.7
Cdn. mortgage	+1.9	OTGIF Mortgage Inc	+3.3	Northwest Mortgage	−0.2
Latin Amer. equity	+1.8	Fidelity Lat Am Gth	+6.6	Dynamic Latin Amer	−12.0
Cdn small-cap equity	+1.6	Trimark Cdn S–Comp	+6.3	BPI Cdn Small Cos	−5.7

• **Tokyo Nikkei average:** A simple price average of 225 of the largest stocks in terms of market capitalization listed on the Tokyo Stock Exchange.

• **Midland Walwyn international equity fund index:** This index is made up of 23 of Canada's largest international equity funds and is said to be "dollar-weighted," meaning that larger mutual funds (by total asset size) have more influence than smaller ones on the overall value of the index. It is intended to track the general performance of international equity mutual funds.

BONDS

• **Scotia Capital Markets universe index:** Represents a broad selection of hundreds of Canadian corporate and government bonds. These include short-term (mature in less than five years but greater than one year), medium-term (mature in five to 10 years) and long-term (mature in more than 10 years) bonds. This index is meant to reflect the broader Canadian bond market, much like the TSE 300 is used to measure the broader Canadian equity market.

• **Scotia Capital Markets short-term index:** Represents a broad selection of Canadian corporate and government bonds with terms of one to five years. Useful for evaluating funds in *FP*'s short-term bond category.

• **Scotia Capital Markets mid-term index:** Represents a broad selection of Canadian corporate and government bonds with terms of five to 10 years.

• **Scotia Capital Markets long-term index:** Represents a broad selection of Canadian corporate and government bonds with terms greater than 10 years. Used in conjunction with the short- and mid-term indexes, this index illustrates the volatility of returns that often go with longer-term bonds.

• **Midland Walwyn Canadian bond fund index:** This index is made up of Canada's 25 largest Canadian bond funds and is "dollar-weighted," meaning larger mutual funds (by total asset size) have more influence than smaller ones on overall index value. It is intended to track the general performance of Canadian bond funds and is useful for evaluating Canadian bond fund performance in general.

• **Midland Walwyn global bond fund index:** This index is made up of 22 of Canada's largest global bond funds and is "dollar-weighted." It is intended to track the general performance of global bond funds.

MONEY MARKET AND OTHER

• **Three-month government of Canada T-bills:** Reflects the average performance of 91-day treasury bills issued by the Canadian government. This widely used, government-guaranteed money market instrument is used by most fund managers – especially in money market funds – to "park" cash balances. It is therefore a useful gauge for evaluating money market funds and the so-called "riskless" rate of investment.

• **Six-month Canada T-bills:** Reflects the average performance of 120-day treasury bills that are issued by the Canadian government. Also useful in monitoring money market funds.

MARKET BENCHMARKS | TABLE

MARKET BENCHMARKS 10.27.98

| | Value | Simple rate of return % | | | | Avg. ann. cpd. rate of ret. % | | | Std. dev |
		1m.	6m.	YTD	1yr.	3yr.	5yr.	10yr.	3yr.
Canadian equity									
TSE 300 total return	13017.91	+10.7	–18.3	–6.1	–7.8	+13.7	+10.1	+9.2	5.5
TSE 100 total return	428.83	+11.2	–17.3	–4.8	–4.6	+14.2	+10.8	+9.5	5.5
TSE 200 total return	376.38	+8.2	–22.9	–12.1	–20.0	+11.7	+7.2	+7.7	5.7
TSE 35 total return	594.93	+11.2	–16.3	–3.1	–1.4	+16.0	+12.6	+10.0	5.6
Russell 100 growth	398.70	+12.3	–16.2	–4.1	–6.5	+11.9	+7.7	+7.7	5.7

- **Five-year average GIC index:** An average of the current five-year GIC rates offered by banks and trust companies in Canada, expressed as a monthly return. This index should be treated as an approximation only.
- **U.S. three-month T-bills:** Reflects the average performance of 91-day treasury bills that are issued by the U.S. government. Useful in benchmarking funds that invest in the U.S. money market.
- **Gold bullion (London p.m. fix):** Tracks the performance of gold bullion by tracking the daily gold price set in London. Useful in evaluating mutual funds that specialize in gold bullion and gold companies.
- **Canadian consumer price index:** tracks the changes in consumer prices by measuring the consumer costs of a fixed basket of commodities. This change in price levels, expressed as a percentage, is computed monthly and is often referred to as the rate of inflation. The inflation rate gives investors a reasonable measure by which to assess how much the general cost of living is eroding one's investment performance.

SEARCHING FOR TRUE MUTUAL FUND RETURNS

"How did I do?" The average mutual fund investor cares only about that seemingly simple question. But in their quarterly performance statements, fund companies are only beginning to work on the answer. Putting aside the consideration that some brokers and financial planners don't really want people to know how poorly their recommendations are doing, it's true that calculating individual, or "customized," rates of returns is no trivial exercise.

For the typical investor buying new fund units monthly and making occasional switches, redemptions and one-time lump sum additions, calculating personal rates of return can entail the sort of mathematics not seen since he or she struggled with Calculus 101 in school. Add to that yearly, quarterly or monthly distributions of dividends from the fund companies and other tax-related phenomena and what appears to be a simple little calculation becomes a major undertaking.

PERFORMANCE FIGURES DON'T ALWAYS REFLECT FUND'S RETURNS

Furthermore, unless an investor buys each fund at the beginning of the month and sells at the end without paying sales charges, the total returns shown in newspaper performance roundups are unlikely to reflect actual performance. And, needless to say, the advertisements showing spectacular performance numbers won't necessarily reflect your returns either. That doesn't mean those numbers are exaggerated. Sometimes an investor can do better than those numbers, sometimes not – it all depends on when they're bought or sold and how markets perform over time. Little wonder, then, that a survey by Toronto-based Marketing Solutions found that 42% of fund investors do not always believe the performance figures provided by their fund companies.

MONTHLY DIVIDEND | TABLE

Almost all mutual funds have "dividend" distributions on a regular basis – monthly, quarterly or sometimes yearly. These payments reflect the proceeds of trading activities by fund management, as well as income earned by the fund. While they're called dividends, they actually can comprise interest income and/or capital gains and/or regular dividends, depending on the nature of the fund and its earnings.

In many cases these distributions are automatically reinvested to buy more fund units on behalf of the investor. But even if they are, you may receive a slip at tax time and have to pay tax on the income. The slip you receive from the fund company should separate the different types of income for tax purposes.

The table that accompanies the monthly mutual fund performance tables lists all dividends issued by Canadian mutual funds during the previous month. Here is a brief explanation of the information in these listings:

Type: This column shows the nature of the distribution. **I** represents income in the form of stock dividends and interest, **C** represents capital gains, and **X** represents a non-taxable return of capital and income distributions during the month.

Amt.: This is the amount of the distribution, expressed as dollars per mutual fund unit.

Pay date: The date the distribution became payable.

Mutual fund dividends

Fund	Type	Amt.	Pay date	Fund	Type	Amt.	Pay date
ABC Fully-Managed	I	0.0234	Sep 30	Altamira S-T Govt Bd	I	0.0800	Sep 30
AGF Canadian Bond	I	0.0270	Sep 30	Altamira T-Bill	I	0.0350	Sep 30
AGF Global Govt Bond	I	0.0379	Sep 30	@rgentum Income Port	I	0.0583	Sep 30
AGF High Income	I	0.0488	Sep 30	@rgentum S-T Asset	I	0.0423	Sep 30
AGF Mny Mkt Account	I	0.0318	Sep 30	Artisan Gth & Income	I	0.0414	Sep 30
AGF RSP Global Bond	I	0.0190	Sep 30	Artisan Income	I	0.0426	Sep 30
AGF US Income	I	0.0338	Sep 30	Artisan RSP Gth&Inc	I	0.0435	Sep 30
AGF US S-T H-Yield	I	0.0299	Sep 30	Artisan RSP Income	I	0.0496	Sep 30
AGF US$ Mny Mkt Acc	I	0.0374	Sep 30	Associate Investors	I	0.0900	Sep 14
AIC American Inc Eq	I	0.0250	Sep 30	Atlas American M-Mkt	I	0.0366	Sep 30
AIC Income Equity	I	0.0250	Sep 30	Atlas Cdn Balanced	I	0.0644	Sep 30

TIME-WEIGHTED RATES OF RETURN SHOW INVESTORS' PERSONAL GAINS OR LOSSES

The standard in the pension and private-client investment industry is "time-weighted" rates of return for clients' segregated portfolios or pooled funds. That calculation is not influenced by the amount of money invested, and the guidelines are set by the Association for Investment Management & Research (AIMR), based in Charlottesville, Va. Pension managers typically have only hundreds of clients, while fund companies must deal with hundreds of thousands of customers, and very few compute unitholders' personal returns.

An exception is Kemper Funds Group of Chicago, which has been using time-weighted individual rates of return on each of its funds since December 1996. More may follow, since the U.S. Securities & Exchange Commission has asked U.S. fund companies to personalize performance data. Canadian no-load firm Altamira Investment Services Inc. has fine-tuned its statements in this area, and Trimark Investment Management Inc., whose funds are sold through brokers and financial planners, has unveiled several new statements. The key concept is what Trimark calls "individual rate of return" and what Altamira terms "internal rate of return."

INVESTMENT FIRMS OFFER STATEMENTS SHOWING CLIENTS' FUND PORTFOLIO ACTIVITIES

The two are not quite the same. Altamira defines internal rate of return as a calculation that takes cash flows and their timing into account. However, Altamira uses the pension industry's simpler time-weighted approach mandated by AIMR and recommended by Glorianne Stromberg of the Ontario Securities Commission. Altamira's semi-annual statements show how much an individual investor's total fund portfolio has risen or fallen, but not the individual fund returns.

Gary Sinner of Wilshire Associates Inc., a Santa Monica, Calif.-based consultant, defines rate of return as "a number that tells us the percentage growth or decline of an investment." The prevalent seat-of-the-pants approach he calls the "popular package" method is a simple division of the dollar return by the dollars invested. The result is a total-period calculation of growth or decline in a portfolio that does not make allowance for weighting of the monthly contributions or withdrawals.

STANDARDIZED CALCULATION OF INDIVIDUAL RATES OF RETURN MAY BE ON THE HORIZON

At the other extreme is the time-weighted returns method. For individual equity fund unitholders there is no standard. But fund companies are leaning toward internal rate of return – or a variant – which requires that a return be recalculated with each new time period. Many investors want to see internal rate of return, says Altamira's Tina De Barbieri. However, AIMR requires the time-weighted return be provided to all investors, which is what Altamira's statements show. Kemper, after getting some input from Altamira, uses both in its statements.

There are several variations on time-weighted return, all of which only approximate a true internal rate of return. AIMR describes three of these. The most accurate is the daily valuation method, but it is an unrealistic process for fund companies. A somewhat simpler approach is the modified Dietz method. It weights each cash flow by the amount of time it is held in the portfolio, but is slightly less accurate than the daily valuation time-weighted rate of return, according to AIMR.

A third method is an extension of modified Dietz and links monthly returns together with a geometric averaging formula for the time-weighted return. It takes into consideration the exact timing of each cash flow. This is the route favored by Trimark. The Investment Funds Institute of Canada is evaluating whether a standardized formula for calculating a personalized rate of return is necessary, says John Kaszel, its research director. Fund companies already have all the necessary information, he says. The only question is "whether to deliver it on a platter" to consumers and what format they really want.

MUTUAL FUNDS | QUARTERLY REPORT

Four times a year, the *Financial Post* publishes the Mutual Funds Quarterly Report, an extensive package of information intended to help investors make decisions on their fund portfolios. These quarterly reports appear the third week in February, May, August and November each year. The largest single element in this supplemental quarterly information is the exclusive portfolio analysis survey conducted by Portfolio Analytics Ltd., using its PAL Trak databases. The survey provides detailed statistics on numerous Canadian and foreign equity funds, Canadian bond funds and Canadian balanced funds. The statistics include portfolio composition, as well as other key measurements such as interest rate sensitivity, relative yields, price/earnings ratios and capitalization. This information is generally calculated as at the end of the preceding quarter and can be very useful for ensuring that a fund is in good financial shape and conforms to unitholders' investment objectives and portfolio requirements.

Here is a guide to reading this table:

CANADIAN EQUITY PORTFOLIOS

Cash/short term: This column represents the percentage of a fund's total assets invested in cash and cash "equivalents" – various types of short-term (less than one year) notes and bonds, at the end of the preceding quarter.

Common equity as % of total: These two columns show what percentages of the fund's total assets were invested in (a) Canadian equities and (b) foreign equities at the end of the preceding quarter. Note that these figures represent common equity only and exclude dividend-generating preferred shares.

Equity sectoral asset allocation: The five columns under this heading show the percentages of each fund's common equity content invested in the following sectoral groups:

- Resource (includes oil and gas, paper and forest products, metals and minerals).
- Precious metals.
- Consumer (includes consumer products, merchandising, communications and media).
- Industrials (includes industrial products, transportation, environment and conglomerates).
- Interest sensitive (includes financial services, utilities, pipelines, real estate and construction).

TSE similarity: This column indicates how closely the sector weightings of each fund correspond to those of the TSE 300. For example, an index fund would have a "high" similarity, while resource or precious metals funds would have a "low" rating. In general, the higher the rating, the closer the yield should be to the TSE 300.

Fundamental analysis: This table provides fund ratings in terms of three key measurements of corporate size and performance – dividend yield, price/earnings ratio and capitalization. These ratings reflect unweighted averages for all the companies held by each fund and are relative to each other.

For example, capitalization represents the average size of companies in the fund and is calculated by multiplying the price by the shares outstanding of each underlying stock. The values are then compared across all of the equity funds and a relative ranking is set. "High" means the fund invests primarily in relatively large-cap companies. "Low" reflects small-cap portfolio holdings.

Similar relative rankings are done for the dividend yield and P/E columns. A fund that invests in small-cap growth companies would typically show a "high" P/E ratio, a "low" capitalization ranking and a "low" dividend yield ranking.

Weighted averages: The Canadian equity statistics are summarized at the bottom of the listings, as weighted overall averages for all funds in the category. Where space permits, these averages are followed by corresponding figures for various stock indexes to provide a means of comparison with overall markets.

CANADIAN EQUITY FUND HOLDINGS 10.27.98

Figures supplied by Portfolio Analytics Ltd.

Fund	Cash/ short term[1]	Common equity % of total Cdn[2]	fgn[2]	Res	Prec. met	Cons	Indus	Int sen	TSE sim.[2]	Yld	P/E	Cap
@rgentum Cdn Equity Portfolio	9.0	88.7	0.0	34.8	2.6	9.1	7.2	46.4	M	M+	M–	H
@rgentum Cdn Small Co. Pfl	19.7	92.2	0.0	6.7	0.0	46.7	27.6	19.0	M–	M–	M+	M–
20/20 Cdn Resources	5.7	85.7	4.9	68.5	22.5	0.9	4.5	3.6	L	L	H	M–
20/20 RSP Aggressive Equity	2.3	83.0	10.3	32.1	5.0	17.3	38.2	7.3	M–	L	H	M–
20/20 RSP Aggressive Smaller Cos.	13.5	77.7	6.9	27.6	5.3	21.7	27.6	17.7	M	L	M+	M–
Acadia Cdn Equity	13.1	86.9	0.0	25.2	3.6	7.7	35.9	27.6	M	M+	M–	H

CANADIAN BOND FUND HOLDINGS 10.27.98

Figures supplied by Portfolio Analytics Ltd.

Fund	Cash & short-term % of total[1]	Bonds % of total	% invested by maturity 1-5	5-10	10+	Avg matur. yrs[2]	% invested by issuer fed govt	other govt	Corp	% fgn exp
Acadia Bond	4.7	92.2	25.7	59.2	15.1	10.1	22.4	58.9	18.8	0.0
Acuity Pooled Fixed Income	39.9	47.8	29.0	71.0	0.0	4.1	100.0	0.0	0.0	0.0
AGF Canadian Bond	3.8	95.1	24.4	45.6	30.0	12.9	80.9	19.1	0.0	0.0
AIM GT Short-Term Income Series A	48.3	18.9	100.0	0.0	0.0	0.6	100.0	0.0	0.0	0.0
AIM GT Short-Term Income Series B	48.3	18.9	100.0	0.0	0.0	0.6	100.0	0.0	0.0	0.0
Altamira Bond	16.2	82.2	0.0	9.5	90.5	22.0	82.6	17.4	0.0	5.4

CANADIAN BALANCED FUND HOLDINGS 10.27.98

Figures supplied by Portfolio Analytics Ltd.

Fund	Cash/ short term[1]	Cdn bond	Fgn bonds	Convert bonds	Pref. shares	Total fixed income	Equity Cdn[2]	U.S.	Int'l	Total	% fgn cont[3]
Acadia Atlantic	15.8	84.2	0.0	0.0	0.0	84.2	0.0	0.0	0.0	0.0	0.0
Acadia Bal.	23.8	34.0	0.0	2.1	0.0	36.1	31.0	9.0	0.0	40.0	9.0
Acadia Diversified	12.9	87.1	0.0	0.0	0.0	87.1	0.0	0.0	0.0	0.0	0.0
Acuity Pooled Cdn Bal.	10.8	11.3	0.0	0.0	0.0	11.3	55.2	13.5	0.0	68.7	13.2
Acuity Pooled Cons. Asset Alloc.	15.4	9.1	0.0	2.6	1.2	12.9	56.8	7.2	0.0	64.0	13.1
AGF Cdn Tactical Asset Alloc.	7.0	30.5	0.0	0.0	0.0	30.5	45.6	8.0	7.8	61.4	16.0

FOREIGN EQUITY FUND HOLDINGS 10.27.98

Figures supplied by Portfolio Analytics Ltd.

Fund	Cash	Cdn.	U.S.	U.K.	Ger.	Fra.	Other Eur.	Jap.	Asia/Pacific H-K	↓	Latin Mex.	Amer.	Other
@rgentum Int'l Master Portfolio	3.3	1.5	48.7	9.1	4.6	2.8	13.7	7.1	-	2.4	2.6	-	4.4
20/20 Aggressive Global Stock	2.7	5.1	16.0	17.4	9.6	13.4	22.2	6.6	-	-	0.0	1.8	5.2
AGF Int'l Group-Intl Stock	5.9	2.7	-	9.9	7.5	9.3	20.1	16.0	10.4	3.9	2.6	9.4	2.5
AGF Int'l Group-World Equity	6.1	3.4	43.1	12.8	2.9	2.7	17.4	6.9	-	0.1	-	2.9	1.7
AGF Int'l Value	5.1	7.8	28.7	4.7	5.5	5.0	6.6	12.0	8.2	2.2	1.0	10.5	2.9
AIC World Advantage	59.6	-6.5	-	17.4	4.2	-	25.2	-	-	-	-	-	-

CANADIAN BOND PORTFOLIOS

Cash/short term: This column is the same as the corresponding column for Canadian equities – cash and equivalents with terms of less than one year.

Bonds: This column shows the percentage of assets invested in bonds (with terms of one year or more).

% invested by maturity: These three columns show the percentages of each fund's bond holdings allocated to short-term (one to five years), medium-term (five to 10 years) and long-term (10-plus years) bond maturities.

Average maturity yrs: This column shows the average maturity of the fund's entire portfolio, including cash/short-term holdings. Cash is assumed to have a zero maturity and short-term notes are pegged at 90 days.

% invested by issuer type: These three columns show what percentages of the bond portfolio are federal government, other government and corporate issues. This information, along with maturity figures, gives some indication of how aggressive or conservative a particular bond fund is.

% foreign expos.: This column shows the percentage of bond holdings that are exposed to foreign-exchange fluctuations (excluding currency hedging instruments unless otherwise noted).

Weighted average: As with the Canadian equity listings, the Canadian bond fund listings conclude with weighted averages for the entire category and comparable index figures where space permits.

CANADIAN BALANCED PORTFOLIOS

Cash/short term: same as above.

Canadian straight bonds: This column shows the percentage of fund assets invested in Canadian straight bonds.

Foreign bonds: Percentage of fund assets invested in bonds issued by foreign countries.

Convertible bonds: Percentage of fund assets invested in corporate convertible bonds that can be traded for equity holdings subject to the conditions set by the bond issuer.

Preferred shares: Percentage of fund assets invested in preferred shares.

Total fixed income: This column provides a total for the preceding four columns (excluding cash and equivalents). It reflects the total fixed-income component in each balanced fund's portfolio.

Equity: These four columns show the percentage of total fund assets invested in Canadian, U.S. and foreign equities respectively, followed by a total figure for the equity component in each balanced fund's portfolio.

% foreign content: This column shows the percentage of fund assets issued by non-Canadian corporations or governments (excluding currency hedging instruments unless otherwise noted).

Weighted average: As with the preceding categories, weighted averages are provided for all funds in the Canadian balanced fund listings.

FOREIGN EQUITY PORTFOLIOS

These listings provide the total percentage of each fund's assets that are invested in cash and equivalents of less than one-year maturities, along with percentages invested in equities from various geographic regions around the world. These figures enable investors to ensure a fund's geographical diversification is in keeping with their own objectives and preferences. As with other categories, weighted averages are provided at the bottom of each column.

The weighted average holdings of funds in the four broad categories surveyed are presented in four pie charts that accompany the Portfolio Analysis survey's introductory article.

The average percentages are adjusted to give more weight to funds with greater assets under management.

This TSE subindex chart compares total returns during the quarter for each of the Toronto Stock Exchange's 14 subindexes, plus the TSE 300, 100 and 200 broad indexes.

The bond indexes chart compares total returns during the quarter for Scotia Capital Markets' benchmark Canadian bond indexes.

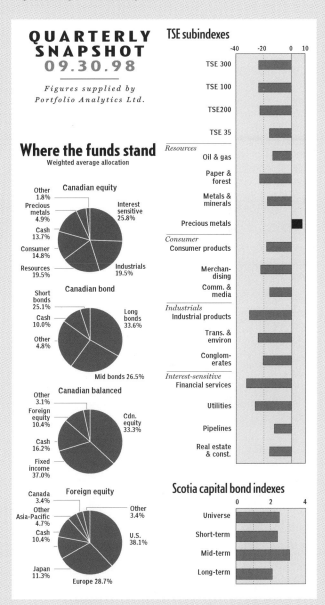

QUARTERLY
SNAPSHOT
09.30.98

*Figures supplied by
Portfolio Analytics Ltd.*

Where the funds stand
Weighted average allocation

Canadian equity
Other 1.8%
Precious metals 4.9%
Cash 13.7%
Consumer 14.8%
Resources 19.5%
Interest sensitive 25.8%
Industrials 19.5%

Canadian bond
Short bonds 25.1%
Cash 10.0%
Other 4.8%
Long bonds 33.6%
Mid bonds 26.5%

Canadian balanced
Other 3.1%
Foreign equity 10.4%
Cash 16.2%
Fixed income 37.0%
Cdn. equity 33.3%

Foreign equity
Canada 3.4%
Other Asia-Pacific 4.7%
Cash 10.4%
Japan 11.3%
Europe 28.7%
Other 3.4%
U.S. 38.1%

TSE subindexes
-40 -20 0 10

TSE 300
TSE 100
TSE200
TSE 35

Resources
Oil & gas
Paper & forest
Metals & minerals
Precious metals

Consumer
Consumer products
Merchan-dising
Comm. & media

Industrials
Industrial products
Trans. & environ
Conglom-erates

Interest-sensitive
Financial services
Utilities
Pipelines
Real estate & const.

Scotia capital bond indexes
0 2 4

Universe
Short-term
Mid-term
Long-term

Each quarterly mutual fund report provides two tables listing the most popular stocks held by top and bottom performing mutual funds at the end of the most recent quarter. The top performing funds are identified as those ranked in the top performance quartile during the two most recent quarters combined. In other words, these were the most popular stocks held by the top performing funds during the quarter. The first table lists the stocks held by funds in the top performance quartile. The second table lists the stocks held by funds in the bottom performance quartile.

Rank: The two columns at the extreme left show each stock's popularity ranking, in terms of total value of that stock held by top and bottom quartile funds at the end of the quarter. The first column shows the current ranking, and the second column shows the stock's ranking at the end of the preceding quarter.

Issuer: The corporation issuing the stock.

Issue: The type of stock being held, such as common, voting or subordinate or non-voting.

 # funds holding security: The number of top-quartile funds holding each security at the end of the quarter.

Value of holdings ($000s): This column provides the total dollar value of holdings by top-quartile funds of each stock, expressed in thousands of dollars. This figure constitutes the basis for each stock's popularity ranking in the first column of the table.

Chg in value ($000s): This column shows the amount by which fund ownership of each stock in the tables grew or declined between the ends of the most recent and the preceding quarters, again in thousands of dollars. A negative figure reflects net sales of the stock by the top-quartile funds during the period.

Chg in # funds vs. 3/98: This column shows the number of additional (or fewer) top-quartile funds holding the stock compared with the number of holders at the end of the preceding quarter.

Best fund performers

Stocks held at 10.27.98, by Canadian equity funds ranked in top performance quartile during the six-month period ended that date.

Rank Sept 98	June 98	Issuer	Issue	# funds holding security	Value of holdings $000s	Chg in value $000s	Chg in # funds vs 3/98
1	12	Shell Canada Ltd.	class A	8	467,336	(47,180)	0
2	1	Bank of Montreal	common	29	457,284	(835,534)	(5)
3	7	Royal Bk. Cda	common	25	439,571	(256,500)	(8)
4	18	Renaissance Energy	common	12	411,354	(2,106)	1
5	15	Alcan Aluminium	common	23	368,346	(81,328)	(1)
6	19	Alberta Energy Co.	common	14	352,513	(35,248)	0
7	2	Fairfax Finl Holdngs	common sub vt	10	315,182	(730,933)	(3)
8	8	Power Financial	common	8	310,581	(330,675)	(10)
9	27	Suncor Energy Inc.	common	15	292,157	(3,617)	(1)
10	26	Anderson Exploration	common	14	281,341	(17,861)	(1)

Worst fund performers

Stocks held at 10.27.98 by Canadian equity funds ranked in bottom performance quartile during the six-month period ended that date.

Rank Sept 98	June 98	Issuer	Issue	# funds holding security	Value of holdings $000s	Chg in value $000s	Chg in # funds vs 3/98
1	4	Royal Bk Cda	common	30	461,561	(182)	6
2	2	Bank of Montreal	common	26	449,144	(201,606)	6
3	6	BCE Inc.	common	31	353,382	(5,124)	4
4	1	CIBC	common	27	335,960	(330,080)	(9)
5	5	Bank Of Nova Scotia	common	21	319,559	(57,902)	(3)
6	40	TransCanada Pipe	common	31	306,997	177,684	15
7	3	Toronto-Dominion Bk	common	25	296,530	(323,211)	(4)
8	10	Suncor Energy Inc	common	30	263,030	19,307	3
9	9	CanWest Global Comm.	sub vtg	13	197,798	(53,975)	4
10	14	Northern Telecom Ltd.	common	25	194,758	(18,561)	3

TOP AND BOTTOM

The quarterly mutual fund portfolio analysis contrast funds' holdings against the fund performance for the preceding three-month period. Tables show the top 10 and bottom 10 funds in terms of three-month simple return in each of the four broad categories surveyed (Canadian equity funds, Canadian bond funds, Canadian balanced funds and foreign equity funds). Each table also provides the overall average return for each table's fund category.

THIRD QUARTER
PERFORMANCE

Figures supplied by Portfolio Analytics Ltd.

Canadian equity funds

Top 10 performers	%	Bottom 10 performers	%
1 First Cdn Precious Metals	8.07	1 Cambridge Resource	-34.68
2 Goldtrust	7.05	2 BPI Cdn Opportunities RSP	-30.75
3 NCE Precious Metals Growth	4.43	3 Cambridge Growth	-29.81
4 CIBC Precious Metal	2.26	4 Cambridge Precious Metals	-29.38
5 C.I. Global Resource Sector	1.54	5 Atlas Cdn Small Cap Growth	-28.84
6 Hirsch Natural Resource	1.26	6 Great-West Life Cdn Equity(G) A	-28.69
7 Green Line Precious Metals	1.18	7 Great-West Life Cdn Equity(G) B	-28.64
8 Scotia Precious Metals	0.06	8 CIBC Cdn Emerging Companies	-28.52
9 Dynamic Precious Metals	0.00	9 Bissett Small Capital	-28.39
10 Cdn Protected	-0.41	10 CIBC Financial Companies	-28.01

MUTUAL FUNDS

The Mutual Funds 15 Year Review is published twice a year and provides tables showing one-year returns for each of the past 15 years. Funds are sorted in the same asset categories as the monthly performance tables. This year-over-year review of one-year returns gives investors an indication of the performance volatility for individual categories and funds.

CANADIAN EQUITY 10.27.98

Fund	15 yr. cmpd.	rate of return %														
		1997	1996	1995	1994	1993	1992	1991	1990	1989	1988	1987	1986	1985	1984	1983
Cdn equity avg.:	**10.5**	**8.3**	**26.8**	**13.2**	**-3.8**	**37.4**	**5.6**	**10.9**	**-12.0**	**17.2**	**8.2**	**2.3**	**10.8**	**25.4**	**-0.4**	**29.9**
Cdn equity med.:	**11.1**	**12.6**	**25.3**	**12.3**	**-3.2**	**30.6**	**2.8**	**11.2**	**-11.7**	**17.3**	**10.4**	**2.0**	**10.1**	**25.7**	**1.2**	**30.5**

Canadian large-cap equity
Invest primarily in portfolio of common stocks and other equity securities of Canadian companies that have market capitalization above $500 million.

Fund	15 yr. cmpd.	1997	1996	1995	1994	1993	1992	1991	1990	1989	1988	1987	1986	1985	1984	1983
Cdn large-cap equity avg.	**11.6**	**14.8**	**24.7**	**13.0**	**-2.1**	**25.1**	**0.5**	**12.7**	**-11.6**	**18.0**	**12.5**	**0.9**	**9.8**	**28.2**	**0.6**	**31.5**
Cdn large-cap equity med.	**11.8**	**13.8**	**24.9**	**12.7**	**-2.7**	**25.0**	**-1.1**	**12.6**	**-10.9**	**17.8**	**11.3**	**0.1**	**8.7**	**26.8**	**1.3**	**31.2**
Allstar AIG Canadian Equity	...	13.0	24.8	9.0	-5.8	19.2	-4.1	12.0	-10.5	12.3	...	...	...	...	...	...
Altamira Capital Growth	9.7	7.8	10.4	9.1	3.3	30.9	10.2	16.6	-6.6	23.5	14.2	-7.2	2.2	20.6	-5.7	25.1
Atlas Cdn Large Cap Growth	...	26.7	29.7	12.5	0.0	16.6	-4.7	11.9	-10.7	16.1	13.1	-5.9	8.5	...	...	...
Atlas Cdn Large Cap Value	...	12.9	16.4	8.9	...	...	...	...	...	...	...	...	...	...	...	...

CHAPTER 6

INVESTMENT | PLANNING

- The basics of investment strategies and styles

- Bonds

- Building a balanced portfolio

- GICs

- Asset allocation and diversification

- Equities

JUST HOW MANY BLACK MONDAYS

CAN YOU HANDLE? | BY JONATHAN CHEVREAU

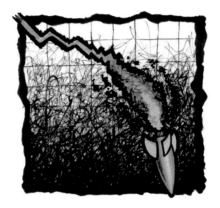

WE'RE ALL LONG-TERM INVESTORS in a bull market it seems. It's easy to get carried away by the big themes – demographics, globalization and the information revolution, for instance – and to end up going overboard on stocks in a portfolio. In good times, it's understandable that investors gravitate to stocks. As the famous charts of Chicago-based Ibbitson Associates show, $1 invested in the U.S. markets in 1926 would have grown to $2,000 by the early 1990s if invested in small-cap stocks and to $700 in large-cap stocks, but only to $11 in government bonds and $10 in treasury bills. The compound annual returns to 1996 are 12.6% for small caps, 10.7% for large caps, 5.1% for long-term bonds and 3.7% for treasury bills, all compared with a 3.1% inflation rate.

Stocks for the long run (that happens to be the title of a fine book on the subject by Jeremy Siegel) is a fine credo for those who have the stomach for it. But in the long run we are also dead. Investors have to live day by day and their capacity to absorb the highs and lows of the roller-coaster varies greatly. The danger in believing we're in a new era where stocks go only up is that investors throw caution to the wind and throw out such traditional safety measures as diversification and maintaining an appropriate balance among the various asset classes – stocks, bonds and cash.

Investors who bought into Asian or gold mutual funds learned this lesson the hard way during the mini-crash of Oct. 27, 1997. When the Asian flu spread to stock markets around the world, many investors found out just how long term their time horizons really were. That decline tested "the resolve of all those who believe in the buy and hold philosophy," said Jon Kanitz, director of CIBC Wood Gundy Inc.'s private client investments division and a contributing editor to the *MoneyLetter* newsletter. Such markets reveal "who is weak and who is tough." The stomach-churning one-day drop in October was followed by one of history's greatest rallies, and it had at least one beneficial effect. It re-acquainted equity investors, some who had never experienced such declines, with the risk side of the risk/return equation.

INVESTORS SHOULDN'T IGNORE THE BASIC PRINCIPLES OF DIVERSIFICATION

The flip side of glorious 40% and 50% single-year returns achieved on individual technology stocks or through specialized equity funds has always been the sharp drops of the type experienced in the 1997 instalment of Black Monday. If you really believe the prevailing axioms of baby boom demographics, stocks for the long run and buying on dips, then you'd take the view of Nathan Mechanic, a broker with RBC Dominion Securities Inc., that whenever such drops occur, "we're having a sale" on stocks and equity funds. If, however, the thought of wading in and scooping up bargains in the next market swoon makes you queasy, you've probably flunked what one financial planner calls the tummy test.

If there was panic late in October, it was likely felt by people who ignored the basic principles of diversification. The big drop may have served as a much-needed wake up call for investors with 100% of their portfolio in aggressive stocks or equity funds. And doubly so for those who borrowed money to maximize returns in a market they thought could only go up. Remember that stocks or equity funds constitute only one of the three major asset classes. The other two, cash and fixed-income investments, also should be represented in the portfolios of most investors. For larger portfolios, 5% or 10% positions are sometimes added in real estate, gold and managed futures.

A BALANCED PORTFOLIO IS SPREAD OUT OVER DIFFERENT ASSET CLASSES

What constitutes a balanced portfolio varies with the risk tolerance and growth objectives of individual investors. At the Rogers Group, the suggested asset mix for a 60-year-old is 50% to 60% equities, 30% to 40% fixed income and 5% to 10% real estate. For a 45-year-old, the mix is 50% to 75% equity, 20% to 30% fixed income and 5% to 10% real estate. Traditionally, the counsel has been to hold fixed income investments inside an RRSP and equity investments outside. That's because fixed income investments are highly taxed outside an RRSP, while capital gains and dividend income get slightly more favorable tax treatment.

Many middle class investors have only nominal non-registered investment portfolios. For these investors, it makes sense to have some equity exposure inside an RRSP. But, as the Asia and gold fund crises showed, aggressive equity funds may not be wise choices for RRSPs. If they go down, you've lost precious RRSP room that cannot be regained. At least outside an RRSP, capital losses can be used to offset capital gains. Most of the big mutual fund companies and banks try to advocate a "portfolio" approach to investments. Generally, whether it's the Mackenzie STAR program or the TD Bank's equivalent, investors fill out a short questionnaire to determine their risk tolerance and objectives, then wait for a computer to spit out a range of suggested asset classes and appropriate products. Such a long-term approach, sometimes called strategic asset allocation, can also be achieved with something as simple as a balanced fund, which typically offers a 60% equity to 40% bond mix.

MARKET TIMERS TRY TO PREDICT HIGHS AND LOWS TO SAVE INVESTOR FROM LOSSES

In opposition to the tried and true "buy and hold" approach involved in strategic asset allocation is the market timing approach. Market timers believe they can predict market highs and lows, thereby saving investors from the gut-wrenching crashes. Of course, many investment professionals believe this is impossible and that market timing also leads to "missing" the market for the powerful one-day ascents that make up most market gains. So-called "tactical asset allocation" consists of short-term attempts to pick the asset class that will outperform and then giving that class more weight. This approach is taken by tactical asset allocation funds but, historically, their performance has been no better than traditional balanced funds.

INVESTORS SHOULD MAINTAIN A STRATEGIC ASSET ALLOCATION MIX

For most investors, occasional (once a year, perhaps) rebalancing of a strategically allocated asset mix is probably preferable to market timing. A market timer is either 100% in the market or 100% in cash. If you're willing to take the risks, by all means engage the services of market timers – Jean Pierre Fruchet of Guardian Timing Services is one – but such drastic calls are beyond the abilities of the average investor. (For more on buy and hold strategies versus market timing, see the other articles on these subjects in this section.) Taking partial profits on the way up is another matter. In mid-1997 a cover story in *Money* magazine suggested investors take profits by cashing in 20% of their shares. The reasoning was that U.S. stocks had more than doubled between 1994 and 1997 and that a portfolio that was in balance in 1994 would have grown out of balance, overweighted in equities, by 1997.

A BALANCED ASSET MIX CONTAINS 60% EQUITIES, 30% FIXED INCOME AND 10% CASH

For example, a 1994 portfolio that was 65% stocks, 25% bonds and 10% cash would have been transformed into a 75% stock weighting, 18% in bonds and 7% in cash. The defensive allocation strategy suggested selling 20% of those equities, thereby reducing the 75% stock weighting to the 60% level. You'd reinvest the proceeds back into the underperforming asset classes of bonds and cash. Such an approach makes eminent sense. It "forces you to go back to your original parameters by selling your most overvalued asset and buying your least valued asset," says Mechanic. But a correction is not the time for rebalancing a portfolio, warns Rogers Group adviser Clay Gillespie. "You hope you have developed a balanced strategy before the correction. Once a correction has occurred, the damage has been done."

He believes Black Monday 1997 had "the very positive effect of lowering the expectations of many investors. If an investor's portfolio was not properly diversified and they didn't like the ride, then they will still have a chance to develop a proper investment strategy." Ideally, by the summer of 1997, investors would have been taking partial profits on stock funds on the way up and rebalancing into long bonds, says Michael Nairne, president of Toronto-based Equion Group. Among alternative asset classes, Nairne advocates a 5% to 15% weighting in real estate, which can be achieved through real estate investment trusts. Nairne forecasts the three-year expected return from REITs will be better than from both stocks and bonds. While gold funds were slaughtered in the second half of 1997, Nairne says a strategic 5% gold position has a place in the average portfolio. "If you're looking for anything but strategic insurance, gold will disappoint you, but if we hit a financial Armageddon that 5% position may go up three- or five-fold, which would allow you to take lots of hits elsewhere."

THE PROSPECTUS IS A COMPLEX TOOL

Prospectuses are required reading for anyone buying mutual funds, but how helpful are these long, complex legal documents for the average investor? And what should the investor be looking for when reading them? Here are some pointers from Riley Moynes, author of *The Money Coach,* co-author of Top Funds 1998, and senior financial adviser and principal of the Equion Group in Toronto.

INVESTMENT OBJECTIVES

This key element of the prospectus is intended to help you ensure the fund's goals are in keeping with your portfolio needs. In general, this section will list any restrictions on permissible investments, and discuss the nature of the risks facing buyers. "This is intended to help investors, but when you read, for example, that every equity fund's stated objective is to provide long-term growth along with security of capital, how much help is that?" asks Moynes. "Prospectuses are not always the best place to get the distinguishing features of different funds."

PORTFOLIO HOLDINGS

A listing of assets, usually presented as of the fund's latest fiscal yearend, is another key element of the prospectus. Do these holdings reflect the fund's stated aims regarding growth versus security? Are some holdings more conservative or aggressive than expected? Is the balance right? Says Moynes: "Assuming you are capable of drawing informed conclusions from this information, holdings can give you a pretty good idea of the fund's style, for example, whether they're small or large cap, growth or value-oriented, and so on. But are you equipped to make sufficiently informed decisions?"

FUND MANAGEMENT

Individual fund managers can have a big bearing on portfolio contents as well as performance since they're the ones who actually make the buying decisions. The prospectus should provide a brief history of the management team along with any recent changes. If there are new people at the helm, how have they performed in the past, and what tendencies did they display? What management style or styles do they employ? What can you expect from them?

FEES AND CHARGES

All funds charge management and expense fees, and sometimes these can have a significant impact on growth statistics. Some funds also charge one-time sales fees ("front-end" or "back-end" loads), complicating the profit equation. The prospectus should detail all these fees, and you should keep them in mind in comparing performance figures with other funds. "Many people are still unaware that funds charge any fees at all," says Moynes. "And I would hope people don't make decisions based only on management expense ratios. As anywhere, you generally get what you pay for. With smaller accounts, no-load can mean no help. This may be fine for those who can make their own decisions, but you should consider what added value those fees provide."

FINANCIAL STATEMENTS

Funds are required to provide complete financial statements, accompanied by an auditor's statement, in the prospectus. "This is essential information, for those who can understand it," Moynes says. A couple of further points: How are transactions performed? Are there restrictions or lead time requirements, as is often the case with real estate funds, that can limit your ability to act quickly? What about transfer fees? How liquid is your capital? What are the dividend distribution policies of the fund? Are dividends automatically reinvested? Also, the timing of distributions in relation to purchases can affect your after-tax results (for instance, if you buy just before the distribution, you might end up with little profit and a year's worth of tax liability).

"One of the other things I would like to see in a fund prospectus is annual performance figures from the date of inception," Moynes adds. "Average annual yields can be very seductive, but they can mask several losing years. Returns for each calendar year would be very helpful in revealing fund performance patterns."

MANAGEMENT STYLE IS IMPORTANT TO WATCH

Diversification is a fundamental tenet of investing, but many investors overlook management style when spreading their money around mutual funds. Yet style can have a substantial impact on the content and trading patterns of a particular fund, not to mention its bottom line. A graphic example of the significance of style was GT Global Canada Inc.'s October 1997 launch of its Canada Value Class fund to complement its Canada Growth Class fund. "These funds will have a completely different management style," says Derek Webb, who manages the Canada Growth portfolio and oversees the Canada Value fund (managed by Roger Mortimer). "But they'll be run dogmatically within their own styles.

"We've found from two years of studies in the U.S. and Canadian markets that style and discipline are the only two things that work," Webb adds. "The two best styles we found for Canada after back-testing for 17 years were momentum [growth] and value investing. Over that period, the TSE averaged about 10%. Growth investing would have yielded 20%, and value investing would have yielded 15% but with lower volatility than the TSE." Value investors seek underpriced stocks, high-quality sleepers that offer good prospects of long-term capital appreciation. Growth investing is more volatile but average returns are higher because, as Webb explains it, "value investors buy at the bottom of the trough and may have to wait a while to make money, but momentum investors buy when a business is already firing on all cylinders and poised for very strong growth." The two styles generally do well in different years, making them complementary elements in an equity portfolio.

FUND MANAGERS RESEARCH COMPANIES LOOKING FOR STRONG MANAGEMENT TEAMS

Another basic style difference relates to company size – "small cap" versus "large cap." Some managers tend to prefer smaller, and therefore generally more volatile, companies for their greater growth potential, while others stick to blue chips. Some managers try to get the best of both worlds with separate funds for each. "We don't have a small cap fund right now but we're looking at it," says Karl Schulz, managing director at TD Asset Management Inc. "We've come through a period when large companies have been out-performing small ones both in Canada and the U.S., but small caps seem to be recovering now, especially in the U.S. They're attracting a lot more investor attention."

Yet another style variant is "bottom up" versus "top down." In the bottom-up approach, managers look for promising stocks based on intrinsic indicators such as price earnings ratios or management resources. Using a top-down style, they look at the macro-economic picture, then focus on the most promising industries and finally the best companies within them. "We do a lot of hard work researching companies, and we don't like to complicate the picture with interest rate trends or politics – they're secondary considerations," says Brad Badeau, president of Trimark Investment Management Inc. and proponent of bottom-up investing.

"For one thing, we're not sure we know the implications of all those macro-economic factors, such as how interest rate trends will affect certain industries. We're basically in the business of buying other businesses," Badeau adds. "We look for stability, and management strength is most important. If a company has the right management team, then presumably they'll make the right decisions, whatever the economic conditions happen to be."

AN INDUSTRIAL SECTOR WEIGHTING DEPENDS ON STAGE OF THE ECONOMIC CYCLE

Sectoral rotation is a variant of the top-down style, one in which different weightings are given to industrial sectors during different parts of economic cycles. For example, companies not affected by economic cycles – the non-cyclicals, such as pharmaceuticals – get emphasis during economic downturns. During periods of economic growth, the retail sector, for instance, will be back in favor.

Then there is technical versus fundamental analysis. "Tekkies" rely heavily on the charting of stock price momentum and trends to try to determine the best buy and sell points. Fundamentalists, on the other hand, look more at intrinsic corporate performance drivers such as financial health, along with macro-economic considerations.

MARKET TIMERS REJECT BUY-AND-HOLD STRATEGY

Bragging about your mutual fund picks is supposedly acceptable cocktail party chatter. But the next time there's a lull in the conversation, try the following experiment: Suggest that everyone who believes in market timing with mutual funds step into one corner, and those who believe in buying and holding funds over the long term occupy another part of the room. If your gathering contains a number of people working in the investment industry, observe how many working directly for the fund companies move to the buy-and-hold camp. Then see how many brokers and advisers opt for the market-timing camp.

Generally, the fund companies eschew market timing. Some, such as no-load firm Altamira Investment Services Inc., limit switches to just 10 a year, on the grounds frequent switchers increase the costs for unitholders and make life more difficult for the fund managers.

"The academic studies we've seen tend to prove over time that you can't add value through market timing," says Altamira president Philip Armstrong. "Funds were designed and are best used for long-term holders." Altamira's 1997 marketing literature indicates someone who bought and held Frank Mersch's flagship Altamira Equity Fund

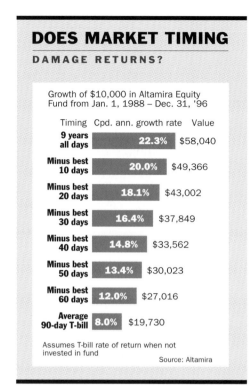

DOES MARKET TIMING
DAMAGE RETURNS?

Growth of $10,000 in Altamira Equity
Fund from Jan. 1, 1988 – Dec. 31, '96

Timing	Cpd. ann. growth rate	Value
9 years all days	22.3%	$58,040
Minus best 10 days	20.0%	$49,366
Minus best 20 days	18.1%	$43,002
Minus best 30 days	16.4%	$37,849
Minus best 40 days	14.8%	$33,562
Minus best 50 days	13.4%	$30,023
Minus best 60 days	12.0%	$27,016
Average 90-day T-bill	8.0%	$19,730

Assumes T-bill rate of return when not
invested in fund

Source: Altamira

from inception would have a 22.3% return. That figure falls to 18.1% if you switched to cash during the best 20 days of the market, and to just 12% if you missed the best 60 days.

Writing in a recent issue of *The FundLetter,* CIBC Wood Gundy Inc. vice-president Jon Kanitz lumped market timers in with sector rotators, asset allocators and momentum investors, concluding that "these techniques are so prone to error that they make fortune tellers look good by comparison." Kanitz, a dedicated stock picker who believes in staying fully invested at all times, adds that some combination of a value or growth approach to stock picking will outperform other styles over the long haul.

Market timers, on the other hand, swear they can beat the buy-and-hold camp and can trot out their own statistics showing the gains to be made by being out of the market on its worst days. The Toronto Society of Technical Analysts recently invited one of the more respected fund switchers, Harland Hendrickson, to reveal some of his secrets. TSTA members normally apply technical analysis to trade stocks or futures directly, and sometimes indexes. Hendrickson takes a similar tack, but switches between mutual funds rather than stocks. His credo is that "sometimes the best fund is no fund at all."

MARKET-TIMING MODELS CAN BE APPLIED TO MUTUAL FUND INVESTMENTS

Hendrickson, who has a PhD in biochemistry, sells load funds from Edmonton and publishes an insightful newsletter, *Market Trend Follower.* He believes funds are better market-timing vehicles than securities held directly because of the instant diversification funds provide, the ability to switch at little or no cost, the lower risk that comes with picking multiple fund managers and the fact funds provide exposure to more than 25 different sectors. Hendrickson uses a momentum strategy to move in and out of major sectors. His approach resembles technical analysis as applied to stock charting, but is applied instead to mutual funds. The premise is that a trend in motion will continue in the same direction until it reverses or until you can find a trend that is doing better. He cites Chicago-based fund manager Richard Driehaus, whose philosophy is to buy high and sell higher. "We apply that to mutual funds," Hendrickson told the TSTA.

The approach is decidedly short term and the opposite of the long-term buy-and-hold approach. Hendrickson tries to incorporate some of the better market-timing models and Windows-based computer programs, all U.S.-made, into his own proprietary FundSoft system. Former TSTA president Kenneth Norquay of Gorinsen Capital Inc. in Toronto, a long-time market timer, agrees that the same timing principles that work for stocks or futures can also be applied to mutual funds. But Norquay disagrees that funds are the optimal vehicle for market timers: "Mutual funds are the dull thud of investing. They hardly move at all. If you're going to time why not do it with something that makes money?" He suggests individual stocks and even bonds or groups of stocks. If going the fund route, he prefers sector funds or closed-end funds.

FUND MANAGERS CAN BE TRUSTED TO MAKE DAILY TACTICAL DECISIONS

There is some irony that so much energy and science are being applied to analysing mutual funds. After all, isn't the whole idea of funds to delegate the decision-making to professionals? A happy middle ground might be to trust your fund manager with the daily tactical shifts of the markets and to rebalance your fund portfolio once or twice a year when major sea changes occur, such as the market crash in October 1997.

THERE IS MORE TO REAL ESTATE THAN BRICKS

It took Oscar Belaiche a year to sell almost $500 million worth of real estate in his old job. In his new one, he could move that much in a week. Belaiche was the real estate executive in charge of selling the big Prudential Insurance Co. of America portfolio of office, industrial and retail buildings. After an intense marketing process and a tight bidding war, Oxford Properties Group Inc. and GE Capital Canada Inc. bought the portfolio in July 1997 for $455.8 million.

Belaiche's new job is managing real estate mutual funds for Goodman & Co. It still consists of buying and selling real estate, but instead of bricks and mortar buildings, he is trading stocks. He's one of the first real estate operators to move over to the securities side of the business. Industry watchers say more will follow. They will move because real estate in Canada is becoming securitized. Property ownership is increasingly held through the stock market – witness the amount of money pouring into real estate stocks and the number of new real estate investment trusts (REITs) launched in the past year.

NEW CAPITAL ENTERING REAL ESTATE MARKET DRIVES INVESTMENT MARKET FORWARD

In 1997, real estate companies or trusts tapped the public markets almost 40 times, raising $5.5 billion, according to CIBC Wood Gundy Real Estate Ltd. The EdperBrascan Corp. real estate giant, Brookfield Properties Corp., has filled its pockets four times, raising $1.6 billion in 1997, surpassing the $1.4 billion the entire industry raised the year before. "Real estate is changing from a privately owned to a publicly owned industry," says Scott White, who has also moved from the bricks to the paper side of real estate.

For 10 years, he was an investment broker at J.J. Barnicke Ltd. Now he's an investment banker with CIBC Wood Gundy. The transformation began in the U.S. four to five years ago and is just beginning in Canada, he says. Even with current market volatility, the wave is expected to continue rolling. "This is a long-term trend and it's not going to be upset by a market correction," says White. About 350 real estate companies are publicly traded in the U.S., many of them relatively new. In Canada, the CIBC Wood Gundy Realty Stock Monitor lists 30 real estate firms. These companies are growing rapidly. The Toronto Stock Exchange real estate subindex, consisting of seven of them, outperformed the TSE 300 index in 1997. "The level of new capital entering the market is unprecedented and is driving the investment market forward at a rapid rate," says Ross Moore, vice-president of research at Colliers International. "Both institutional and retail investors are anxious to increase their exposure to real estate and are fuelling the demand for more real estate securities."

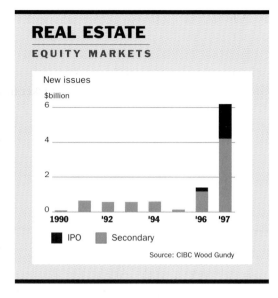

REAL ESTATE
EQUITY MARKETS

New issues
$billion

Source: CIBC Wood Gundy

■ IPO   ▨ Secondary

POPULARITY OF REAL ESTATE MUTUAL FUNDS IS GROWING IN CANADA

"Real estate is an emerging industry in the stock market," says Anne MacLean of Goodman's Dynamic Canadian Real Estate Fund and the global Dynamic Real Estate Equity Fund. "There's a lot more information in the public domain today than there was two or three years ago on real estate, so there's a lot more to evaluate."

Expertise like Belaiche's helps. "We're merging the portfolio management theories of the stock side with the portfolio management theories on the real estate side," he says. "It's a merging of the skills of the traditional CFA [chartered financial analyst] working with an operating person. Before, I was directly buying and selling real estate. Now, I'm buying the companies that are buying and selling real estate."

"Oscar [Belaiche] is going to find that liquidity is tremendous relief," MacLean says, mimicking Belaiche in an imagined scenario. "I don't like that building any more: Oh! Gone!" MacLean says with a wave of her hand. The growth of Dynamic's global real estate fund illustrates how rapidly investments are being funnelled to real estate. In January 1996, with assets of $3 million, the fund was, in MacLean's words, "teenie, teenie, teenie, teenie, teenie, teenie tiny." A year later, assets had climbed to $50 million and now stand at about $220 million. The much newer Canadian fund was launched last February. Total assets at the end of June were $100 million. Its top five holdings are familiar real estate names: Oxford Properties, RioCan REIT, Cambridge Shopping Centres Ltd. and Gentra Inc.

Until recently, the Dynamic funds were the only real estate mutual funds in Canada.

But in October 1997, Mackenzie Financial Corp. launched its Universal World Real Estate Fund. And in September, CIBC Securities Inc. created the CIBC Canadian Real Estate Fund. One reason Dynamic had little competition is that it's tough to find a fund manager for the specialized field of real estate, says MacLean. "Who else would you name?" she asks. "There is a real shortage of real estate analysts in Canada, not so much on the sell side, but there is for sure a lack of them on the buy side."

Ted Cadsby, a vice-president in CIBC's mutual funds group agrees. "There are very few qualified real estate managers in Canada." Instead of forming a new team, CIBC has appointed Morguard Investments Ltd., an established real estate investment management firm, to do the job.

THE RIP VAN WINKLE STRATEGY MIGHT WORK

There are now more than 1,600 mutual funds available in Canada, not to mention hundreds more closed-end funds, offshore funds and other products. Little wonder investors are confused. An entire industry has sprung up to help them pick funds. There are more than 20,000 brokers and financial planners, dozens of seminar speakers, a slew of newsletters and a gaggle of book authors all claiming expertise in the field. This army of experts makes the topic of fund selection far more complicated than necessary. A vast library of esoteric information has sprung up, involving asset allocation, performance and style analysis, comparisons of volatility, relative expenses and risk/reward tradeoffs.

A TWO-FUND PORTFOLIO CAN BE AS GOOD AS A 20-FUND PORTFOLIO

Much of this is geared to fund switching, which usually means investors sell funds just when they should be buying and vice versa. Some investors emulate their financial planners by spending hundreds of dollars a year for monthly computer disk performance updates. Investors can now spend as much time analysing mutual funds as they used to spend analysing individual stocks. Wasn't the whole idea of mutual funds to delegate security selection to the professionals? Investors were supposed to be able to choose a fund or two, pay the 2% or so annual management fee and forget about it, spending their lives on more congenial pursuits.

Not now, however. Everyone is chasing the latest hot fund, frantically switching between regional equity funds and, lately, different industry sectors. If you're not worrying about bailing out of Europe and jumping into Asia, you have to decide between the computer industry, health sciences, financial services and consumer products sectors.

Anyone with more than eight mutual funds is probably overdiversified. Enter the Rip Van Winkle two-fund portfolio. At the risk of scuttling sales of The Financial Post's annual *Smart Funds* guide, the idea that all you really need is two funds is an idea I've floated at seminars and bounced off a few advisers, and no one has refuted its logic. Both funds are from proven, credible fund families, both with below-average management fees. The idea is to buy these two funds and hang on for the next 40 years. No need for rebalancing, switching or even paying close attention to daily market changes. I'd argue anyone who adopts this approach will match the performance of the complex 20-fund portfolios of the gurus and pundits.

PORTFOLIO HAS BALANCE OF STOCKS, BONDS, CASH AND FOREIGN INVESTMENTS

Rip Van Winkle is, of course, the fictional bearded character who falls asleep one day and awakes decades later to a very different world. The idea of the portfolio is to pick two funds that run on automatic pilot: if you leave the country for 30 years, or fall into a long coma, you should awaken to an investment portfolio that has grown considerably. You do nothing, nor does your financial planner. That doesn't mean the portfolio is static: at least two fund managers are continually engaged in stock picking, moving in and out of geographical regions and modifying asset allocation on your behalf.

I'm assuming an average RRSP/RRIF investor who wants a balance of stocks, bonds and cash and maximum foreign content. Growth and a little income.

SO WITHOUT FURTHER ADO THE ENVELOPES PLEASE

• Fund No. 1 is Trimark Income Growth, a basic low-fee Canadian balanced fund with a management expense ratio, or MER, of 1.6%, compared with the category average of 2.15%. This constitutes 80% of the Rip Van Winkle portfolio. There's a good cross-section of mid- to large-capitalization Canadian stocks, some bonds, cash and mortgage securities. The asset mix is the classic 60% equity to 40% bonds. The fund maximizes its permitted 20% foreign content with mostly U.S. and some European and Japanese stocks. Average compound annual growth rate for the five years ended May 31, 1997, was 14.2%, well above the 11.6% median return for the category.

• Fund No. 2 is Templeton Growth Fund, the classic global equity fund created in 1954 by the legendary Sir John Templeton. Again, a lower than average MER of 2% (compared with the 2.5% average), a five-year performance track record of 16.2% through May 1997 versus the median 13.3% and a good value-oriented geographical mix that buys bargains around the world at the time of maximum pessimism.

Use Templeton for the 20% foreign content portion of a registered plan; coupled with the 20% of the 80% from Trimark Income Growth, you'd have 36% foreign content.

I realize the combined asset allocation of these funds is skewed slightly to equities. That should be fine for any young investor. Older people could bring the total portfolio into a traditional asset mix by substituting Templeton Global Balanced Fund. Purists

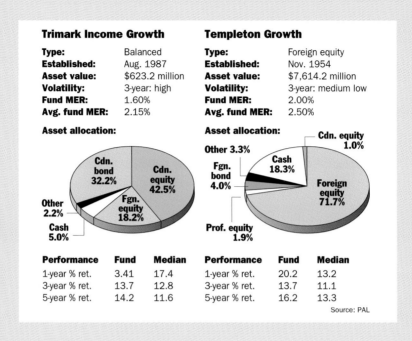

THE RIP VAN WINKLE | TWO-FUND PORTFOLIO

Trimark Income Growth

Type:	Balanced
Established:	Aug. 1987
Asset value:	$623.2 million
Volatility:	3-year: high
Fund MER:	1.60%
Avg. fund MER:	2.15%

Asset allocation:

Cdn. bond 32.2%
Cdn. equity 42.5%
Fgn. equity 18.2%
Other 2.2%
Cash 5.0%

Performance	Fund	Median
1-year % ret.	3.41	17.4
3-year % ret.	13.7	12.8
5-year % ret.	14.2	11.6

Templeton Growth

Type:	Foreign equity
Established:	Nov. 1954
Asset value:	$7,614.2 million
Volatility:	3-year: medium low
Fund MER:	2.00%
Avg. fund MER:	2.50%

Asset allocation:

Other 3.3%
Fgn. bond 4.0%
Cash 18.3%
Cdn. equity 1.0%
Foreign equity 71.7%
Prof. equity 1.9%

Performance	Fund	Median
1-year % ret.	20.2	13.2
3-year % ret.	13.7	11.1
5-year % ret.	16.2	13.3

Source: PAL

who say Trimark is overweighted in North America could substitute Templeton International for Templeton Growth. Similarly, you could use Templeton International Balanced Fund instead of Templeton Global Balanced. Those already in particular families could substitute for the balanced fund: Dynamic Partners, Industrial Income, PH&N Balanced, etc.

RIP VAN WINKLE STRATEGY SUITS BEGINNING INVESTORS

The only caveat I'd make is that I wouldn't move from 100% cash to these mostly equity funds right now while global stock markets are still quite high. If, however, you plan to begin buying on a monthly or quarterly basis, taking advantage of dollar-cost averaging, then in the event of another correction like the one in October, you'd be getting units cheaper. This two-fund portfolio takes the fun out of the fund tracking and switching game, but it's doubtful all the energy spent on these pursuits would add to performance.

The table on the following page, prepared with Portfolio Analytics Ltd.'s PAL Trak software, shows that Rip would have done very well with an initial $10,000 investment made in 1987, adding $1,000 a month under the 80/20 asset-allocation ratio. Joy Wolfson, a planner with Manulife Securities International Ltd., questions the one-size-fits-all advice, but concedes the Rip strategy is "appropriate for beginning investors with modest portfolios. I agree that overdiversification is a common and expensive mistake made by many novices."

Christopher Horan of Equion Group, a financial planning firm, agrees that constant fund switching is pointless and that "people's investment failures usually result from such big mistakes as overweighting asset classes that have gone up or underweighting assets that have gone down. An experienced adviser is needed to keep their clients on course."

Toronto-based planner Glenn Neuman likes the Rip portfolio, and notes that "one of the major hurdles I encountered was the clients' will to diversify into several different funds. They have ascribed to the 'don't put all your eggs in one basket' theory and simply see a mutual fund as only one egg. Some clients get very suspicious if you try to concentrate their assets into two or three funds."

WHEN CHOOSING A FUND, LOOK AT THE MANAGEMENT EXPENSE RATIO (MER)

Fees-only planner Warren Baldwin, of T. E. Financial Consultants Ltd. says the Rip portfolio "makes sense" for portfolios between $30,000 and $50,000. Beyond that, he'd like to see more diversification of management. With $75,000 or more, Baldwin says he "would use a couple more funds immediately. In both cases, I would consider an appropriate fund from Phillips, Hager & North Ltd. or Bissett & Associates." Baldwin puts even more stress on low MERs: "Mr. Van Winkle's 'Dream Portfolio' is 54 basis points below the MER for the same portfolio using average MERs for the fund categories selected. Assume we are starting with zero in the RRSP portfolio and adding $12,000 per year over the next 25 years. Assume also that the portfolio grows at a compound rate of 10% per year. Assuming that an alternative average fund portfolio only grows at an annual rate of 9.46% [reduced due to the additional MER costs], the difference in accumulation after 25 years is almost $100,000. The MER on both PH&N and Bissett would further reduce the average MER for Mr. Van Winkle."

Baldwin adds that if going the broker-sold route, "we would negotiate the front-end load as low as possible." That's why Trimark Income Growth was selected over the higher-MER, normally rear-load Trimark Select Balanced, which some brokers will try to

RIP VAN WINKLE
PORTFOLIO

Allocation

Fund	Original investment at 9/87 $	Monthly contrib. $	Value at 5/97 $
Templeton Growth	2,000	200	58,124
Trimark Income Growth	8,000	800	200,914

Performance

Simple rate	Rip Van Winkle portfolio	Canada Savings Bonds	Inflation	5-year GIC
Last month %	3.64	0.25	0.00	0.40
Last quarter %	3.36	0.74	0.22	1.20
Last year %	17.24	3.93	1.70	5.25

Annualized rate

2 years %	16.27	4.69	1.45	5.78
3 years %	13.71	4.83	1.94	6.51
5 years %	14.67	5.22	1.49	6.57

Source: company reports

push first because of the immediate 4.5% commission. Ted Cadsby, CIBC Securities Inc.'s vice-president of marketing, believes that high net worth investors should strive to lower fees further by moving to "discretionary or pooled management, which can be cheaper and more tailored."

LABOR FUNDS' POTENTIAL OVERLOOKED

It's just as well the brave souls who invest in Canadian labor-sponsored venture capital funds are compelled to hold on for eight years. It's not just because they must repay the generous tax credits if they sell before the end of that period. A glance at the performance charts makes this special category of investment fund pale besides regular mutual funds. In a bull equity market, labor funds had an average return of -0.7% for the year ended Aug. 31, 1997, with the five-year and 10-year compound annual returns just 4.4% and 5.9% respectively. But comparisons to regular mutual funds are odious, says Denzil Doyle, chairman of the Capital Alliance Ventures Inc., an Ottawa-based technology labor fund. Doyle's $40-million fund was down 4.3% in the same one-year period, well below the 14% registered by labor-fund frontrunners Canadian Venture Opportunities and VenGrowth Investment.

LABOR FUNDS PAY OFF IN THE LONG TERM

Doyle says a labor fund should start to outperform a regular equity mutual fund after four or five years. But he would prefer investors pay more heed to the growth in employment rates and revenues of the underlying investments. He says that despite the unit-value decline of his fund, employment among the companies in Capital Alliance's portfolio has risen 39% since the investments were first made, and annualized revenues have increased 58%. As hybrids of venture capital funds and mutual funds, labor funds are "very different investment instruments than those the investment community has worked with in the past," he says. Their venture capital attributes mean they are long-term instruments unlikely to show any significant appreciation in the first five years. That's consistent with Ottawa's treatment of these funds: generous tax credits of 30% (half federal, half provincial) are proffered in return for a commitment by the investor not to redeem for at least eight years.

CASH LEVELS IN LABOR FUNDS NEVER DROP BELOW 20%

But their mutual fund attributes necessitate calculating unit values that reflect the values of the underlying companies. Those don't change much in the short term – the way publicly traded stocks do – because most companies held by labor funds are not publicly traded. Their values only change if there is a new round of investment, an initial public offering, a sale of the company to a third party, or a termination or bankruptcy, Doyle says. All labor funds start out with capital invested in government treasury bills or bonds, and they are compelled by legislation never to drop their cash levels below

20%. This provides liquidity for redemptions but also acts as a significant drag on performance, says Ron Begg, president of $823-million Working Ventures Canadian Fund.

As capital is invested, cash flow dries up and the value of the fund may drop, Doyle says. The only short-term prospect for appreciation is a second round of financing by another investor at a much higher price. Sometimes a venture capital firm may experience an IPO in one of its investee companies within months of the investment, but this is unlikely for labor funds because they are required to place much of their investments in early-stage

HOW LABOR FUNDS

COMPARE

Labor-sponsored funds with one-year track records

Fund name	Assets $ mil.	Simple rate of return		
		1mo.	6 mo.	1 yr.
C.I. Covington	104.6	1.8	2.2	11.2
Cdn Medical Discoveries	251.2	0.2	-3.8	1.1
Cdn Venture Opportunities	16.7	1.9	-0.6	14.2
Capital Alliance Ventures	40.1	-0.1	-2.0	-4.3
DGC Entertain. Ventures	7.5	-0.7	0.2	5.2
Enterprise Fund	8.5	1.2	-2.4	8.9
First Ontario	22.7	0.1	0.1	2.4
Fonds de solidarité	2,182.7	0.0	3.1	6.5
Retrocom Growth	34.7	1.3	3.6	4.2
Sportfund	13.0	-0.3	-1.8	5.8
Tourism & Enter. Growth	1.2	-12.9	-57.5	-84.6
Triax Growth	164.5	-0.6	-1.3	2.2
Trillium Growth Capital	8.3	0.6	-4.8	-3.8
VenGrowth Investment	139.5	0.1	2.4	14.0
Working Opportunity (EVCC)	161.4	1.1	3.1	5.8
Working Ventures Cdn.	827.7	-0.5	0.7	0.7
Average	190.7	-0.2	-2.5	-0.7
Median	16.7	0.0	0.0	4.7

firms. Another difference is the way investments are made and managed. Mutual fund managers rely on current and past financial information, while venture capital managers rely on business plans and operational scenarios.

CASHING IN LABOR FUNDS BEFORE MATURITY CAN RESULT IN LOSSES

"Testing the validity of those plans can be a complex task," Doyle says. To pick a labor fund, investors should analyse the potential of each of the companies in which the fund invests, he says. They should show incremental sales or rising market share and preferably "gaining market share in a growing market." Labor funds may also invest in firms with no sales at all, but which are still in research mode. Here the labor fund manager has to assess the capabilities of the entrepreneurs behind the firms.

A well-managed labor fund will invest in companies that will survive what Doyle terms the "death valley" period of its first three or four years. He expects that of 10 investments, three will be losers, four will be so-so survivors and three will be exceptional performers. While investors may expect little more than the generous tax credits, industry watcher Mary Macdonald predicts many will get a pleasant surprise when they see the growth of these funds five or eight years from now. A Macdonald study presented at an industry conference said $1.1 billion in venture capital investments would be made in Canada in 1997, much of it through the labor funds.

Macdonald is concerned because some of the original money invested with a five-year horizon will come free this year – the first big selling year was 1993, especially for

Working Ventures. She says the pressure to redeem at a time when the portfolios still are not mature will not be to anyone's benefit. That's why investment advisers like Patrick McKeough, editor of newsletter *The Successful Investor,* are wary about latecomers to labor funds, who in effect help pay for the early birds' liquidations.

BROKERAGE WRAP PROGRAMS ARE BOOMING

In what may be an admission that their constant tinkering and switching may be hurting their clients' investment returns, Canada's major brokerage firms are making an aggressive push into wrap accounts. Assets of Canadian wrap programs grew 94% to $4.6 billion between December 1994 and March 1997, according to Investor Economics Inc. Wrap accounts provide investment management, brokerage and custodial services, all "wrapped" together for one set fee, typically between 2.5% and 3% a year. These accounts appeal to clients who want custom-tailored managed products, full service and one-stop shopping, says ScotiaMcLeod Inc. president David Wilson.

WRAP ACCOUNT FEE STRUCTURE FEATURES A DIFFERENT WAY TO PAY FOR SERVICE
The fee-based approach of wrap programs eliminates the potential conflicts of interest that exist in a transaction- or commission-based model. Of course, as high net worth consultant Kelly Rodgers points out, "you pay a premium to have that transaction bias removed." The popularity of wrap programs also begs the question of what exactly brokers and financial planners have been doing all along to justify the generous commissions and trailer fees they get from stock and mutual fund transactions.

Rodgers points out roughly 1,200 of the 1,800 mutual and segregated funds in Canada are broker-sold load funds. Choosing among them, setting overall asset allocation and matching funds to investor temperament and objectives have presumably been the job of investment advisers all along, she suggests. "Clients don't like the commission aspect of traditional brokerages," she says. "[The wrap account] is a different way of paying for the advice and service brokers say they've been giving us for the past 20 years."

HIGH NET WORTH INVESTORS WILL BENEFIT THE MOST FROM WRAP ACCOUNTS
At the top of the market, wrap programs are often offered as a segregated service – they select individual securities. In Canada, this segment grew 177% in the 15-month period studied by Investor Economics. In the "middle" market are wrap accounts that use mutual funds or pooled funds as the underlying product. They grew 72% and 56% respectively over the same period. ScotiaMcLeod's Pinnacle program has joined RBC Dominion Securities' Sovereign program and AGF Trust's Harmony program in this middle ground of mutual fund and pooled fund wraps. ScotiaMcLeod was already in the upper end of the wrap business, with its three-year-old Weir program, which offers segregated investment management for investors with more than $500,000. Weir has $400 million in assets, according to associate director Robert Stiles.

Like the pioneering five-year-old $1.7-billion Sovereign program, Pinnacle is available to retail investors with a minimum $50,000 to invest. Pinnacle's annual fee is 2.5% for the first $250,000 of assets, dropping to 2.25% for up to $500,000; 2% for up to $1 million; and 1.5% thereafter. These are comparable to Sovereign's fees. Any additional fund expenses will be capped at 50 basis points. Nesbitt Burns Inc. has been developing a similar program called Quadrant, also with a $50,000 minimum investment. Pinnacle, Harmony and Sovereign use what Rodgers calls "private-label" mutual funds, which are available only in those particular wrap services. "They have been structured to resemble pooled funds, with fees charged outside, but are offered by prospectus to allow investments of less than $150,000," Rodgers says. Pooled funds, which are sold by offering memorandum, require a minimum $150,000 investment in Ontario.

INVESTMENT FIRMS PACKAGE SELECTED FUNDS TO OFFER ONE-STOP SHOPPING

Pinnacle employs various "model portfolios" built from 12 specially created funds. That's in contrast to the popular ($2.3 billion in assets) STAR program of Mackenzie Financial Corp., which uses various Mackenzie funds that are already available as the underlying products. STAR imposes a nominal 0.1% annual fee on top of the regular fund management fees. Pinnacle uses 12 mutual funds selected and monitored by NT Global Advisors, a subsidiary of Northern Trust Co. of Stamford, Conn. Each fund bears the Pinnacle prefix, and most are available in value and growth versions.

There are, for example, three Canadian equity funds: Pinnacle Canadian Growth Equity Fund, managed by Aurion Capital Management Inc.; a value fund managed by BonaVista Asset Management Ltd.; and a small-cap fund managed by Ultravest Investment Counsellors Inc. The service is non-discretionary, in this case meaning the individual investor works with a ScotiaMcLeod investment adviser to determine individual risk tolerance and to develop a customized asset allocation strategy. Pinnacle's target audience is investors whose assets lie mostly in directly held stocks or mutual funds or those with cash from business sales or inheritances. ScotiaMcLeod expects to generate $1 billion from the program over the next two years, according to Chris Hodgson, managing director of private client financial services.

WRAPPED FUNDS MAY NOT CONTAIN TOP PERFORMERS BUT VOLATILITY IS LESS

Bank of Nova Scotia has a third wrap program. The minimum investment in its Scotia Leaders program has been lowered to $10,000 from $25,000. Leaders uses a number of third-party load funds selected by economist Ranga Chand, but charges a hefty 1% annual fee on top of the 2% or so charged by the funds themselves.

Allen Clarke, vice-chairman of AGF Trust and the creator of Sovereign and Harmony, says brokers stand to make less money initially with wrap accounts than through transactions. The break-even point is four or five years, which benefits the client because "they don't switch around, so they get much better performance and no up-front fees. The client is better off, but so is the broker as the assets grow and he retains the business." For this reason, beginning brokers may shy away from wrap accounts. "It takes a mature broker with a big enough base" for wraps to pay off for the broker, Clarke says.

Investors also need to be aware that, by design, the mutual funds in these programs will never be top-performing funds, more likely falling into the second quartile. "But the volatility will be a lot less. That's the thing to watch," he adds.

LEVERAGE GENERATES BIG GAINS — OR LOSSES

Leverage is the strategy of trying to magnify your investment gains by borrowing money. Say you buy $1,000 worth of a stock and borrow from the bank to buy another $4,000 worth, and the stock value rises 20%. You end up with $6,000 in shares which, after the bank loan is repaid, means you have doubled your money (excluding carrying costs and broker's fees) rather than earning just $200.

That's great when stock markets are rising and money is relatively cheap. But you'd better be confident that your stock prices will appreciate and you're not near the beginning of a bear market. As anyone who has borrowed in the past and been hit with a correction knows, the downside can be scary. "Never forget you have a fixed liability against a variable asset," says Warren Baldwin, regional vice-president at T.E. Financial Consultants Ltd., a fees-only financial planning firm.

INTEREST CHARGED ON LEVERAGE FUNDS IS TAX DEDUCTIBLE

Still, government tax policy encourages the practice of leverage, since the interest charges are tax-deductible (although you can no longer write off RRSP loan interest). If you invested the tax refunds from investment interest charges, you could go even further in magnifying the potential gains, or any losses, as illustrated by the accompanying tables prepared for *The Financial Post* by financial author and speaker Talbot Stevens. The table's top section shows what happens after one year to an investment of $50,000, to which you add $117,000 on margin. This represents a 70% margin: your $50,000 represents 30% of the total investment of $167,000. The other 70% is borrowed from your broker at 7.5% interest. The table factors in taxation, assuming a 50% marginal tax rate, and assumes all the investment comes in the form of capital gains, three-quarters of which are taxable. It also assumes capital losses are used to offset capital gains.

PERCENTAGE OF LEVERAGE AVAILABLE IS DETERMINED BY STOCK VALUE

You'd be ahead if the stocks or equity funds you bought returned more than 7.5%, which is the typical current rate for an investment loan. If the stock fell by 10%, though, your losses would be much greater than the gains from a 10% increase in the stock price. Margin rates on stocks vary with their price. According to Greg Clarke, vice-president of the Investment Dealers Association of Canada, dealers are not supposed to lend any money at all for illiquid securities or stocks selling for less than $1.50. For stocks between $1.50 and $1.75, brokers will lend you 20% and you have to put up 80%. Between $1.75 and $2, they can lend 40%. Above $2, it's 50%.

Finally, there is a list of about 300 highly liquid stocks on which dealers will lend you 70%. This group of stocks has to meet the criteria for listing of options under the Canadian Derivatives Clearing Corp., Clarke says. Many firms set their own margin rates, and may be even more (or less) selective. Mutual fund investors generally can get 50% margin from their broker, but Stevens said they can often leverage 100% of the purchase by arranging their own financing. And because of their inherent diversification, mutual funds are less exposed to downside risk than single stocks. "[The downside is why] I educate and only endorse conservative leverage that is long-term [minimum 10 years] and diversified, and where the margin call is eliminated, with a trusted adviser," Stevens says.

THE BREAK-EVEN POINT ON LEVERAGED INVESTMENT IS LOWER AND DECREASES OVER TIME
He defines conservative leverage as the type in which long-term annual cash flow is able to finance at least the interest expense and possibly repay some principal, too. That way, the interest expense does not compound and risk is reduced. The break-even point is lower and decreases over time. Given the variety of personal situations, Stevens calcu-

AFTER TAX VALUES
AND COMPOUND RETURNS AFTER ONE YEAR

Investment of $50,000, with 70% margin borrowed at 7.5% interest rate

Before-tax return %	From	After-tax value after 1 year $		After-tax compound annual returns %	
		Unleveraged	Leveraged	Unleveraged	Leveraged
12.0	A good stock gain	53,750	57,031	7.5	14.1
10.0	A good equity fund	53,125	54,948	6.3	9.9
7.5	Current 5-year money	52,344	52,344	4.7	4.7
0.0	A mediocre investment	50,000	44,531	0.0	-10.9
-10.0	Recent gold funds	48,875	34,115	-6.3	-31.8
-43.0	Bre-X collapse	36,562	0	-26.9	-100.0
-85.0	Bre-X collapse	23,437	(44,010)	-53.0	-188.0

Losses would be greater if capital losses can't offset capital gains.

After-tax values and compound returns after 10 years

Before-tax return %	Unleveraged	After-tax value after 10 years $		Unleveraged	After-tax compound annual returns %	
		Leveraged, R0%	Leveraged, R100%		Leveraged, R0%	Leveraged, R100%
12.0	115,808	191,992	247,160	8.8	14.4	17.3
10.0	99,804	138,648	190,545	7.2	10.7	14.3
7.5	83,157	83,157	131,363	5.2	5.2	10.1
3.9	64,565	21,182	64,767	2.6	-8.2	2.6
2.4	58,364	0	42,388	1.6	-36.7	-1.6
0.0	50,000	game over	12,019	0.0	game over	-13.3
10.0	29,646	game over	game over	-5.1	game over	game over

R0% means refund from interest expense deduction is not reinvested; R100% means refund reinvested.
Game over means leverage loan would be terminated; therefore can't have negative balances
Source: Talbot Stevens for *The Financial Post*

lated the average annual compound return a leveraged investor needs to break even – that is, to cover the interest on the loan as well as the capital gains tax due when the investment is sold. Using present value math, he adjusted for inflation ($1 of interest paid today is inherently worth more than $1 of earnings realized 10 years from now). As can be seen from the table on the previous page, the longer a leveraged investor holds on, the lower the break-even rate of return.

RETIREMENT-ORIENTED INVESTORS SHOULD CONSIDER 10- OR 20-YEAR HORIZON

Thane Stenner, vice-president of Midland Walwyn Capital Inc., doesn't go so far as some planners who suggest that houses be remortgaged to provide investment capital. He recommends a home be paid off first and maximum RRSP contributions be made each year. Stenner then suggests high income earners borrow one year's worth of discretionary income against their home – say, $22,500 on an annual income of $100,000 – and invest that money in a conservative global equity fund. The second part of the table shows Stevens' leveraging analysis over the 10-year horizon that most retirement-oriented investors should be considering. (Twenty years would be better.) It does not track the downside of the poor investments shown in the top chart because no rational investor would keep reinvesting in such money-losing investments.

LOWER INTEREST RATES MEAN LOWER ADVANTAGE TO LEVERAGING

The table entries labelled "game over" do not show negative balances because the leverage loan would be quickly terminated by the broker. The table also shows how further gains (or losses) would arise by reinvesting the tax refund generated by the interest-expense deduction. "Leveraging may not be as effective a way of generating financial wealth in the 1990s" as it was in the 1980s, concludes Jim Rogers, chairman of Vancouver-based Rogers Group. In . edited by John St. Croix (Uphill Publishing Ltd.), Rogers writes, "though we are now experiencing relatively low interest rates, the spread between the cost of borrowed money and the rate of return is often much lower too, reducing the potential advantage of leveraging."

POOLED FUNDS OFFER EASY DIVERSIFICATION

Pooled funds do not receive nearly so much ink as mutual funds but, at certain levels of wealth, the "pooleds" have several advantages. Think of pooled funds as mutual funds sold wholesale by big banks, trust companies, pension managers and independent investment counsellors. Typical pooled funds will cost 1% or 1.5% a year in management fees, or about half the retail cost of 2% to 3% that goes with most equity mutual funds.

You do not see pooled funds advertised on television, nor are they accompanied by road shows or direct-mail blitzes. All that costs money. With pooled funds, about 1% a year stays in your pocket instead of going to brokers, ad agencies and other middlemen. However, pooled funds carry a higher than normal minimum investment. In Ontario, under "sophisticated investor" rules, the pooled fund minimum is $150,000, which puts them out of reach of many Canadians. Unlike mutual funds, pooled funds are not sold with a prospectus. Instead, they are accompanied by an offering memorandum. Conceptually, though, pooled funds are similar to mutual funds. As the name implies, assets of many clients are combined, or pooled, into one account and the investors receive units of the account proportional to their investment.

A FUND CAN BE MARKETED AS A POOLED OR A MUTUAL FUND BY THE SAME FIRM

The distinction between pooleds and mutual funds is particularly fine at certain firms. For instance, Vancouver-based Phillips Hager & North Ltd. has pooled funds for its pension clients, but almost identical no-load mutual funds for its individual investors. Usually, the mutual funds have more securities. Investment adviser Patrick McKeough suggests pooled-fund managers typically buy and hold stock. They are under less pressure than their mutual fund counterparts to show short-term performance gains. Internal trading costs, therefore, may be lower than with aggressively run mutual funds. Affluent investors seeking to hand over their nest eggs to a discretionary investment manager usually have the choice of pooled funds or separately managed accounts. The difference is that a manager is picking and holding stocks for the investor in a segregated or "separately managed" account. That means it can be tailored to individual preferences.

On the other hand, the distinctiveness of segregated portfolios may be overstated. Paul Starita, former chairman of CIBC Securities Inc., says "the reality is almost all the private managers pool their funds, no matter how they report them to you. It is efficient and consistent with good management."

POOLED FUNDS ARE A GOOD INVESTMENT IF YOU COME INTO A LARGE INFUSION OF CASH

Kelly Rodgers, author of *The Insider's Guide to Selecting the Best Money Manager,* says discretionary managers who offer both segregated and pooleds often "try to push people into pools." That is because it's easier for the firm, with the administrative and other efficiencies that pooling makes possible. Pooled funds can offer quick and easy diversification, particularly for investors who come into a large one-time infusion of cash. "But they're not so good if you have existing holdings because to go into pooled funds you have to sell your holdings," Rodgers says. "That can create a tax event, which is not advantageous for some people." Buying pooled funds late in the calendar year also makes you liable to tax on distribution of capital gains at the end of the year, even though you did not benefit from them most of the year. That is the same problem faced by mutual fund investors.

Over the past 10 years, information technology has developed to the point that cost-effective management can be made available to smaller asset pools. That same technology also makes it possible to run segregated portfolios for about the same cost as pooleds.

Pooleds may appeal to investors who are seeking a particular management style – for example, an actively traded bond portfolio for an RRSP.

DISCONTENT SPURS GIC ALTERNATIVES

These are desperate times for people living on a fixed income. As GICs roll over at rates less than half what they were five years ago, the siren call of the stock market or equity mutual funds is getting louder. But moving out of fixed-income products into today's stock markets is a scary proposition for those who can't afford to lose their precious capital. As a seminar given recently by Bank of Nova Scotia made all too clear, senior citizens in particular are facing a triple-barrelled dilemma.

In addition to what appear to be chronically low interest rates, the average person's life expectancy is rising. Meanwhile, the federal government is slashing universal benefits and, by moving up the RRSP maturity deadline to age 69 from 71, has reduced the retirement-savings period.

NEW GICS LET YOU PLAY THE STOCK MARKET WHILE PROTECTING INVESTMENT CAPITAL

Seniors whose RRSPs have been converted to registered retirement income funds (RRIFs) are facing a yearly erosion of their capital if their plan is invested solely in traditional GICs, warns Scotiabank manager of investor services Bob Lamb. That's because the current average 5% yield of a five-year GIC is lower than the 7.38% minimum annual RRIF payout. As a result, Scotiabank and several rivals have introduced what at first blush appear to be ideal solutions to the GIC dilemma: varieties of GICs that

HOW INDEXED-LINKED INVESTMENTS | COMPARE

Name	Underlying equity index	Cap on return	Term	How interest computed
Scotia two-year Stock Index GIC	TSE 35	20% (formerly 30%)	2 years	index level at maturity
Scotia G7 Stock Indexed GIC	7 global indexes	30% over 3 yrs.	3 years	index level at maturity
Scotia McLeod TSE 35 Bull Note	TSE 35	90% over 4 yrs.	4 years	index level at maturity
TD GIC Plus	TSE 100	no	3/5 years	based on averages
CIBC Stock Market Advantage	TSE 35	no	3/5 years	averaging over term
Sun Life Trust Global Index GIC	MSCI world index	no	5 years	averaging
Credit-union index-linked term deposit	TSE 35	no	3/5 years	monthly averaging
London Life	TSE 35	no	3 years	averaging formula

promise some participation in the stock market but also protect invested capital from the market's downside.

These new hybrids are called index-linked GICs. They're not perfect but it's true that, should markets crash, you get back your principal (but no interest). If stocks continue to rise, they offer potentially higher interest payouts, although some issuers limit the gains by capping the payout at a predetermined level.

These hybrid GICs don't pay dividends. You are participating only in the capital gains of the underlying stocks. Most are eligible for RRSPs but few, if any, can be held inside a RRIF.

INDEX-LINKED GICS LOCK UP MONEY FOR TWO, THREE OR FIVE YEARS

You also are locking up your money for two, three or five years. And, unlike cashable GICs, Canada Savings Bonds or the new Canada RRSP bonds, index-linked GICs are not redeemable. Finally, if held outside an RRSP, you pay tax on interest income, not the more favorably treated capital gains. There are also significant differences in how the interest is paid out. Most payouts are based on some averaging formula, but some are based on the final level of the index when the GIC matures. There are advantages and disadvantages to both.

Credit unions and National Bank of Canada pioneered index-linked GICs several years ago, with limited sales success. In 1996, Scotiabank also launched an index-linked GIC – a two-year version tied to the return of the Toronto Stock Exchange's Toronto 35 index. In early 1997, Scotia added two new variants: a fully RRSP-eligible global stock-indexed GIC under the bank's label, and the Toronto 35 index bull note, marketed by its ScotiaMcLeod Inc. stock brokerage. The latter is not a GIC, but rather a four-year note redeemable at any time.

OTHER GIC ALTERNATIVES

• Canada Trust introduced World Market GIC in early 1997, a five-year GIC capped at a 100% total return, or the equivalent of 15% compounded annually. It is fully RRSP-eligible but, unlike global mutual funds, currency exposure is limited to the C$.
• CIBC launched Stock Market Advantage GIC around the same time. It's available in three- and five-year terms and tracks the TSE 35.
• Toronto Dominion Bank's GIC Plus, introduced in the fall of 1996, is available in terms of three and five years, with returns based on the TSE 100 index.

Bank of Montreal has come up with Savings Portfolio, which packages a GIC with bond and dividend mutual funds. Royal Bank Financial Group has introduced GICs linked to the TSE, as well as to world market indexes. Financial institutions are reluctant to describe what they're doing behind the scenes to make these GICs tick. Essentially, they lock in most of the principal (say, 70% to 90%) with a zero-coupon bond. Equity participation is achieved through derivatives, typically call options that provide a gain if the underlying index rises.

Critics of index-linked GICs say you can do all this on your own and cut out the middleman's mark-up, an amount that banks are reluctant to divulge. But it's believed to be comparable with mutual funds' annual management expense ratios of 2% to 3%. "My one-liner on these are they're all junk," says Moshe Milevsky, a professor of finance at York University's Schulich School of Business. Milevsky gives some compelling arguments that investors would be better off cooking up their own combinations, such as putting 70% of their capital in a regular GIC and investing the balance in equity mutual funds.

FOR THE RISK-AVERSE INVESTOR, INDEX-LINKED GICS MAY BE THE WAY TO GO

But some financial planners say the new hybrid GICs may be appropriate for extremely risk-averse investors or those who do not want to create their own capital-protection scheme. Equity or balanced funds may be better investments for younger investors. But if forced to choose between basic GICs and index-linked GICs, even Milevsky concedes the latter might be the better choice. "What may be intellectually the thing to do is less important than what will sit well in the oldsters' tummies," says Jim Rogers, chairman of the Rogers Group, a Vancouver-based financial planning firm. "The banks know their market and the ultimate test of whether an investment is appropriate is the tummy test."

STRIP BONDS ARE FIXED-INCOME ALTERNATIVES

The recent global wave of stock market jitters has caused more than a few investors to reconsider the fixed-income portion of their portfolios. For Canadian RRSP investors, strip bonds, "strips" for short, have long been a favorite fixed-income alternative to the popular GIC. Understanding the concept of strips requires some knowledge about normal government or corporate bonds. Basically, bonds are debt instruments used by corporations or governments to borrow money. They "bond" or promise to repay the lender (you) the money at some point in the future (the maturity date), along with an agreed-upon interest rate paid periodically, also called the "coupon."

However, an investment dealer can "strip" this coupon from the bond, leaving a "residual." Both portions can be sold separately to investors. The coupons are normally sold to individual retail investors. Because they come in maturities of up to 30 years, they are ideal investments for RRSPs or RRIFs. Institutions tend to use the residuals because they can take advantage of time horizons that are often longer than those that apply to coupons. The "coupon" is a promise to pay interest. The bond residual, also called a "zero-coupon" bond, is a promise to pay the principal amount when due, along with any interest coupons that were not stripped away.

Both the coupons and the residual generate interest income because they are sold at a hefty discount to their face value. For this reason, Nate Mechanic, broker with RBC Dominion Securities, compares a strip with "a long-term treasury bill. Instead of maturing in three months, it matures 10 or 20 years later." While some brokers charge a $5,000 minimum to buy strips, there are some who will put through a trade for as little as $1,000. When you buy a strip, you specify the face value – what it will be worth on maturity. The further out that is, the less it will cost per $100 of face value.

THE MARKET PRICE FOR STRIPPED COUPONS RISES AND FALLS WITH INTEREST RATES

In the fall of 1997, for example, it cost $14.61 to purchase a $100 coupon maturing in the year 2028, for a yield of 6.58% annually. A $100 coupon maturing in 2020 would cost $24.52 for a yield of 6.52%, says Mechanic. These prices include brokerage commissions. A good explanation is contained in the book Investing for Income by Hugh Anderson (Penguin Books, 1996). Like regular bonds, the market price of coupons and residuals "varies as interest rates rise and fall but usually in much bigger swings," Anderson writes. "Their price will, however, gradually rise toward their face value as the time for payment of the face amount approaches."

IF YOU HOLD YOUR STRIPS TO MATURITY, YOU KNOW HOW MUCH THEY ARE WORTH

One advantage of strips is they eliminate re-investment risk. With regular bonds, fluctuations in interest rates can change your return assumptions when it comes time to re-invest – something investors facing rollovers of GICs have found to their dismay. With a strip, there are no interest payments to re-invest. As long as you hold it till maturity, you know exactly how much it will be worth.

The disadvantage may arise if you wish to sell strips before maturity. As Anderson notes, the absence of regular interest payments makes their market prices very volatile. When interest rates rise, strip prices fall further and faster than regular bonds. On the other hand, when interest rates drop, strip prices rise more than regular bonds.

TO AVOID TAXES, KEEP YOUR STRIPS IN AN RRSP

Even though you don't actually receive income from a strip bond every year, Revenue Canada takes the position that you have received the imputed interest for the year. Therefore, strips are best held inside registered plans rather than outside. Most financial advisers suggest creating a laddered series of strips maturing at different times in your projected retirement.

For RRSP clients, Warren Baldwin, vice-president at no-fee planner T.E. Financial Ltd., prefers strips to most fixed-income alternatives and particularly to bond mutual funds with their hefty management expense ratios. Mechanic likes strips for the fixed-income component of a 45-year-old's portfolio. But he also sees a place for bond funds in RRIFs or for elderly clients who aren't equipped to keep on top of interest rate and bond market shifts.

SEEKING PROFESSIONALLY MANAGED MONEY

It's probably safe to say most Canadian investors end up with a stock broker or financial planner more or less by default. At some point you decided to buy 100 shares of IBM or Bell Canada. Odds are you got a name from a friend or colleague or finally consented to give a shot to a cold-calling new broker. Alternatively, you may have stumbled on a mutual-fund-dispensing "financial planner" at a free "educational" seminar. Either way, you were sold on the services offered. In contrast, discretionary investment management or managed money is bought, says Kelly Rodgers, president of Toronto-based Rodgers Investment Consulting.

Just as people progress through a life cycle that includes adolescence, youth, marriage, parenthood and on up to retirement, there is also an investing life cycle. What Rodgers calls the "life cycle of the high net worth investor" starts with high income, moves to affluence (net worth of between $250,000 and $2 million) and finally to true wealth ($2 million plus). Somewhere along this upward trajectory, the objective changes from "aggressive growth" to "capital preservation."

IF YOUR ASSETS ARE AT LEAST $500,000, YOU NEED AN INVESTMENT COUNSELLOR

Beginning investors tend to start with stockbrokers or mutual funds, in part because they haven't accumulated enough wealth to hire a professional investment counsellor. True discretionary management tends not to be available until you have at least $500,000 in assets, although broker-sold mutual fund "wrap" accounts are available to those with $50,000. The role of investment counsellors is "to meet the unique needs of each client," Rodgers says. Since individual objectives for income and growth vary widely, the first step is for the client and counsellor to determine objectives and develop a portfolio that will meet them.

This process is documented by creating an investment policy statement. The portfolio manager may work with a client's accountants, lawyers, financial planner or other consultants to devise the final investment plan. Responsibility for security selection rests solely with the portfolio manager. This "discretionary" nature of investment counselling is a distinguishing feature of the industry. "For some clients, relinquishing control is initially difficult to accept," Rodgers writes, "but given the education and experience required to qualify as a portfolio manager and the high standards of professionalism that govern the industry, it is more readily accepted over time."

A FINANCIAL COUNSELLOR EARNS PERCENTAGE OF MARKET VALUE OF PORTFOLIO

Counsellors do not receive any compensation or commission for buying and selling stocks, bonds or other securities. "Being free from this potential conflict of interest means that the investment counsellor is rewarded only for managing the portfolio in accordance with the clients' objectives," Rodgers says. This freedom from transaction bias may be the most appealing feature for many investors.

Fees are calculated as a percentage of the market value of the portfolio being managed. Most counsellors have a set fee schedule that tapers down as a portfolio size grows. These charges are considerably lower than those of retail mutual funds or full-service stockbrokers, Rodgers says. Funds invested by investment counsellors are held by an independent custodian, usually a trust company. Custodial service fees may be billed separately or be included in the investment counselling fee. Investment counsellors are regulated by provincial securities commissions and must have distinct educational and work qualifications to become registered.

AN INVESTMENT COUNSELLOR FOLLOWS STRICT ETHICAL AND PROFESSIONAL STANDARDS

Most investment counselling firms are members of the Association of Investment Management & Research. This Virginia-based organization supervises strict ethical and professional standards and awards the chartered financial analyst (CFA) designation carried by many portfolio managers. This does not mean affluent investors do not or should not patronize stockbrokers. The decision to make your own stock picks, with some input from a broker, or to recognize your incompetence or lack of interest and delegate investment decisions to a professional counsellor will obviously vary with your temperament, ability and the time available to spend on your investments.

If you had perfect information, it's true a concentrated portfolio of a few well-chosen stocks may outperform highly diversified managed products. At one point, super-investor Warren Buffett had US$2 billion spread among just three stocks. But most of us are not Warren Buffetts and neither are our brokers. The brokerage channel accounts for 20% of the $1.2 trillion of Canadian financial assets. Only the deposit-taking branch networks of the banks hold more of our savings, according to Earl Bederman of Toronto-based Investor Economics Inc. Brokerage firms continue to grow. The traditional transaction-based portion of the business (where brokers charge commissions for buying or selling investments) is expanding at 15% a year. Significantly, the fee-based portion is growing at 44%, Bederman says.

EXPECT PERFORMANCE FROM YOUR INVESTMENT COUNSELLOR IN A BEAR MARKET

Many an investor has fled to professionally managed money after experiencing losses on ill-considered stock trades. Such losses may be minimal in a bull market. Investment counsellors have more trouble finding clients when all is going well. It's during a bear market that counsellors really earn their keep, Rodgers says. The hazards of amateur stock-picking have been depicted in such books as Fred Schwed Jr.'s *Where are the Customers' Yachts?* (written in 1940 and republished in 1995 by Wiley Investment Classics). With commissions ranging from 8.5% on small trades to 1.5% on large trades, there's always the temptation for a broker to "churn" your account, contributing to a down payment on a yacht for him, not you.

Some investors who have got to the high net worth stage may opt to keep some of their "fun money" with a broker, the better to bet on junior golds like Bre-X Minerals Ltd. or obscure technology stocks that promise to be "the next Microsoft." But many opt to place the bulk of their assets – their "serious money" – with a discretionary manager. The hard part is to convince yourself you are an amateur investor and that you may have been expecting too much from your broker. You must realize that you and your broker are sharing responsibility for your investment health. "Brokers advise and make recommendations, they do not manage," Rodgers says. "Some people with serious money continue to deal with brokers because they think they're getting management, but they're not."

STOCKBROKERS DON'T HAVE TIME TO EFFECTIVELY MANAGE A HIGH NET WORTH PORTFOLIO

Investors have to be aware of what a broker is licensed and qualified to do and where the final responsibility lies. "If you're the type of client that does what your broker says, then you're abdicating responsibility and should be in a managed product or with a manager," Rodgers says. One investment adviser who works in a brokerage and caters to the high net worth market agrees and recommends using consultants such as Rodgers to pick an investment counsellor. "There are all kinds of strong reasons to go to a fee-based manager over a commission-based broker and probably over a fee-based broker," says the adviser, who asked not to be identified.

A typical broker tracks hundreds of stocks for hundreds of clients. Either they spend so much time on service they can't keep on top of the market or the reverse. More experienced brokers may have fewer, more affluent clients and be better able to juggle those twin demands. For the average investor, "it's a mug's game picking stocks," says the adviser. "Trading stocks on your own is reckless. The only time it may be appropriate is if you buy them for dividends and you hold them for decades."

WHAT ARE STOCKBROKERS' COMMISSIONS?

Do you know how much commission you're paying when you buy stocks through your full-service broker? Odds are you don't. Brokerage houses used to operate on a schedule of fixed commissions, but following deregulation in 1986, they were free to set their own rates. Now, most investors have to wait until they get a confirmation slip to find out how much they've paid the broker.

Shopping around is difficult because many brokerages refuse to provide commission schedules even to existing clients. This appears to be the way Canada's mostly bank-owned brokerages like it. While the banks' discount brokerage firms freely give out their commission schedules, their full-service arms – with the exception of CIBC Wood Gundy Securities Inc. – wouldn't provide them when asked. The few large full-service independents, such as Midland Walwyn Inc., also would not co-operate. "The firms are sensitive" about commission rates, said one broker. "The discrepancies can be enormous."

Nor does the Investment Dealers Association of Canada centralize this information for investors. Thomas Dalzell, IDAC's vice-president of government and member relations, says there's wide variation among firms. In an informal survey, he found average commissions worked out to a fairly stiff 3.75% to 4.25% for trades of $2,000 or less. Because of minimum commissions, many investors unwittingly pay 8% or more on trades of $1,000 or less. Most brokers use some variation on a commission grid in which different rates kick in at certain break points. Dalzell found the key break points are at trade values of $2,500, $5,000, $10,000, $25,000, $50,000 and $100,000. The biggest discrepancies are at the lower levels. For a $10,000 trade, most commissions were between 1.36% and 1.8%. They fell to 0.7% to 1.1% at $50,000.

INVESTORS CAN AND SHOULD NEGOTIATE COMMISSION FEES
Based on calls to brokers, the average commission on a Canadian stock trade seems to hover around 2% plus a small per share charge. One RBC Dominion Securities Inc. broker says he charges 2% on all stocks, similar to the average mutual fund commission. If you're a particularly valuable client, a commission of 0.5% to 1% would be considered normal. In fact, at some point the full-service commission may actually be lower than at a discount brokerage. Firms don't like setting rates in stone because investors can and should negotiate better ones. "There's really no such thing as normal commission rates," says TD Evergreen Investment Services vice-president Ana Escubedo. "We allow our investment advisers to be flexible."

Some brokers will give discounts of 20% to 50% or more from the house grid; others won't budge. Commissions also drop rapidly on U.S. trades. If the principal exceeds US$2,500, Wood Gundy's commission on a U.S. trade is 0.9% of the principal value plus $22. Commission on US$20,000 worth of U.S. stock (priced above US$1 a share) is 0.6% plus $82. Beyond US$30,000, it drops to just 0.4% plus $142. Some brokers make a distinction between "unsolicited" trades initiated by the client and those that originate with the brokerage. In the first case, a discount would be appropriate since the broker did little more than execute a trade that any discount brokerage could have done. Beware of the minimum commission of $75 to $85. On a $1,000 trade, that's a hefty 8.5%, or 17% on a round trip (a buy followed by a sell). The minimum charge reflects about half an hour of administrative work.

COMMISSION DISCOUNTS ARE RARELY AVAILABLE ON SMALL TRANSACTIONS
A similar situation crops up in the case of parents or grandparents buying a few shares for their children or grandchildren. The trade doesn't make sense on the numbers alone, although some firms will put them through with a discount for customer goodwill purposes. Commissions on small trades can be three times lower at the discount brokers. But as the full-service firms' grid kicks in at bigger trades, the difference becomes less

dramatic. Responsible full-service brokers advise waiting until you have $5,000 to buy a stock. The alternative for smaller amounts is to use a discount brokerage or to buy additional units of a mutual fund.

If you value the services of your full-service broker but don't want to get dinged on small trades, you may get the best of both worlds by maintaining both a full-service and discount brokerage account.

Such a hybrid strategy is now feasible since the discount brokerages have waived their fees on self-directed RRSP accounts of more than $25,000. An alternative is to use DRIPS and SPPs (dividend reinvestment and share purchase plans). This strategy is described in the book *Commission-Free Investing* by Cemil Otar (Uphill Publishing), which focuses on three dozen Canadian blue chips, including BCE Inc. and most of the banks, that allow you to make regular commission-free investments.

CHAPTER 7

TAX | PLANNING

- Tax basics

- Measuring after-tax investment returns

- Income splitting

- Drawing up a strategy

- Trusts

FIVE STEPS TO SIMPLIFYING

TAX-PLANNING UNCERTAINTIES | BY ARTHUR DRACHE

IT IS INTERESTING, IN LOOKING BACK over the past two decades, to see that in terms of the fundamentals of tax planning, not much has changed. Arguably, there are five main rules that have to be followed, and that was as true in 1978 as it is now.

TAX DEFERRALS

There is little doubt one of the most significant planning techniques revolves around the deferral of tax payable. There are two potential benefits from deferral: the fact that marginal tax rates may be lower in the future (much retirement planning, such as the use of RRSPs, is based in part on this premise) and the fact that deferring taxes in effect discounts the final bill. Lately, with interest rates low, the discounting effect is less significant than it was. But the value of deferring taxes cannot be underestimated, whether we are looking at short-term deferral or longer-term deferral through the use of companies, tax-sheltered investments or the holding of appreciated assets for later sale.

INCOME SPLITTING

So long as we have a progressive tax system and individuals within the family are separately taxed, there will be major tax benefits in shifting income from the higher-income taxpayer to the lower-income individual. Most often, this is done between spouses or between parents and children. In some cases, the tax system itself allows such splitting (for example, through spousal RRSPs) but more often, splitting can be arranged only through careful and sophisticated tax planning. There is little doubt that for the most part, a major trend in amendments to the income tax system in Canada over the past 15 years has been an attack by the government (both through statute amendments and court challenges) on income splitting, which in itself is testimony to the effectiveness of this approach.

CONVERSION OF INCOME

Because different types of income are taxed in different ways, a significant amount of planning revolves around setting the stage to characterize income receipts. Until a few years ago the main focus was on achieving capital gains, and while the bias in their favor is not as great as it once was, it still exists. But now, Canadian corporate dividends may be taxed at an even lower rate. It is important to decide whether you would rather get an investment yield as interest, dividends or capital gains. An important facet of incorporating is the ability to decide the form of remuneration taken from a company, taking the tax consequences into account. Also, older Canadians should annuitize some funds to get pension income eligible for the pension income tax credit.

OFFSHORE PLANNING

This technique includes all forms of tax planning involving the use of offshore business plans and residence. As with most forms of tax planning, the laws have been changed so often that planning has become much more difficult and sophisticated than in the past. But greater international mobility means a greater segment of the population is in a position to consider offshore planning, up to and including giving up Canadian residence.

MAXIMIZING CREDITS

One of the major changes in the tax system since 1978 has been the replacement of many deductions with tax credits, including refundable credits. Especially for people on lower incomes, planning to maximize everything from child benefit credits to provincial low-income credits, not to mention avoiding clawbacks on tax credits and transfer payments, has become a key element of sophisticated tax planning, one which barely existed 15 years ago. Related to this is the avoidance of other levies, such as high probate fees (in Ontario especially) as part of estate planning.

Also linked to this technique is the need to ensure maximum use of allowable deductions, such as for child-care costs, moving expenses and relocation reimbursement, all of which may require sophisticated planning. The tax system has become ever more sophisticated and complicated over the past 20 years. Almost all the changes – even the massive rate cuts in 1981-82 and 1987-88 – have carried a price: added complexity and a system designed to limit the use of basic planning techniques.

Even socially progressive changes, such as the recognition of common-law relationships, were prompted not by a desire to bring the tax system into line with reality but to protect government revenue against "undue" claims for tax credits associated with children born to couples who have chosen not to get married. There is no doubt that tax planning is significantly harder now than it was in 1978, but the basics remain the same. There are only a handful of true tax-planning techniques. All the rest simply represent an attempt to maximize the use of these basic rules. To borrow from an ancient story: "This is the law. All else is commentary."

MAKE TAX RULES WORK TO THE ADVANTAGE

For most people, tax planning is much the same as flossing your teeth. You can't argue with the benefits, but the process is less than toothsome. And while it doesn't make you any extra money, it can help you keep more of what you have already earned. So to help you beat the taxman, here are 10 suggestions for tax planning.

1. A BIG REFUND MAY SEEM LIKE A WINDFALL, BUT IT MEANS POOR TAX PLANNING.

If you have large tax deductions (such as alimony or maintenance, high RRSP contributions, tax shelter investments, business losses, etc.), tell the source deductions department at your local Revenue Canada office. Request permission to have your employer withhold less tax from your paycheque so you can take home more.

2. AVOIDING MORTGAGE INTEREST IS IMPOSSIBLE (WELL THAT'S MY PERSONAL EXPERIENCE).

But how can it be made tax deductible? Interest incurred to finance investments or a business is generally tax deductible. Your goal should be to convert your mortgage debt (or some of it) into an investment or business loan. For example, you may have a $125,000 mortgage and a $125,000 investment portfolio (if you're lucky). Sell the portfolio and use the funds to pay off the mortgage. Immediately borrow the funds again, using the house as security, to repurchase the portfolio. As the purpose of the loan is to buy the investment portfolio (as opposed to a house), the interest is tax deductible. However, don't forget about the income tax that may arise on the sale of the portfolio, the selling and buying commissions and early mortgage repayment fees. If you don't have an investment portfolio equal to your mortgage, perhaps you have a portfolio that could be liquidated to take advantage of your annual "up to 10%" mortgage principal paydown opportunity. The result – part of your mortgage interest becomes tax deductible. If you're self-employed and work out of your home, a portion of your mortgage interest can be deductible, too.

3. CAN YOU EXCHANGE SOME TAXABLE BENEFITS FOR NON-TAXABLE BENEFITS?

How about giving up a little salary in return for employer-funded pension and/or profit-sharing plans? How about club fees where your membership helps further your employer's business opportunities? Changing jobs? This is the best time to negotiate. How about stock options? Do you have to move? Ensure moving expenses and related matters are designed to be tax-free. How about a no- or low-interest home purchase loan? These are not completely tax-free, but less costly than regular mortgages.

4. FOR THE MOST PART, LEAVING CANADA LETS YOU LEAVE OUR TAX SYSTEM BEHIND.

There is, however, a "departure tax." It's an income tax calculated on the assumption you sold all your assets. This "sale" will trigger taxes on accrued capital gains. However, there are many exceptions that you will want to fall into and you should talk to a tax adviser before leaving the country. Don't forget about the tax system of your adopted country. It will want a piece of you, too. Knowledge of your new country's tax system is a must.

5. IS THERE ANYTHING ELSE YOU CAN DO TO BEAT THE TAXMAN?

If your only income is from your job and you are already making your maximum RRSP contributions, is there anything else you can do? Maybe – and you only have to look as far as mom and dad. Parents can have significant income tax liabilities when they die. The "death" tax is based on the capital gain calculated under the assumption that the parent's assets are sold at the time of death for a price equal to the current value. The capital gains are taxed in the deceased's final return. Tax is owed but no cash has been received as the sale occurred for income tax purposes only. This tax reduces the value of the estate available to be passed on to the heir. You say your parents have no assets with accruing capital gains?

Don't forget the full value of RRSPs and RRIFs goes into the final return to be taxed. Ouch! Also, if your parents have U.S. assets, there is another tax system to worry about. The U.S. has both income and estate taxes. Ensure your parents' taxes on death are minimized as well as their exposure to U.S. estate tax and provincial probate fees. It's called estate planning – making sure your parents' affairs are organized to the benefit of their heirs and not to the benefit of Revenue Canada.

6. OUR TAX RULES PERMIT MOST OF US TO SELL OUR HOMES ON A TAX-FREE BASIS.

This is true where a home is designated as a principal residence. However, a principal residence does not have to be a city home. It can be the cottage, vacation condo, ski chalet or trailer.

Also, it is not necessary to designate which place is the "principal residence" until one is sold or considered sold (as in the case of death). The general rule is to select the property that has (or will likely have) the greatest capital gain per year of ownership, but remember, this is not always the city place. Until 1982, a husband and wife were both permitted to have their own principal residences and could be eligible for two exemptions. Tax planning in the '70s suggested one spouse own the city home and one spouse own the cottage – no joint ownership of either. This sweet deal ended in 1981 but the current rules still allow a partial principal residence exemption on a second family property basically equal to the gain accrued before 1982.

Even better, you can adjust your ownership retroactively to take advantage of these rules. Do it now as the death of one spouse before the ownership change will void the advantage.

7. AFTER TAKING CARE OF YOUR PARENTS, TAKE CARE OF YOUR SPOUSE AND CHILDREN.

Exact tax-planning strategies depend on your income tax rate versus your spouse's and whether your children are older than 18. Your focus should be on family income splitting. You'll have to go through a few hoops to retain the constant level of family income (remember tax planning doesn't increase your income), but have the income spread among family members who are taxed at a lower rate than yourself.

What can you do?

• The spouse with the lower income-tax rate (spouse A) should do all the family's investing. The spouse with the higher rate (spouse B) should pay all living expenses (mortgage, groceries) including spouse A's income tax bill and RRSP contribution. All family investment income is taxed in spouse A's hands.

• Loan spouse A funds to invest, but make sure that the terms of repayment and interest charged are similar to those in the marketplace. The investment return must beat the interest rate on the loan to make this effective. This is your investment adviser's role – not your tax planner's.

• Invest in equity-based mutual funds in the names of your minor children. As the accounts are "in trust" you have control to ensure your children don't blow the money travelling around North America following Pearl Jam or Green Day. Capital gain allocations from these funds will be taxed in the children's hands – not yours. (What tax rate is your 11-year-old at?)

The end result: you have control of the funds and you can take advantage of your children's lower tax rates. Warning: equity funds may also allocate dividend and interest returns. These will be taxed in your hands. This is not a cost to you as it would be taxed in your hands anyway. The win here is the shifting of the capital gain tax to your children. This is a great way to help with a child's education costs. Don't forget you are the trustee of your children's money. Your role is to ensure the funds are used for the benefit of the children – not yourself.

Children over 18? It gets easier. Give funds (hey, an early inheritance) to adult children. Even if they're in the same tax bracket as yourself, you may be ahead as your estate has been reduced for probate fee purposes and your lower income may minimize or remove the Old Age Security clawback. If you are the adult child, explain this to mom and dad. Make sure they realize you have their best interests at heart. Also, there is no problem in giving a financial gift or loaning funds to children to start a business.

8. WHY NOT HAVE YOUR CHILDREN OWN PART OF YOUR INCORPORATED BUSINESS?

Tax rules permit young children to be shareholders of non-investment businesses in Canada. The children's shares are owned on their behalf by a family trust. The incorporated business pays dividends to the trust, which are then paid to the children. The funds can then be used to pay the child's tuition, music lessons, sporting activities, etc. Again, the funds are in your control as a trustee. The win? If a child's sole source of income is dividends, he or she can receive about $23,000 and pay no tax. In setting up a trust situation, professional advice is essential to make sure you stay within the law.

9. SORRY – THIS ONE'S NEITHER SEXY NOR FUN.

I'm an accountant, what do you expect? However, don't miss out on the RRSP because it's an easy way to save taxes and prepare for your retirement. It's easier to sell the idea of an RRSP than to persuade people to focus on the investment yield. Talking to a bank teller on Feb. 28 may not be the smartest move. Take a chance – talk to someone who has the ability to advise you on a variety of RRSP investment alternatives. You can make your RRSP contributions less painfully with automatic monthly payment plans. Take full advantage of the spousal RRSP rules to split retirement income. Don't forget the Home Buyer's Plan. Take advantage of it while it's still around. First-time home buyers can borrow up to $20,000 from their RRSP. The loan is repayable over the next 15 years. If you already have a home, why not give or lend your adult child funds to maximize his or her RRSP tax-deductible contribution, which can then be turned into a Home Buyer's Plan loan?

10. THE BEST WAY TO BEAT THE TAXMAN IS TO BE ACTIVE.

None of us, on our own, can influence tax rates or tax rules. So "kwityerbitchin" and start taking advantage of the tax rules (they are not loopholes) now to minimize the tax you and your family pay.

TAX EFFICIENCY THE NEW STANDARD FOR FUNDS

Tax efficiency has recently become one of the buzzwords of mutual fund analysis, and for good reason. Expectations of high investment returns have continued to fall amid low inflation, shrunken yields from fixed-income investments and, more recently, turbulence in equity markets. In this investment climate, putting together a portfolio that shields your returns as much as possible from the ravages of taxation has become all the more desirable. Mutual funds, because of their flow-through characteristics and the various types of income that they generate, present numerous opportunities to reduce taxes. Many tax-saving techniques have to do with funds' underlying assets and the different types of payouts they make.

HOW TO USE | TAX-EFFICIENCY DATA EFFECTIVELY

The PAL Trak tax-efficiency ratio is a measure of the percentage of a mutual fund's total return retained after tax by an investor holding the fund in a taxable account. The ratio is calculated over three-year or five-year periods. The highest possible score is 100%, which is achieved by funds that have paid no distributions and whose returns are reflected entirely in an increase in their net asset value.

The tax-efficiency ratio is based on assumptions that, while having the advantage of standardizing the calculations, do not purport to represent the actual tax situation of individual investors. It also assumes the investor is in the top tax bracket.

Interest income is assumed to be taxed at a marginal tax rate of 50%. As a result, almost all money market funds have a tax-efficiency ratio of 50% since their distributions are in the form of interest.

The most favorable treatment by PAL Trak is given to capital gains. This type of distribution is assumed to be taxed at a marginal tax rate of 37.5%. The greater the proportion of a fund's distributions that is generated by capital gains, the more tax efficient it is presumed to be.

An oversimplification in PAL Trak's methodology is the 50% marginal tax rate attributed to distributions of dividends from Canadian corporations.

Although PAL Trak's creator, Portfolio Analytics Ltd., acknowledges that dividends are taxed at a more favorable rate than interest income, the company says it lacks "comprehensive data" on dividend distributions.

"One can assume, therefore, that funds distributing dividends from Canadian corporations will have an understated tax efficiency," Portfolio Analytics cautions its users.

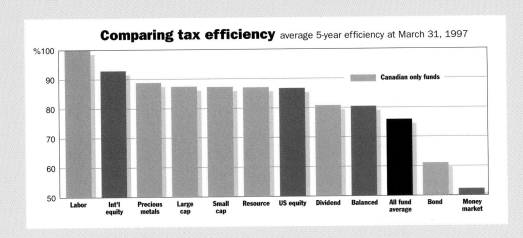

Comparing tax efficiency average 5-year efficiency at March 31, 1997

Categories (left to right): Labor, Int'l equity, Precious metals, Large cap, Small cap, Resource, US equity, Dividend, Balanced, All fund average, Bond, Money market

Most tax-efficient Canadian equity funds

at 12/31/97

Name	Tax efficiency 5 years	Total assets $M	$ distrib. 12/31/97	1-year % ret.	5-year % ret.*
20/20 Canadian Resources	100.00	285.1	0.00	−9.4	17.9
Mackenzie Sentinel Cda. Eq.	100.00	11.4	0.00	0.9	15.9
CT Special Equity	100.00	401.0	0.00	22.8	13.6
Cambridge Growth	100.00	20.0	0.00	−31.5	−0.9
AGF Growth Equity	100.00	888.2	0.00	17.1	19.9
Quebec Growth Fund Inc.	100.00	18.6	0.00	40.5	17.2
Cote 100 REER	100.00	36.0	0.00	18.4	18.0
AIC Advantage	100.00	1781.3	0.00	43.3	35.1
Dominion Equity Resource	100.00	16.7	0.00	−11.6	14.3
Investors Retirement	100.00	3026.9	0.00	10.0	14.4
National Trust Special Equity	99.84	46.5	0.00	12.0	14.0
AGF Canadian Equity	99.64	721.1	0.00	0.5	10.4
Atlas Cdn Large Cap Growth	99.47	318.0	0.00	26.7	16.6
GBC Canadian Growth	99.42	207.9	0.23	27.0	20.1
Green Line Canadian Equity	98.51	831.2	0.45	24.4	18.0
Trans-Canada Value	98.19	3.0	0.00	1.0	11.5
Industrial Future	98.10	702.3	0.00	14.4	20.0
Green Line Canadian Index	97.79	367.7	0.00	13.7	16.1
BPI Cdn Small Companies	97.73	524.7	0.00	−18.6	14.5
Royal Precious Metals	97.71	238.9	0.00	−33.7	15.8
Templeton Canadian Stock	97.57	282.7	0.17	17.5	16.4
First Canadian Equity Index	97.44	366.1	0.02	13.5	15.3

Least tax-efficient Canadian equity funds

Name	Tax efficiency 5 years	Total assets $M	$ distrib. 12/31/97	1-year % ret.	5-year % ret.*
Emerald Private Cap Equity	37.89	0.4	12.82	28.9	19.0
Middlefield Growth	39.73	21.9	0.00	3.6	9.0
CentrePost Canadian Equity	49.93	18.9	1.93	1.2	13.4
Canadian Protected	55.15	1.6	0.00	2.9	5.8
Guardian Monthly Dividend C	56.99	130.1	0.05	3.1	8.5
BPI Cdn Resource Fund Inc	58.50	40.9	0.00	−30.3	3.6
Multiple Opportunities	60.87	12.9	0.00	−13.7	35.6
AGF High Income	60.90	518.1	0.06	6.2	9.2
Altamira Resource	62.90	198.4	0.00	−27.0	5.9
Cambridge Special Equity	63.85	4.9	0.00	−43.9	7.2
MAXXUM Natural Resource	65.51	52.7	0.00	−39.2	15.5
Altamira Equity	66.18	1,980.7	3.69	4.1	15.8
All-Canadian Compound	66.74	12.2	1.33	6.3	11.5
All-Canadian Resources Co.	68.71	3.3	0.20	−18.3	10.7
Mawer New Canada	69.34	32.5	4.29	16.4	22.9
Cambridge Resource	69.67	12.8	0.00	−42.3	7.4
General Trust Cdn Equity	70.36	37.5	7.84	1.1	11.9
First Heritage	71.96	4.0	0.41	−19.4	8.7
Cornerstone Cdn. Growth	72.79	74.5	0.07	−1.6	12.1

* Compound annual return

Source: PAL Trak

By understanding tax efficiency, an investor is better equipped to choose an optimal mix of assets and decide which funds are best held inside or outside an RRSP or RRIF. Other tax-saving opportunities arise from the timing of an investor's purchase or sale of fund units and when the fund pays out its capital gains. To complement the analysis of the pretax returns and risks of funds, there is now an emerging body of knowledge on tax efficiency. Portfolio Analytics Ltd. of Toronto, for one, has developed a tax-efficiency ratio published monthly on its PAL Trak software, which is sold mainly to financial advisers. A common way to measure tax efficiency – and the approach used by Portfolio Analytics – is to do a breakdown of how a fund's total returns after fees and expenses were achieved.

IN GENERAL, THE LEAST TAXED FORM OF INVESTMENT INCOME IS DIVIDENDS

For mutual funds structured as trusts (which include the vast majority), distributions to unitholders are made in one of four ways: capital gains, dividends originating from Canadian common or preferred shares, interest from Canadian sources or foreign income from either dividends or interest. These various sources have different implications for taxpayers, depending on individual situations. But, in general, the least taxed form of income is dividends. "People still have the misconception that capital gains are the most tax-efficient source of income," says Ed Legzdins, vice-president of investment funds at Bank of Montreal. He notes tax changes in recent years have wiped out the previous advantage enjoyed by capital gains. For example, three-quarters of capital gains are taxable, compared with just half 10 years ago. And the $100,000 capital-gains exemption was eliminated in 1994.

For someone in a high tax bracket, the after-tax difference between capital gains and dividends is relatively small. Legzdins estimates Canadian dividends for a typical high-income investor would be taxed at an effective rate of 33%, compared with about 37% for distributions of capital gains. But for individuals with taxable income of up to $30,000 – which is the case for many retired people – the advantage widens considerably in favor of dividends. The tax rate on dividends plunges to only about 7%, compared with a 20% marginal rate payable on capital gains distributions and 27% on interest income.

BUYING IN TO A FUND LATE IN THE YEAR INCURS UNWANTED CAPITAL GAINS TAXES

Because of the very favorable treatment afforded to dividends, conservative savers should consider looking beyond fixed-income asset classes. One of Bank of Montreal's MatchMaker savings portfolios, for example, has a model asset mix of 50% in one-year GICs, 33% in the bank's First Canadian Bond Fund and 17% in First Canadian Dividend Income. "Dividend-yielding stocks are a very good component for retirees," Legzdins says. Regardless of what might make up the distributions that a fund pays out, the timing of an investment can make a big difference tax-wise. This is because mutual funds – mostly those in the equity category – commonly flow through their distributions to unitholders at the end of the calendar year.

The biggest pitfall to avoid is making a purchase late in the year of a mutual fund that has had substantial trading profits during the year and is about to declare a fat yearend capital gains distribution. After the distribution, the fund's net asset value falls by a corresponding amount. "Investors should recognize that investing immediately prior to a fund distribution could dramatically affect their after-tax returns for that year," says Eric Grove, vice-president of marketing at AGF Management Ltd. As a result, the unitholder who bought before the distribution is stuck paying capital gains tax on profits that he or she didn't really make.

The common solution is to buy into the fund early in the new year so that, if it makes a lot of capital gains during the year, you'll be in on the action. There are exemptions to the buy-early rule that help prove the point there are no funds that are tax-inefficient in all situations and that, ultimately, there are only inefficient situations for individuals. Andrew Roblin, president of University Avenue Funds, a Toronto-based mutual fund company that annually distributes a tax guide to clients, notes some investors might benefit from buying late in the year and accepting a capital gain.

HIGH-TURNOVER PORTFOLIOS ARE BEST HELD IN AN RRSP

For example, says Roblin, individuals who have started a business this year or those who are expecting a big inheritance next year would have tax rates lower this year than next. They might be better off earning capital gains this year at a lower marginal tax rate. "You would have to be the judge as an individual investor which is the best for your tax requirements," Roblin says, emphasizing it's not enough to rely on guidelines. "The generalities can often be quite misleading to the individual." One of the most controversial aspects of tax efficiency is the debate over whether funds with high portfolio turnovers are less tax efficient than those whose managers practise a long-term buy-and-hold style. Turnover matters because there are two ways to earn capital gains on a mutual fund investment.

One source of gains results from the fund manager's trading profits, which are paid out annually to unitholders. The other is entirely up to the individual investor and occurs when fund units are redeemed at a profit, after sales fees. The greater a fund's portfolio turnover, the more likely capital gains will be distributed annually, instead of being built up over time and reflected in the fund's net asset value. The conventional wisdom is that funds with high portfolio turnover should be held inside RRSPs, where tax efficiency doesn't matter, and that low-turnover funds are more suitable candidates to be held outside RRSPs.

BUY-AND-HOLD INVESTING MAY RESULT IN HEFTY DEFERRED TAX LIABILITY

Exemplifying this school of thought is Richard Charlton of Infinity Funds Management Inc., who contends that buy-and-hold investing is the surest path to wealth, and portfolio turnover triggers taxes that eat into the investor's returns. "We believe wealth is created by investing in good businesses and holding for the long run," says Charlton, who cites as a prime example the AIC Advantage Fund, of which he was formerly an active promoter. But unless a fund does no trading at all, it's untrue to suggest it can avoid tax liability. "A fund that has a policy of buying and holding can, in fact, generate tax consequences each year if they sell some of their holdings each year," says University Avenue's Roblin.

Furthermore, fund analyst Duff Young of Midland Walwyn Capital Inc. suggests low-turnover funds such AIC Advantage may build up a hefty deferred tax liability. A heavy tax load, as he calls it, might deter a fund manager from selling a security in a portfolio that has become overpriced. By comparison, he says, a high-turnover fund like Altamira Equity has "almost no tax liability" embedded in its net asset value. It's difficult to reconcile the radically divergent views on the impact of portfolio turnover. But it is safe to say the tax efficiency of a fund will vary. Market conditions, a portfolio manager's investment style or changes in a fund's objectives or managers all can have a significant impact.

TAX EFFICIENCY OF A PORTFOLIO IS DIFFICULT TO PREDICT

"A value style and a growth-momentum style could have very different impacts on the after-tax returns," says AGF's Grove, who is a chartered financial analyst. "But both could be volatile year after year, depending on the level of the market and the trading patterns of the manager." Nor, warns Grove, should investors base their expectations of year-to-year distributions on what happened in previous years, unless the fund is a fixed-income fund with low volatility and a low rate of portfolio turnover. Since the degree of consistency associated with yearly equity returns isn't high, neither is its measure of tax efficiency.

Portfolio Analytics' Mackenzie agrees tax-efficiency ratios can vary. In addition, he cautions against attaching any significance to precise percentage measures, recommending instead that investors or advisers look at tax efficiency in terms of which funds fall into various ranges. Mackenzie shares the consensus that the most valid measure of tax efficiency is how it affects the individual investor.

"Tax efficiency is not a good or bad thing," he says. "It simply is a factor you should consider when constructing your portfolio."

DIVIDEND SHIFT CAN PROVIDE SAVINGS

Most tax-planning techniques are carried out well in advance of the actual day you sit down to complete your tax return. Exceptions include a decision on which spouse is to claim charitable donations. Another is deciding who claims the family medical expenses.

A third, which can be very useful to those who qualify, is the ability to shift dividend income from one spouse to another. This can be a significant tax saver in some circumstances. The basic rule is found in subsection 82(3) of the Income Tax Act and applies only if the receipt of dividends by one spouse will reduce the other spouse's claim for a dependent spousal tax credit. Thus, this option is available only to couples in which one spouse is taxable and the other is not and in which the non-taxable spouse receives Canadian source dividends.

In effect, the rules allow the supporting spouse to remove dividend income from the dependent spouse's income and add it to that of the supporting spouse, who can also claim the associated dividend tax credits. For 1997, the federal tax credit on a dependent spouse was reduced when the dependent spouse's income exceeded $538. Thus, shifting the dividends only applied if the dependent spouse's income, including the grossed-up dividends, exceeded $538. The actual calculation for the spousal income credit as shown on the tax return was $5,918 minus net income. The product was multiplied by 17% (as part of the calculation on non-refundable tax credits) but the actual value of the credit had to be boosted by roughly 50% to take into account provincial tax rates. For the purposes of the examples to follow, this assumes a maximum spouse credit of $1,372 (i.e. [$5,380 x 17%] + 50%).

EXAMPLES OF HOW THE DIVIDEND TRANSFER WORKS AND ITS BENEFITS

Example 1: Suppose Sarah, who stayed at home in 1997 to have a child, had dividend income of $1,000 from a taxable Canadian company. This had to be reported as $1,250 because of the required 25% gross-up but also carried a potential dividend tax credit of $250 (taking into account provincial taxes). If no election is made, Sarah pays no tax. Joshua, her husband, will have a reduced claim for spousal tax credits. That amount would now be $5,918 – $1,250, or $4,668. The value of the credit at 17% is $793.56 and, when the provincial tax rate is taken into account, jumps to about $1,190. Joshua has "lost" $181 in tax credits.

Example 2: The facts are the same but Joshua elects to bring Sarah's dividends into his own income, making the election under subsection 82(3). If we assume that Joshua's marginal rate is 40%, he increases his income by $1,250 and increases tax by $500. But he also gets $250 in dividend tax credits, meaning his additional tax liability is $150. But he is able to claim the full spousal tax credit, leaving the family $31 ahead of the game. If Joshua's marginal tax rate were 50%, he would be worse off by making the election, so caution must be exercised. Conversely, if Joshua were in the lowest tax bracket (about 26%), the gain would be more substantial.

Example 3: Suppose Sarah had $3,500 in dividends, which were grossed up to $4,375, with $875 of dividend tax credits. Sarah still pays no tax, but Joshua's spousal tax credit drops to $262.30 [($5,918 – $4,375) x 17%]. Taking into account provincial tax, this equals about $393. If Joshua makes the election, his income rises by $4,375, which costs $1,750 in the 40% tax bracket, reduced by a dividend tax credit of $875 for a cost of $875. But the tax credit he can claim for Sarah returns to the maximum of $1,371. His increased credit exceeds his increased tax by a little over $100.

While the savings may be modest, it is important to realize that they are free tax dollars to be saved simply by making the right choice.

Unfortunately, there is no rule of thumb to quickly determine whether an election is beneficial, since it will depend on the amount of the dependant's income, whether there is income other than dividends, and the marginal tax rate of the supporting spouse. Revenue Canada's Interpretation Bulletin IT-295R4 offers more information.

DIVIDEND TAX CREDIT HAS BENEFITS

Under the Income Tax Act, individuals who receive dividends from taxable Canadian corporations must report 125% of the cash dividends received. The extra 25% is known as the "gross-up" and the full amount is reported on line 120 of the income tax return. The theory behind this gross-up is that when a corporation pays taxes, some part of the tax burden is paid on behalf of shareholders. Today, that figure is arbitrarily set at 25% of the dividends received. In the past it has been as high as $33^1/3$%. To offset this gross-up, the taxpayer also gets a dividend tax credit. Thus, if a $100 cash dividend is grossed up to $125, there should be a $25 tax credit.

HOW IS THIS CREDIT COMPUTED?

This is where many taxpayers truly get confused. Before looking at the actual percentages, we remind you that, except in Quebec, the system must take into account the fact that an individual's overall tax bill is split on a ratio of approximately two to one between the federal government and the provinces. That is to say, two-thirds of the tax bite goes to Ottawa and one-third to the province in which the taxpayer resides, assuming the provincial tax rate is roughly 50% of the federal tax liability.

THE GROSS-UP AND BENEFITS SYSTEM WORKS TO TAXPAYERS ADVANTAGE

If you look at the individual tax return, you will find that the federal portion of the credit is 13.33% of the taxable dividends reported – that is, 13.33% of the grossed-up dividend on line 120 of the return. Thus, if you had a $100 dividend and grossed it up to $125, the federal dividend tax credit is ($125 x 13.33%) about $16.67. On the other hand, most tax planners calculate the credit using a formula from the act itself, which indicates the dividend tax credit is two-thirds of the rate of the gross-up. Since the rate of the gross-up is 25%, two-thirds of this amount is 16.67% – which is applied to the dividend before it is grossed-up. In other words, it is 16.67% of $100, or $16.67, the same as using the other formula. In both cases, assuming a provincial tax rate of 50%, the dollar value of the tax credit for combined federal/provincial purposes rises to about $25, the amount of the

TOTING UP | THE GROSS-UP

Dividend	$100
Gross-up amount	$25
Taxable dividend	$125
Combined fed/prov tax (at 52%)	$65
Combined dividend tax credit	$25
Net tax	$40

gross-up itself. So when many tax planners offer examples of how the dividend tax credit works, they simply show a combined credit equal to the amount of the gross-up.

The gross-up and credit system benefits taxpayers. It adds $25 to income, meaning a tax increase of perhaps $13 or $14 at the top end of the income range. But the value of the credit is $25, so the system reduces the tax bite overall. The higher the gross-up and credit rate, the better off the taxpayer is. When the rate was reduced from 33^1/$_3$% to 25% as part of tax reforms in 1988, it represented an increase in taxation of Canadian source dividends.

TAXATION ON DIVIDENDS VARIES FROM PROVINCE TO PROVINCE

Finally, the figures used here are all approximations, because of variations in provincial tax rates and use of surtaxes. But for quick calculation purposes, the rules of thumb as set out above are accurate enough to determine the approximate impact of taxation on dividends.

SOME BASIC RULES OF INCOME SPLITTING

Income splitting is the art of transferring income from a person in a high tax bracket to someone in the same family with a low tax bracket. Done legally, the family ends up with more after-tax cash. However, there are rules to keep you from simply shifting assets to your spouse or children. They're called "attribution rules" because they attribute the income from those assets back to you and tax it in your hands. Here's a quick walk through those rules.

SPOUSES

If you simply give your spouse investment money, you face tax on the proceeds. But not if you "sell" assets to your spouse at fair market value, in exchange for other property (or cash). So, maybe you hold an asset that's likely to soar and your spouse will be in a low- or no-tax bracket when it's sold for real. By selling or trading to your spouse, you'd pay tax now on appreciation to date, but all future growth would be taxable for your spouse.

If your spouse doesn't have enough property or cash to do the deal, you can grant a loan, but attribution will apply unless you charge interest. The same goes if you want to lend your spouse money to make an investment.

The rate you charge must be no less than Revenue Canada's quarterly "prescribed rate" – a relatively low 4% at the end of 1997. The prescribed rate is adjusted every quarter, based on 90-day treasury bill rates in the first month of the preceding quarter. Any fraction is rounded upward to the nearest full percentage point. But once the loan is established, the rate can be locked in indefinitely, no matter where future prescribed interest rates go. The loan must be fully documented, including proof of funds moving from one bank account to another. The lower tax bracket spouse has to make real interest payments to the high tax bracket spouse within 30 days of each calendar yearend.

Like all income, that interest must be declared on the annual tax form of the high earner. But the low-bracket spouse normally gains a tax deduction on the interest paid.

Brian Quinlan, a chartered accountant, uses the example of a couple named Richard and Fiona to show the results of this strategy. Richard is taxed at the top bracket of 52%. He lends Fiona $50,000 to invest. As she earns much less, she is taxed at just 26%. The couple documents the loan with a promissory note prepared by a lawyer, stating interest is 4% and is payable no later than Jan. 30 following each calendar year. Richard would pay tax on the first 4%, since that is the interest he receives from Fiona.

At the same time Fiona would claim a deduction based on the same 4% charge. The investment income beyond the initial 4% is taxed in Fiona's name at her lower marginal tax rate. For example, if the investment yielded 9% a year, Fiona would pay tax on 5%.

Louis notes this same strategy could be applied to children. The easiest way to take advantage of the tactic is to make a loan, but if you do not have ready cash, it is possible to transfer investments owned outside an RRSP to low-bracket family members. The family member would pay you by giving you a promissory note. The transferred investment must be treated as if it had been sold at its current value.

A similar opportunity is also available if your employer lends you money to acquire a home. The prescribed rate would be deemed a taxable benefit, but can be locked up for five years. And if you receive a qualifying home relocation loan, you could gain an additional tax break.

There are two alternatives to the loan route. One involves "second-generation income." Say you give – not lend – your spouse $10,000 to buy a GIC that compounds at 10%. Each year you face tax on the first-generation income – the $1,000 of interest on $10,000 of capital. But all interest subsequently earned by that $1,000 belongs to your spouse without attribution. Attribution rules also do not apply to income from an active business. So you can lend or give money to an entrepreneurial spouse. But it must be a true business.

MINOR CHILDREN
The attribution rules also apply to children under 18 as well as grandchildren, great-grandchildren, nieces and nephews, with two exceptions. There is no attribution on capital gains earned by a minor. So you could give your child money for an equity mutual fund. But attribution is supposed to apply to interest and dividends on the capital. Also, with gifts – as opposed to loans – a minor's attribution stops at the end of the year in which the child turns 18.

ADULT CHILDREN AND OTHER FAMILY MEMBERS
Attribution applies to loans – but not gifts – to family members such as parents, siblings, grandparents and grandchildren. But that's if it's an investment loan aimed at reducing your taxes. The rules do not prevent mom and dad from funding a child's home mort-

gage. This attribution does not apply to nieces or nephews. Nor does it apply if you charge interest on the same terms as the spousal loan discussed above. Be careful about getting clever, though. There are anti-avoidance rules aimed at preventing you from funnelling money through a third party to your spouse or child.

There are also rules to keep you from avoiding attribution by replacing initial assets or loans with new ones.

FAMILY EXPENSES

Each spouse has a separate bank account. The higher-taxed one pays all family expenses, leaving the other's full income for investment. If the lower-taxed spouse owes tax when the yearly return is due, the other can foot that bill so the low-taxed money stays invested.

GIFTS AND INHERITANCES

The same as above. Say you earn far less than your mate and receive money from your parents. Invest that in your own name so its earnings are taxed at your lower rate. Many people have relatives outside Canada. There is no attribution on money from someone who's not a Canadian tax resident. Say your parents send your newborn $10,000. That can be invested in trust for the child.

SPOUSAL RRSP

This is usually a long-term plan aimed at balancing a couple's retirement income. But the new Seniors Benefit may negate the advantage for many. Spousal RRSP contributions can work in the short term, too, if one spouse plans to stop work in a few years.

TESTAMENTARY TRUST

This trust is created on the death of the person providing the money. Say you'll leave a pile of cash to your spouse to support the family. The investment income would all be taxable in his or her hands. Instead, your will could create a trust for each family member so his or her share of the income gets taxed at his or her progressive rates.

CHILD TAX BENEFIT

This cheque can be invested in your child's name without attribution. Save it for post-secondary education.

REGISTERED EDUCATION SAVINGS PLANS

Investment earnings are tax-deferred until withdrawn and then get taxed in the student's hands. Child tax benefit money already carries the same tax breaks, though, so don't use that cash flow to fund an RESP.

CHILD'S ALLOWANCE

Pay all your teenager's expenses so he or she can save all part-time and summer job money for college or university. Children who file tax returns will be able to make RRSP contributions. So part of the savings could be tax-sheltered until withdrawal for school.

CPP/QPP SPLITTING
Retirees can have up to half their Canada or Quebec Pension Plan payments made to their spouses if both are at least 60. The split depends on a formula that factors in the contribution periods and marriage duration.

SELF-EMPLOYMENT OPPORTUNITIES
You can pay your spouse and child reasonable salaries for bona fide services.

FIVE CREDITS CAN BE TRANSFERRED TO SPOUSE

If one spouse's income is so low that he or she does not pay any taxes, then the other spouse can claim his or her unused non-refundable credits to reduce taxes further. There are actually five tax credits that can be transferred from one spouse's tax return to the other. They are the amounts for:
- tuition fees
- education
- age (65 or older)
- pension
- disability credits.

You are entitled to claim only the unused portion of these credits, meaning your spouse must use as much of them as required – along with credits for the basic amount, Canada Pension Plan contributions and employment insurance premiums – to reduce income taxes to zero first. These credits are transferred using Schedule 2 of the income tax return.

SPOUSE CAN CLAIM UP TO $5,000 OF EDUCATION EXPENSE
The tuition fee credit may be claimed if course fees during the year are greater than $100, in which case the actual amount of tuition can be claimed. The education credit is available only to full-time students, although the rules on what constitutes full time have been liberalized in recent years. Up to $5,000 in combined tuition fees and education amount – or a credit of $860 – may be transferred to your return from your spouse's. Receipts and forms to support claims for the tuition and education credits need not be submitted to Revenue Canada when a tax return is filed. But they must be retained by the taxpayer, since the tax department may ask you to submit them later.

VARIOUS OTHER CREDITS CAN ALSO BE CLAIMED BY SPOUSE
You can claim the age 65 or older credit but bear in mind that it will be reduced 15¢ for

each dollar of income above $25,921. The credit disappears entirely if the taxpayer's net income is $49,134 or more. Amounts eligible for the pension credit include annuity payments from pension plans, RRSPs, RRIFs and other pension-related sources. But Rob Davis of KPMG's national tax department says some tax planning could allow a person to use the credit – and thus transfer it to a spouse – in future years.

"If it is possible, it may be worthwhile to arrange your affairs so that your spouse receives at least $1,000 of eligible income annually to take advantage of this tax break," he says.

Finally, the disability credit is available to taxpayers who have a severe and prolonged mental or physical impairment. To qualify for the credit, a physician must certify on a Revenue Canada form T2201 that the individual suffers from an ailment that significantly restricts his or her daily activities. The impairment must be expected to last for a continuous period of at least 12 months.

CALCULATING OTTAWA'S CUT CAN BE TAXING

With the loss of the $100,000 lifetime capital gains exemption in 1994, small investors with stocks, mutual funds or other non-RRSP investments that generate capital gains face complications when filing their income tax returns. If you have sold securities outside your RRSP or RRIF, you're obliged to report the transactions on your tax return and pay capital gains tax if you made a profit. While your broker's statement should provide details of such transactions, there is no tax information slip to attach to your return when reporting capital gains, as there is for dividends and interest. But don't assume that because no one sent you a tax slip on the transaction that Revenue Canada will not be aware of it. All capital gains realized during a taxation year must be reported on Schedule 3 of that year's tax return.

ONUS OF CLAIMING CAPITAL GAINS IS ON THE INVESTOR

The tax department used to rely on the honor system for reporting capital gains, and that's still the case for real estate transactions and interest payments under $50. However, investment dealers now are required to file a Statement of Securities Transaction – form T5008 – with Revenue Canada, which reports sales of securities held directly by investors. Most fund companies have permission to file the T5008 electronically, so no form is sent to the unitholder. However, the information to make computations is provided to unitholders in the annual statements. Stocks not sold through an investment dealer, such as through employee stock purchase plans, may escape this net, which puts the onus on the taxpayer to report gains.

Unfortunately, it's no simple matter to calculate your resulting tax bill. The biggest problem involves calculating an investment's adjusted cost base (ACB) ACB typically must be computed by a mutual fund investor who buys units of a fund on a monthly basis, or engages in frequent switching, buying and selling of units. Obviously, you can-

CALCULATING | ADJUSTED COST BASE

Mutual fund investment		Cost A $	No. of units B $	Adjusted cost base per unit (ACB) A÷B $
June 15, 1993	Purchase	35,000.00	2,278.6458	15.36
Dec. 31, 1993	Reinvested distribution @ $17.09	2,738.93	160.2651	17.09
		37,738.93	2,438.9109	15.47
Dec. 31, 1994	Reinvested distribution @ $19.05	1,444.08	75.8047	19.05
		39,183.01	2,514.7156	15.58
Dec. 31, 1995	Reinvested distribution @ $20.96	3,175.83	151.5186	20.96
		42,358.84	2,666.2342	15.89
June 12, 1996	Purchase @ $22.96	10,000.00	435.5401	22.96
		52,358.84	3,101.7743	16.88
Nov. 20, 1996	Redemption @ $23.17	(1,688.00)	(100.0000)	16.88
		50,670.84	3,001.7743	16.88
Dec. 31, 1996	Reinvested distribution @ $23.06	1,350.80	58.5776	23.06
Dec. 31, 1996	Balance	52,021.64	3,060.3519	17.00

1996 capital gain calculation on redemption of 100 units	$
Proceeds @ $23.17 per unit ($23.17 x 100)	2,317.00
Adjusted cost base @ $16.88 per unit ($16.88 x 100)	(1,688.00)
Redemption fees (deferred sales charge)	(76.68)
Capital gain **552.32**	
Taxable capital gain (@ 75%)	414.24

not compute a capital gain without first calculating your original cost. What's worse is that your fund company can't always do this for you because you may have purchased the same fund from more than one broker. And your broker can't do it for you because you may have bought through more than one broker.

DISTRIBUTIONS FROM FUNDS MUST BE CLAIMED BY TAXPAYER

Revenue Canada is in no better position, which puts the onus squarely on the taxpayer, or on a competent tax preparer or other independent adviser working on your behalf. This is an area that confuses many brokers and financial planners, so it's worth figuring it out on your own. The effort is worth it because you might otherwise end up paying too much capital gains tax. An excellent source of information on this subject is a brochure from Trimark Investment Management Inc., *Taxation of Your Trimark Mutual Fund Investments.*

Capital gains realized when mutual fund units are sold should not be confused with those on T3 slips that itemize distributions, which are capital gains, dividends and interest flowed through to investors by a fund. Funds distribute this income because Revenue

Canada classifies funds as flow-through entities. As a result, investors generally must pay some tax on a fund investment each year – even if you do not sell any units of the fund. Distributions usually occur once a year, but sometimes more frequently. Instead of a fund paying capital gains tax or being taxed on dividends or interest at the top marginal income tax rate, unitholders are taxed on these amounts, possibly at lower marginal rates. Distributions are deemed for tax purposes to have been received by the investor in cash, even if they are automatically reinvested in additional fund units.

PAYING TAXES ANNUALLY REDUCES TAXABLE CAPITAL GAINS AT REDEMPTION

This is where considerable confusion arises over a fund investment's adjusted cost base. The cost of the new units increases the ACB of your total investments, says Nathan Mechanic, a broker with RBC Dominion Securities Inc. The result is good news designed to prevent double taxation: a reduced taxable capital gain when you redeem your total holdings some time in the future. "Failure to note this increase in ACB could result in subsequently overpaying your capital gains tax over time, especially in a situation where an estate is filing returns and proper records haven't been kept," Mechanic says.

UMBRELLA STRUCTURES ALLOW SWITCHES, WHICH AVOID CLAIMING CAPITAL GAINS

When you do redeem fund units, calculate your capital gain by subtracting the ACB and expenses from the sale price of your units in the fund. Expenses can include commissions, redemption fees and transfer fees. Keep in mind that the "average unit cost calculation" provided in annual account statements is not the same as the ACB, nor will the statement take into account deemed redemptions, which can occur when beneficiaries change upon death, for example. Note, too, that transferring between funds is considered a redemption for tax purposes; hence the popularity of "umbrella" structures that shield such switches, available through CI Mutual Funds' sector funds and similar products at AGF Management Ltd. and GT Global. Under these structures you can switch, for example, between a fund family's European equity fund and its Asian fund, without creating a disposition and realizing a capital gain.

IT IS THE INVESTOR'S RESPONSIBILITY TO CALCULATE ACB ON INCOME TAX FORMS

If you deal with just one broker and a few fund companies, you can ask the broker to get the companies to calculate the ACB for you. If you simply take a stab at guessing the ACB, don't assume Revenue Canada's computers are going to recalculate and rule in your favor. Trimark warns that deemed dispositions for tax purposes don't normally appear on client statements as specific redemptions or transfers, nor does the company have to report them to Revenue Canada.

The onus is on the taxpayer to report them. Failure to do so is considered tax evasion. Another situation to be wary of is a financial institution mistakenly issuing a tax information slip for income that is meant to be sheltered within an RRSP or RRIF. If you own the same fund inside and outside an RRSP, make sure you're being taxed only on the one held outside.

TAX RULES HAVE MAJOR IMPACT ON RETURNS

Investors should always be guided by two rules. First, investment decisions should be made on the basis of investment data, not tax issues alone. Second, tax issues must be taken into account in determining your final return from an investment – a key element in deciding whether to make dividend-paying or interest-bearing investments. The issue is often joined when it comes to deciding whether to sell or hold an investment. The timing of a sale, which triggers a capital gain or a loss, may best be determined by an impending yearend.

CAPITAL LOSSES CAN ONLY BE USED TO OFFSET CAPITAL GAINS

Generally, if you want to realize a gain, a delay until after yearend postpones tax liability. If you want to trigger a loss, the sale should be made before yearend. However, since capital losses can only be offset against capital gains, not against ordinary income, some matching makes sense. Consider a not-uncommon situation. You rode the 1997 stock market wave and held your stocks and bonds when the market fell in late October. Common sense may have told you to lock in those gains (or what you had left) by selling. But on the other hand, some of those stocks may have been good long-term holds. And to complicate matters, if you locked in the gains, you locked in the potential tax liability for 1997, too. Ironically, those who jumped on the bandwagon late and undoubtedly suffered, may have had the easiest way out. The financial pain associated with the sale of shares at a considerable loss could at least be mitigated in the long run by using the losses to offset gains on other investments.

INVESTORS SHOULD PLAN TO SELL LOSERS IN SAME CALENDAR YEAR AS WINNERS

While this sort of planning will never recoup dollar for dollar what has been lost on a stock, it can ease the overall tax bite. The general rule of thumb many investors follow when liquidating winners is to try to sell losers in the same calendar year to ease the tax bite. If you have winners you want to stick with, you have two options. You can simply hold them until you feel it is right to sell them or you can sell them now, take the gain and repurchase them. Realizing the gain should be done with a recognition that either you have offsetting losses or a tax bill will be forthcoming.

CAPITAL LOSSES CAN BE CARRIED FORWARD INDEFINITELY

If your losers in a year are in excess of your winners or if you want to dump losers while retaining winners, bear in mind that capital losses can be carried forward indefinitely and set off against future capital gains. Repurchasing winners after a sale to realize the gain is easy. But in the case of losers, the issue is more complicated from a tax perspective. Suppose you have a loss on a stock in which you still have confidence over the longer haul. If you just hold on, no loss is recognized. But you may choose to sell to offset gains realized on winners. If you do this, you have to understand the superficial loss rules.

In a nutshell, if you or a person "affiliated" with you sells a stock at a loss and acquires the same stock within 30 days of the sale (either before or after), the loss will not be recognized for tax purposes. ("Affiliation" basically means your spouse or a corporation with which you do not deal at arm's length.) The amount of the loss will simply be added to the cost base of the repurchased shares. Having a good understanding of the basic rules relating to when gains and losses are realized for tax purposes, how losses can be used against gains and the pitfalls of the superficial-loss rules will help minimize the tax bite associated with having stocks that have made a large move.

A LOOK AT SOME KEY TAX NUMBERS

Here are some tax numbers that may prove to be handy in your financial planning. They were compiled in the national tax office of chartered accountants KPMG and reflect federal and provincial budget changes during 1997.

• Canada Pension Plan contribution rates have been raised to 6.4% of pensionable earnings for 1998.

• If you turn 69 in 1998, you must "mature" your RRSP by the end of the year. To prolong the tax-sheltering effect, your options are to convert to a RRIF and/or an annuity.

• New rules kicked in for child support agreements signed or changed after May 1, 1997. Payments under these agreements will no longer be taxable for the recipient parent nor deductible for the payor.

• The new reporting requirement for assets over $100,000 held outside Canada has been deferred until 1999.

• The 1998 threshold for Old Age Security recipients is unchanged at $53,215 of net income. Recipients lose benefits based on whichever is less, the amount received or 15% of net income over the threshold. The seniors' $3,482 age credit is reduced by net income over $25,921 and is lost entirely when income passes $49,134 (separate rules apply to the Quebec seniors' benefit).

• Tax brackets and surtax: The three federal tax brackets are unchanged: $0-$29,590, $29,590-$59,180 and $59,180-plus. The federal individual surtax for 1998 will be 3% of basic federal tax. The high-income surtax is unchanged at 5% of basic federal tax over $12,500.

• The maximum RRSP contribution limit has been frozen at 18% of earned income to a maximum of $13,500 per year until 2003, after which it is slated to increase by $1,000 a year until it reaches $15,500; thereafter, it will be indexed to growth in the average industrial wage.

The 1997 federal budget introduced a "pension adjustment reversal" to augment the RRSP contribution room of individuals whose pre-retirement departure from an employer's pension plan or deferred profit sharing plan results in excess loss of contribution room.

- Basic personal amount: No change. $6,456.
- Disability amount: No change. $4,233.
- Medical expense threshold: No change. $1,614.
- Married amount: No change. $5,380 if spouse's net income is up to $538. Partial credit may be available if spousal income is above that level.
- Charitable donation credit: The federal credit is now 17% on the first $200 of donations and 29% on the excess. The maximum annual claim was increased to 75% of annual net income in the 1997 federal budget, and this limit now applies to gifts to the Crown as well. The limit is 100% of net income in the year of death. (Special rules apply in Quebec.)
- RESPs: The maximum contribution to a Registered Education Savings Fund has been increased from $2,000 to $4,000 a year per beneficiary, although the cumulative lifetime limit remains at $42,000 per beneficiary. Also, the rules regarding forfeiture of earnings have been relaxed.
- Those who acquired cars or mini-vans in 1997 will be able to depreciate $25,000 in value, plus sales taxes. That's up from $24,000 in the preceding year.
- Deductible leasing costs for newly acquired vehicles are capped at $550 a month plus taxes. That's down $100 per month from the 1996 tax year. The maximum interest deduction for new car loans is $250 a month, down from $300.

DEBT REDUCTION IS A GOOD INVESTMENT

Having a tough time with your investments? Would you like to earn 15% to 20% or more, risk-free? Just pay down your debts – and don't add to them. The accompanying tables show why accountants and financial planners nag clients to pay off debts that are not tax-deductible. Few investments pay anywhere near as well. That's mainly because of taxation. Now that the $100,000 capital gains exemption is dead, nearly all personal investment income is earned in pretax dollars. Meanwhile, payments on consumer loans are made in after-tax dollars.

PAYING DOWN DEBT CAN PUT PRETAX DOLLARS IN YOUR POCKET

The key is your marginal tax rate – the tax on your last dollar of income. Say you have taxable income this year of about $50,000. Your marginal rate on fully taxed income is about 40% (depending on province). So you must earn $1.67 to be able to pay $1 of interest on a loan. Since capital gains are taxed more lightly, the break-even point for earning that after-tax dollar would be $1.42. Now, suppose you have $5,000 parked in a money-market fund, waiting for a clear sign that the stock market is turning up again.

MARGINAL | TAX RATES

1998 combined federal-provincial marginal tax rates

for top-bracket taxpayers, including surtaxes and provincial flat taxes, based on budgets brought down in 1997

Province	Dividends %	Capital gains %	Other income %
British Columbia	36.6	40.6	54.2
Alberta	31.4	34.6	46.1
Saskatchewan	36.5	39.0	52.0
Manitoba	36.3	37.8	50.4
Ontario	34.4	38.2	50.9
Quebec	39.4	39.5	52.6
New Brunswick	33.8	37.6	50.1
Nova Scotia	33.5	37.2	49.7
Prince Edward Island	34.0	37.7	50.3
Newfoundland	36.0	40.0	53.3
Yukon	31.4	34.9	46.6
Northwest Territories	30.0	33.3	44.4

Suppose you also have a 9% car loan. Look at the tables on the following page. Use the column for a 40% marginal tax rate and read down to the row for a 9% loan. Using that $5,000 to reduce the car loan is about the same as earning 15% in pretax interest or 12.9% in capital gains.

CASHING IN INVESTMENT FUNDS TO PAY OFF DEBT CAN EARN YOU MORE

Here's the logic. At 9%, a $5,000 loan costs $450 in interest payments for the year. For simplicity, I've ignored compounding or whether the loan payment consists of a blend of principal and interest. Earning 15% in fully taxed interest brings you $750, but – at a 40% marginal rate – the tax collector takes $300. That leaves you with $450 to pay the interest on the loan. Earning a 12.9% capital gain brings you $645. Three-quarters of that – or $483.75 – will be taxed. At a 40% marginal rate, that costs you $193.50. Subtract that tax from the $645 gross gain and you net just about $450 – the amount due on the loan. The last row on the tables – 28.8% – is the rate for some charge cards issued by retail stores. Rates on Visa and MasterCard credit cards from financial institutions have ranged from 10.9% to 18.9%. But the gap between charge cards and credit cards is actually even greater. Charge cards typically compound interest monthly, so the posted 28.8% rate really works out to 32.9% if the balance is outstanding for a full year. Credit cards, however, don't compound interest.

Yet, in an Angus Reid poll done for Ernst & Young in 1996, 58% of respondents with outstanding balances said they'd prefer to pay down their bank cards than their charge cards. In the above example, debt reduction means you'll lose use of that $5,000. But you'll free up cash flow that can then be invested. Why not calculate your monthly interest savings from the loan paydown and invest that amount each month in an equity mutual fund? You'll build wealth over time and sleep a lot easier as you average out the market's ups and downs.

DEBT REDUCTION | VERSUS INVESTMENT

Debt reduction versus fully taxed investment

| Loan rate % | 25% | Approximate marginal tax rate | | | 55% |
| | | 40% | 45% | 50% | |
		Equivalent pretax investment return %			
8.0	10.7	13.3	14.5	16.0	17.8
9.0	12.0	15.0	16.4	18.0	20.0
10.0	13.3	16.7	18.2	20.0	22.2
11.0	14.7	18.3	20.0	22.0	24.4
12.0	16.0	20.0	21.8	24.0	26.7
13.0	17.3	21.7	23.6	26.0	28.9
14.0	18.7	23.3	25.5	28.0	31.1
15.0	20.0	25.0	27.3	30.0	33.3
16.0	21.3	26.7	29.1	32.0	35.6
17.0	22.7	28.3	30.9	34.0	37.8
18.0	24.0	30.0	32.7	36.0	40.0
19.0	25.3	31.7	34.5	38.0	42.2
28.0	38.4	48.0	52.4	57.6	64.0

Source: KPMG

Debt reduction versus capital gains investment

| Loan rate % | 25% | Approximate marginal tax rate | | | 55% |
| | | 40% | 45% | 50% | |
		Equivalent pretax investment return %			
8.0	9.8	11.4	12.1	12.8	13.6
9.0	11.1	12.9	13.6	14.4	15.3
10.0	12.3	14.3	15.1	16.0	17.0
11.0	13.5	15.7	16.6	17.6	18.7
12.0	14.8	17.1	18.1	19.2	20.4
13.0	16.0	18.6	19.6	20.8	22.1
14.0	17.2	20.0	21.1	22.4	23.8
15.0	18.5	21.4	22.6	24.0	25.5
16.0	19.7	22.9	24.2	25.6	27.2
17.0	20.9	24.3	25.7	27.2	28.9
18.0	22.2	25.7	27.2	28.8	30.6
19.0	23.4	27.1	28.7	30.4	32.3
28.0	35.4	41.1	43.5	46.1	49.0

Source: KPMG

YOU'RE NEVER TOO YOUNG TO FILE A TAX RETURN

When the annual blizzard of tax returns hits homes across Canada, there may well be some people – including a great many young people – who should consider filing even though they haven't received forms from Revenue Canada. The Income Tax Act says that if tax is payable, an individual must file a return. But these days, about one-third of the more than 20 million tax returns are filed by individuals who do not owe any tax. This is because in the past 10 or 15 years there has been a steady blending of the federal transfer system with the tax system so that many payments, ranging from Old Age Security to Family Benefits, are in fact linked to the tax system. The net result is that anybody eligible for federal or provincial transfer payments or refundable tax credits must file a return to ensure they receive those benefits.

MANY TAX CREDITS ARE CALCULATED BASED ON YOUR TAX RETURN

For many years, low-income parents have effectively been forced to file a return to get benefits associated with having children. When the goods and services tax came into force, the associated tax credit required a tax return to be filed even if the person has no income. When the tax system started to recognize common-law marriages, it meant many young people were deemed to be married and thus had to file to be eligible for the GST credit. Almost all students at post-secondary schools should file tax returns, not only for the GST credit but because they may, depending upon the province, be eligible for a range of provincial tax credits that are linked to the tax system and require filing to make a claim. (Experience indicates many students fail to file unless prodded by parents and thus lose benefits, including the GST refund and credits linked to rent paid while away at school.)

INCOME CLAIMED BY YOUNG PEOPLE CAN BE CARRIED FORWARD FOR RRSP PURPOSES

The 1996 federal budget contained a provision that should have had the effect of increasing tax filings by young people. The seven-year limitation for the carry-forward of RRSP contribution eligibility was eliminated, meaning all earned income will qualify for RRSP contributions indefinitely. But that's only if Revenue Canada is aware of the earned income. Suppose a young person living at home with parents gets a summer job and earns $1,200. In the past, he or she probably wouldn't file a tax return since no tax would be payable and the person was too young to be eligible for any of the other credits available. Furthermore, if the child were planning on attending a post-secondary school, the likelihood of having an RRSP within seven years was slight.

But with an unlimited carry-forward, things have changed. If the youth earns $1,200 a year from age 15 to 18, say a total of $4,800, he or she can contribute 18% of this amount, or $864, to an RRSP any time in the future. The key is that a return would have to be filed so Revenue Canada knows the income was earned. (If there had been withholding tax, the filing of the return might also produce a modest refund.) Most individuals would normally start filing at age 19 in any event, to be eligible for the GST credit, but voluntary early filings might offer a deferred tax opportunity in the form of extra RRSP room when they do go to work.

HELPING TEENAGERS FILE THEIR OWN RETURNS IS A FIRST LESSON IN TAX PLANNING

If a young person has never filed a return before, one must be procured from one of the myriad sources at which they are available. Once filing has occurred, the appropriate return will be sent automatically in future years. We also suggest that the youth, with parental help, do the return personally so the significance of filing is brought home at an early age. Obviously, one wouldn't want to pay a fee for having this sort of non-taxable return prepared. Since few youngsters truly understand the nature of the income tax system and the obligations and opportunities it offers, this can be a very useful exercise. The benefits are long term, not immediate, but that too is a lesson in tax planning that is worth imparting.

BE CAREFUL SETTING UP "IN-TRUST" ACCOUNTS

Parents and other relatives often put child tax benefit cheques and other cash into bank accounts in a child's name, usually as an "in-trust-for" account so they can make deposits and withdrawals on the child's behalf. Interest from savings stemming from child tax benefit payments (and its predecessor, the family allowance) is taxed in the child's hands. Interest from other deposits is attributed back to a parent or other relative. Mutual funds and even company shares or bonds also are frequently held in an in-trust investment account, the assumption being any interest or dividend distributions will be reported on the contributor's tax return but capital gains will be taxed in the child's hands.

However, Lorn Kutner, a tax partner with Toronto-based chartered accountants Mintz & Partners, warns capital gains from these informal accounts may well be attributed back to the contributor.

THE PERSON WHO SETS UP AN "IN-TRUST" ACCOUNT MUST CLAIM ANY CAPITAL GAINS

For a trust to be a valid entity, Kutner says the settlor – the person who sets up (and usually funds) the trust – must formally transfer the property to the trust's trustees. "Revenue Canada's published opinion is that an in-trust-for account is an informal trust arrangement which permits the transferor to withdraw the investment for their personal benefit. Therefore a true transfer of the funds has not taken place and any income, or capital gains, will remain the client's."

Even if there is a formal trust, you must ensure it is set up properly so that attribution of capital gains will not occur. Kutner cites subsection 75(2) of the Income Tax Act, which says clearly that any income or loss from property, as well as any taxable capital gain or allowable capital loss from the disposition of property, is attributed to the person from whom the property was directly or indirectly received, if the trust states that the assets may revert to that person or that other beneficiaries may later be named by that individual. There also may be attribution if distribution from the trust requires the consent of the source of the assets. "Many in-trust-for arrangements seem to fit these criteria since [the person who contributed the assets] will have the power to withdraw funds or must consent to any sale," Kutner says.

BEFORE ENTERING A TRUST AGREEMENT, DETERMINE WHO PAYS TAX ON INCOME GENERATED
There is another potential problem, says Kutner, which often lurks in some brokers' off-the-shelf trust agreements that define the person setting up and funding the trust as the account's beneficial owner, not the trustee. "This will be fatal from Revenue Canada's perspective and attribution of income will occur," he warns. He adds that if subsection 75(2) is applicable to a trust, the assets cannot be distributed to the beneficiaries at their tax cost. "The property is distributed at fair market value so that, if it had gone up in value, a capital gain – and a tax liability – is created." These concerns might seem extreme for many taxpayers, but it appears Revenue Canada has the right to tax capital gains in the hands of many parents, grandparents, aunts and uncles who are either too casual about how they transfer money to children or who concoct elaborate trust arrangements with too many strings attached.

DISABILITY CREDIT SCRUTINIZED BY TAXMAN

A generation or so ago, it seemed the vast majority of tax appeals had to do with capital gains, driven in part by the favorable treatment given this form of income. Nowadays, a large percentage of cases have to do with the disability tax credit. This credit is worth a maximum of $720 at the federal level, or about $1,100 for combined federal-provincial purposes in most provinces.

THE STATUTORY REQUIREMENTS FOR CLAIMING THE CREDIT
• An individual has a severe and prolonged mental or physical impairment.
• The effects of the impairment are such the individual's ability to perform a basic activity of daily living is affected.
• A medical doctor, or where the impairment is an impairment of sight, a medical doctor or an optometrist, has certified in prescribed form that the individual has a severe and prolonged mental or physical impairment the effects of which are such the individual's ability to perform a basic activity of daily living is markedly restricted.
• The individual has filed the certificate with the minister for a taxation year.
• No amount in respect of remuneration for an attendant or care in a nursing home, in

respect of the individual, is included in calculating a deduction under section 118.2 of the Income Tax Act for the year by the individual or by any other person.

If an individual does not have enough income to claim the credit, a supporting family member can make the claim. The number of cases being heard on appeal has increased, probably because of the use of the informal appeal system, which allows individuals to argue their own cases. In decisions by Tax Court Judge Donald Bowman on two cases heard in Cornerbrook, Nfld., Bowman upheld the claim in one but rejected it in another. Bowman made some interesting points in the second judgment. The case was being argued by the wife of the taxpayer, but the latter was not called as a witness.

IF DISABILITY CREDIT IS DENIED, TAXPAYER HAS A RIGHT TO APPEAL

In such cases, Bowman said it is useful for the court to see the person to help in making a judgment about physical capacity. In that same case, the physician's certificate did not check the long-term disability space on the claim form, and Bowman was forced to wonder whether this was intentional or inadvertent. The problem is deciding whether, to use the Tax Act's words, "the individual's ability to perform a basic activity of daily living is markedly restricted" is, in the end, a subjective call by the judge. These two decisions thus ended up being based on the particular facts of each case and it is difficult to find a common thread, since so much, as Bowman noted, depends upon how the person "looks" to the judge.

We suspect that in most cases, judges are faced with emotional situations in which personal sympathy vies with the protection of the public purse. But there is a conundrum here. On the one hand, the legislation itself is sound and tax relief is appropriate. However, the statutory tests are appropriate, and it is difficult to dispute the right to appeal when Revenue Canada denies a claim. Having said all that, there is an enormous cost associated with these appeals, not only of money but in terms of the court's time. But there appears to be no alternative process that offers tax justice to the individuals who are affected while at the same time producing a reasonable cost-efficient method of providing that justice. Meanwhile, those who feel they are entitled to the credit should claim it – and hope for the best in court if the claim is rejected.

CHAPTER 8

RETIREMENT PLANNING

- Estate planning

- Calculate the costs of your retirement

- RRSPs

- Maximizing foreign content

- Carry-forward options

RETIREMENT COULD COST YOU

A LOT MORE THAN YOU THINK

BY BRUCE COHEN AND
JONATHAN CHEVREAU

HOW MUCH MONEY DO YOU NEED to be able to retire? That depends largely on how much you spend each year and how many years you'll live. The first is fairly easy to determine. The second depends on your lifestyle and the genes you inherited. However, calculating your retirement costs can be a sobering experience and may bring you to the scary conclusion you'll have to become an RRSP millionaire two or three times over if you are to retire in style. If so, most Canadians are in for a rude awakening. Even a more modest retirement nest egg of $1 million is likely to be reached by only 6% of Canadians, according to a Gallup poll released by Deloitte & Touche chartered accountants. Of 1,002 adults surveyed, 12% expect to save between $500,000 and $1 million, 18% between $250,000 and $500,000 and fully a quarter of them less than $100,000.

MOST CANADIANS UNDERESTIMATE WHAT THEY WILL NEED FOR RETIREMENT

Of course, even $1 million isn't quite what it used to be, and will buy even less 20 years from now than it does today. Investing $1 million in a 5% guaranteed investment certificate (GIC) would yield just $50,000 a year before tax – hardly a fortune. A survey conducted by Toronto-based Marketing Solutions in November 1996 suggests 60% of Canadians have not even tried to calculate how much they'll need to retire. As the old saying goes, if you don't know where you're going, you'll likely end up somewhere else. The survey found that many people "grossly overestimate how early they can retire," says president Dan Richards. On average, 45-year-olds think they can retire at 58. The younger the investor, the earlier they expect to retire.

RETIREMENT INCOME PROJECTIONS MUST CONSIDER INFLATION AND INVESTMENT RETURNS

Most financial planners use complex planning software like RRIFmetic to come up with scenarios appropriate for their clients' needs. But there are plenty of simpler software programs you can play with on a home computer. Most allow you to make multiple projections by changing variables such as inflation or investment returns. Just bear in mind that any projections are very sensitive to rates of return and assumed rates of inflation. Say you're 45, would like to retire in 10 years and figure you'll need $30,000 a year in today's money to top up whatever you get from the government and your employer. That's $30,000 before tax.

If we assume annual inflation will average 3% over the next 10 years, you'll need $40,320 for your first year of retirement. That's $30,000 times the 10-year factor of 1.344. Assuming 3% inflation and 8% growth, you'll need $17,489 of capital at 55 to fund a fully-indexed $1,000 payment each year for 35 years, until you're 90. For $30,000 a year in today's money, use the inflated 10-year figure of $40,320. You'll need a nest egg of $705,156 – that's 40.32 times $17,489. Depending on what you've already saved, and what it's earning, that may be achievable.

HERE ARE SOME POINTS TO PONDER

• The sooner you retire, the longer your money must last. Put another way, each additional year of work is one less in which you'll have to tap your savings. A 40-year-old man has just over a 10% chance of living into his 90s, according to StatsCan's general life expectancy tables. A 40-year-old woman has a 26% chance of passing 90 and a 10% chance of passing 95. At 8% growth and 3% inflation indexing, a 30-year income stream requires about 24% more capital than a 20-year stream. A 40-year stream requires about 39% more than a 20-year stream and about 12% more than a 30-year one.

• Generally, early retirement cuts off your buildup in savings and investments just when you can afford to set aside the most money. I use the qualifier "generally" because this assumes your children are on their own, your mortgage is paid off and you're not supporting your parents – three very big assumptions.

• People generally hit their peak earnings in their 50s – again, watch that qualifier. Whether you fit that profile will depend on the extent of restructuring in your employment field.

• The longer your retirement, the more threat you face from inflation. Even if inflation is held at 2%, today's $1 would lose one-third of its purchasing power over the next 20 years. Goods and services that now cost $1 would run about $1.49.

• How much will you spend in retirement? Many people believe their expenses will fall but later find they don't. That's especially true for those who are healthy and active – big consumers of travel and expensive hobbies.

• Are you counting on your employer's defined-benefit pension plan? Actuarial reductions for early retirement mean a smaller monthly cheque because the pension will have to be paid over a longer period. That could be a major concern unless your plan provides for unreduced early retirement.

• Your Canada or Quebec Pension Plan cheque may also be lower than you expect. That's because of a feature called the "dropout." C/QPP computers automatically exclude low- or no-income months for up to 15% of your credited years dating back to Jan. 1, 1966, when the plans began. That's meant to cover career interruptions such as unemployment, illness and schooling. But it can hurt early retirees if the zero-credit years before age 60 total more than 15% of their records. Say you'll turn 60 on Jan. 1, 2006. Your C/QPP "career" will have spanned 40 years. The 15% dropout will cover six years. If you already have four low- or no-income years, full retirement at 55 would reduce your C/QPP entitlement.

• What employment benefits – such as a company car – would you give up? What about employer-subsidized drug, dental and medical insurance? How much would it cost to replace them?

• What will you do with your time? About half the affluent boomers in the Royal Trust poll said they work more than 50 hours a week. Research has found healthy retirees usually maintain the lifestyles developed during their working years. Do you have a fulfilling hobby or are you totally devoted to your job?

• Will close friends be retiring about the same time as you? If not, what would happen to your social life?

• Where will you live? Often retirees move to havens in British Columbia or the U.S. Sunbelt only to find they miss their friends and families. Even if you've vacationed in your prospective retirement haven for years, you may find it unsuitable as a permanent residence. Try living there a while before selling your current home

In the end, how much you need to save for retirement boils down to common sense. Because of the power of compounding, the earlier you start the better. If you're behind, you'll have to save more now and/or increase the return on your investments. If you're unwilling to do that, you'll have to face the fact that you'll either have to lower your expected retirement lifestyle or delay your retirement.

LACK OF PLANNING BODES POORLY FOR MANY

Half of Canadian adults claim to have a financial adviser but two-thirds do not have a financial plan for retirement, according to a recent survey prepared by A.C. Nielsen for Canadian Imperial Bank of Commerce. The CIBC Financial Health Poll of 1,000 people aged 18 or over found that younger Canadians are even less well prepared – four out of five people aged 18 to 35 have no retirement plan. While many Canadians seem appallingly ignorant about financial matters, the CIBC survey can also be interpreted as showing a significant minority of financial planners are not doing their jobs properly. The poll data suggest 17% of people claiming to be financial planners have not put a retirement plan in place for their clients.

YOUR FINANCIAL ADVISER CAN HELP WITH A RETIREMENT PLAN

In further analysis by A.C. Nielsen for *The Financial Post,* of the 50% without a financial adviser (defined broadly), 15% have a plan and 85% do not. Of the 50% who have an adviser, 52% have a plan and 48% do not. The extra data analysis also shows that of the 67% without a financial plan, 36% have an adviser and 64% do not; of the 33% with a plan, 78% have an adviser and 22% do not.

MANY FINANCIAL ADVISERS ARE TRANSACTION ORIENTED RATHER THAN PLANNING ORIENTED

Linda Hohol, CIBC executive vice-president, concedes some financial planners are transaction-oriented and more interested in the commissions from selling mutual funds or stocks than in long-term financial planning. The term "financial adviser" is fairly loose, she said, and providers of financial advice, as opposed to products, are not regulated. "I wouldn't necessarily conclude they are not doing their jobs," said Terry Taylor, executive director of the Canadian Association of Financial Planners. "Someone may not have accepted their recommendations or not have enough dough to start the plan." Clients may agree a financial plan is a great idea but delay implementing it, Taylor added. But the Asian currency meltdown of October 1997 and the resulting fallout in global stock markets seem to have sparked renewed interest in seeking proper advice now, not later.

MARKET VOLATILITY FORCES PEOPLE TO SECURE A FINANCIAL PLAN

One CIBC interview subject, Joanna Mackie, does not yet have a financial plan but is now thinking about rectifying the situation. "Recent volatility in the market has made me a little more uncomfortable about my current investments and certainly has reinforced to me the importance of securing a firm financial plan." Not surprisingly, higher income Canadians are more likely to have a plan: 59% of those with more than $75,000 in annual income have a plan. Because of the failure to plan, fewer than two in five Canadians know how much money they will need to retire comfortably. One in five (22%) fears not having enough money at retirement age. Yet the average Canadian expects to retire at 59.

RRSPS ARE THE MOST IMPORTANT EXPECTED SOURCE OF RETIREMENT FUNDING

Those saving for retirement began doing so on average at 28, though they feel they should have begun at 25. One in four has yet to put aside a single dollar for retirement; of this segment, 41% cited "lack of money" for their slow start. Registered retirement savings plans are by far the most important expected source of retirement funding. The 57%

expecting to rely on RRSPs is almost double the number counting on the Canada Pension Plan or company pension plans. Despite saturation media coverage of mutual funds, 25% still rate themselves "not knowledgeable" about funds. While 43% are unsure of how to invest their money, 54% would place their money in mutual funds or stocks, 35% in fixed-income products like bonds or GICs, and 11% in other investments.

ONE-FIFTH OF RRSP INVESTMENTS CAN BE HELD IN FOREIGN SECURITIES

Those who own funds are most likely to be in Canadian equity funds (69% of the time); 45% have foreign bond or equity funds, 43% balanced funds, 40% money market funds, 39% U.S. equity funds and 29% bond funds. Two-thirds do not know 20% of an RRSP can be invested in foreign securities and more than half do not know one-year GICs pay about 3%. Among the 50% of Canadians who do not have a financial adviser, 32% say they would turn first to a bank or trust company employee for advice. Another 28% would use spouses, family or friends and 12% would rely on their own instincts. Only 9% would seek out an independent financial planner and only 7% would turn to a stock broker or investment adviser.

So, is retirement all it is cracked up to be? A subset of the CIBC survey focused on those already retired or semi-retired. Asked to cite the main lifestyle change they have experienced, only 32% said more free time to relax or pursue hobbies and 4% said they can now "enjoy life." About 20% feel they have less money than they used to or not enough to live on. Only 4% felt financially secure and 3% are still working.

RRSPS TOP THE RETIREMENT-SAVINGS HEAP

Everyone should try to take advantage of tax-assisted ways to save for retirement. But many people fall short of the mark when it comes to investing in registered retirement savings plans, financial industry experts say. People shy away from setting up an RRSP for many reasons. "I know there are lots of excuses all across the board as to why people don't do it," says Gena Katz, senior principal at Ernst & Young's national tax group. "For those who are young, they don't do it because they have 40 years to retirement. And, once you get into a stage of life where you find you've got a lot of financial burdens, you've got other things you have to spend your money on, like mortgages. So you just can't see your way clear to saving for retirement."

RRSPS NOT ONLY SAVE TAXES, THEY ARE AN INVESTMENT FOR YOUR RETIREMENT

But, financial experts say, people have to come to terms with their need for income in retirement. The reasons for being concerned are manifest. People are living longer than ever, company pensions are often not overly generous – in some cases, not even available – and there are concerns about the viability of the public pension system. Even those with modest incomes should be setting aside sums for retirement, and the RRSP is the best vehicle for doing so. "I don't think anybody – from the upper to the lower-income tax brackets – can afford to ignore the RRSP. It's a tax-saving measure, and it's an investment, and it's your retirement planning," says Michele Wood-Tweel, a chartered accountant and principal in personal advisory services at KPMG. "The plans have become more accommodating over the years. Even somebody who can afford to put away $25 a month from their spending can benefit."

MAKING REGULAR RRSP CONTRIBUTIONS THROUGHOUT THE YEAR HAS TAX BENEFITS

The financial experts say there are a few straightforward strategies that allow those with modest incomes to take advantage of the RRSP. The toughest thing is to make the commitment to put aside some money for an RRSP, says Ann David, manager of wealth management at Royal Trust. "The key is to set aside monthly amounts and to make regular contributions. Don't get discouraged, don't give up, and don't put it off until tomorrow," David says. One strategy is for people to arrange to have money automatically deducted from their pay or from their bank account each month. Financial institutions will accommodate savers so that money is automatically transferred to an RRSP investment, she says.

Some companies offer group plans for RRSP contributions. "Employers are getting on the bandwagon through group plans, where they will withhold amounts from your salary, which is actually a really good way to do it. If you don't see the money, it doesn't hurt as bad," Katz says. By withholding source deductions and transferring the amounts to an RRSP, people get the benefit of the RRSP tax deferral right from the start, instead of having to wait until tax time for a refund or rebate, Katz says.

Individuals who don't have such a group plan at their place of work can still take advantage of this strategy. This option of making RRSP contributions before income tax is levied on your earnings is also generally available to individuals. "[This form of savings] subsidizes you as you go through the year because your taxes are reduced as you're making those RRSP contributions. You are effectively getting your refund throughout the year, instead of getting this lump sum at the end of the tax year," Wood-Tweel says. Individuals can have this type of source-deduction RRSP benefit by obtaining the appropriate documents at Revenue Canada or from financial institutions that have the Revenue Canada forms available at their branch locations.

INTEREST-BEARING INVESTMENTS CAN BE HELD IN AN RRSP

Another way of putting money into an RRSP is through borrowing, the experts say. Individuals who don't have the free cash right away can usually borrow from a financial institution. Part of the repayment for the loan can be derived from the expected income tax refund. Any borrowing for an RRSP should be based on an individual's ability to handle the loan repayments. "It can make sense to borrow for an RRSP, but you have to

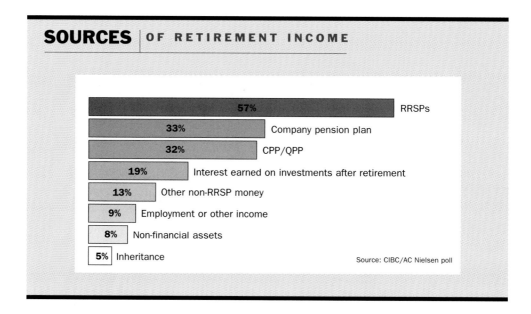

SOURCES OF RETIREMENT INCOME

57%	RRSPs
33%	Company pension plan
32%	CPP/QPP
19%	Interest earned on investments after retirement
13%	Other non-RRSP money
9%	Employment or other income
8%	Non-financial assets
5%	Inheritance

Source: CIBC/AC Nielsen poll

consider that your refund is not going to be 100% of what you borrowed, it's only going to be part of it, so you're going to have pay the amount back," David says.

Deciding on individual investments to place in the RRSP, you need to consider what, if any, investments are being held outside the RRSP: the so-called "taxable" or "open" part of your investment program. If you have sizable wealth outside the RRSP, financial advisers counsel holding the interest-bearing vehicles – such as a GIC, Canada Savings Bond or bond fund – inside the RRSP and equities and dividend-paying stocks (or mutual funds investing in them) outside. That's because capital gains and dividends are not taxed as harshly as interest income.

SELF-DIRECTED RRSPS LET YOU MAKE YOUR OWN INVESTMENT CHOICES

If, as is often the case for people still paying off mortgages, your only financial assets are in your RRSP, you will want to include all major asset classes in you plan; that is, equities for long-term growth, bonds or income mutual funds for a stable earnings flow, a small amount of cash perhaps in the form of money market funds and maybe some special asset classes such as gold/precious metals or commodities, also available through mutual funds.

The process of asset allocation – deciding on the appropriate mix of stocks, bonds, cash and other assets – is critical. This can be done in consultation with a fee-only financial planner or with a mutual fund broker/dealer or financial planner who makes a living selling "load" (i.e. with a sales charge) mutual funds. Alternatively, you can choose domestic or global "balanced" funds or more tactical asset-allocation funds that let the fund manager decide for you.

Typically, a balanced fund maintains a mix of about 60% equities to 40% bonds, with only minor fluctuations from that formula. A tactical asset-allocation fund makes shorter-term tactical shifts: the fund manager attempts to time the markets by over-weighting asset classes expected to outperform and underweighting those expected to underperform.

Whatever the case, you also may need to decide whether to buy a regular "managed" RRSP investing in mutual funds as decided entirely by the issuing institution or a "self-directed" plan in which you can call all the investment shots. Self-directed RRSPs offer much more flexibility in terms of your investment choices.

MAXIMIZE FOREIGN CONTENT FOR REDUCED RISK

During the past decade, the permitted foreign content of registered retirement savings plans has doubled to 20% and RRSP experts advise taking full advantage of the allowance. "Over time, your returns will be higher and your risk level lower with a glob-ally diversified portfolio," says Steve Wilson, president of Hongkong Bank Securities Inc. "We strongly advise our clients to max out their 20% foreign content," Wilson adds. "We find to our dismay that usage of foreign content is overlooked in many cases."

MAXIMIZE THE FOREIGN CONTENT OF YOUR RRSPS

The ability to diversify RRSP investments to include foreign content is available both for self-directed plans and managed plans. Most plan managers now offer clients a basket of mutual funds, including funds that invest in foreign markets. Those funds provide the opportunity for adding foreign assets to an RRSP portfolio. A self-directed RRSP offers additional flexibility for investment directly in foreign stocks or bonds or other assets. The basic rule is set out in accounting firm KPMG's *Tax Planning for You and Your Family.*

"Generally, only 20% of the cost amount of all property held by your RRSP can be invested in foreign property," the KPMG authors write. "The calculation is performed at the end of each month. Foreign property values over the 20% threshold are subject to a special tax of 1% per month payable by the RRSP. The 20% limit is generally based on the property's cost at the time of purchase, not its market value." KPMG says the RRSP administrator "should monitor" the foreign content "and warn you if it is in danger of going offside." Wilson adds it is "up to you" to act on the administrator's warning.

MARKET GROWTH CAN PUT YOUR FOREIGN CONTENT INVESTMENTS OVER THE 20% LIMIT

"Give yourself a little leeway," advises Adrian Mastracci, a partner at Macdonald, Shymko & Co., a Vancouver firm of financial advisers. He prefers investors to keep in hand a cushion of perhaps 2% as protection against the unexpected. One example of the unexpected can be a capital gains distribution from a mutual fund held within the RRSP that could put the investor offside if the full 20% is used.

Michael Ryan, a vice-president at Leith Wheeler Investment Counsel in Vancouver, warns the cap can affect decisions about the RRSP. For example, it is conceivable that several years of growth in the value of investments held can take the foreign content well beyond the 20% measured by the market value of the RRSP fund. That does not trigger an infraction as content is measured by cost. However, if the investor decides to take his profit and sell some or all of that foreign holding, he will only be able to reinvest up to the 20% cap. Ryan says there can be a tendency for investors to delay taking the profit because they can't find an acceptable foreign replacement.

INCREASING FOREIGN CURRENCY EXPOSURE MAKES RRSP SUBJECT TO FLUCTUATIONS

There are ways of increasing the foreign exposure of an RRSP portfolio above 20% without violating the 20% rule. "Invest up to 20% of the RRSP book value in qualifying foreign content investments and then allocate the other 80% to mutual funds which themselves have 20% of assets in foreign content areas and are also RRSP-eligible," Mastracci says. "This will approximate a total of 36% foreign content within the RRSP." Other strategies for increasing foreign content within an RRSP include investing directly in Canadian companies that operate in US$s or which have shares denominated in US$s. This increases foreign currency exposure. Mastracci cautions against taking on too much foreign currency exposure as currency fluctuations can trigger a gain or a capital loss in the RRSP. He warns that a real capital loss within a RRSP hurts because it cannot be deducted against gains.

CARRY FORWARD OFFERS RRSP OPPORTUNITIES

In a move that surprised many observers, the March 1996 federal budget eliminated the seven-year limitation for unused RRSP contributions and offered an unlimited carry forward for unused room. This opens up some significant additional planning opportunities, especially for young people. Many youngsters, those in their teens or early 20s, have earned income within the definition for RRSP purposes. A lot of that income goes unreported because there is no need for the earners to report just a couple of thousand dollars of casual employment (or self-employment) income, especially if there has been no withholding tax at source. Thus, money earned delivering newspapers, baby-sitting, shovelling snow and other casual work can become the basis for future RRSP contributions, if that income is reported on a tax return.

CANCELLATION OF SEVEN-YEAR RULE MEANS UNLIMITED CARRY-FORWARD OPPORTUNITY

The benefits of reporting have increased substantially, especially for those 18 and older, because of the possibility of getting GST refunds, provincial tax credits and other payments that are income-linked. In fact, generally speaking, there is no reason why anybody with earned income, no matter how low, shouldn't file a tax return – not only for those reasons, but also now to create an earned income base for RRSP purposes. Although this was also the case before the budget, the difference is the cancellation of the seven-year rule, which in most cases would have meant wasting the eligibility because the earner might not have sufficient income within seven years to take full advantage of the carry forward.

The new situation provides more opportunity for income splitting because a parent could make the contribution on behalf of the child without income attribution (each child having reached age 18), giving the child a deduction and a shift of income between generations.

REPORTING EARNED INCOME AT A YOUNG AGE OPENS TAX-SHELTERING DOORS

Even if the child were under age 18, the income-attribution rules wouldn't create a problem – as long as no income came out of the RRSP while the child was under that age. Presumably, a parent would only make such a contribution when the child could actually use the deduction to reduce tax liability, though some may feel that deductibility is secondary to the ability to earn a tax-free return within an RRSP.

If a child had earned $4,000 a year in each of the past four years, for a total contribution base of $16,000, a parent could give the child $2,880 for an RRSP contribution (18% of $16,000). This money could be used either as part of a genuine retirement fund or could be used a few years down the line (with accrued interest) to pay for further education or to help start a business or buy a home.

The bottom line is that reporting earned income even for a fairly young child can open future tax-sheltering opportunities with little or no cost. All that is required is the paperwork ensuring Revenue Canada has a record of past earned income.

RRIFS OFFER FLEXIBILITY IN POST-RRSP PLANNING

For most of your working years, the pressure is on to salt away as much in tax-free RRSP savings as you can. Eventually, however, you'll be forced to start spending it, and that requires a major change in the way you think about your finances. There are several things you can do with your RRSP savings, which must be "matured" no later than the end of the year in which you turn age 69. One option is to cash in the plan, but this is undesirable because it can result in a huge one-time tax hit on the entire proceeds at your top marginal tax rate. Another option is to buy an annuity, which pays out a guaranteed fixed amount for life but which is based on interest rates, currently at low levels. Or, you can roll your RRSPs into registered retirement income funds (RRIFs), which offer more investment and withdrawal flexibility. It's also possible to arrange combinations of these options.

ALMOST EVERY INVESTMENT PRODUCT IN YOUR RRSP CAN BE HELD IN A RRIF

RRIFs are generally the recommended place for relatively healthy people to put their money because they allow you to invest in mutual funds, bonds and other products that can potentially bring a higher return than current interest rates offer. "There is a definite concern about people outliving their money," says Bernard Roy, assistant vice-president,

MINIMUM RRIF | WITHDRAWAL RATES

Age at Jan. 1	RRIF opened Pre 1993 %	Post 1992 %	Age at Jan.1	RRIF opened pre-1993 %	post-1992 %
65	4.00	4.00	80	8.75	8.75
66	4.17	4.17	81	8.99	8.99
67	4.35	4.35	82	9.27	9.27
68	4.55	4.55	83	9.58	9.58
69	4.76	4.76	84	9.93	9.93
70	5.00	5.00	85	10.33	10.33
71	5.26	7.38	86	10.79	10.79
72	5.56	7.48	87	11.33	11.33
73	5.88	7.59	88	11.96	11.96
74	6.25	7.71	89	12.71	12.71
75	6.67	7.85	90	13.62	13.62
76	7.14	7.99	91	14.73	14.73
77	7.69	8.15	92	16.12	16.12
78	8.33	8.33	93	17.92	17.92
79	8.53	8.53	94+	20.00	20.00

Source: The Rogers Group

retirement services with Canada Trust. "If you've been used to a certain lifestyle, you have to consider how you will be able to maintain it based on current interest rates." Generally, almost every investment product that you held in your RRSP can be held in a RRIF. The mix of products you choose should be based on your age, how much income you need to maintain your standard of living, how much risk you are willing to tolerate and what other sources of income you have, if any. "We recommend that you have up to 20% of your RRIF portfolio in equities to really make it worthwhile," Roy says.

MONTHLY PAYMENTS EVEN OUT IMPACT OF MARKET HIGHS AND LOWS
You must withdraw at least the minimum payment by the end of the year after you open your RRIF (see above table). The financial institution that handles your RRIF will calculate its value at the end of each December, and the amount of your withdrawals are based on that value.

If you want to minimize the size of the payments, you can have the valuation done based on your spouse's age, if your spouse is younger than you are. You also can vary the amount of the payments, so long as the scheduled minimum is taken. You also determine how often to take the payments, annually, semi-annually or monthly.

Rob Whipp, branch manager for Fiscal Agents, an Oakville, Ont., deposit brokerage firm, recommends payments be taken monthly to reduce the impact of market and interest rate fluctuations. "Say you have a lot of mutual funds, and the market has gone up a lot" before the yearend valuation of your RRIF. "If you elected to take your annual payment in July or August and the market suddenly dropped, you still would have to take the amount out that is based on your December valuation, which was high." That means you'd have to redeem extra units, which could use up your RRIF faster than you planned, he says.

Taking payments monthly evens out the impact of highs and lows of the market when you're selling off units of mutual funds, Whipp says. It also helps protect bondholders, for similar reasons. Once you start receiving RRIF income, you must pay quarterly income tax instalments. If you take payments annually at the end of the year, that income must be included in your quarterly payments, and you must pay the tax, even if you haven't received the money, Whipp says.

RRIF THEN ANNUITY IS WORTH LOOKING AT

The spectre of outliving your money is one that haunts many investors in these days of low interest rates. That in part accounts for the current equity cult, as baby boomers and other investors stuff their RRSPs with stocks and equity mutual funds. Those already retired face similar concerns. This accounts for the relative popularity of registered retirement income funds (RRIFs), with their RRSP-like flexibility, compared with life annuities, which invest strictly in long-term fixed-income securities.

Ironically, though, one of the chief advantages of a life annuity is precisely that you can never outlive your money. A life annuity is a contract between you and a life insurer, under which you pay a non-refundable lump sum in return for a promise to provide you with a guaranteed income for life, no matter how long you live.

INSURANCE COMPANY ANNUITIES GUARANTEE INCOME FOR LIFE

As York University finance professor Moshe Milevsky explained in an article for *Benefits Canada* magazine, the insurance company can provide a lifelong guarantee because it pools many annuitants' money and makes conservative yield assumptions. Pooling means individuals who do not reach their life expectancy subsidize those who exceed it. Because a RRIF can be converted to an annuity, but not vice versa, it's possible to have your cake and eat it too by using a RRIF early in retirement and switching later to an annuity. The trick is picking the right moment for the switch. That entails making a guess about life expectancy, future interest rates and investment returns.

FINDING THE RIGHT MOMENT TO SWITCH FROM RRIF TO ANNUITY CAN BE A HARD CALL

Making such estimates is no trivial task. Milevsky applies some surprisingly complex mathematics to arrive at a few cogent conclusions about how to maximize the benefits of annuities. He uses what is called a "Monte Carlo Simulation," a computer algorithm that examines all possible combinations of interest rates, equity markets, mortality rates, inflation rates and annuity prices. For most people, Milevsky recommends starting with a RRIF and delaying an annuity purchase until the last possible moment. "Buying an annuity is synonymous with betting that you will live longer than average." He

The potential benefit of investing in a RRIF during the early years of retirement and switching to an annuity later for someone age 69 with a $200,000 RRSP.*

Age switched to annuity	Success probability %		Median bequest $	
	Male	Female	Male	Female
69	100	100	0	0
74	94	97	33,688	19,920
79	89	93	80,825	56,653
84	83	87	141,664	124,166
89	78	81	209,713	240,456
Never	76	79	310,138	683,409

* Annuity payable at age 69 on that amount would be $1,820 for a female and $1,540 for a male. Assumes RRIF is invested in a diversified portfolio with expected return of 13% and volatility of 17%. Mortality assumes IAM 1996 basic rate for life annuities, plus 10%

Source: York University Schulich School of Business, Statistics Canada

argues the case for what he calls a "do it yourself and then switch" strategy. That means making your own investment calls with a RRIF, then switching at the right moment to an annuity.

PUT OFF SWITCHING TO AN ANNUITY UNTIL THE TIME IS RIGHT

Given the way life annuities are structured, mortality trends and the long-term strength of equity returns, Milevsky says "it makes very little sense for males under the age of 75 and females under age 80 to annuitize any additional non-pension wealth." One would choose otherwise only if interest rates were very high or if you have reason to believe you are much healthier than average, and therefore likely to live longer than most people.

ENJOY THE LIQUIDITY OFFERED BY RRIFS WITH DIVERSIFIED PORTFOLIO OF EQUITIES

The accompanying table shows two examples that correspond to the payout a $200,000 life annuity "would have" provided at age 69. This strategy involves consuming from your RRIF the monthly amount that an annuity would have provided and deferring actual annuitization until later. In the first example, a 69-year-old woman stays with a $200,000 RRIF for 10 years, withdraws $1,540 a month (the amount an annuity would have paid), then switches to an actual annuity at 79. She stands a 93% chance of being able to purchase a life annuity paying out an identical $1,540 a month with her remaining wealth. In the second example, a 69-year-old male uses a $200,000 RRIF to generate a monthly income of $1,820. He gets more because males have shorter life expectancies. He has a 94% chance of purchasing a comparable annuity five years from now, and an 89% chance of doing the same 10 years from now.

This strategy depends on investing in a well-diversified portfolio of equities. "Putting the funds in a GIC defeats the point and will likely make it impossible to ever purchase the same annuity in the future," Milevsky says. Among the advantages to the strategy are that the retiree maintains complete control over the funds at the RRIF stage, which means liquidity is maintained. Any emergency or unforeseen cash crunch – for long-term care, perhaps – can be met from the non-annuitized pool. Second, the retiree can annuitize at any future point. "Why pay for something today if, in all probability, you can pay the exact same thing 10 years from now, yet maintain the benefits of the purchase?" Milevsky asks.

A LIFE ANNUITY LEAVES NOTHING FOR YOUR ESTATE

Yet another consideration in putting off the decision to annuitize is leaving an estate for your heirs. A pure life annuity leaves virtually nothing for your estate. Milevsky says it may sound morbid but "the longer you delay annuitization, the greater the chances that you will die prior to purchasing the life annuity, which will mean that your estate gets the proceeds of the RRIF." A less risky alternative is to use Milevsky's strategy alongside a deferred annuity. Not to be confused with his "delayed" annuity strategy, a deferred annuity allows the retiree to lock in a mortality table and interest rate early in retirement, with the payout "deferred" – typically for 10 or more years. A 69-year-old male with $200,000 might use $160,000 in Milevsky's strategy and put the other $40,000 into a 10-year deferred annuity. For a female, the mix might be $145,000/$55,000.

WHAT DOES YOUR COMPANY PENSION PLAN OFFER

Every year companies that offer their employees a pension plan must send each staff member a statement outlining his or her pension entitlement. Chances are, the employee's eyes will glaze over before getting to the bottom of the first page. While most working people want a pension, few pay attention to the details of the company plan. Yet there are pointed questions employees should ask to get answers that will help inform them about their post-retirement finances. Read that statement, says Janet Downing, lawyer and consultant at Watson Wyatt & Co., pension and benefits consultants in Toronto. And read the booklet about your company pension plan that you got when you joined the firm.

If it's not in plain English, or any other plain language, don't despair. There should be a pension provider, someone at the company or a union representative who can answer questions in a way everyone can understand.

COMPANY PENSION FUNDS ARE PROTECTED FROM BANKRUPTCY

As pension regulations have multiplied, the jargon surrounding pensions has mounted. But the rules protect pension money, even in the case of a company bankruptcy, Downing says. This is because pensions must be segregated from other company funds and will survive a bankruptcy. Paul Love, a partner in the pension services group at Price

Waterhouse, outlines some questions that will bring out the most pertinent information around the company pension

WHAT TYPE OF PENSION ARE YOU ENTITLED TO?

Traditional defined-benefit plans, in which the employer guarantees a defined income for life, often based on a formula involving years of employment and average or peak earnings, represent the vast majority of Canadian plans. However, they are losing popularity because of their inherent complexity and cost, as well as their shortcomings when early retirement is considered. Many smaller and mid-size companies are opting for defined-contribution plans in which the amount of money you get at retirement depends on the amount contributed to the plan and the investment yields it earns during your working life. The employer or employee, or both, contribute a defined amount to the plan, which is managed by a professional investment manager. In some cases, the employee has a choice of how the pension money is to be invested.

Do you have a profit-sharing plan or group RRSP in which employees pool money for RRSP investment? Unlike the more paternal defined-benefit plans, these plans leave the risk – and the investment choices – in the hands of employees. In this sense they are like defined-contribution plans.

Many people welcome the opportunity to make their own investment decisions, says Denise Castonguay, vice-president and general manager of Trimark Pensions, a division of Trimark Mutual Funds Ltd. However, she says employees with these types of plans need some investment education. Many Canadians prefer such safe investments as GICs, which may not grow sufficiently to provide an adequate yield in real after-inflation terms.

ARE THERE PROGRAMS OVER AND ABOVE THE COMPANY PLAN?

Some companies offer supplementary entitlements for anyone earning more than $80,000 (see "Finding the Money to Retire"). Pension plans give up to 60% of income after retirement to those earning up to about $86,000. After that, the portion of earnings received after retirement from a company plan declines. If there is a supplementary plan, check how it is funded, Love suggests. Some of the funding may come from employer profit and amount to little more than a promise.

AT WHAT AGE WILL YOU BE ENTITLED TO A COMPANY PENSION?

What is the normal retirement age? What is the penalty for early retirement? Some firms offer reduced benefits for those who retire early. Others apply tests to determine entitlements.

HOW DOES YOUR COMPANY PLAN MESH WITH YOUR RETIREMENT STRATEGY?

You may want to check out the tax implications of when you begin taking income from your RRSP and other investments. With a pension that's not indexed, you may take little from your RRSP in the early years and let the money grow. When the pension money starts to be insufficient, that may be the time to start using the RRSPs.

FINDING THE MONEY TO RETIRE

John is 53 and has just been laid off from a $100,000-a-year executive position. Is his original goal of retiring at age 63 still realistic? We asked Alain Quennec, financial adviser at Vancouver's Rogers Group, to run some projections using a planning package called RRIFmetic for Windows, from Fimetrics Systems Ltd. of Vancouver.

HERE ARE THE KEY INPUTS
• John was part of a defined benefit pension plan before being laid off. That will generate a non-indexed pension income of $30,000 at age 63.
• He has a new job at $50,000 a year, with no pension.
• John has only $60,000 in his RRSP, but has established a spousal plan for his 50-year-old wife, Mary, worth $290,000.
• Mary earns $25,000 a year as a part-time consultant.
• In two years, the couple expects a $150,000 inheritance.
• Inflation averages 4% a year.
• Investment returns average 8% a year.
• Their income goal in retirement is $45,000 a year after taxes (70% of what his executive job paid after taxes).
• They will live 30 years after retiring. The house is paid off, children grown.

HERE ARE RRIFMETIC'S OUTPUTS
John must contribute $6,000 a year to the spousal RRSP plan until retirement. Assuming $4,250 a year of income from the Canada Pension Plan, he will have $25,000 a year after tax, in today's dollars. Mary must contribute $1,500 a year to her own plan. Assuming another $4,250 a year of income from CPP, Mary will have $20,000 of after-tax income.

PENSION EXPECTATIONS MAY BE TOO GREAT

Employees in private pension plans are more optimistic than they should be about their prospects for enjoying a sustainable retirement income, a study released last year shows. Canadians are going to have to become more actively involved in their retirement planning, chiefly because of the continuing shift from the traditional defined benefit (DB) pension to more portable defined contribution (DC) plans, says Warren Laing, president and chief executive at HRL Funds Management Ltd. of Toronto. DB pension plans guarantee members a set amount of money in retirement. With DC plans, members set aside a regular amount, often in equity mutual funds, and end up with variable and less predictable income.

The next generation of pensioners may be in for a shock when they realize that "investment returns are going to shrink, the cost of living isn't going to go down and people are retiring earlier and living longer," Laing says. He predicts the average pension

PENSION PLAN
WISH LIST

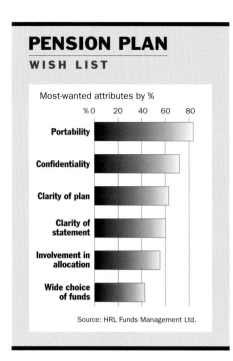

Most-wanted attributes by %

Source: HRL Funds Management Ltd.

plan's annual investment returns will fall to 3.9% in 1997 and continue in the low single digits for the foreseeable future. That prospect is more frightening when one considers investors have become complacent because of the high returns enjoyed so far in the 1990s. Laing says pension plans generated an average compound annual return of 14.8% between 1991 and 1996. Over the long term – 1926 through 1996 – the compound return managed 8.4%.

MANY HAVE FAITH IN COMPANY PLANS

The HRL-commissioned survey, conducted by Andover Research Associates and Intel-liPulse, restricted itself to people aged 25 to 60 who are in a private pension plan. Almost half (48%) were optimistic they will be able to retire at age 65, compared with only 21% who were pessimistic. A telling result was that 53% of DB members were optimistic, versus only 45% of DC members. Nearly three-quarters of high-income earners were optimistic, compared with less than half of all survey respondents classified as baby boomers. Among DB members, 45% believed they could live comfortably even if they retired before age 65, versus only 37% of DC members.

A majority of respondents still had faith their company pension plan would be there when they need it. Nearly two-thirds disagreed with the suggestion firms might reduce or scrap their support for company-sponsored pension plans. "We are amazed" by the level of optimism revealed by the survey, Laing says. "These results raise serious issues."

DEFINED CONTRIBUTION PLANS ARE LESS PROFITABLE BUT MORE PORTABLE

Many Canadians appear to be ignoring the implications of the shift to DC plans. If the trend continues, Canadians will have to "increase their retirement savings substantially if they want to retire comfortably." The survey identified shortfalls of up to 30% between what DC members say is important and how satisfied they actually are with their plans. This gap showed up in every demographic group. "Are DC plans delivering? The answer is a resounding no," Laing says. "The industry has a long way to go before [these] plans meet their needs."

Pension consultant Malcolm Hamilton of William M. Mercer Ltd. says employees' optimism over their retirement prospects may be misplaced but is understandable. "Investment results have been so good for so long that even if they return to normal it's going to feel like it's bad."

But retiring at age 65 is no great accomplishment, Hamilton says, since few employees will be retiring based only on the investment results of their DC plans. "Many of these people will get Canada Pension Plan, Seniors Benefit or sell their principal residences." Nor did Hamilton interpret the survey as a reason for employees to embrace DB plans again. "DB plans are the least portable of plans," he says. "According to the survey, portability is the No. 1 concern."

DEFINED CONTRIBUTION MEMBERS WANT MORE SAY IN HOW MONEY IS INVESTED

The survey found 83% of respondents want plans that can easily follow them from employer to employer. About three-quarters cited confidentiality about the assets in their plans as important. Two-thirds said it was important their plan and its supporting statements be easy to understand. More than half said they want a strong say in how their contributions are invested. Among DC members, 44% believed it is important to be given expanded investment choices, defined as access to most mutual funds and guaranteed investment certificates.

CPP A CASE OF EVERY LITTLE BIT HELPS

When you're assessing your retirement finances, don't forget the Canada Pension Plan – it won't make you rich but it can be a good source of supplementary income. And unlike many other income sources, CPP benefits are fully indexed to inflation, meaning they won't lose value over time. The maximum annual CPP retirement benefit for 1997 is $8,840. This dollar figure will increase every January based on inflation for the preceding year. The amount you eventually receive depends on when you retire and how much and for how long you contributed to the plan.

CPP BENEFITS WILL BE BASED ON PREVIOUS FIVE-YEAR PENSIONABLE EARNINGS

Benefits are based on the average of yearly maximum pensionable earnings (YMPE) over the most recent three years, but this is slated to become five years. (See box on the following page for details of the proposed premium changes.) According to Malcolm Hamilton, at the actuarial firm of William Mercer Ltd. in Toronto, the benefit reduction stemming from the formula change will be roughly equivalent to the average inflation rate. If inflation averages 2% a year, your benefits will be about 2% less than they would have been with the three-year average.

If you're nearing retirement, you can get a pretty close idea of your CPP entitlement from the Statement of Contributions the government sends you every three or four years. If you want more details, you can contact your nearest Income Security Programs (ISP) office. David Conway, national director at CIBC Trust, urges some caution in interpreting future CPP benefit estimates. "The changes being made to CPP now mean there's a greater chance it will exist in future. I just hope they don't change the rules down the road and start clawing back payments like they're planning to do with the Seniors Benefit."

HERE ARE SOME POINTS TO CONSIDER ON CPP'S ROLE IN RETIREMENT PLANNING

• **Want to split income?** Couples who are both at least 60 and in different tax brackets can "assign" some of their CPP retirement benefits to each other and possibly save on taxes. The amount that you can split with your spouse depends on how long you have lived together while contributing to the plan. For example, if you lived together for 20% of both your contributory periods, you can split 20% of your benefits. (The same type of pro rating formula is applied to the division of CPP benefits upon divorce.) If you retire in the middle tax bracket (about 42% depending on province) and your spouse has no income, the first $538 transferred to him or her will generate a tax saving of $225 annually. Any further transfers would reduce your ability to claim the spousal credit, but even so, you stand to save about 16¢ on each additional dollar. The savings are even greater if you are in the top tax bracket.

• **Thinking about retiring early?** You can start drawing CPP benefits as early as age 60 provided that your income from other sources at the time is less than your benefit entitlements, or you have "substantially ceased working." This requirement does not apply once you reach 65. If you do opt for early retirement, your CPP payments will be reduced 0.5% for every month before age 65 that you begin to collect. So, for example, if you were to retire at the age of 62 (36 months before age 65), you would be entitled to 18% less than your regular benefit. At age 60 the regular benefit would be reduced by 30%. Conway says collecting reduced benefits before 65 could affect your entitlement for the proposed Seniors Benefit after age 65.

"If smaller CPP payments are included in your Seniors Benefit clawback calculation, then depending on your circumstances, this could result in your getting an increased benefit." You also can defer CPP benefits until after age 65 if you wish and will receive 0.5% more benefit for each month's deferral, to a maximum of 30% extra per year if starting at age 70.

CPP PREMIUMS GOING UP, | WAY UP

Canada Pension Plan premium payments are up and going higher over the next five years. For 1997, the contribution rate was 6% of pensionable earnings between $3,500 and $35,800. That rate increased to 6.4% for 1998 and will go to 9.9% by the year 2003. At the same time, the pensionable earnings ceiling is indexed to average industrial wages while the floor is fixed, meaning the amount of earnings subject to contribution will increase over time. For example, if wages rise with inflation at 2% a year, pensionable earnings will increase from $32,300 for 1997 to more than $36,800 for the year 2003.

The combined impact of these changes would see maximum CPP premiums rise from $1,938 in 1997 to about $3,645 in 2003. Furthermore, since CPP contributions generate only a bottom-bracket tax credit (as opposed to a full deduction as is the case with RRSP or pension contributions), anyone in the middle or top tax bracket will get only a partial offset. For someone currently in the top marginal bracket, the net after-tax cost would be the same as for an RRSP or pension contribution of almost $5,400.

- **Change your mind about retiring early?** You can cancel your decision up to six months after starting to collect CPP benefits. You must repay any benefits you have received to date and your future entitlement will be unaffected.
- **Worked in another country?** You may be entitled to a pension from that country for your work. If not, you may be able to have the working time factored into your CPP benefit calculations.
- **Planning to leave Canada when you retire?** CPP benefits can be collected anywhere in the world. If you move to the U.S. Sunbelt and arrange to have the money deposited to your U.S. account, it will even be converted into U.S. funds automatically. However, you should ascertain the tax implications of receiving this government pension in your destination country before you move. A financial adviser familiar with the tax regimes of both Canada and the other country could be of great value.
- **Make sure to apply early.** You must apply to receive CPP benefits – they do not come automatically, and ISP may not be able to backdate payments. You should allow at least six months for your application to be processed and for the cheques to start arriving.

PLAN CAREFULLY BEFORE CHANGING COUNTRY

Canadian income tax liability is based on residence, so the date on which an immigrant or emigrant becomes or ceases to be a Canadian resident is a key factor in determining how, and how much, income will be subject to Canadian tax. Generally, the date of commencement or cessation of Canadian residence is the date of the physical move. However, business, financial and social considerations may also affect the factual determination of residence status. It is even possible an individual will be considered to be a resident of more than one country for tax purposes. In such situations, income tax treaties between the countries will usually resolve the residency question.

In the year in which an individual establishes or relinquishes Canadian residence, he or she is considered a part-year resident and is taxable on worldwide income for the portion of the year he or she is a resident of Canada. A part-year resident is also subject to Canadian tax on certain Canadian-source income received for the relevant part of the year.

IMMIGRATION

When an individual becomes a resident of Canada, he or she is deemed to have disposed of and re-acquired each property, except taxable Canadian property, owned immediately prior to establishing residence, for proceeds equal to the fair market value of the properties at that time. Taxable Canadian property includes Canadian real property, capital property used in carrying on a business in Canada, shares of Canadian private corporations, certain shares of public companies and Canadian resource properties.

For properties deemed to be acquired, a new cost base is struck and any gains that accrued before commencement of Canadian residence will not be subject to Canadian tax. Once Canadian residence is established, your world income becomes taxable in Canada at our graduated rates. Any foreign source income received after becoming a resident of Canada will likely be subject to foreign as well as Canadian tax, but to avoid double taxation, any foreign taxes paid in respect of this income generally are eligible for a foreign tax credit in Canada.

THESE RULES GIVE RISE TO THE FOLLOWING CONSIDERATIONS

• If tax rates in the country from which you are emigrating are lower than Canadian rates, try to receive all foreign source remuneration before establishing Canadian residency.

• Review your investment portfolio before establishing Canadian residence. It may be advantageous to sell investments with accrued losses to avoid a future Canadian capital gain combined with a foreign capital loss.

• If marginal tax rates are lower here than in the other country, try to plan the date of commencement of Canadian residence to take advantage of this. For example, if you were to take up residency in Canada in September and earned $30,000 during the remainder of the year, it would all be taxed at the lowest marginal rate; if you immigrated in April and earned $60,000 in Canada, more than half would be taxed at the much higher middle rate.

• If you own significant foreign investments, consider establishing a non-resident trust before becoming a Canadian resident to shelter income from these investments from Canadian tax for up to five years. Consult your tax adviser about this planning opportunity.

• Review the tax consequences of any employer benefits paid relating to the relocation to Canada. Where possible, try to structure the benefits so that they will not be taxable in Canada. For example, moving-expense reimbursements and some mortgage subsidies are not considered taxable, while a standard-of-living equalization payment has been held to be taxable by the courts.

• If you were a member of a foreign pension plan, your employer may be able to continue to contribute to that plan. However, such contributions will reduce your ability to use registered retirement savings plans, registered pension plans and deferred profit sharing plans.

• If you were a member of a foreign pension plan, you may be able to transfer your plan holdings to an RRSP on a tax-free basis.

• You may be able to continue coverage under the social security system of your former country and opt out of the Canada Pension Plan.

• If you own stock options from your foreign employer, it may be wise to exercise the options before establishing residence if the foreign country taxes the benefit more favorably than Canada does.

EMIGRATION

When an individual ceases to be a resident of Canada, he or she is deemed to dispose of all property owned for fair market value at that date. Exceptions to this rule include real property situated in Canada, capital property used in a business carried on by the individual through a permanent establishment in Canada, pension rights (from RPPs, RRSPs and registered retirement income funds), employee stock options and, for certain short-term Canadian residents, property owned when the individual became resident here. This means any accrued gains on non-exempt property will be taxed in the year of departure. However, instead of having to pay the tax immediately, emigrating taxpayers are permitted to post security with Revenue Canada and pay the tax when the property is actually sold.

If the value of assets you own when you cease to be a resident of Canada exceeds $25,000, you must report their total value and details of each property, other than personal-use properties individually valued at less than $10,000. Once you cease to be a resident of Canada, you are no longer taxed in Canada on your worldwide income. However, if you receive Canadian-source income as a non-resident, such income generally will be subject to Canadian income tax. Certain types of Canadian-source income, such as interest, dividends, rents and pension income, will be subject to Canadian withholding tax at a general rate of 25% (which may be reduced under a tax treaty with your new country).

If you earn Canadian-source employment or business income or sell taxable Canadian property as a non-resident, you will be required to file a Canadian tax return reporting this income and pay the resultant tax. If you are required to report this income as taxable income in your new country, you may be able to claim a foreign tax credit for the Canadian tax paid.

CONSIDER THE FOLLOWING

- Establish the date you became a non-resident and ensure this date can be supported by the facts.
- Make RRSP contributions in the year of departure if you have contribution room. (It is generally advantageous to leave RRSPs in place when leaving Canada, as long as keeping money in an RRSP does not create tax problems in your new country.)
- If you rent out your Canadian home or another property after ceasing Canadian residence, you will be subject to 25% Canadian non-resident withholding tax on the gross rental income. A better alternative may be to elect to file a Canadian tax return, reporting net rental income (after deducting applicable expenses), which will be subject to marginal tax rates.
- If you plan to retain any Canadian bank accounts or investment accounts after ceasing residence, notify the Canadian payers of interest and dividends to withhold and remit the appropriate amount of Canadian withholding tax.
- It may be advantageous to sell property with accrued gains if these gains could be taxed in the new country.

SUCCESSION IN FAMILY BUSINESS CAN BE TRICKY

Who's going to take over the family business when you pass on? It's a question almost every company owner must confront at one time or another, and it can give rise to many problems if not addressed well in advance of the actual event. "The first piece of advice I would give to anyone contemplating a business succession is to start planning early," says Debby Stern, a partner at KPMG in Toronto. "It can take five years or more to arrange a proper and orderly transition. At the least, early planning reduces problems if you suddenly become disabled," Stern adds. "What if the children are too young to take over – do you bring in professional management? Can your wife cope with the responsibilities? If nobody knows what you want done, the result could be a distress sale. That's to no one's benefit but the buyer."

THERE ARE MANY QUESTIONS TO CONSIDER IN SETTING A SUCCESSION PLAN

Even when you've made a succession plan and have a successor in mind, there may be conflicts and problems to resolve. "You may have children already in the business, but are they up to the task of running it?" Stern asks. "Do they need more training or expertise? How much, and where do they get it?" Timing can be a problem too. Stern cites the example of a client who wants to retire in five years, but has two sons who think they can run the business as a team right away. "This is fairly common. They're trying to pressure him to leave, but he doesn't want to go just yet. He's going to have to resolve this conflict somehow."

What if you don't want to retire completely? Have you made arrangements to continue on in a reduced capacity, perhaps as a consultant or an honorary board member? What if you want to retain control over the company even though you are no longer actively involved? "You have to be careful, because there can be a lot of points of dissension and conflict between family members," Stern says. "The situation can get quite emotional and contentious, so you have to identify all the issues and stumbling blocks, and discuss them with everybody in advance. You have to develop arrangements acceptable to everyone concerned."

IN PLANNING A SUCCESSION, YOU HAVE TO BE FAIR TO ALL FAMILY MEMBERS

Sometimes, for example, an owner wants to pass the business title to a spouse but place the son in charge of its operation. This could result in making the spouse dependent on the son for income to survive – not an ideal situation. One way around this problem is to provide for the spouse separately through life insurance. That way his or her needs can be covered regardless of what happens with the business. The situation can be more complicated if more than one child is involved, especially if the business is your single biggest asset. "What if you have a son who is in the business, and you also have a daughter who wants no involvement in the company?" Gordon asks. "Do you still give them both half shares? This can create tensions for the son, who is doing all the work and getting only half the rewards.

"In planning a succession, you have to think about what's fair for your children and not necessarily what's equitable," Gordon adds. "If you have substantial personal assets, maybe they can be given to the daughter while the son inherits the business. But if not, then again, life insurance can be used to help ensure everyone is treated fairly, without causing problems for the business."

ESTATE PLANNING IS ESSENTIAL

 In the cavalcade of life's pleasures, estate planning probably ranks below trips to the dentist for most people. But the cost of a disorderly estate to your loved ones, your favorite charities and your business (if any) can be enormous. What happens when you die without any preparations – that is, you die "intestate" without a properly drafted will? In general, all your last year's income and any as-yet untaxed assets – including RRSPs and RRIFs, real estate (other than your principal residence), shares and mutual funds with accrued gains – are lumped together in your estate and taxed as income for the final year.

So, for example, the estate of someone with $30,000 in pension income for the year, plus $200,000 in RRSPs or RRIFs and perhaps real estate or other equities with accrued gains of $100,000 could face a tax bill approaching $150,000. And that's just the beginning – your provincial government will take over the estate, perhaps liquidating non-cash assets for fire-sale prices to pay the tax bill and other liabilities, then distributing whatever's left to family members according to a strict formula.

The distribution formula can vary somewhat by province, but generally leaves a share to your spouse and splits the rest between children. If there is no immediate family, it goes to your nearest relatives. If no relatives can be found, the province keeps all. If you happen to own a business, there's more. Your ownership shares will be thrown into the estate pot and taxed as well, before being passed on to family or relatives as per the above list. Without clear instructions on succession, the business could founder or be torn apart by rivals within and without.

There are, of course, lots of wrinkles and exceptions to the above scenarios, but the point is that if you have any wishes regarding your estate, you will have to set them down for yourself. No one will be able to second-guess what you want after you're gone. Despite this harsh reality, though, many people still try to ignore the inevitability of death and final taxes. In her book *You Can't Take it With You: The Common-Sense Guide to Estate Planning for Canadians*, author Sandra E. Foster suggests the top five reasons for not preparing an estate:

1. You like to pay taxes.
2. Your family always gets along.
3. The government will look after it for you.
4. You're not old enough.
5. You will live forever.

Except perhaps for number 4, she notes, the other reasons are hardly legitimate justification for deferring this chore. So what should you do, and when should you start? To answer the second question first, you should start planning your estate as early as possible, if only to avert nasty consequences in the event of an untimely accident. And certainly you should set down your testamentary wishes once you have begun to raise and support a family, to ensure they'd be cared for in your absence.

SOME SUGGESTIONS ON GETTING STARTED

1. Make and update your will. The first step in organizing your estate is to draft a proper will. You can simply write one yourself and have someone witness it – a "holograph" will – but there are potential legal snags that could leave it open to dispute. In most cases it would be better to have a lawyer versed in estate law vet the document. You also should update the will periodically. Most experts suggest once every three years or so. That way you can allow for changes in tax and other laws or in personal or business circumstances. The classic example here is the man who divorces and then remarries without changing his original will, in which case the original spouse could get the lion's share of his assets.

2. Appoint an executor. You will need someone to administer your estate and ensure your testamentary wishes are executed. This individual can be anyone – your spouse, a relative or friend or a professional. But bear in mind that the executor's duties can be numerous and complex. The person you choose will be responsible for making funeral arrangements, locating the will and obtaining probate (many financial institutions will refuse to release assets in the absence of letters of probate), locating and valuating all your assets, arranging for their safe keeping where appropriate, advertising for creditors, preparing a statement of assets and liabilities, discharging liabilities, liquidating assets in the most tax- and cost-effective manner where required to settle debts or meet the terms of the will, preparing and filing tax returns (there could be as many as three different returns), notifying beneficiaries . . . and the list goes on. Your spouse probably will be unable to handle all these duties during a period of bereavment. Friends and relatives may understand your personal wishes but lack the necessary skills to do everything in a cost-effective and efficient manner.

For this reason, many people opt for a professional executor or joint executorship between a professional and a friend or relative. The executors' compensation depends on several factors, including the size and complexity of the estate and the duration of the administration. Courts have approved a percentage-based tariff, which is applied in most instances involving an estate of average complexity. Roughly, the tariff invokes an annual charge of 5% of the income earned in the estate plus a management fee of two-fifths of 1% of the assets of the estate under investment. There is also a capital charge equal to 5% of the value of the estate assets, payable as the estate assets are realized and disbursed to beneficiaries or used to meet capital expenditures of the estate. Courts will deviate from the tariff for cause, but you should generally assume executors' compensation will be calculated on that basis, if there is no contract.

3. Assign a power of attorney. This should be done at the same time you draft your will. Basically, the power of attorney provides for someone else to take over your financial as well as health-related matters if you should become incapacitated. Don't assume your spouse could simply take over your affairs because unless a POA exists, your affairs could be frozen until a court or public trustee determines what should be done and allows the spouse to take over.

4. Prepare for business succession. If you own a business, the issue of succession can be highly complicated. As with personal matters, you should start early and give consideration to individual as well as financial implications (see "Succession in Family Business Can Be Complicated").

5. Organize your affairs. You want to arrange your finances to maximize the benefits for those you love, while minimizing taxes. In this regard, there are many strategies you can undertake including:

- Transferring assets to family members or others beforehand.
- Freezing your estate with a trust.
- Placing assets into joint ownership.
- Triggering gains when the tax bill will be lower.

Any of these strategies involve complications, though. For example, some people trying to avoid probate fees will transfer assets while alive, or put them into joint ownership so they pass directly to the co-owner upon death. But this will result in a deemed disposition and unless you're transferring the assets to your spouse at cost – the only person other than certain dependents entitled to this treatment – you may be hit with an immediate hefty tax bill. Joint ownership transfers also mean that earned income from the portfolio will now be divided equally between all joint owners.

LIFE INSURANCE SHOULD BE A PART OF GOOD ESTATE-PLANNING STRATEGY

Some people try to reduce their final tax tab by giving away assets to their children while alive. This may also trigger a large tax liability right away. And the assets revert to the recipient, for them to do with as they please, not an appealing option if you want to keep a rein on a child's profligate ways. Many good estate preservation strategies involve the use of life insurance. When the first spouse dies, RRSPs, RIFs and other assets can be rolled over to the surviving spouse tax-free. But when the second spouse dies, the government takes the taxes deferred on those assets before they are passed on to children or other beneficiaries. An insurance policy can cover that liability with proceeds that are tax free. Proceeds from permanent insurance are most commonly used to pay off Revenue Canada when capital gains are realized on death. But many also use them to generate cash for their estate to equalize payments to all beneficiaries or to donate money to their favorite charities.

Another planning point: Many couples have one spouse with a company pension plan and one without, either because they have been out of the workforce or because their job provided no pension plan. The spouse with the pension plan has the choice of a life annuity for a single person only or a joint-life annuity, which extends over the life of both partners but gives a lower benefit. An alternative is to buy a life insurance policy that will provide the spouse with a lump sum that can be invested to provide income. The increased benefits of the life annuity may be high enough to support the cost of premiums. Whatever the case, estate planning can be complicated. It behooves most people to seek professional help in arranging their estate and thus avoid many of the potential pitfalls that await the unwary.

TRUSTS LET YOU CONTROL YOUR MONEY

A trust arises when a person transfers legal title of property to another person (the trustee) with instructions as to how the property is to be used for designated beneficiaries. All types of assets can be placed in trust, including bank accounts, stocks and bonds, mutual fund units, real estate, even private businesses. There are two main purposes for trusts: They let you control how money is used, and they can generate tax savings. Sometimes, too, trusts can help protect assets from creditors.

A trust set up while you're alive is called an inter vivos, or a "living," trust, but you also can also set up in your will a "testamentary" trust, which will allow your wishes to be carried out after you die. For example, a charitable remainder trust allows you to donate a cottage or artwork to charity, generating a tax credit now and allowing you use of the item while you're still alive. Or, you could put assets into trust to support disabled family members when you're gone.

Many small investors may already have trusts and not realize it. If you are putting money into a mutual fund for a child's education, it may be held "in trust" for them. There's no written document but there is an intention to create a trust in that situation, says Sean Foran, vice-president of client services for Trust Company of Bank of Montreal. But this may not cover contingencies such as what happens to the assets upon premature death of the child, so a more formal trust has advantages.

TRUSTS MUST BE PROPERLY DRAFTED TO PROTECT INDIVIDUAL'S WISHES

Because a formal, irrevocable trust cannot be changed, it's essential the trust agreement, or will, be properly drafted and accurately reflect the individual's wishes. The trust agreement should be drawn up by an estate and trust lawyer but any estate-planning expert can help frame the issues and wishes. Typical one-time start-up legal costs are between $2,500 and $5,000, while associated income-tax preparation services can run about $500. There are also recurring annual trustee fees that can run 0.8% to 1% of assets.

CHOOSE RRSP BENEFICIARIES CAREFULLY

Designating a beneficiary for your RRSP or RRIF seems simple enough. But last-minute designations – and even those made more carefully – can produce a minefield of problems. The seemingly fair division of your estate can easily become unfair because there are two types of beneficiaries for registered plans. The first category, i.e., spouses, qualify for tax-free rollovers to their own plans. If you have no spouse, the money can be rolled into a plan for an infirm child or grandchild who's dependent on you or be used to buy an annuity to support a healthy dependent child or grandchild until age 18.

All others fall into the second category. They do not qualify for tax-free rollovers, and that's where unfairness can come roaring in. Since there's no rollover, the institution will treat the transaction as a withdrawal and issue a T4 tax slip – but to your estate, not the beneficiary. Consider the case of a widower who has $200,000 split evenly between an RRSP and some term deposits. He wants to treat his adult son and favorite niece evenly, so he leaves the $100,000 in term deposits to his son through a will and names the niece beneficiary of his RRSP. Unfortunately, the niece will get her full share but the son won't. He'll get only what's left after the estate pays $50,000 income tax on the RRSP cashout that went to the niece. The only way the niece would be hit for tax is if the estate didn't have enough money to pay the bill. Only then does the law let Revenue Canada go after the RRSP beneficiary.

A better plan would have been for the widower to leave the RRSP to his estate and name the son and niece equal beneficiaries. They would evenly divide the term deposits and share what's left of the RRSP after tax. But leaving the RRSP to the estate means it might face probate fees – a big concern in Ontario where the levy is $15 per $1,000 of estate value over $50,000 (plus $5 per $1,000 up to $50,000). Some people try to avoid probate by naming joint beneficiaries so the RRSP money will be paid to them outside the estate and won't face probate – unless the financial institution holding the plan insists on it. But this can cause problems too.

NAMING JOINT BENEFICIARIES CAN LEAD TO COMPLICATIONS

Say our widower named his son and niece as joint beneficiaries of the RRSP. The son, who has a child of his own, dies first and his grief-stricken widow soon afterward. The niece will get the entire RRSP while the orphaned grandchild gets far less than the share intended for his father. That's because the niece was the only named beneficiary alive at the time the RRSP was cashed out and, of course, the tax bill went to the widower's estate, reducing the amount available for the grandchild. To avoid this problem, some institutions allow only one person to be named RRSP/RRIF beneficiary. Or, say you have two sons aged 19 and 12. Since the 12-year-old would qualify for a tax-free rollover, you name him as beneficiary of the RRSP and, in your will, leave the other assets of equal value to the older son. Six years later you die without having updated either document. John, now 18, no longer qualifies for a tax-free rollover but still gets the full RRSP, while Sam's inheritance gets reduced because the estate has to pay the tax on the RRSP cashout.

- You can make RRSP/RRIF designations in your will or the plan contracts. If you do both, make sure they match and get updated together.
- Say you name your spouse beneficiary in your RRSP contract and then divorce. Make sure to change that designation – divorce automatically revokes designations in a will but not necessarily in an over-the-counter form. If you remarry, make a new will with a clear statement revoking all previous RRSP beneficiary designations.

DONATIONS IN WILLS NEED A SECOND LOOK

Much personal giving comes by way of bequests in wills – given that most people make large donations only when they are certain that giving away money or other assets will not jeopardize the family lifestyle. However, recent tax changes have made it important for many individuals to revise their approach to bequests. Thus a review of wills, particularly of charitable bequests contained in them, is necessary.

The key donation-related tax change of recent years is that gifts (including those made through a will) made in the year of death and in the preceding year can be claimed as a tax credit of up to 100% of the deceased's income. This may prompt many people to modify their wills to increase charitable donations. The same change has created a major opportunity with regard to donating money in RRSPs or RRIFs. Until 1996, RRSP/RRIF money paid to an estate was fully taxable and if transferred by will to a charity, only 20% of the amount would be eligible for a tax credit. Now, donations from estates can be transferred to a charity tax-free.

However, a charity cannot be named directly as a beneficiary of an RRSP or a RRIF, so the gift must be made in two steps. First, the money must be paid to the estate, which usually can be done only if there is no surviving spouse or dependent child. Then there must be a will that states the money must be transferred to one or more named charities.

Another change of significance: many wills directed charitable gifts to Crown agency foundations, which provincial governments often set up for certain charities such as universities and museums, because until 1996 only such gifts qualified for a tax credit of up to 100% of income. Now that the 100% tax relief is available for a donation to any registered charity, it may be more desirable to have money bequeathed directly to a charitable organization rather than its Crown agency foundation. If so, the appropriate change to the will should be made.

FAMILY ISSUES IMPEDE TO ESTATE PLANNING

Estate planning is aimed at providing for the orderly tax-effective distribution of your assets at death. Entrepreneurs should embrace the idea since so much of their lives – and their family's well-being – is tied up in their companies. But that's often not the case, says Wally Howick, Toronto-based vice-president with Bank of Montreal's private client services: "The minute you start talking about estate planning, many of them get antsy. They're just not ready to deal with succession; family issues are the single biggest impediment to estate planning."

AN ESTATE FREEZE CAN AVOID A LARGE TAX BILL

The incorporated business owner is caught in a dilemma between prudent tax planning and preserving family harmony, Howick says. Without planning, the harder you work, the bigger that bill. Say your company was incorporated at $100 and is now worth $1 million. If you died today, the tax hit would be about $400,000. Say you continue to build the business to $10 million and then die. The tax would be about $4 million. You can turn off the tax clock by doing an "estate freeze" that revamps the company's ownership. Normally, the entrepreneur converts his or her common shares to preferred shares frozen at today's value. Other family members – typically adult children – get new common shares that grow in value as the company grows.

Howick has found many entrepreneurs understand the tax rationale but still shy away because they're not ready to work out who gets what and are afraid of blowing apart the family. Those who don't plan add to their family's burden during a time of grief and can leave the business vulnerable, he warns. "Your competitors may smell blood and go after your customer base, and even long-time suppliers may want to revisit their relationship."

Tax and succession planning don't have to be done together, Howick stresses. He outlined a way to freeze your tax liability but still buy time to work out the company's future with your family. For simplicity, Howick uses the example of a $1-million business, even though he feels the fees involved make a full freeze worthwhile only for companies worth at least $4 million. As above, the founder's current cost base is $100.

THE PLAN CALLS FOR THREE SETS OF SHARES

• Normal freeze preferred shares for the entrepreneur, valued at $1 million. Though non-voting, they're retractable so he or she can always demand the money.
• Special preferred shares for the entrepreneur. There would be 1,000 valued at $1 each. These would be voting shares.
• New common shares for family members. There would be 100 valued at $1 each.

A discretionary trust is created. If the entrepreneur has a living parent, Howick says it's technically best if the parent creates the trust with a gold coin or other nominal asset that does not produce income. The trust then borrows $100 from an arm's-length lender. Now, the key. Instead of going directly to the adult children, the new common shares are bought by the trust. The trust deed names the children as beneficiaries but does not set their allocations. There might be three trustees: the entrepreneur, a reliable friend and a professional adviser. That caps the entrepreneur's tax exposure but leaves time for the family to focus on succession. The trustees can determine how much the various children are willing and able to get involved in the business.

THERE ARE THREE WAYS THE PLAN KEEPS THE ENTREPRENEUR IN CONTROL OF THE COMPANY

• The retraction feature allows him or her to demand redemption of all or part of the regular freeze preferred shares at any time.

• The special preferreds give the entrepreneur 1,000 votes compared with just 100 for the common shares.

• The entrepreneur is one of the trustees.

"Control is very important to entrepreneurs because they see the business as the key to the family's well-being," Howick says. His example assumes all the children are adults. More complex planning is required if there are minors. Usually, Howick adds, an entrepreneur wouldn't do a full freeze until he or she is over 50, though a younger owner-manager might consider a partial one in certain cases.

A non-profit organization – the Canadian Association of Family Enterprise – can help with communication and other issues and has chapters across Canada.

CHAPTER 9

PERSONAL | PLANNING

- Strategy
- Protecting your credit rating
- Mortgage options
- Buying a home and renting
- Financing your family's education
- Bankruptcy

DEALING WITH THE OBSESSION

KNOWN AS PERSONAL FINANCE | BY JONATHAN CHEVREAU

PERSONAL FINANCE IS NOT A NEW TOPIC, although the recent proliferation of financial Internet sites, books, television shows and repositioned publications seems to suggest it is a brand-new journalistic beat. The reason for this renewed and intense multimedia attention is not hard to fathom and almost too obvious to mention. Money is one of the three gods of modern society, the other two being power and sex. And arguably, money can buy those two. You could more succinctly use the term "My Money" to describe Personal Finance. After all, other people's money is nowhere near as fascinating as your own.

The obsession with personal finance is intensified by the ongoing demographic trends in North America and around the world. This is well documented in such books as *Boom, Bust & Echo* and *The Pig & the Python*. The baby boomers have become affluent and, as they turn 50 in large numbers, they are becoming obsessed with having enough money for retirement. Most boomers are now closer to retirement than they are to the pivotal event of their youth: 1969's Woodstock festival. Few worried about retirement then and they are frantically trying to make up for lost time, taking on perhaps more risk than many are comfortable with.

This generation has bought into the notion that stocks are the best vehicle for growing their RRSPs, to the point they rely on them for retirement income. Hence their keen interest in the stock market and their angst over the Oct. 27, 1997, mini-crash. Many also realize that investing in stocks or bonds is best left to professionals, which accounts for their willingness to delegate security selection to mutual fund managers and the current mutual fund mania.

THERE IS MORE TO FINANCIAL PLANNING THAN GUARANTEEING RETIREMENT INCOME

The generation that has followed the boomers shares their concerns about retirement, if only because it has little confidence the Canada Pension Plan is going to be there for them. While getting a job is their predominant worry, they too see their future in stocks and mutual funds held inside RRSPs. Then there are today's seniors. Down the road, they have a keen interest in the government's proposal to merge the current Old Age Security program with the Guaranteed Income Supplement, creating the much-debated Seniors Benefit. While saving for retirement is the single biggest topic in personal finance – and the subject of an earlier primer in this series – it encompasses much more than this. In this section, for example, we have primers for the first-time home buyer, how to be a cheapskate, 10 reasons for ditching the car and taking the train and others that originally appeared in *The Financial Post*.

Clearly, the average consumer is suffering from information overload. Apart from what we in the business term "pure editorial," there is also a bombardment of advertising, mostly from the banks and mutual fund companies. Face it, there's big money in personal finance. The journalistic waters are being muddied by pseudo journalists who have a toehold somewhere in the media to flog their personal business interests. Beware the shill in journalist's clothing. There's a difference between the objectivity of full-time journalists on the staffs of newspapers, magazines or broadcast outlets, and those whose real business is public speaking, financial planning, mutual fund sales or computer software.

PERSONAL FINANCE ADVICE COMES IN ALL SHAPES AND SIZES

Before you make a financial decision based on what appears to be legitimate media commentary, you need to understand the nature of journalism and expertise. You need to be selective if you want to find some value in this surfeit of personal finance coverage. At some media outlets, there is a thin line between editorial and advertising. Many Web sites, for example, amount to little more than electronic brochures for various financial institutions. Also suspect are the hundreds of newsletters issued by financial planners. Marketing Solutions has created a package of materials that allows "Joe Planner" to stick his picture on top of a pre-written story and pass off a bunch of pre-written marketing bumf as his personal summary of the great financial events of the day. Some of this information may be good, but be aware that the underlying agenda is to get you to buy more financial products.

The same sort of discrimination needs to be applied in the burgeoning field of seminars. If the speaker is being sponsored by two or three mutual fund companies, how critical is he or she likely to be about mutual funds in general and those particular companies in particular? I'm not saying you should disregard their statements – I myself have given a few such talks – but at least take it all with a grain of salt and doublecheck all assertions afterward. As the conduit between the investor and the financial services industry, the watchword for the consumer of the media's prodigious output on personal finance topics should be "let the reader/viewer beware."

TIPS ON BUYING YOUR FIRST HOME

Thinking of buying your first home? It's not a bad time to do it as mortgage rates are low. Lots of people realize this, of course, which is why it has been a seller's market in most major Canadian cities since the fourth quarter of 1996, according to housing economist Mary McDonough. That puts first-time buyers in a more precarious position than they were in the bargain basement market of earlier this decade.

A friend just taking the plunge insists he has no time to read the various primers on the subject and that "surely it can all be summarized in a single column." It can't really, although you can get the free Ontario Real Estate Association (OREA) book, *How to Buy Your Home,* from a real estate agent or by calling 1-800-563-HOME. Unable to resist my friend's challenge, however, the rest of this section reflects my personal experience of buying a first home, moving up once and renovating.

LOCATION, LOCATION, LOCATION STILL CARRIES WEIGHT

The first thing this writer told him was that, like marriage, children and entering a lobster trap, buying your first home is easy to do. But if you make a mistake, getting out is a tricky, costly proposition. Luckily, first-time buyers are shielded from the realities of real estate commissions, which run at 5% or 6% and are paid by the seller. Sure, the price the house is listed at may reflect that commission but as a first-timer you get about the only free ride you're likely to get over a lifetime of home ownership. So you may as well use an agent, but be aware that agent may have the vendor's interest at heart more than yours. The OREA guide goes into this fully.

You can find an agent at any open house. There's no central place to check out agents' credentials, so don't rush to commit to the first random encounter. Try to get one to share their bible: the weekly updates of the Multiple Listing Service (MLS) covering the district you're considering. They're not supposed to give them out, but you can sometimes snag a copy of the previous week's edition. "Location, location, location" is the well-worn cliche about what's important in a home. Again, the decision is a bit like marriage. You're not just marrying a person, you're marrying into a family.

Same with a house. You don't want to live next to rental properties or crack houses or next to an alleyway. You don't want the traffic noise of a major street steps from your front door or be under airplane flight paths. You do want to be near public transportation, schools, day care, churches, parks and convenience shopping. Ideally, you'd find this all out by renting first in your proposed district – it's like living together before marriage. The corollary of location, location, location is "price, price, price." Obviously, the best locations cost the most and worst locations are cheap.

Young newlyweds may have to get a starter home in a lesser district and later pull up stakes and get the dream home in the classy district. Older first-timers with hefty down payments may be better off choosing their "dream district" right off the bat, even if it entails a slightly larger mortgage. The commission to later sell a $350,000 home would be $21,000. Add moving, legal and other expenses and there seems little point in compromising now and moving to the perfect situation later.

HOUSING OPTIONS INCLUDE CONDOS, TOWNHOUSES AND THE TRADITIONAL DETACHED HOME

There are condos, townhouses and those trendy lofts you see sprouting everywhere. I'm biased in favor of traditional detached houses on real land, where you can grow vegetables in the event of economic cataclysm or put on additions if boom times continue. Condos have maintenance fees, elevators and possibly noisy neighbors. Townhouses have you running up and down three flights of stairs, a negative as you age. Lofts seem an overpriced fad. It may have been a novel thing to have bought a genuine loft years back, but the current wave strikes me as artificial and blatantly commercial. I doubt there are bargains to be had. So we're back to a good old detached home on terra firma. Avoid semi-detached homes unless you're really strapped for cash, and avoid shared driveways. In both cases, the unknown variable is your immediate neighbor. I know a couple who were assaulted by an insane neighbor with whom they shared a driveway.

DECIDE ON YOUR "MUST" FEATURES BEFORE YOU BEGIN YOUR SEARCH

Another basic decision is new house or old. You have to pay GST on new homes, which tend to be out in the suburbs. Consider how you plan to commute to work in this case. New home construction schedules can be problematic and you need to be aware of various unforeseen closing costs. If you like "new" and the ability to customize to your needs, there are hundreds of full-page ads in the major newspapers. Old homes (resales) don't have GST on them but obviously are "used" homes. There are all sorts of potential maintenance problems to check out, such as roofs, furnaces and termites. Resales tend to be in established and more central districts and have lots of fully grown trees. The vendor may be more flexible on price.

Full two-storey houses are better than storey-and-a-half houses, which tend to have chopped-off room corners. A basement doesn't have to be renovated yet, but it should be full height so you can add a recreation room down the road. Many old houses are heated by hot water radiators. If you want central air conditioning, then look for houses heated with forced-air gas. Their furnaces can be later upgraded to air.

In Toronto, pick up the *Real Estate News* every week, since it's free on most any street corner, or try *Smart Seller* from various coffee shops. They list properties outside the agency loop. Also check out the Toronto Real Estate Board's Web site. Understand the concept of tradeoffs. There is no perfect house. If there was, you couldn't afford it. List the "must" features and those you prefer but can live without. You can do this on the Web search. I suggest leaving out small features that can be cheaply added at a later date. What you want is a good solid structure at a bargain price in the district you want, with the potential to later add your dream features. If you plan a major addition, make sure the lot size is large enough to conform to the building permit guidelines.

RESOURCE BOOKS HELP SORT OUT HOME BUYERS' QUESTIONS

Beware the costly glamor features. Pools drown children and are hard to resell, lakeside properties have a $100,000 premium for the privilege of stepping in goose poop, and hot tubs and skylights may be more trouble than they're worth. You need to find out about insurance, lawyers, inspectors and mortgage financing. A good overview is provided in *The Complete Guide to Buying, Owning and Selling a Home in Canada,* by Margaret Kerr and JoAnn Kurtz (John Wiley & Sons, 1997). For mortgage strategies, try Gordon Pape's *The Canadian Mortgage Book.* I don't agree with all of Garth Turner's leveraging advice in *The Strategy: A Homeowners Guide to Wealth Creation* (Key Porter, 1997). But Turner's insights on the type of homes that will sell in the future (i.e. bungalows) versus the white elephants (i.e. 6,000-square-foot monster homes) are well worth reading. I think 2,000 or 2,500 square feet of space is all that the average three- or four-member family needs.

RENOVATING CAN BE CHEAPER THAN MOVING

Renovate or move? The dilemma is a common one for many homeowners. There's an army of real estate agents eager to get you to move, but there's a cost involved in listening to them. In addition to their 5% or 6% commission, there's the difference in price between your old home and your new one, the legal expense of buying one and selling the other and the actual shifting of furniture and other worldly goods. On top of the big costs are lesser ones, such as painting or installing new carpeting in a resale home.

On the other hand, when you stay put and add a bathroom, update your kitchen or build an extension, you pay provincial sales tax on materials and the hated GST on both labor and materials. Having moved into a first home and neighborhood, you can become attached to neighbors who become friends, nearby schools, day care, church, shopping and the whole package deal of home and district.

Real estate agents naturally tend to downplay the loss of community involved in the decision to move. But if you do have good material to work with in your first home –

great neighbors, large enough lot, and so on – then renovating can make sense. You can make 100% on your investment in a kitchen and 80% on a bathroom should you later decide to resell. Basement renovations or swimming pools may not be fully recouped but any time you add new space, such as a family room or fourth bedroom, you stand to win on the subsequent resale, says Ross Gilmore, partner at Gilmore & Harris Custom Builders and Renovators.

BEFORE YOU RENOVATE, CHECK THE CONTRACTOR'S CREDENTIALS

If you do decide to stay and renovate, there are plenty of pitfalls in choosing a contractor. You should make a short list of three or four possible firms. Rene Cantin, president of Rosewood Construction and host of CFRB Radio's *Home Improvement Show* in Toronto, says you should always check the references and licences of a potential contractor. Visit the sites of one or two satisfied customers whose projects were of the scope you are contemplating. Check with the Better Business Bureau and call the Canadian Home Builders Association (1-800-387-2422), which can give you the names of provincial and municipal associations that can comment on your proposed contractor. Call your local building department to find out what permits are needed, and insist the contractor obtain them all. Also, make sure they have $1 million or $2 million in liability insurance.

THE LOWEST QUOTE IS NOT NECESSARILY THE BEST DEAL

Get everything down in writing and, if the project is large, have the contract checked by a lawyer. Do not give deposits of more than 10%. You have the right to hold back 10% of value of the project for 45 days after substantial completion. There is considerable variation in the ability of contractors to tackle large projects, Cantin says. "The problem with a reno or an addition is you're tying new into old." Prices can be negotiated but recognize that a contractor has only so much leeway in this tough business. The markup on small jobs may be 20% or 30%, but it may be 15% or less on large jobs.

Watch out for low-ball cash deals from possible fly-by-night operators, warns Kelly Reynolds of the Greater Toronto Home Builders Association. "If the price sounds too good to be true, where they say do this under the table and avoid the taxes, you have nothing to fall back on." But even on legitimate bids, going strictly with the lowest bid could be a mistake. If you leave the contractor with no profit, you can hardly complain if they respond by substituting lower quality materials or skimming on intangibles such as service. "You have to be leery of someone priced really low," says Cantin. "In the commercial business, they say he who makes the biggest mistake in the price gets the job."

RENTING MAY BE SMARTER THAN BUYING

Renting a house or apartment is dumb because after years of monthly payments, you'll have nothing to show for it, right? That's what just about every real estate agent and a large part of the public will tell you. But you won't hear it from Sean Hennessey, an asso-

SHOULD YOU | BUY A HOME OR RENT?

% annual appreciation		Renting wins if initial monthly rent is less than: $200,000 house		$150,000 house	
Funds	House	25% down $	50% down $	25% down $	50% down $
14	5	1,909	1,982	1,361	1,486
	4	1,970	2,038	1,403	1,529
	3	2,016	2,081	1,435	1,560
	2	2,050	2,113	1,459	1,584
12	5	1,600	1,709	1,200	1,282
	4	1,681	1,790	1,260	1,343
	3	1,742	1,852	1,307	1,389
	2	1,842	1,898	1,341	1,423
10	5	1,350	1,402	1,013	1,051
	4	1,462	1,517	1,097	1,138
	3	1,548	1,605	1,161	1,204
	2	1,613	1,671	1,210	1,253

After-tax values compared after 30 years. Assumes 3% inflation and that closing costs equal 2% of house price, mortgage is 8 % paid monthly and amortized over 20 years, property tax equals 2 % of purchase price, repairs and maintenance equal 1.5%, mutual fund capital gains realized only at end and taxed at 37.5%, and first month's rent due as deposit with no interest paid.

ciate professor at the University of Prince Edward Island. Hennessey, who teaches personal finance, wrote a paper showing that by retirement an informed renter can beat a home buyer by more than $5 million in Canada – and by more than $2 million in the U.S., where buyers get generous tax breaks. That's after 40 years, with the last 20 years mortgage-free for the homeowner and the renter paying a huge capital gains tax bill.

THE NUMBERS DON'T ADD UP IN THE HOME BUYER'S FAVOR

"I went into the analysis thinking there's no question that buying a home is a good investment because that's what you always hear," says Hennessey, a homeowner himself. "But as I worked through the numbers and logic, I never figured it would come out nearly as bad as it did." Using average housing price figures for North America, Hennessey compared the purchase of a $140,000 home paid off over 20 years at 8% to renting at $950 a month, rising 3% a year. The home buyer's initial $2,800 property tax bill and $2,000 for repairs and maintenance per year also rose 3% annually. He assumed the renter invests the $35,000 that would have been used as a down payment. During the first 17 years, the renter pays less for shelter and invests that difference, too.

THE RENTER'S ADVANTAGE LIES IN INVESTING FUNDS EQUAL TO THE DOWN PAYMENT

"This is a very structured investment approach and you have to be willing to follow it," Hennessey stresses. "If the down payment or the net cost of buying are not invested, the analysis is invalid." Indeed, nearly 80% of the renter's ultimate edge over the buyer is due to compound growth on the down payment. Hennessey assumed this cash and all top-ups go into good international mutual funds averaging 14% a year.

Is that reasonable? Hennessey says the Toronto Stock Exchange 300 index averaged about 12% over the past 45 years and "better-performing mutual funds will get you a much better long-term return than the TSE 300." He assumed a buy-and-hold strategy with no tax until the end of his 40-year analysis period, when he taxed the capital gains at 42.7% – considerably higher than today's top marginal rate on gains.

Eighteen international funds have five-year "tax efficiency" ratings of at least 98%, according to Portfolio Analytics' PALTrak database. A 98% rating means taxable distributions cut the fund's reported returns by just 2%, so an investor averaging 14.3% would net 14%. Hennessey also assumed the home's value will just track inflation at 3% a year. That will startle many but not those who've read *Boom, Bust & Echo,* the bestseller by baby boom analyst David Foot.

WE MAY NOT SEE A HOUSING BOOM LIKE THE 1980S UNTIL 2010

Foot, a University of Toronto professor, suggests the 1980s real estate runup was due to the demographics of the baby boom. But for much of Canada he predicts the baby bust that followed the boom means less demand for housing – at least until after 2010. Tinkering with Hennessey's model, I produced the table on the previous page. It spans 30 years, since I suspect even a veteran renter would likely want to buy a house or condo for retirement. Say you're eyeing a $200,000 purchase with 25% down and accept Hennessey's assumptions of 14% for long-term mutual fund returns and 3% for house appreciation. Renting can match or beat ownership as a long-term investment if you can find suitable rental accommodation for $2,016 a month or less. Housing economist Mary McDonough says the $150,000 and $200,000 house price assumptions have been in line with averages in Canadian cities, "although there are tremendous differences among neighborhoods."

HOME BUYERS LOSE OUT IF THEY ARE FORCED TO SELL BEFORE REALIZING A PROFIT

In consultation with McDonough, I set closing costs and property taxes each at 2% of the purchase price and budgeted 1.5% for repairs and maintenance. I used Hennessey's 3% inflation assumption, but tested investment returns of 10% and 12% as well as his 14%. House appreciation ranged from 5% down to 2%. I assumed a 50% marginal tax rate, which meant taxes took 37.5% of the taxable capital gain after 30 years. "Many households choose to buy a home based on emotional, social and psychological factors and, likely, in the belief that it is a wise investment choice," Hennessey's paper says. "For some, this may be the case; for others, however, it is a mistake from which it takes many years to recover."

For example, by not questioning common wisdom, people concentrate the bulk of their wealth into an illiquid holding that's subject to speculative swings and they become exposed to "extreme unsystematic risk," he argues. Consider the plight of someone forced to sell by marital breakdown, job loss or transfer, a major change in the neighborhood or perhaps because an obnoxious rock band just moved in next door.

HENNESSEY SUGGESTS PROSPECTIVE HOME BUYERS CONSIDER THE FOLLOWING

- Will the house increase in value over time and, if so, by how much?
- Will the house require expensive renovations or repairs now or in the future?
- Do you require greater portfolio diversification than a house can provide?
- Do you have the discipline for a strict investment strategy and appreciate that stock prices fluctuate?
- Is suitable rental accommodation available? Is a long-term lease possible?
- Are there rent controls? To what extent do you face the risk of an unreasonable rent increase?

All these factors can affect the buy/rent equation. But one thing is fairly clear in the wake of Hennessey's analysis: Buying a house simply for investment reasons may not be the wise decision that realtors invariably suggest.

MORTGAGE INSURANCE GETS PORTABLE

The market for mortgage insurance – more accurately referred to as "default insurance" – has undergone substantial change in Canada over the past few years. The changes include the portability of mortgage insurance, the insuring of mortgages held by self-directed RRSPs and the percentage of a home's value that is insurable under a high-ratio situation.

Spearheading this innovation has been GE Capital Mortgage Insurance Canada (known in the industry as Gemico). Neither Gemico nor Canada Mortgage & Housing Corp. – the federal agency that continues to dominate the Canadian default insurance market – offer their products directly to the public. They deal primarily with the large number of financial institutions that lend out mortgage money. The mortgage insurance market began a transition in 1992, when CMHC began insuring mortgages for first-time home buyers who had only a 5% down payment. Previously, the maximum insurable financing for all buyers was 90% of the first $180,000 of purchase price plus 80% of the balance.

INNOVATIONS IN MORTGAGE INSURANCE INCLUDE HIGH-RATIO MORTGAGES AND PORTABILITY

For example, on a $250,000 purchase, the maximum financing previously possible was 87.2%, or $218,000, compared with 95% or $237,500 after the new program took effect. Then, in January 1995, Gemico acquired the assets and operations of Mortgage Insurance Corp. of Canada (MICC), the only other source of mortgage insurance in Canada besides CMHC. Gemico subsequently introduced some innovations, including the ability to insure a mortgage held by a self-directed RRSP. This previously had been available through MICC and was revived by Gemico. It has broadened the appeal of this strategy.

Another innovation is the ability through both Gemico and CMHC to insure almost all of the mortgage amount for homebuyers other than first-timers, compared with the more conservative sliding scale that was used previously. Typically, they will cover up to 90%, depending on the size of the mortgage and other circumstances. For example, they now will cover $450,000 of a $500,000 loan.

Probably the most significant development for the average homebuyer has been the introduction of mortgage insurance portability. In the past, high-ratio borrowers would pay an insurance premium to either CMHC or MICC and if they moved to a different home, the insurance was lost. That was fine, provided the mortgage on the new property was for a low-ratio loan (covering less than 75% of the property's value). But if they needed insurance on their next property, they'd have to pay another premium. And with the significant drop in property values in many cities between 1990 and 1993, chances were that many people repurchasing would still require a high-ratio mortgage.

SELF-DIRECTED RRSP MORTGAGES CAN NOT BE CONVERTED TO A RRIF

Gemico's portable policy, introduced in 1995, provided homeowners with the comfort of knowing that, with some limitations, their original insurance premium was all they would ever pay if subsequent purchases required default coverage. CMHC was fairly quick to follow suit, announcing a portability feature in April 1996, although it will still not allow you to switch lenders when selling one property and buying another. CMHC coverage, however, does offer some advantages. The National Housing Act, which governs CMHC's operations, allows any borrower to pay off a CMHC-insured mortgage with a maximum of three months' interest penalty after three years, regardless of the number of times the mortgage is renewed.

Gemico, by contrast, operates under the lender's prepayment policies, which vary among institutions. In many cases, the lender will charge a penalty to cover the interest rate differential and require the borrower to continue dealing with them (if a mortgage is still needed) until the current term would have expired. CMHC also will not terminate insurance on a self-directed RRSP mortgage when the time comes to convert the RRSP to a RRIF, allowing the customer to convert the plan in an orderly fashion. Gemico requires full replacement of the mortgage money by discontinuing coverage after the RRSP is converted to a RRIF.

NO ONE PAYS THE STICKER PRICE

Competition has driven down mortgage rates as lenders increasingly show willingness to discount their posted rates. In fact, in *The Canadian Mortgage Book,* authors Gordon Pape and Bruce McDougall "strongly advise" that no one accept the posted rate these days. In most cases, there's room to negotiate up to a full percentage point, depending of course on the length of the term, Pape said. "Negotiating a mortgage has become rather like buying a car. No one pays the sticker price." You can also negotiate away hidden costs such as appraisal fees, which are usually between $150 and $500, survey fees of another $150 to $400, renewal fees, mortgage transfer fees and mortgage insurance in the case of high-ratio mortgages.

The implications for people shopping around for mortgages are clear. If you want a mortgage below the posted rate at your local bank, make it clear that you're aware of what Citizens Bank or Trimark Trust are charging. If they won't budge on the posted rate, then try to get them to waive one or more of the related fees. If that doesn't work, it's time to pull out the heavy artillery. You represent much more than just potential mortgage business to the banks. If you give them your RRSP, credit card and other business, odds are they will be more willing to give you a mortgage below the posted rates.

THE WEB CAN SERVE UP MORTGAGE BARGAINS

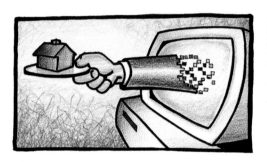

For consumers looking to beat lenders' posted mortgage rates, the Internet is becoming a money-saving tool. The big banks enjoy a dominant position in the mortgage market. They have two advantages: a bricks-and-mortar presence on almost every street corner and the ultimate weapon of "relationship" banking. Industry insiders say a two-tiered mortgage rate system developed in the depressed real estate market of the 1990s. One tier is the posted rate the banks would like you to pay, somewhat like the sticker price on a new car. The second is the discounted rate the consumer wishes to pay.

The banks have been willing to discount since 1992, particularly if they think they can also win, or retain, your registered retirement savings plan (RRSP), credit card, commercial banking and other business.

USING YOUR PERSONAL COMPUTER, YOU CAN APPLY FOR A MORTGAGE AND GET APPROVAL
If you are willing to spread your business around and shop for the best mortgage, you should be able to improve on the posted rate by 50 to 100 basis points. To find the best deal, you can go to a traditional mortgage broker or to the new electronic equivalents on the Internet. This exercise may still lead you back to one of the big banks, or it may take you to unfamiliar but aggressive newcomers such as Trimark Trust or new branchless banks such as Citizens Bank. It's now possible to arrange an electronic mortgage from your personal computer. You can apply for a mortgage and have it approved over the Internet without an in-person visit to a branch. (The accompanying table gives Internet addresses for some leading Web sites.) A good place to start the search is the Online Mortgage Explorer Web site. This allows the prospective borrower to compare

rates at several major lenders. You can find out whether you qualify in privacy before having to fill out the online application form.

Tony Humble, Online Mortgage Inc.'s chief operating officer, says posted rates are artificially high. The two-tiered rate schedule is becoming a problem as the Internet reveals the extent of the competitive alternatives. Branchless virtual banks such as Citizens can post rock-bottom rates because they have "disintermediated" the branch system, he says. The new competitors instead process documents by secure Internet transmission, e-mail, telephone and fax. Humble says Internet mortgage technology remains "relatively primitive." Only the largest of the banks provide "truly capable" software to obtain new mortgage business, he says. However, "virtually every financial institution claims to be working actively on adding or improving this capability."

FINANCIAL | SERVICE SITES

One-stop shopping

Online Mortgage Explorer Inc.	www.themortgage.com
i Money Corp.	www.imoney.com

Directly through financial institutions

Bank of Montreal	www.bmo.com
Canada Trust	www.canadatrust.com
CIBC	www.cibc.com
Citizens Bank	www.citizens.com.
Royal Bank	www.royalbank.com
Scotiabank	www.scotiabank.ca
TDBank	www.tdbank.ca
Trimark Trust	www.trimarktrust.com

CONSUMERS CAN NOW PURCHASE MORTGAGES, INSURANCE AND MUTUAL FUNDS ONLINE

While many banks offer mortgage information on their Internet sites, not all yet permit the entire cycle of mortgage application and approval. Bank of Montreal was a pioneer in Internet mortgages. This is not surprising since one of its subsidiaries, Cebra Inc., is Online Mortgage Explorer's distributor. Bank of Nova Scotia has joined the Internet mortgage fold following extensive work to make access secure. It is unclear how, or if, consumers can negotiate for better rates electronically. "We don't believe the Internet will provide customers with any better pricing," says Ted Taylor, Scotiabank's senior vice-president of mortgages. "It's just a service for those who prefer dealing with automated methods of communications." The Internet service i Money Corp. offers an electronic supermarket approach to financial services. Its Web site permits consumers to purchase not only mortgages but also insurance, mutual funds and other financial products.

MORTGAGE BROKERS CAN HELP YOU FIND THE BEST DEALS

Borrowers not yet tapped into the computer age do not have to be locked out of this mortgage cornucopia. Just as there are real estate brokers, stockbrokers and mutual fund dealers, you can also find a mortgage broker to help you negotiate a better deal. (The bank pays a finder's fee, typically 0.5%.) It used to be the case that mortgage brokers dealt primarily with poor credit risk borrowers who could not obtain loans from the banks, says Rick McGratten, president of the Mutual Group's residential mortgages division. That started to change about 1990 when TD Bank started to use mortgage brokers to win "prime" business.

Consumers can find a mortgage broker by calling the Canadian Institute of Mortgage Brokers & Lenders toll-free at 1-888-442-4625. One such broker, Andy MacDonald of Killian Mortgage Services Inc. of Toronto, says it is becoming tougher to obtain the big rate discounts that were possible until recently. Tom Alton, president of Bank of Montreal Mortgage Corp., says some "dysfunctional pricing" has crept into the marketplace, where people are using price as a primary weapon. He says brokers may be trying to turn mortgages into a commodity. "But if that is all they have to offer, it is the easiest mortgage to steal."

Here is what *Financial Post* reader Morton Katz learned after using the services of mortgage broker Norlite Financial in Mississauga, Ont.: "I have a pretty amazing mortgage and everyone pays way more than me. I am not in any special circumstance – I just did my homework. I figure I have put more equity in my house in 1.5 years than a 7.5% five-year big bank mortgage does in 10 [years]. Tell the others there are millions to be saved."

VARIABLE RATE MORTGAGES GIVE FLEXIBILITY

The mortgage marketplace has changed considerably over the past few years, as lenders scramble for customers. Deals abound, and variable rate mortgages are one recent innovation that can also save you money.

But as always, make sure you understand the contract details. Variable rate mortgages have been around for many years but only became popular among Canadian homeowners about five years ago, when interest rates began a prolonged drop. These most flexible of mortgages give homeowners the freedom to change mortgage terms or switch lenders at any time. They also charge the lowest interest rates, usually the institution's prime lending rate. The rate changes with the prime rate.

INTEREST CHARGED ON VARIABLE RATE MORTGAGES IS OFTEN THE LOWEST AVAILABLE

In its basic form, the variable-rate mortgage has many advantages over its fixed-rate, fixed-term counterparts. It is fully open for additional payments – called prepayments in mortgage lingo – at any time. It is convertible at any time to another mortgage type without penalty or transferable to another institution, also without penalty. Some lenders will insure a variable rate mortgage against default as a high-ratio mortgage (with some restrictions), thus making this mortgage option available to borrowers with lower down payments.

Fixed-term, fully open mortgages are available at most institutions for terms of six months and one year, but also charge significantly higher rates than variable rate mortgages. This past fall, for example, some vendors' variable rate mortgages charged 4.75%, compared with 5.95% for a six-month open mortgage and 6.25% for one year. The only additional protection afforded by fixed-rate open mortgages is a few extra months at the fixed rate should the prime rate shoot up.

Variable rate mortgages tend to be underpromoted by lenders. For instance, you can pay down a variable rate mortgage at any time during the year, not just on the renewal anniversary. The money enters the mortgage account sooner, and interest costs are reduced accordingly. Over time, this might shave a year or two off the mortgage's amortization, more if substantial prepayments are made. To the lender, however, frequent small prepayments are a big clerical headache when everything else on the mortgage system is automated, save for a once-a-year additional payment. Because it is human nature not to take advantage of a single-shot prepayment opportunity, the fixed-rate, fixed-term mortgage tends to keep mortgage balances – and thus interest payments – at the maximum level.

SOME HOME OWNERS USE THE DOUBLE-UP MORTGAGE LIKE A LINE OF CREDIT

An innovation of the late 1980s was the "double-up" mortgage payment. At the time, some lenders also allowed borrowers to skip a payment, doubling up on a later payment. Many have taken advantage of the double-up option, but it has also turned out to be a blank cheque for spur-of-the-moment expenditures, with mortgage-holders skipping a payment and then having to make it up later. A variable rate mortgage, by contrast, cannot be used as a credit line. Once a prepayment has been made, it's irretrievable. Using the double-up/skip-a-payment combination is like paying off a credit card and then running up the balance again. Prepaying a variable rate mortgage, on the other hand, is like paying off a car loan – the only way to get the amount of the prepayment back is to take out another loan.

An interesting variation is the capped variable rate mortgage, which charges an "insurance premium" of about one percentage point over prime for the security of a pre-determined ceiling over a long term. These are closed mortgages with terms that vary from three to five years and are convertible to a fixed-rate, fixed-term mortgage at any time. That's an expensive rate premium, although it is somewhat reassuring in volatile times. However, in a period of prolonged rate stability, their appeal is limited.

MANY VARIABLE RATE MORTGAGES LET YOU LOCK IN AT BELOW-MARKET RATES

Another variable rate mortgage derivative is available from FirstLine Mortgages, a subsidiary of Canadian Imperial Bank of Commerce. Introduced in 1990 as the "ARM [adjustable rate mortgage] with a Trigger," this mortgage charges an exceptionally low rate, compounded semi-annually instead of the monthly compounding used by basic variable rate mortgages. The borrower gets at least one entire calendar quarter at this rate, plus whatever part is left of the quarter in which the transaction closes. For example, if your mortgage closes Dec. 31 you get three months – the entire first quarter to March 31 – at that rate. If you close Jan. 2, you get that rate for almost six months, until June 30.

The ARM has an impressive array of below-market-rate lock-in options. These options – the longer term rates – are priced as much as one-quarter of a percentage point below posted rates for similar terms. This route becomes even more attractive after the initial term, because the rate is adjusted at the end of the calendar quarter to the Canada three-month treasury bill bid-side rate on the last Thursday of the calendar quarter, plus 1.5 percentage points.

RRSPS CAN FINANCE A HOME PURCHASE

Tapping a registered retirement savings plan to finance a home purchase is an attractive strategy, but you have to have enough money in the RRSP to make the exercise worthwhile. You have to weigh the investment return, too. Do the advantages of paying mortgage interest to your plan outweigh the lost opportunity of investing in potentially more lucrative arenas?

First, the basics. What you are doing is borrowing from your RRSP (only self-directed plans are eligible) to finance a home purchase or to refinance an existing mortgage. "Your mortgage principal and interest payments go back into your RRSP to help finance your retirement," says Leona Tranter, a principal with Canada Trust's financial advisory services group. "These payments generally represent a secure, high-quality investment, usually offering a higher rate of return than other fixed-income investments like GICs."

A few months ago, for example, the big banks and trust companies were charging 5.35% for a one-year closed mortgage and paying 3% on a one-year guaranteed investment certificate. They were charging 7% for a five-year mortgage and paying 4.75% on a five-year GIC. You may have to sell existing investments in your RRSP to raise the cash to finance the home purchase or refinance your mortgage. What you are doing is selling securities held in your RRSP and using the proceeds to set up a mortgage within your plan. The new mortgage holder – your RRSP – then pays off the home vendor or the current mortgage holder.

THE RRSP MORTGAGE ARRANGEMENT CAN ONLY APPLY TO YOUR PRINCIPAL DWELLING

You do not have to pay income tax on the money that ultimately leaves your RRSP – as is the case with normal RRSP withdrawals – because that money, in effect, is remaining within your RRSP in the form of a mortgage security. You are obliged to repay the debt, with interest, to your RRSP, and that debt is secured by the asset being financed – your home.

Revenue Canada, which polices RRSP contributions and withdrawals, requires that an RRSP mortgage be set up and administered by an approved lender – usually a bank or trust company – and must be insured by Canada Housing & Mortgage Corp., a federal agency, or a private mortgage insurer such as GE Capital Mortgage Co. (Gemico). The RRSP arrangement can only be applied to "non-arm's length" mortgages, Tranter says, "which means you must own and occupy the mortgaged property either individually or jointly."

The terms of the mortgage – interest rate, semi-annual interest compounding and administration details – must reflect normal commercial practice, she says. You must pay your RRSP the same rate a bank or trust company would charge over a similar term. "Any changes to your mortgage during its term must follow your financial institution's regular lending policies and do not receive preferential treatment," she says. "For example, if you wanted to accelerate payments or pay the mortgage off early, you would have to refer to the terms of your mortgage loan." The mortgage payments that will be made to your RRSP in no way affect your RRSP contribution room since each payment's principal portion represents money already contributed to the plan and the interest portion is income paid on the investment.

THERE ARE ADDITIONAL SET-UP AND ANNUAL FEES WITH A SELF-DIRECTED RRSP

Then there are fees. A self-directed RRSP has annual trustee fees of up to $150, although some institutions have reduced or waived this charge. In most cases there is also a one-time set-up fee of $100 to $200. On the mortgage side, the institution that sets up the mortgage for your plan charges fees for the application as well as for property appraisal. You also will have to pay legal or notarial fees, which typically total $1,000 to $1,200, when the mortgage is set up. And if you have a high-ratio mortgage – 75% or more of the property value – you will also have to pay a one-time mortgage insurance premium, generally 0.5% to 2.5% of the mortgage principal (this can be amortized along with the outstanding principal). On the new mortgage's anniversary date, you will have to pay annual mortgage administration fees of up to $200. And finally, many of the above fees are also subject to sales tax.

Tranter says a self-directed RRSP mortgage is suitable only for mortgages of at least $50,000. And do not overlook the RRSP investment angle, she adds. "Your adviser should help you determine the suitability of this type of investment, taking into account your investment objectives, risk tolerance and considering other investments that may yield higher returns. A self-directed mortgage can be a valuable part of a well-diversified portfolio," Tranter concludes, "but it should not be the only investment in your RRSP."

LAWS TRY TO BE FAIR TO CREDITOR AND DEBTOR

After nearly four years of tinkering, Canada's amended bankruptcy laws came into effect in 1997. Bill C-5, which amends the Bankruptcy and Insolvency Act and the Companies' Creditors Arrangement Act (CCAA), tries to strike a balance between a creditor's right to share in a bankrupt's assets and a debtor's right to a fresh start – or, as the legislation puts it, a "balance between rehabilitation and obligation." Some bankruptcy trustees have applauded the changes, saying they should overcome the perception that bankruptcy is too easy an option for consumers. Others are skeptical that widespread abuses by "professional bankrupts" will be curbed.

CHANGES TO THE BANKRUPTCY LAW REFLECT INCREASE IN CONSUMER BANKRUPTCIES

Most of Bill C-5, including the section that addresses commercial matters, came into force in the fall of 1997, but some changes to the bill's consumer side will require more regulations and may not take effect until later this year. In changing the law the government recognized that business bankruptcies had been relatively stable over the past few years but consumer bankruptcies were on the rise. More than 85% of the 93,860 bankruptcies filed in 1996 were by individuals. The new law raises the ante on debtor responsibility with new provisions on payment of debts from surplus income. The Superintendent of Bankruptcy is to set standards as to what constitutes surplus income in various situations and regions of the country. If the amount is disputed, it will go into mediation.

The law also provides changes on discharge, which is the process of releasing a bankrupt's debts. Trustees are required to make a report on the bankrupt's conduct. That report now includes a recommendation as to whether the debtor should be discharged, based on the bankrupt's conduct and ability to make payments.

TWO NEW GROUNDS ON WHICH A CREDITOR CAN OPPOSE A BANKRUPTCY DISCHARGE

• If the debtor has failed to pay surplus income according to the bankruptcy agreement.
• If the debtor chose bankruptcy instead of a viable proposal to a creditor – one that would have been accepted by the creditors.

The law is tougher on the thousands of students who abuse the Canada Students Loans program before they've even begun their working life. Students were able to declare bankruptcy even before they graduated. Under Bill C-5, students are not to be released from their loans within two years of declaring bankruptcy, unless a court rules otherwise. The government estimates student bankruptcies cost it more than $70 million in unpaid loans in 1996, and that figure excludes Quebec. Students are aided and abetted by the credit card companies, who, as one insolvency specialist put it, "are just throwing cards at students." But students are already flocking to bankruptcy trustee Chee-Kong Leong with plans to go bankrupt two years from now. "I think it's still too soft," he says. "There's a lot of potential for creative bankruptcy."

THE LAW ENCOURAGES BUSINESSES TO REORGANIZE RATHER THAN LIQUIDATE

Leong sees plenty of scope for continued abuse by high-income professionals who go bankrupt to avoid the biggest creditor of all: Revenue Canada. The law is designed to encourage insolvent businesses to reorganize rather than liquidate their affairs. Liability protection for company directors encourages this. Previously, directors vulnerable to personal claims were unlikely to rebuild an insolvent firm. It also harmonizes the CCAA with the Bankruptcy Act. Companies now need liabilities of more than $5 million to get access to the CCAA. There are also special rules dealing with insolvency of securities firms and international insolvencies. Bryan Tannenbaum, president of Mintz & Partners Ltd., a trustee in bankruptcy, says C-5 "will go a long way to improve things." He says it will be possible to refine the law over time, unlike many other pieces of legislation.

DECLARING BANKRUPTCY IS STILL TOO EASY FOR CONSUMERS

But some bankruptcy lawyers are skeptical the law will make a difference. "I doubt whether the new provisions will encourage any significant change," says Frank Bennett of Bennett & Co., author of *Bennett on Going Broke.* "It's too easy to go into bankruptcy and likewise just as easy to get out." The Bankruptcy and Insolvency Act was never intended to apply to consumers, Bennett says. The surge in individual bankruptcies has occurred only since the Second World War. Amendments in 1992 intended that consumer debtors would attempt to make proposals or arrangements to pay a portion of their debts in an orderly fashion. "Unfortunately, the laws of going into bankruptcy and getting out are so easy that consumers elect not to make such consumer proposals," he says. "Until Parliament recognizes the problem, I suspect that our bankruptcy statistics will continue to be on the rise for many years to come."

THE INCREASE IN PERSONAL BANKRUPTCIES MAY BE AN AFTER EFFECT OF THE RECESSION

Bankruptcy rates have been rising despite the end of the recession of the early 1990s. That's because of what John Owen, principal of Omega-one, a credit consulting firm in Streetsville, Ont., refers to as "the bankruptcy echo." Today's bankruptcies are spurred by root causes that occurred five or 10 years earlier, such as a foreclosure on a home or the rash of white-collar layoffs at the height of the 1990s recession. Senior managers were initially shielded by generous severance packages. If their joblessness extended longer, they next plundered their RRSP savings. Only after that avenue was exhausted did some take recourse to bankruptcy. Owen says the situation has been aggravated by the rise of financial planners, some of whom advise individuals to "consider bankruptcy as just one more element in a comprehensive personal finance plan, as legitimate as making an RRSP contribution to reduce one's tax liability."

10 REASONS TO DITCH THE CAR FOR THE TRAIN

For most families, automobile expenses represent a sizable chunk of the monthly budget. But if you live in or near a major city, do you really need a car? Driving a car to work is an overrated and expensive luxury. As traffic congestion intensifies in big cities and driving manners deteriorate, it may be time for some commuters to re-evaluate their attitude to taking public transit. The government of Ontario's GO transit system experienced its first-ever annual decline in ridership in 1992. But it's been rising again recently.

To take a leaf from David Letterman, there are at least 10 reasons to consider com-

WHAT YOU CAN SAVE | BY LEAVING THE CAR AT HOME

Savings based on 35-kilometre commute at 35.9¢/kilometre, not including parking

Cost of	Car $	GO Train $*	Savings $
Two-way trip	25.14	9.20	15.94
Weekly (5 days)	125.70	41.50	84.20
Monthly (20 days)	502.80	145.00	357.80
Yearly	6,033.60	1,740.00	4,293.60
10 years	60,336.00	17,400.00	42,936.00
40 years	241,344.00	69,600.00	171,744.00

* includes cost savings of GO 10-ride ticket and monthly pass

muter rail, many of them directly or indirectly financial. I base the following observations on my experience of trains on GO's Toronto region Lakeshore West route. But they apply to similar systems in Vancouver and Montreal: B.C. Transit's West Coast Express and the Montreal Urban Community Transit Corp.

HERE ARE 10 GOOD REASONS TO DITCH THE CAR IN FAVOR OF THE TRAIN

10. Save money. You can extend the life of your car and save money on gas, parking and maintenance. According to the Canadian Automobile Association, the average cost of running a car is 35.9¢ a kilometre. That figure consists of gasoline costs and all variable and fixed ownership and maintenance costs. As the accompanying table for an Oakville, Ont., resident commuting to downtown Toronto shows, the yearly cost for the car would be $6,033, versus $1,740 for commuter rail. That's an annual saving of $4,300. Taking the car just half the time would still generate an annual saving of more than $2,000 a year. Based on this analysis, over a 40-year working life, you could buy a house on the savings. And if you ditched the car altogether, you'd also save a ton on insurance. Even if you drove just half as much, you'd gain a few years on the life of the car. A two-car family that opted for one car, with each spouse alternating between car and transit, would also save thousands a year.

9. Help the environment. Anyone whose only contribution to the environment consists of using blue boxes can feel twice as good by also using commuter rail. A 1982 study found car commuters used as much energy in four years of driving as a transit rider consumes in 40 years. One 10-car GO Train carries the same number of people as 1,000 air-polluting cars. If you used transit for a year instead of driving to work, the environment would be spared 13.5 kilograms of hydrocarbons, 100 kilograms of carbon monoxide, seven kilograms of nitrogen oxides and 1,517 kilograms of carbon dioxide, according to the Ontario Ministry of Municipal Affairs. To put the last figure in perspective, that level of carbon dioxide is 20% of the amount removed by one hectare of forest. Do you really want all that on your conscience?

8. Health and exercise. The environment is a macro health issue, but transit also can impart direct health benefits to the individual user. The four walks a day involved in going between home, rail stations and work can easily add up to the half-hour daily exercise many doctors recommend. The related health benefits may well ultimately save you money.

7. Safety. Driving every day increases the odds of having an accident, which may well result in higher subsequent insurance rates. Recent studies showing the appalling number of red lights being run in Toronto are alone reason to consider public transit. The hazards of drunk driving are equally evident.

6. Reduce highway congestion. Many commuter rail users also own cars and occasionally need to take them to work. No one says you have to take the train every day of the week – if you have a meeting and need the car, take it. A single 40-foot transit vehicle replaces 46 cars in rush hours. If all car drivers used the train just half the time, that would leave the highways that much less congested for those who need to use the car on a particular day. The reduced stress could also help your health and cut future medical expenses.

5. Increase reading and work time. Depending on the length of your commute, you can gain nearly an hour a day of reading time on the train. You may even develop your speed reading skills, as you master the technique of squeezing an entire chapter of a book in during a ride. You can also crunch spreadsheets or do word processing on a laptop computer or make cell phone calls. These productivity gains may translate into increased earning power.

4. Buffer zone. The combination of walking and riding the train makes a nice transition between the leisure of home and stresses of the workplace. In the morning, you can mentally plan your day; at night, you can decompress, without the adrenaline surges involved in coping with discourteous car drivers or the stress and waste of time of traffic jams.

3. Window on pop culture. The train is a great place to check out tastes in popular literature. Seems to be an even mix between trash novels and literary and philosophic classics.

2. Music appreciation. Most motorists aren't really listening to music; they're operating a complex mechanical device that could inflict death at any moment. *Listen!*, a primer on classical music, says that to properly appreciate good music you need to close your eyes and concentrate. You can do this with a Walkman on a commuter train, but it's definitely not recommended for car drivers.

AND THE NO. 1 REASON FOR TAKING THE TRAIN INSTEAD OF DRIVING?
Contemplation and meditation. As transit veterans know, commuter rail cars are the quietest place on earth. Commuters are generally quiet, law-abiding, middle class people who value their privacy and solitude. Conversations on the train are rare. At home, you can't escape the demands of spouse and children and are subject to door-to-door solicitations at any time. If the phone rings, you're compelled to answer. And then there are the incessant demands of the workplace. Only on the train can you grab a few minutes of contemplation or meditation.

BEING A CHEAPSKATE CAN BE GOOD STRATEGY

There are two types of spenders in this world – cheapskates and spendthrifts. If you act under the illusion that you're already rich, spending indiscriminately day after day, you'll end up poor. Conversely, if you act poor, you have a far better shot at ending up rich. While the average consumer tends to drive a hard bargain on big-ticket expenses – going to elaborate lengths to keep taxes to a minimum or shave half a point off mortgage rates – it's the little day-to-day living expenses that really cut into your financial prosperity.

Most of us fritter away at least $10 a day in items we're barely conscious of purchasing. The problem is there are 365 days in the year, which means the habit of daily impulse buying can cost you almost $8,000 a year. That's not a math mistake. In today's overtaxed climate, a penny saved is not a penny earned. In the 50% tax bracket, a penny saved is worth two pretax pennies. If you count consumption taxes such as the 7% GST, an after-tax penny is even more valuable. So $10 in after-tax dollars thrown away every day is $20 pretax.

THESE HELPFUL HINTS SHOW YOU HOW TO SAVE MONEY EVERY DAY

To mangle metaphors further, if you respect these after-tax pennies, the after-tax dollars will take care of themselves. There are plenty of examples of cheapskates who became rich. In his younger days, Sir John Templeton loathed personal debt, including even mortgages. He furnished his early households with used furniture and other bargains, buying things only when he had the cash. Today, the founder of the Templeton mutual fund empire doesn't have to worry about money. But he still tells investors the best time to invest is "when you have the money" and frowns on leverage.

There are some obvious potential cost savings. Take lunch. So-called fast food is neither fast nor cheap and, in some cases, barely qualifies as nourishing food. Bag lunches of fruit, granola bars, sandwiches or microwaveable products such as Lean Cuisine should cut your average lunch bill from about $7 to $3. That's $80 to $100 a month in after-tax dollars saved, which can be applied to paying down your mortgage (priority No. 1 for genuine cheapskates). How much do we waste on coffee? It's almost $1 a throw these days and closer to $2 at Starbucks. A Brita water filter at your desk is cheaper and probably healthier.

The little consumption items at home also add up. I happen to be an audio buff and used to spend a lot on compact discs. I'd bought in early to the idea the CD sound was superior to old-fashioned vinyl records, and for years happily forked out $20 or more for each CD. I'm not so sure CDs are superior anymore. Their very popularity has led to such volume manufacturing that I find quality has slipped. Second, modern popular music leaves me cold. Third, portable CD players aren't as light and convenient as cassette Walkmans. And fourth, CDs are still expensive. Being a cheapskate, my solution has been to phase out CDs and frequent the few stores that still sell used vinyl records. The best in Toronto is Peter Dunn's Vinyl Museum, with locations on Bloor Street West and Lakeshore Boulevard.

Peter sells good-quality vinyl from the 1950s to 1980s for $2.50, $3.99 or $4.99. Regulars get a 20% discount and there are occasional half-price sales on the cheaper records.

You can purchase almost the entire output of a particular artist for $20 or $30, about the same cost as a single CD. I buy cheap 90-minute cassettes at the Bi-way and record two vinyl albums on each cassette for use in the car or Walkman. Of course if you're a dedicated cheapskate, you can simply go to the library and borrow music CDs or tapes, not to mention books, videos and magazines.

A CHEAPSKATE STRATEGY IS GOOD FINANCIAL PLANNING

Another common household expense is batteries. If you have children, you know how expensive it can be to power the multitude of toys and electronic gizmos that clutter the average home. And if a child ever leaves a flashlight on overnight, as mine has, you know how fast $5 can go down the drain. That's five "after-tax" dollars! The solution is rechargeable batteries.

I used to buy the blue nickel-cadmium batteries sold at Radio Shack, but there's a new type of battery technology out called "reusable alkaline." They are similar to the use-once-and-throw-away alkaline batteries you buy at any convenience store. But you can't recharge regular alkaline batteries, which, apart from being expensive, also makes them environmentally unfriendly.

Rayovac Canada Inc. of Mississauga, Ont., is marketing Renewal rechargeable alkaline batteries. They cost about the same as regular throwaway batteries, work right out of the package like throwaways, but can also be recharged 20 or 30 times. They degrade a bit with each recharge, but hold a charge much longer than the older nickel-cadmium rechargeable technology. Just be warned, rechargers for one type of battery won't work for other rechargeable batteries. There are also a handful of competitors to Renewal. They're not as widely available as regular alkalines but Radio Shack carries the new batteries and the rechargers.

There are plenty of other cheapskate opportunities out there, too. Don't overlook their value in your financial planning.

DO RESPS ANSWER THE EDUCATION QUESTION?

Which method of saving for a child's education is better: registered education savings plans (RESPs) or equity mutual funds held in trust? While the RESP acronym resembles the RRSP, there is a major difference. RRSPs provide a tax deduction on the initial principal, RESPs don't – they merely shelter the income or growth created by that principal.

All capital gains, dividends and interest compound untaxed and become taxable only when withdrawn by the student. The idea is that the student will be in such a low tax bracket that, even though the income becomes taxable, the tax bill will be negligible.

RESP INVESTMENTS ARE INTENDED TO FUND POST-SECONDARY EDUCATION

RESPs come in two main flavors: pooled RESP plans and plans administered by financial institutions or mutual fund companies, which offer flexible and simple "self-directed" RESP plans. The main pooled RESP vendors are Canadian Scholarship Trust, USC Education Savings, Heritage Scholarship Trust and Children's Education Trust of Canada, some of which go back to the early 1960s. You'll typically see their brochures in waiting rooms of maternity wards or retail stores selling children's goods. RESPs were intended to help finance the cost of sending children to universities, community colleges, CEGEPs in Quebec and Canadian junior and technical colleges or universities outside Canada. RESP money can also pay for books, lab fees, equipment, accommodation and transportation.

The 1998 federal budget introduced a grant of up to $400 a year to match an individual's RESP contribution. The 1997 budget doubled the RESP contribution limit to $4,000 a year per child (the lifetime limit remains at $42,000), and other provisions made them more attractive than in past, but they still have a number of warts. For example, pooled RESPs charge large enrolment fees upfront, somewhat like a mutual fund front-end load at the 10% level. If you cancel in the first year or two, you'll forfeit most of that fee.

IN-TRUST FUNDS HAVE SEVERAL ADVANTAGES OVER RESPS

The 1997 budget changes did overcome the single biggest objection to RESPs: the forfeiture of the plans' growth if the child did not go on to higher education. This led to arguments about how much education was needed to keep the RESP earnings. Revenue Canada's minimum education requirement was a three-week course with at least 10 hours a week of study and homework. It also insisted the school had to consider the child a full-time student.

Those arguments are hardly relevant now, since the budget allows parents to take back capital contributions and roll over the income accumulated in the RESPs into their RRSPs. "If RESPs were a bad idea at $2,000, they're twice as bad at $4,000," says Warren Baldwin, regional vice-president of T. E. Financial Consultants Ltd., though he adds the RRSP rollover may create some new opportunities, particularly for wealthy investors.

The RRSP rollover may also mean the "tontine" aspect of pooled RESPs has been diluted. Under tontine financial schemes, income forgone by plan contributors whose children opted not to go to university was added to the pool shared by those still college bound, typically about 85% of the beneficiaries who started. There is also a 10% a year dropoff between second-year university and fourth year.

"It's a bit of a dilemma," says Tom O'Shaughnessy, senior vice-president of Canadian Scholarship Trust. "Irrespective of what the budget says, the contracts say if you

RESPs VS. IN-TRUST ACCOUNTS

	RESPs	In-trust accounts
Availability	Some financial institutions	Most financial institutions
Contribution limit	$42,000 per child	None
Annual cont. limit	$4,000 per child	None
Taxation	Tax-deferred growth in plan Income taxable to child on withdrawal	Interest/dividends taxable to contributor Capital gains taxable to child
Uses	Post-secondary education*	Any purpose at any time

* 1997 federal budget allows rollovers into RRSPs, or cashout with penalties.

Source: The Rogers Group, Vancouver

withdraw, you'll forfeit" the earnings. The fund companies do not use the tontine. They also have a simpler alternative that does not use the RESP: the equity mutual fund held in trust.

A Dynamic Mutual Funds advisory argues "astute advisers will find an equity mutual fund properly set up in trust for a child is still more flexible than an RESP and offers greater potential tax savings." Some independent financial planners agree. Vancouver-based Rogers Group Ltd. prefers trust accounts because "they remain more flexible, especially for longer-term investment horizons."

Pooled RESPs can invest only in fixed-income securities. If you believe stocks or equity funds provide greater longer-term growth, pooled RESPs won't be your best bet. If that's your preference, you needn't have a mutual fund RESP either: just opt for the simpler course of holding the fund in trust for your child.

A FORMAL TRUST LETS YOU SPECIFY HOW THE MONEY IS TO BE SPENT

Capital gains taxes will be paid by the child, but, unless the child is making more than $6,500 a year in taxable income, he or she should have negligible taxable income and will pay no tax. The downside is that while the trustee – usually the parent – controls the assets, the child gains control at age 18 and could decide to blow it on a new car or a trip to Europe instead using it for school. That's why some planners, like Leslie Mezei, an associate with Brightside Financial Services, prefer a formal trust to the informal trusts set up by the fund companies. A formal trust can allow you to specify how the money is to be spent. They cost $500 to $1,000 to set up.

SURE KIDS COST A LOT, BUT HOW MUCH?

Any parent will tell you it costs a lot of money to raise a child, but few people have bothered to count the actual dollars spent. Manitoba Agriculture can tell you right down to the last penny from its annual surveys of child-raising expenses. Taking fads and fash-

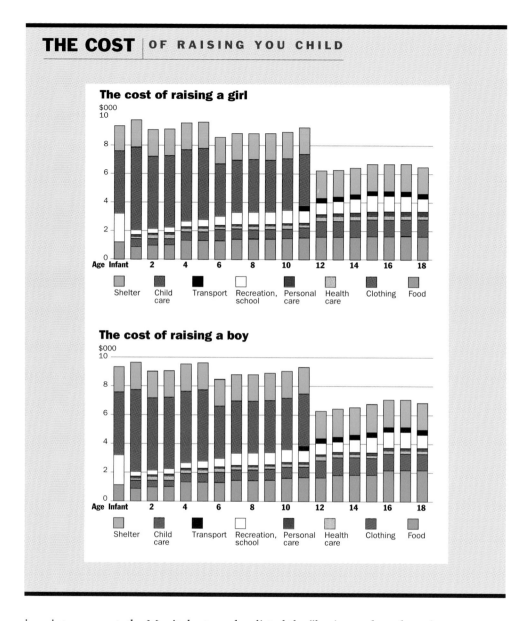

The cost of raising a girl

The cost of raising a boy

ions into account, the Manitoba team has listed the "basic goods and services necessary to maintain physical and social well being." Then they priced each item. As much as possible, they used the Sears catalogue. If the desired item was not available or unsatisfactory, they visited one or more Winnipeg area stores.

BOYS EAT MORE FOOD AND GIRLS NEED MORE IN CLOTHING

They sought well-made items that offered good value, and selections tended to fall between the most and least expensive. In some cases, researchers visited several stores and averaged the prices. As shown on the accompanying chart, total costs of raising a child in 1996 ran to about $9,348 for an infant of either sex. At four years old, the tally was $9,471 for a boy and $9,492 for a girl. At eight years, it was $8,828 for a boy and $8,832 for a girl. At 12, when day care is no longer needed, a boy cost $6,258 and a girl $6,247. At 16, the totals were $7,046 for a boy and $6,724 for a girl. Boys devour far more food and girls need more in clothing.

For boys, except infants, total costs were barely up from the previous year. That was also true for girls aged one to 11. Total costs for girls 12 to 18 rose roughly in line with inflation. The total cost for an infant rose 3.9%, but lack of supply forced shoppers to switch from a generic formula to a more costly name brand.

In May 1997, the federal government enacted child support guidelines for divorce orders, with the figures varying by province and the income of the payor parent. At the average industrial wage, about $35,500 (in 1996), the $3,540 federal standard for Manitoba would have covered about 40% of the estimated cost for a child under 10. At the $45,000 income level, the $4,476 federal standard would have covered about 50%.

HERE IS HOW SOME OF THE FIGURES WERE COMPILED

- Durables, such as clothing, were depreciated over their expected life.
- The food list was based on Agriculture Canada standards for a nutritious diet.
- Health-care costs reflected the difference between single and family coverage under Blue Cross. That category included one annual dental checkup and cleaning, but no eyeglasses or special needs.
- Recreation included a bicycle and lessons in one activity. Significantly, it did not include expensive popular pursuits such as hockey or private music lessons.
- School needs covered just supplies. There was no provision for savings for college or university.
- There was no special weekly allowance. That money came from the categories shown.
- Transportation reflected Winnipeg public transit fares. Manitoba Agriculture says car owners "roughly estimated" that child-related trips and teenage use added about 8.8¢ per kilometre to overall vehicle ownership cost.
- Child-care costs were based on licensed day care in Winnipeg.

The shelter cost reflected the difference between rent for a one and two-bedroom apartment in Winnipeg. Manitoba Agriculture also estimated that each child adds 10% to family utilities bills. Having two children would not double the stated cost because some expenses, such as health insurance, were set per family while others, such as furniture and clothing, can be reused.

MAKE SURE YOUR CREDIT RATING IS ACCURATE

Have you ever wondered what your personal credit history looks like? If you're like the vast majority of Canadians, chances are you've never even glanced at this all-important piece of paper. Even if you're not applying for a loan or a mortgage, you should make it a priority to examine your credit report, if for no other reason than to make certain the information it contains is accurate. And in case you're wondering, it's free for the asking.

I always believed I was in possession of an unblemished credit history, a document festooned with "R1" notations – credit-bureau-speak for credit card balances being "paid as agreed and up to date." But when my eyes gazed upon my two-page credit history, which I had requested from Montreal-based Equifax Canada, you could hear the sound of cartilage on linoleum – my jaw dropped to the floor. I'm the kind of fellow who looks upon debt as a four-letter word. So, you can understand the jolt to my system when I discovered that my personal credit report – the document that banks, utilities and employers use to approve (or assassinate) my character – contained a sprinkling of condemnation.

IT IS WORTH OBTAINING YOUR CREDIT REPORT AND VERIFYING THE INFORMATION

First, there was this Bank of Montreal MasterCard. It was originally activated in December, 1992, my report noted, and was currently carrying a balance of $978. The account had been 30 days past due five times; 60 days past due three times; and 90 or more days past due, three times. There was only one not-so-insignificant hitch. This piece of plastic doesn't belong to me. Other information was awry as well. Gazing on the box listing my former address, my eyes met the name of a street I've never strolled past, much less lived on. And the company I used to work for was listed as being my wife's present employer.

To their credit, a call to the people at Equifax resulted in assurances that the errors would be put under investigation and likely rectified within a few weeks. A telephone representative explained that, based on the evidence at hand, I had been cross-filed with another person of the same name. Somehow my credit and residence history had been merged with bits and bytes of his, and not even Equifax, which is a major player in the consumer-credit information business, knew why. If there is something to be learned from my experience, it's simply this: If you don't know anything about the Equifax and Trans Union credit bureaus – the two largest credit bureaus in the land – you should. They know a lot about you, and sometimes their data are not entirely on the money.

PERSONAL CREDIT RATINGS ARE THERE FOR THE ASKING

A few years ago CBC's *Marketplace* aired a segment in which 100 consumers requested copies of their personal credit reports from Equifax. A staggering 47 found errors. Thirteen reports had errors so significant the misinformation would have affected the consumers' chances of getting credit. "It is definitely a problem, because so much data is being retrieved and entered [by the credit bureaus], errors can easily be made," says Laurie Campbell, a program manager with the Credit Counselling Service of Toronto. "One thing we always ask individuals to do, whether they think their credit rating is good or bad, is to get a copy to check it out."

Yet, for whatever reason, many Canadians look upon credit reports as being documents shrouded in mystery. A national opinion survey conducted for Equifax Canada by Louis Harris and Associates Inc. determined that only 13% of Canadians have seen a copy of their credit report or had the contents of their credit report read to them over the phone. (The corresponding U.S. figure is 38%.) As well, only 56% of Canadian adults believe they actually have a legal right to see their personal credit bureau reports. But there shouldn't be any mysteries about personal credit ratings – credit-bureau information is there for the asking.

INACCURACIES IN YOUR CREDIT REPORT WILL BE CORRECTED BY THE CREDIT BUREAU

By law, personal credit information can be released to third parties only if the person is applying for credit, employment or insurance, or if there's a legitimate business need for this information. (For example, utilities are included under this principle because new customers can run up whopping bills and then skip town.) But anyone can gain access to their own information at any time. And what about those errors? Ken Porter, vice-president and general manager of Toronto-based Trans Union of Canada, Inc., says despite sophisticated information-gathering technology, mistakes are sometimes made on people's reports because amassing data often boils down to "garbage in, garbage out."

Most credit grantors supply the bureaus with information that is accurate and legible. But there are other firms, says Porter, "that give us applications that seem to have been filled out on scrap paper." And that's when mistakes are likely to be made. Michel Globensky of Equifax Canada says hundreds of thousands of Canadians obtain copies of their credit reports each year and Equifax is diligent when it comes to eradicating errors. "If inaccuracies creep in, despite the best of our intentions, it's our job to correct them," he says. "Information is our lifeblood."

Even so, before negotiating a mortgage or applying for a loan or credit card, Campbell of CCS advises people to review their own credit ratings first. "This way, you can

CHECKING UP | ON CREDIT CHECKERS

Some people believe they actually have to pay so-called credit doctors a fee (typically from $300 to $500) to gain access to their credit history, but it's not true.

Here's how to get the documentation the financial institutions are judging you by for free: Equifax Canada requires photocopies of two pieces of identification such as a driver's licence, birth certificate or passport. Sign the photocopies and include a note indicating current address, former address, date of birth and daytime phone number. Mail to: Equifax Canada Inc., 7171 Jean Talon E., Anjou, Que., H1S 2Z2. Trans Union of Canada also requires photocopies of two pieces of valid ID, as well as a photocopy of a utility bill to verify your address. Mail to: Trans Union Consumer Relations Department, P.O. Box 338-LCD1, Hamilton, L8L 7W2. Information is usually processed in 10 to 14 days and then mailed out. If there are anomalies, call the credit bureau (Equifax: 1-800-465-7166; Trans Union: 1-800-663-9980) and your file will be investigated and, if necessary, corrected. An updated credit report should be on its way to you in 15 to 20 days.

correct the inaccuracies before you're sitting across the table from the bank manager," she says. "And if there's any justified black mark on your record that you've forgotten about, at least you know what it's there for."

FINANCIAL PLANNERS DO MORE THAN INVEST

Panicky investors who considered bolting for the equity exits in October 1997 probably have their financial planners to thank for keeping them invested. In such situations, good advice is worth thousands of dollars, while poor advice or none at all can cost you big-time. Financial planners like Jane Baker see their job primarily as keeping clients invested in such situations, holding them to long-term plans made in calmer times. They call this hand holding, something do-it-yourself investors miss out on. But the seemingly simple question of "How do I find a good financial planner?" almost stumped me the other day when a television interviewer posed it.

My flip TV answer was: "Don't worry, financial planners will find you" at the multitude of free seminars that appear as registered retirement savings plan season approaches. I neglected to say there is a free directory available from the Canadian Association of Financial Planners. Call 1-800-346-CAFP or check the association's Web site at www.cafp.org. It contains 800 names of financial planners who have at least a CFP (chartered financial planner) designation or the more rigorous RFP (registered financial planner).

DO SOME BACKGROUND WORK BEFORE CHOOSING A FINANCIAL PLANNER

As of April 1, 1999, the CFP will be restricted to those who pass an exam set by the Financial Planners Standards Council of Canada, a body established in November 1995 to set uniform minimum standards. Ideally, financial planners also have an RFP, which means they have been in the business at least two years, have liability insurance, have met educational requirements and are bound by the CAFP's code of professional ethics. Keep in mind that, except in Quebec, financial planners are not formally regulated as yet. Financial products are regulated but financial advice about how to put those products together is not.

Based on the 22,000 brokers and dealers Mackenzie Financial Corp. and Trimark Financial Corp. say sell their funds, and another 3,000 representatives of the captive Investors Group Inc. sales force, there must be at least 25,000 people claiming to be financial planners. By contrast, there are only 800 RFPs in Canada, according to Steve Gobel, investors division manager and CAFP president. The CAFP directory is broken down provincially and reveals degrees and professional designations and how the planner is compensated. Most are paid by commission; but there are some who charge fees and some who use both methods of remuneration.

Fee or fees-only means, in theory, you pay a separate fee for advice and a financial plan. Such a planner is supposedly pure and uninfluenced by front or rear loads, trailer fees and other enticements that may compromise objective advice. But you must recognize they have to be paid. There is nothing wrong with being compensated through commissions, as long as this is made clear. Toronto-based planner Jane Baker, for example, charges commissions, a percentage of assets under management and/or fee-for-service, depending on what the client prefers. She spells out each option to all prospective clients.

If you located a planner through a trusted friend or colleague, you are expecting a measure of integrity and competence in the person being considered. But before handing over your life savings, ask for references. The CAFP advises meeting with a prospective planner "to ensure that you get along well." Ask about the planner's education and related experience and establish whether an assistant will be handling your account. If so, ask to meet that person too. Explore the planner's areas of expertise. Where there are gaps, establish how good connections are with accountants, lawyers, investment counselors and other professionals.

YOU HAVE A RIGHT TO KNOW HOW MANY CLIENTS THE PLANNER SERVES

The CAFP does not suggest it, but I would want to know how many clients the planners and their staffs are serving. Ask commission-compensated planners how big their "book" of business is. If it is huge – and many have a book well beyond $100 million – ask yourself how much service you, the small client, are likely to receive. If the book is tiny, is it because the planner is new in the business or has the advice been so bad many clients have left?

Gobel suggests finding a planner who deals with people with situations similar to your own. You can check the planner's average client asset size by dividing the book value by the number of clients, and seeing how your portfolio size compares. Gobel also says planners should advocate a broad approach to financial planning. This includes clarifying the client's financial situation; identifying goals and making recommendations with regard to cash flow management, retirement planning, tax planning, estate planning, and particular investment products.

SINCE YOU ARE THE SOUGHT-AFTER CUSTOMER, YOU CAN DRIVE A HARD BARGAIN

Products, such as mutual funds, are only one component of a financial plan. If you view the planner as primarily a seller of products, be clear on the nature of these products and how the planner is compensated for selling them. If the planners are primarily fund salespersons, they probably sell six or seven fund families. Find out which ones. Remember, you are the prospect and a highly sought-after customer. Be fussy and drive a hard bargain.

CHAPTER 10

INSURANCE | PLANNING

- The fundamentals
- Home, car and travel insurance
- Group plans
- Disability, critical illness and long-term care insurance
- ABCs of life insurance

INSURING FOR A HEALTHY LIFE

AND AGAINST AN UNTIMELY DEATH | BY JONATHAN CHEVREAU

LIFE IS ALL ABOUT RISK. Insurance is the art of hedging against the multiple risks we all face as we move through our lives. "Even the best designed financial plans for individuals, families and their businesses face three fundamental risks," says Bill Strain, executive vice-president with PPIFinancial Group. The family breadwinners may die too soon, become disabled or live too long. He defines insurance as being a "business of risk intermediation."

This chapter explores the various types of insurance available in the Canadian market. These include the traditional big three of life insurance, auto insurance and house insurance. But, increasingly, it's becoming necessary to provide for "living benefits" that kick in not when we die but when we become disabled (disability insurance); critically ill through cancer, stroke and similar calamities (critical illness insurance); and to care for us in an advanced but perhaps infirm old age (long-term care insurance). As Strain points out, there is risk living too long as well as dying young. As he puts it, "increasing longevity increases the risk of outliving your money and incurring greater long-term health care costs."

INSURANCE POLICIES CAN BE TAILORED TO YOUR INDIVIDUAL NEEDS

As insurance products evolve, they are becoming more complex, he says. The pace of innovation in the life insurance marketplace has been particularly frenetic, as products move from concept to delivery in months rather than years. The rise of the personal computer has allowed insurance agents to build many more options into product offerings, empowering financial planners and agents to tailor insurance products to various "what-if" scenarios involving their clients. "No longer does one size fit all," Strain says. Insurance professionals also must accept greater responsibility for keeping clients informed about the risks as well as the rewards of some of the more aggressive strategies.

Examples of this are provided in the articles on leveraged life insurance in the Retirement Planning section of this Investing Guide. Leveraged life plans aim to provide high

*Insurance professionals must accept responsibility for keeping
clients informed about the risks involved*

net worth investors with a tax-free flow of retirement income. This is achieved through
a type of life insurance known as universal life and by using the investment savings portion of the policy as collateral for a series of bank loans. The loans are repaid with the
death benefit and, theoretically, a tidy nest egg remains for your beneficiaries. With participating whole life and universal life insurance products, the policyholders assume an
underlying investment risk, whether or not they realize it, Strain says.

DIFFERENCES IN POLICY PREMIUMS AND BENEFITS CAN BE VAST
Faced with a precipitous decline in interest rates in recent years, disgruntled policyholders have found the actual returns on their universal life and participating whole life
polices have not lived up to the initial promises. This has given rise to "vanishing premium" cases in North America. In either case, Strain and other insurance professionals
counsel full and fair disclosure of the assumptions and guarantees laid out in sales illustrations of such products. Insurance is generally available through "group" plans at
work or purchased individually to supplement group coverage. There is also a measure
of insurance in certain government programs, such as the disability provisions of the
Canada Pension Plan and Workers Compensation.

If you want to buy individual insurance, you'll generally have to choose between captive sales people married to one supplier or more independent brokers who try to shop
the market for you. Differences in policy premiums and benefits can be vast, as is appar-

ent in the case of automobile insurance in Ontario. In this case, consumer hotlines like the Consumer's Guide to Insurance, can help you choose.

Strain says innovations in insurance will be driven by clients, especially the demographic wave of aging baby boomers. That alone will make long-term health care and related insurance a booming business. The U.S. is well advanced in this market but as health costs rise in Canada, more families here will look to privately financed care through insurance. Strain envisages an era in which well-off consumers build pools of investments through the tax-deferred mechanisms of universal life policies.

INSURANCE POLICIES WILL NOW COVER LONG-TERM CARE, CRITICAL ILLNESS AND DISABILITY

Increasingly, these will be used to fund benefits for long-term care, critical illness and disability. Products may combine various combinations of what to date have been sold on a piecemeal basis. "Rather than using stand-alone products to indemnify a particular risk, tomorrow's products may adopt a more holistic approach," Strain predicts. Such policies would not only insure but "offer the ability to accumulate tax-sheltered supplementary retirement savings" over and above registered pension plans and RRSPs. Even more revolutionary would be flexible multiple life policies that would cover several lives and "introduce the potential for some co-insurance with the policyholder."

ALL YOU NEED TO KNOW ABOUT LIFE INSURANCE

Life insurance is a financial tool whose main purpose is to replace income that is lost when a wage earner dies. It's an efficient way to protect your survivors and dependents against financial hardship and to ensure that they are not burdened with significant debt when you die. Life insurance can also be a useful way of ensuring that your mortgage or tax bill is paid off or be a mechanism for leaving money to organizations or charities of your choice.

HOW MUCH LIFE INSURANCE DO I NEED?

To determine how much life insurance you require, it is important to carry out a financial needs analysis. You can do this yourself, but a trained and licensed life insurance agent can help you conduct a more thorough review. You should take into consideration what immediate financial needs there will be after your death to cover such expenses as medical bills, funeral expenses and estate taxes. Keep in mind also what costs would be involved in a readjustment period for family members or friends who relied on your financial support. Other items to factor in are monthly bills and other ongoing expenses, rent or mortgage payments, day-care costs and tuition fees. A general rule of thumb is that you should buy life insurance that is equal to five to seven times your net income.

WHAT KINDS OF POLICIES ARE THERE?

There are two basic kinds of life insurance: permanent and term. As the name implies, permanent insurance is best suited to cover long-term and permanent financial needs, such as funeral expenses, income for your survivors and dependents, and capital gains taxes and other liabilities at death. Term insurance, on the other hand, is designed to look after shorter-term financial needs, such as mortgages, education and other expenses when children are young and some business commitments. Permanent insurance provides life-long protection and it is known by several names: whole life, universal life or variable life. This kind of life insurance has several distinguishing features.

WHO BUYS | INSURANCE?

Age of insured	% of policies	% of amount*
Under 18	17	7
18-24	12	10
25-34	30	38
35-44	22	29
45-54	12	12
55 or over	7	4

Total: 16 million Canadians covered.
* the dollar value of individual policies

Size of policy $	% of policies	% of amount*
Under 15,000	10	1
15,000-24,999	8	1
25,000-49,999	16	5
50,000-99,999	22	14
100,000-300,000	40	60
300,001 and over	4	19

Source: Canadian Life and Health Insurance Assoc.

First of all, premiums remain level over the lifetime of the policy. Second, reserves in the policy accumulate as a cash value. You may borrow against this cash value, or you may receive it if you surrender your policy. Third, non-forfeiture options allow you to use the cash value to pay premiums, to buy a lesser amount of permanent insurance with no further premiums or to purchase an equal amount of term insurance. Participating policies receive their share of the financial success of the life insurance company in the form of dividends that are declared annually and paid to policyholders.

Term insurance provides protection for a specified period of time (one, five, 10 or 20 years or to age 60, 65 or 70) and it pays a benefit only if you die during the term of the policy. Premiums remain level during the term chosen, but they increase when the term is renewed.

This kind of policy does not have a cash value or non-forfeiture options. One form of term insurance, called Term to 100, provides protection to age 100, but generally doesn't pay dividends or include cash values.

Group life insurance is made available by most employers and unions. It is usually term insurance to age 65 and often does not require a medical examination or other evidence of insurability. Care should be taken to determine if your insurance coverage can be converted to individual insurance at the termination of your employment.

WHOM SHOULD I NAME AS A BENEFICIARY?

You can name an individual to receive the proceeds of the policy or you can name your estate or a trust. If you name a beneficiary in your policy, the money goes directly to that person or organization and does not go through your estate, thus avoiding having to pay probate fees or taxes. Another advantage to naming a spouse, child, grandchild or a parent as a beneficiary is the money is exempt from seizure by creditors. You also have the option of naming an irrevocable beneficiary, which means that the policyholder cannot change the name of that beneficiary without his or her consent. This money is also protected from creditors and doesn't become part of your estate. You may also name a contingent beneficiary, in the event that the primary beneficiary you have named is not alive at the time of your death. Otherwise the money will go to your estate. Finally, you can name a registered charitable organization as beneficiary, in which case the premiums can be tax deductible.

WHEN DO I PAY MY PREMIUMS AND WHAT HAPPENS IF I STOP PAYING THEM?

Most people choose to pay their premiums on a monthly basis, often through automatic bank withdrawals, but you can opt for annual, semi-annual or quarterly payments. You may choose to determine the number of years you want to pay premiums, so that at some point your policy will be fully paid up. If you stop paying your premiums for whatever reason, you have 31 days to make the payment after the due date. If you do not pay within that time, your policy will lapse, or terminate. It can be reinstated but this will require payment of overdue premiums, with interest, and may require a medical examination. In most policies there are riders that can help you in the event that you are having difficulties paying your premiums.

HOW SHOULD I USE MY POLICY DIVIDENDS?

If you purchase a participating life insurance policy, you will receive policy dividends (these are not to be confused with regular dividends issued by corporations to their shareholders). You can use them for a variety of purposes: to increase your insurance coverage; to increase future cash values through paid-up additions or bonus additions; or to purchase one-year term insurance. You can also use your dividends to reduce your premium, or you can take them in cash.

Some people choose to leave these dividends on deposit to earn interest or to be invested in a segregated fund, which is the insurance industry's version of a mutual fund.

WHAT IS GROUP CREDITORS' LIFE INSURANCE?

Many people don't realize that your mortgage or car loan may become payable in full if you die. Lending institutions and car dealers sell creditors' group insurance that will pay off these debts in the event of death or in some cases, disability. When purchasing this kind of insurance, pay close attention to restrictions, exclusions or age limits. Also check to see if you own other policies that already offer the same coverage.

SHOULD I BUY LIFE INSURANCE ADVERTISED ON TELEVISION?

As with all purchases of life insurance, before you buy a policy, insist on a thorough explanation of its benefits and read all the fine print for exclusionary clauses. Direct marketing of life insurance is a legitimate business, but a life insurance policy purchase should not be entered into without careful thought and consultation.

HOW DO I CHOOSE AN AGENT?

Selecting a life insurance agent is no different from choosing any other kind of professional adviser. It is important to shop around and to ask the advice of someone you trust. Ask friends or family members whether they can recommend an agent. If not, check the Yellow Pages or call an insurance company. Keep in mind that you are looking for someone who is knowledgeable, who can relate well to you and to your financial situation and who can explain insurance in terms that you understand. Don't meet with just one agent. Take the time to interview two or three.

SOME OF THE QUESTIONS YOU SHOULD ASK YOUR PROSPECTIVE FINANCIAL ADVISER

- How long has the agent been in the business?
- What companies does the agent represent? Some work for only one company, while others, known as brokers, represent several companies.
- What professional designations does the agent have (CLU, chartered life underwriter, or CHFC, chartered financial consultant) and does the agent belong to a professional association (Life Underwriters Association of Canada, Independent Life Insurance Brokers of Canada)?
- Will the agent give you references from other clients?

Once you have chosen an agent, you can begin the discussion of your financial needs and goals. It is important to be open and frank with your agent so he or she can offer you suggestions and options that will truly meet your requirements. Make a point of asking for proposals in writing and be very cautious if your new agent suggests you surrender or replace policies without clear explanations why this is appropriate for you. As with all important financial transactions, read the application form carefully before signing. By signing you authorize the company to carry out a confidential investigation of your medical history. Confirm with your agent that he or she will deliver the policy in person within a specified period and that at that time both of you will review the policy in detail.

WHAT HAPPENS WHEN I APPLY FOR LIFE INSURANCE?

Be sure that you are honest in answering the questions on the application form. Life insurance is a "good faith" legal contract, and if you lie or withhold information, the policy could be null and void. Your signed application allows the underwriting department of the insurance company to verify your medical records and to assess the risks you present, by virtue of your health, age, gender, family history, financial situation and occupation. If you are a non-smoker and can state that you have not smoked for at least a year, you will qualify for lower premium rates. Depending on all these factors, the insurance company may ask that you undergo some form of medical examination.

SHOULD I WORRY ABOUT AN INSURANCE COMPANY HAVING CONFIDENTIAL INFORMATION?

Everyone working for an insurance company must comply with strict and elaborate privacy rules. Your consent is required for any information to be gathered about you, and this information may not be used for purposes other than qualifying for life insurance. Medical information about you can be released only to you and only by your personal physician. You may also request that an insurance company reveal what information it has on file for you. Medical information is shared among some 750 life insurance companies in North America through a non-profit organization called the Medical Information Bureau. The purpose of this sharing of information is to alert against potential fraud. Even though confidentiality is closely protected, you may see if there is a file on you and verify its contents by contacting the Medical Information Bureau at 330 University Ave., Toronto, Ont., M5G 1R7, telephone (416) 597-0590.

WHAT IF I CHANGE MY MIND AFTER I APPLY FOR LIFE INSURANCE?

If you decide that you do not want to go through with your purchase of life insurance after you have applied, you can return your policy to the insurance company within 10 days of receiving it. The policy will be cancelled and your paid premiums will be refunded to you. This is called the "10-day free look" or the "rescission right."

WHAT SHOULD I KNOW BEFORE I REPLACE A POLICY?

If you are thinking about replacing a life insurance policy, do not make a hasty decision. A precipitous decision could result in a loss of coverage, an unnecessary increase in cost or the need to offer proof of insurability through medical exams because of your older age or of being in poorer health. Review your reasons for changing policies and seek trustworthy advice on the pros and cons of other policies. Also explore whether your existing policy can be changed to meet your new needs at a reasonable cost. And by all means ask your agent to assist you in this review of your financial situation and your insurance needs.

If you decide to go ahead and replace a policy, your agent must fill out a disclosure form that explains the pros and cons of both the old and the new policy. Read this document carefully before you sign it. And finally, make certain you do not cancel your old policy until you have the new one in hand. A termination notice must be signed for the old policy to be cancelled.

CAN I BORROW AGAINST MY LIFE INSURANCE POLICY?

You can borrow any amount up to the cash value of your permanent life insurance policy by requesting a loan through your agent or directly by calling your insurance company. No credit checks are required and the interest you will pay on this loan will usually be very reasonable. You can pay back the loan in a lump sum or in instalments. In some cases these loans may be taxable, so check this out before you request the loan. If you die before you have paid back the loan, the outstanding balance and interest will be deducted from the death benefit.

WHAT KIND OF INSURANCE DO I NEED AS AN ENTREPRENEUR?

If you are self-employed or are running a small business, you should look into liability and disability insurance, as well as group life and health insurance for yourself and your employees. Many insurance companies have very attractive packages of insurance for small companies of five or more employees.

CAN I GET LIFE INSURANCE OTHER THAN FROM A LIFE INSURANCE COMPANY

In many cases you can obtain life, health and disability insurance through membership in professional associations, alumni groups, unions or affinity groups. This is a growing market, so shop around. This kind of plan can also be used to top up your other insurance coverage.

WHAT ARE LIVING BENEFITS?

On a voluntary basis, and upon request by policyholders, insurance companies make available to terminally ill patients a portion of their death benefit, usually up to 50% of the benefit, or in the range of $50,000, although awards can be higher. Your request must be accompanied by medical documents indicating you are terminally ill, and often you must seek a release from the beneficiary agreeing to this prepayment. Living benefits, or accelerated benefits, as they are also called, can make a significant difference in the quality of health care terminally ill patients can afford, and they can also improve the quality of life for people in the latter stages of their illness. Another option for AIDS or cancer patients wishing to obtain an early payment of a death benefit is a viatical settlement company. These are not insurance companies. They sometimes offer up to 80% of the death benefit, but the remainder of the benefit does not go to the beneficiary. Care should be taken in dealing with these organizations and you should check to make sure that they are legal, since in some jurisdictions they are deemed to be trafficking illegally in life insurance.

WHAT HAPPENS WHEN SOMEONE FILES A CLAIM?

To file a claim the beneficiary must contact the agent or the insurance company and provide them with proof of death, a doctor's statement or a death certificate. Claims should be made within 90 days to 12 months after the death. The claim is usually paid within a week to 10 days, unless an investigation is needed to determine the cause of death or if death occurs during the first two years the policy has been in force (the contestable period). Interest will be paid from the date of death. Most beneficiaries prefer to take the proceeds of the policy in a lump-sum payment, although there may be other settlement options for leaving the money with the insurance company.

ARE DEATH BENEFITS TAXABLE?

The death benefit of a life insurance policy is not taxable in the hands of a beneficiary.

WHAT HAPPENS IF THE CAUSE OF DEATH IS SUICIDE?

If death by suicide occurs during the first two years the policy is in force, the claim will not be paid. After that two-year period, the claim will be paid.

WHAT KIND OF CONSUMER PROTECTION LIMITS APPLY TO LIFE INSURANCE?

The Canadian Life & Health Insurance Compensation Corp. (CompCorp) is the industry-funded consumer protection plan. In the event of the insolvency and winding up of a life insurance company, CompCorp provides protection and continued coverage to Canadian policyholders up to certain limits. Coverage is per policyholder, per company, and includes group as well as individual insurance:

- $200,000 for life insurance.
- $60,000 for non-registered accumulation policies and cash values in life insurance policies.
- $60,000 for RRSPs and RRIFs combined.
- $2,000 per month for annuities and disability income policies,
- $60,000 for other health benefits.

WHERE CAN I GET MORE INFORMATION ON LIFE INSURANCE?

To receive more information on life insurance or issues of consumer protection, to talk with a knowledgeable counselor or to request consumer publications, you can call the Information Centre free of charge from anywhere in Canada at 1-800-268-8099 or in Toronto at (416) 777-2344. You can also write to The Information Centre, Canadian Life & Health Insurance Association Inc., 1 Queen St. E., Suite 1700, Toronto, Ont., M5C 2X9

BOOKS TO SURVIVE IN LIFE INSURANCE JUNGLE

Murphy's Little-Known Law of Life Insurance states: "Any product designed to favor the consumer will ultimately be withdrawn or have its rates increased to the level where it favors the company."

That little gem and 34 more life insurance gags come from Richard Gilbert, the maverick president of Megacorp Insurance Agencies Inc. of Mississauga, Ont. Gilbert is a refreshing breeze in an industry that seems to go out of its way to bury simple concepts under a mountain of confusing jargon. Or, as another Gilbert quip goes: "The more complex a policy's language and conditions, the greater the probability that the promises are carved in Jell-O." He warns consumers should never buy a policy without reading the fine print.

Stripped to its essentials, life insurance should be simple. Just don't expect easy or frank disclosure from the insurance companies. A more objective source is a concise primer called *Insure Sensibly* by James Bullock and George Brett (Penguin Books Canada Ltd.). Bruce Cohen's recently updated *The Money Adviser* (Stoddart, 1997) also has several cogent chapters on insurance. *Insure Sensibly* concedes "life insurance is still sold using a lot of smoke and mirrors; make sure you look past all the fast talk. You need to know what you are buying and why it will work for you. Before you buy, insist on being shown a number of alternatives involving at least a couple of companies and scenarios."

GUIDEPOSTS FOR THE ANNUAL SNOWBIRD TREK

Heading south? Tighter conditions on out-of-Canada health insurance and changing tax rules make it harder for snowbirds each year, but there is help available in making your choices. If you're on the Internet, check the Web site set up by chartered accountants KPMG. The Snowbirds Tax Page offers explanations and advice on Canadian and U.S. tax rules, immigration and customs, cross-border estate planning, property ownership, health care and pensions. There's also a section where you can leave questions: http://snowbird.kpmg.ca. (The standard www prefix is not needed.)

SHOP AROUND CAREFULLY FOR HEALTH COVERAGE BEFORE LEAVING THE COUNTRY

If you're not on the Net, visit your local Royal Trust branch and ask for their free booklet called *Planning a Winter Out of the Country*. It also deals with tax and customs rules as well as banking. It's on the Net too, at http://www.royalbank.com. Here's yet another handy information source. The Canadian Life & Health Insurance Association offers a free consumer brochure on out-of-Canada health insurance along with a list of companies and associations that sell the coverage. The list includes their toll-free numbers. For a copy, call CLHIA at 1-800-268-8099 or, in Toronto, 777-2344.

It's more important than ever to shop carefully for health insurance, says Milan Korcok, a Florida-based Canadian who tracks that market. "The process is becoming more exclusionary and there are more pitfalls to watch for," he warns. Korcok's biggest concern involves the medical exclusion questionnaires that are now a standard part of purchasing coverage. "Those forms are now very complex with very ambiguous language," he says. For example, one form asks if you've had dizziness or lightheadedness in the past five years. "What constitutes that, how many times and how dizzy?" Korcok wonders.

PREMIUMS PAID FOR HEALTH COVERAGE QUALIFY FOR MEDICAL EXPENSE TAX CREDITS

A common question asks if you've had a change in medication. Korcok says the insurer may include a switch from a brand-name drug to a generic. Or even a reduction in your prescribed dosage. Also, he points out, doctors advise many seniors to take an aspirin a day for preventive reasons. That's medication but Korcok says many people don't realize that. When buying coverage, remember the premiums qualify for the medical expense tax credit. Also, make sure you take the insurer's toll-free emergency phone number with you. Those lines are run by companies that will arrange or oversee your care. If they're not called within 24 or 48 hours, your plan likely slashes coverage, perhaps to $25,000 or less.

HERE ARE SOME OTHER POINTS TO CHECK WHEN SHOPPING FOR COVERAGE

• Are you already covered by an employer or association plan? To what extent? For leisure trips? Your family or just you?

• Do you rely on coverage from a credit card? Some cover just 17 to 22 days. You can't cover a few weeks with one card and a few more with another; all card coverage starts on departure. Card issuers sell extended coverage but a standalone policy might be cheaper. And does your card insurance only cover trips charged on the card?

• Don't assume all policies have the same exclusions and don't assume the insurer you used last year has the same exclusions this year. Korcok says some plans have widened exclusions to conditions present within the past five years.

• Don't top up one plan with insurance from another. The second insurer may view a problem that developed during the first period as a pre-existing condition.

• More insurers are requiring doctors' statements for certain conditions. Normally you pay for that, but Korcok suggests getting your annual checkup just before your trip so medicare foots the bill.

• Check multi-trip plans if you travel more than once a year. For example, a 30-day plan covers any number of trips, each lasting up to 30 days. If you go south after Thanksgiving, head home for Christmas and then go back, a 90-day multi-trip would cover both stays for one price.

• Save money by taking a high deductible. Check your employer-sponsored coverage, if any. Korcok says the plan may cover the first $5,000 of medical expenses. So you can easily go for a $5,000 deductible on your privately purchased plan. "That's a terrific way to cut your cost by one-third," Korcok says.

• There are low-priced plans that cover just enough care to stabilize you for return to Canada. Check the limit. Some offer only 72 hours of care or $10,000, whichever comes first. Korcok says $10,000 may cover less than two days of intensive care at a U.S. hospital where daily fees run about US$4,000. Some plans have raised their limits to $25,000.

INSURANCE MAY OFFER RETIREMENT TAX BREAK

A little-known leveraged life insurance strategy known as an insured retirement plan (IRP) can be used to generate tax-free income in retirement and leave more for your heirs, according to many investment advisers and life insurance agents. Although these plans have been around for more than a decade, many people have never heard of IRPs, or they think they're too good to be true.

In fact, Tim Henry and Michael Kraik, two investment advisers who are licensed to sell life insurance products through RBC Dominion Securities Financial Services (they are among the minority of advisers who straddle the worlds of traditional investment banking and life insurance) call the IRP "the most effective tax-neutralization strategy that exists in Canada today."

Some insurance vendors, on the other hand, are far less enamored of the IRP concept. For example, Bob Porter, associate broker with Megacorp Insurance Agencies Inc. of Mississauga, Ont., suggests these insurance-based plans are being flagrantly misrepresented by vendors with vested interests. He refuses to sell IRPs to his clients, and suggests they "will come back to haunt' those who deal in them.

UNIVERSAL LIFE INSURANCE

Technically, an IRP is not an insured retirement plan. Rather, it is a retirement plan inside a universal life insurance policy, plus an exit strategy. In addition to life insurance, a universal life policy includes a tax-sheltered cash-value fund that cannot exceed the policy's face value. The policy is funded with contributions well in excess of the cost of the underlying insurance. Deposits are made over several years into investments selected by the policyholder, and an annual premium is withdrawn from the policy to pay for the insurance coverage. Henry and Kraik stress the plan best suits affluent or middle-income people who have maximized their registered retirement savings plan contributions.

LEVERAGING THE CASH VALUE

The key to the tax minimization strategy is to borrow money from a bank on retirement, a loan that is ultimately repaid with a tax-free death benefit. This is also called leveraged life insurance, which admittedly flies in the face of traditional retirement advice to clear all debts. When the policyholder wants to draw on the income in retirement, the accumulated capital is used as collateral for a series of bank loans. These, in effect, provide tax-free income. Interest is tacked on to the outstanding loan balance. The loan isn't paid off until after the policyholder dies, but is structured so the sum of loans plus interest never exceeds 75% of the accumulated investment account. If designed properly, there should be a hefty nest egg left to go to your heirs, also tax free.

PAYMENTS NOT TAX-DEDUCTIBLE

Unlike RRSP contributions, IRP payments are not tax-deductible. But IRP payouts are tax-free, while RRSP proceeds (normally taken through a registered retirement income fund, or RRIF) are taxable. For that reason, people in certain income bands may even want to consider an IRP instead of an RRSP, although the investment performance of an RRSP or RRIF is likely to be superior. That's because IRPs do not invest directly in stocks or mutual funds but in indexes, such as the Toronto Stock Exchange 300 or Standard & Poor's 500 composite stock indexes, or bond indexes. As the RBC advisors put it: "Life insurance companies can only pay interest on the surplus account values in policies. The companies do, however, have the ability to tie the rate of interest to certain stock market indexes." "You should consider an IRP if you currently own or require life insurance and can wait at least 15 years before you require the supplemental income produced by the IRP," Kraik says.

How whole life, universal life policies compare

Policy type	Whole life	Universal life
Period of coverage	Life	Life
Premiums	Guaranteed, usually remain level	Flexible. Can be increased or decreased by policyholder within certain limits.
Death benefits	Guaranteed in contract. Remain level. Dividends may be used to enhance benefits	Flexible. May increase or decrease according to fluctuations in cash value.
Cash values	Guaranteed in contract.	Flexible. May increase or decrease according to investment returns and level of policyholder deposits
Other non-forfeiture options	Guaranteed in contract.	Guaranteed in contract.
Dividends	Payable on 'participating' policies. Not guaranteed.	Most policies are 'non-participating' and do not pay dividends.

Pros and cons of permanent insurance

✔ Provides protection for entire life – if kept in force.

✔ Premium cost usually stays level, regardless of age or health problems.

✔ Has cash values that can be borrowed, used to continue protection if premiums are missed, or withdrawn if the policy is no longer required.

✔ Other non-forfeiture options allow the policyholder various possibilities of continuing coverage if premiums are missed or discontinued.

✔ If the policy is participating, it receives dividends that can be taken in cash, left to accumulate at interest, or be used to purchase additional insurance.

✘ Initial cost may be too high for a sufficient amount of protection for your current needs.

✘ May not be an efficient means of covering short-term needs.

✘ Cash values tend to be small in the early years. You have to hold the policy for a long time, say over 10 years, before the cash values become sizable.

Source: Canadian Life & Health Association

How IRP, RRSP compare
Leveraged insurance can preserve cash flow after retirement

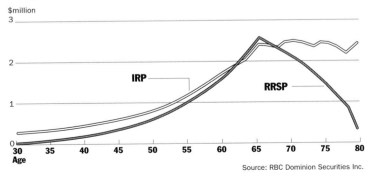

Source: RBC Dominion Securities Inc.

SAMPLE COMPARISON OF IRP VERSUS RRSP

The accompanying chart, provided courtesy of RBC Dominion Securities Inc., shows one example of the difference between making annual RRSP contributions of $10,000 from age 30 to 65 and making annual contributions of $6,000 to an IRP. These amounts are equivalent in after-tax dollars. The total death benefit when the IRP is first set up is $270,000, and is augmented by investment growth and annual $6,000 IRP premium payments. The example assumes a person is in the 40% marginal tax bracket before retirement and in the 50% bracket afterward.

The money is projected to compound at 9% a year, with 3% annual inflation. That return can't be guaranteed, however. Note the RRSP growth stops at age 65 and decelerates when it becomes a RRIF at age 69. The IRP, worth $2.5 million at age 66, is used as collateral to borrow $141,000 each year for 14 years, tax free. At the end you owe the bank $2 million, or $4 million with interest. The cash surrender value of the policy, worth $1.5 million at 65, grows to $5.4 million by age 80. With the $1-million death benefit, the policy is worth $6.4 million in total at the end, Kraik calculates. So after your estate pays back the bank upon your death, your heirs are left with $2.4 million, tax free. Meanwhile, the RRIF's assets have fallen to zero by age 82.

SOME RISKS TO IRPS

There are, however, some risks to an IRP. One is interest-rate uncertainty, says Bill Strain, senior vice-president of Toronto-based PPI Financial Group. The interest rate on the loan will be linked to the bank's prime rate, while the interest earned by the policy's side fund is linked to bond or equity indexes. Strain warns that interest credited on the fund could be as much as two percentage points below the relevant market index. So if the benchmark index is up 8%, you might get as little as 6% interest. That creates the spread the insurance company needs to cover its investment expenses and pay a special 15% federal tax due on investment income credited to exempt policies.

The insurer also might adjust the side fund interest rate because of factors unrelated to investment performance. These include the insurer's expense levels, tax rates, and the accuracy of assumptions on how many people cancel policies early (the "lapse" rate), or die sooner than expected. "You have to look very carefully at just what's guaranteed," Strain says.

CAREFUL MONITORING ESSENTIAL

There is a formula that makes the guaranteed rate a floor rate, well below the rate that would normally be credited. "At any time, the company would have the ability to unilaterally adjust the rates they are currently crediting down to that guaranteed rate," Strain says. So, for example, when five-year money earns 7%, you might find you are receiving as little as 5.4%. Strain says careful planning and ongoing monitoring and management of the arrangement is essential to ensure that the value of the insurance asset is properly matched with the amount of the related debt obligation, no matter how long the insured may live.

For his part, Porter is much more critical of IRPs. "Contrary to its name, the IRP is absolutely not a retirement plan that is insured, or in any way secure or guaranteed," he says. "Most are loaded with charges and fees – either open or hidden – that are not fixed. These are deducted from the policy's premiums with each payment, thus depleting what is available for investment. The name is a disgraceful deception." As for the earnings projections accompanying these policies, Porter calls them "a crock. . . . It was refreshing to see [the accompanying table] projecting less than 10%, but because of factors such as provincial sales tax and CompCorp levy, the UL's investment would have to return 10% or more just for 6% to be credited to the plan investment fund."

According to one actuary, if UL lapse assumptions are out by one percent the costs upon which these assumptions are made will be out by between 18% and 20%. On one policy which had projected annual growth of 10%, the real growth turned out to be minus 3% after three or four years. These UL illustrations are not worth the paper on which they are written.

Richard Gilbert, president of Megacorp, is even more vehement: "These policies are the worst possible buy for the consumer. They contain more fallacies than you can shake a stick at, and are a classic example of why the insurance industry gets a bad reputation. To illustrate [in the accompanying chart] that the IRP, which is no more than a life insurance policy, would have a greater cash value than an RRSP, borders on a criminal act of deception."

EMPLOYERS CO-ORDINATE GROUP BENEFITS

Employers who provide generous group insurance plans or who absorb a significant share of the costs, often wind up covering spouses who should be covered by their own employers. Co-ordination of benefits has always existed but was sparsely enforced. What is new is the strategy used to enforce it. More employers have switched to "positive enrolment." Using this approach, details of dependants, including information on the spouse's coverage, are requested at the time of their enrolment. This way, co-ordination can be applied when claims are processed.

Co-ordination standards are the same for all companies. An employee's claims go first to his or her insurer and the spouse's claims to his or her carrier. Any portion not paid can then be submitted to the other carrier for reimbursement, assuming dependant coverage was selected. When both parents have dependant coverage, children's claims are submitted first by the parent whose birth date comes first during the year. Special provisions apply to children of parents who are divorced or legally separated.

What will it cost you? There is no simple answer, as cost-sharing, rate structures and experience levels vary from plan to plan. You may contribute less and your spouse more, or vice versa. What is certain, however, is that claim costs will be distributed more fairly between employers. Who knows, your employer may be able to share the savings with you.

DISABILITY COVERAGE IS OFTEN IGNORED

Statistically, the risk of being disabled before retirement is greater than that of death. Yet many people fail or refuse to link their health and income, and many insurance agents shy away from selling disability policies because contracts are complex, coverage can be quite costly and there's stiff competition from group plans. That came to mind as I heard about three people, all around 40, who had become disabled. Two of my colleagues at a previous employer were having a hard time pressing claims, while a third was on welfare because she was a contract worker and had no coverage.

Ironically, I had just met John Paterson, a Calgary insurance broker who also advises insurance agents across the country on how to sell disability plans. Paterson, president of Paterson Insurance Services Inc., is walking, talking proof of the need for adequate coverage. In 1988 Paterson was a prosperous orthodontist, but then an eye disease ended his dental career at age 34. A top-of-the-line disability plan ensured income for life, but idleness demolished his self-esteem. In 1990 he decided to become a disability insurance consultant.

A DISABILITY INSURANCE CONSULTANT GIVES SOME HELPFUL TIPS

Paterson tells his story in a small booklet called *Russian Roulette: Gambling with Disability*. It's a quick, easy read, albeit very much a sales pitch. In any event, here are some key points to consider:

• On average, it takes at least six months to sell a professional practice. It took Paterson 18 months, even though he worked at the task full-time and eventually accepted a fire-sale price. He later learned that a pre-arranged buy-sell agreement with a colleague "would have eliminated all my effort, time, worry and costs associated with selling my practice [and] I would have received close to its full value."

• Like many self-employed people, Paterson had business overhead coverage to a set limit. That let him keep his staff to help sell the business. Significantly, without realizing it, Paterson had included an "extension of benefit" clause. That let him take, as a lump sum, the difference between his actual overhead costs and the coverage limit. He used that to buy out his office lease.

•Because of their strong cash flows, it's easy for many professionals to get loans. But Paterson says bankers are quick to show concern if the practitioner is sidelined. Paterson's business loans were insured but the demand loan for his house wasn't, and his banker quickly called it. Paterson's disability policy allowed benefits to be "assigned" so, if the bank insisted, the insurer could make the loan payments directly. The contract was sent to the bank's head office and two weeks later the bank manager relented.

• Based on his experience as a broker, Paterson stresses the need for full and complete disclosure when a policy application is made. Disability can mean big-money payouts so claims are investigated thoroughly. In particular, he warns professionals against over-stating their income. Also, report any medical condition that might affect your work. The insurer may exclude or limit coverage for that condition, but if you don't report it, the insurer can challenge any claim you make. (A Saskatchewan court upheld an insur-er's refusal to pay disability to a man who did not disclose what turned out to be symp-toms of multiple sclerosis. Significantly, the man did not intend to deceive the insurer; he just thought he had a temporary condition that was successfully treated at the time.)

• Be careful about fine-print differences among policies. Paterson cites the case of a man whose group plan refused to pay because doctors felt his slow-growing cancerous tumor began several years before his employment. The policy only covered conditions "con-tracted and commencing" after enrolment in the plan. Paterson says a better clause would have defined sickness as "a disease or disorder which first becomes apparent" after enrolment. Imagine the plight of a dentist who cuts off a finger while doing car-pentry. Paterson says one was denied benefits on grounds it was a self-inflicted injury at a time when there was a cash crisis in his practice.

Many group plans halt benefits after two years if you can perform "any occupation" for which you're reasonably qualified. Paterson hastens to point out that "any occ" claus-es are based on ability to work, not the availability of a job.

• "Filing a claim can be one of the most stressful experiences of your life," Paterson warns. But there are ways to ease the process. First, if disability strikes, contact your insurance adviser immediately. If he or she is not available, have a lawyer review the pol-icy to make sure you meet all the deadlines and conditions. Ask the insurer to put in writing all requests for action on your part. That avoids disputes over what was or was not said in a telephone conversation.

Make sure the examining physician understands how your ability to work is impaired. "It is easy for a physician to assume a condition may not affect your work if he or she is unfamiliar with the actual duties of your occupation," he says. After your claim is approved, make sure a physician doing a follow-up exam has a copy of the orig-inal report. Doctors often use similar yet different technical language, and inconsistent wording can lead to a stressful case review.

NEW CHOICES IN LONG-TERM CARE INSURANCE

Long-term care insurance is a market that's only beginning to attract the attention of Canadian insurance companies. And Canadian consumers are largely unaware such insurance even exists.

By contrast, there is a large and growing long-term care, or LTC, insurance market in the U.S. Policies have been available there for almost 15 years. Paying for long-term care yourself can be very costly. In the U.S., the price of one year in a nursing home averages US$38,000 (more than $50,000 Canadian). Home care costs between US$8,400 and

US$12,300 a year. According to one U.S. study, the single biggest reason for buying LTC is to avoid being dependent on others.

LONG-TERM CARE INSURANCE EASES COSTS OF CARING FOR AGING PARENTS

A big potential market for the product in Canada are "junior seniors" aged 50 to 65 who want to take care of their aging parents, according to Ian Shaw, president of Oakville, Ont.-based Interplay Consulting Service. Over the next five to 10 years, it's also expected the giant baby boom generation will gravitate to LTC insurance as it faces the reality that its parents are coming into the long-term care years. Currently, only 8% of the elderly are in assisted-living or LTC programs. The rest live by themselves or are supported by their families.

Since the wealthy can afford long-term care without insurance and the poor can get various government services or subsidies, the middle class is seen as the group most in need of LTC coverage. Measured by the number of days of use, LTC facilities are almost exclusively the domain of those age 65 and over, while about half of hospital use is by this age group.

The families of people who receive LTC are well aware of the emotional cost of providing such care themselves and of the financial cost of hiring professionals. The insurance is not cheap but, should it prove necessary, it could be preferable to wiping out a family's assets or those of a future estate.

Hamilton-based Westbury Life and Burlington, Ont.-based ITT Hartford Canada have sold policies for at least two years.

SALES OF LONG-TERM CARE INSURANCE ARE SLOW TO TAKE OFF IN CANADA

"The market is huge but sales have been minuscule," says Denis Scodallaro, senior vice-president of ITT Hartford. "It's difficult to convince Canadians there is a need." ITT has an in-home care insurance policy, with riders that can be added for facility care outside the home. However, awareness of LTC insurance may get a boost from the marketing muscle of Toronto-based Commercial Union Canada. In September 1996, the company took the wraps off its Living Care program, which provides tax-free LTC benefits for people requiring home care or nursing home care.

THE COST OF LONG-TERM CARE CAN EAT AWAY AT ASSETS

Like all insurance, the cost rises steeply with age. If you qualify for benefits, coverage is for life, but the insured must be between the ages of 40 and 80 at the time the policy is issued. Commercial Union says benefits are payable in the case of "cognitive impairment" (inability to think, perceive, reason or remember) or if the claimant can no longer perform unaided two of the following five "activities of daily living:" bathing, eating, dressing, toileting or changing positions of the body.

A private Canadian nursing home can cost between $3,000 and $6,000 a month, according to Commercial Union. Even at $100 a day, the cumulative costs of long-term care can quickly eat into savings. At that rate it amounts to $36,000 a year, or $180,000 for five years. Government nursing homes can cost less, but have long waiting lists. Even with government subsidies, ward coverage in Ontario can cost $1,225 a month.

Home care may cost $35 to $48 an hour for a private registered nurse or $70 an hour for an occupational therapist or physiotherapist. Less skilled personal care to help with eating or light housework can run $15 an hour. Government programs may only provide 60 hours a month for home care, or two hours a day.

One advantage of Living Care over other policies is the benefits paid are for a set amount rather than reimbursements for actual expenses. They range from $20 to $300 a day.

THERE ARE SEVERAL COVERAGE OPTIONS AVAILABLE

You can choose between unlimited benefits, or 2,000 times the daily benefit amount selected, or 750 times, with premiums varying accordingly. For example, under a $200 daily benefit and 2,000-times limit, the maximum payout would be $400,000. An inflation option, which carries higher premiums, increases the daily benefit amount by 2% a year for 20 years.

Premiums can be reduced by choosing a longer elimination period, which is the number of days between the commencement of care and the beginning of benefits. For example, a 90-day elimination period results in premiums that are roughly 30% less than if costs are paid as soon as the care begins.

However, Commercial Union's elimination period is based on the number of care days, not calendar days, as is the case with Westbury Life. So if you needed only three days of care a week, a 30-day elimination period would preclude benefits for 10 weeks. (This feature drew groans from the agents attending the product launch.)

As the chart shows, Living Care premiums start getting expensive around retirement age. For $100 a day of benefit, the cheapest premium would be $140 per year for a 40-year-old choosing the 750-times option and a 90-day elimination period. At the other extreme would be a $19,730 a year annual premium to insure an 80-year old for a $100 a day benefit under the unlimited maximum plan and a zero-day elimination period. The accompanying table shows a portion of Commercial Union's scale for a $100 daily benefit under the 750-times option.

A LONG-TERM CARE POLICY CAN BE EXPENSIVE

The policy is a good one but expensive because of the way it is designed, says Dick Gilbert, president of Mississauga, Ont.-based Megacorp Insurance Agencies Inc. "They're paying for everything: the assessment in the first place, for a co-ordinator to go out and do a whole plan and interview the family and then arrange it all."

Gilbert doesn't expect the product to take off immediately because, when it comes to insurance, Canadians are the "world's worst procrastinators." He foresees a "slow, gradual acceptance" over the next five to 10 years. "Lots of boomers will do it because they're selfish and will want it for their parents. Some wealthier people will buy it for asset protection."

BETWEEN DEATH AND DISABILITY INSURANCE

We all want health, wealth and happiness. But without health, your wealth is going to decline and along with it your happiness. That's why comprehensive financial planning includes life insurance and disability insurance. Life insurance pays your beneficiaries if you die, and disability insurance kicks in if you're unable to work. However, one dreary possibility baby boomers are starting to face is that of a critical but not fatal illness, such as breast cancer, severe heart attack or stroke. It's that netherworld between death and permanent disablement that pop star Bruce Springsteen described in the song "Jungleland," where inner-city warriors ended up "wounded and not even dead."

Consider, for example, that one in four Canadians suffers from some form of cardiovascular disease and 75,000 a year suffer heart attacks, according to private health insurers Blue Cross Life Insurance Co. of Canada. There are 125,000 new cancer cases reported every year, and one in three Canadians will eventually develop some form of life-threatening cancer. The good news is that these diseases are becoming much less fatal.

HOW TWO POLICIES COMPARE

Illness	Canada Life LifeAdvance	Commercial Union LifeCheque
Cancer	excludes stage A prostate cancer. excludes Duke's stage A colon cancer. excludes tumors in presence of HIV or any cancer diagnosed within 90 days.	same as Canada Life. 60-day waiting period before claim paid.
Stroke	states that a measurable neurological deficit must persist for 30 days.	must persist for 24 hours.
Coronary artery disease	only one affected artery necessary for claim.	two or more abnormalities necessary.
Multiple sclerosis	requires two or mor well-defined neurological abnormalities.	needs only one episode of neurological abnormality.
Paralysis	180-day waiting period.	90-day waiting period for accidents 180-day waiting period for illness.
Major organ transplant	five organs (pancreas not covered).	six organs (including pancreas).
Heart attack	death of portion of heart muscle.	same as Canada Life.
Kidney failure	chronic irreversible failure of two kidneys.	chronic irreversible failure of one kidney.
Blindness	covers blindness where acuity worse than 20/200 or less than 20 degrees field of vision.	total, permanent and irreversible loss of all vision in both eyes.

Source: Sean Long Insurance Agencies Inc., company information

For example, 75% of stroke victims now survive the initial event. The bad news is that strokes result in high costs, particularly one-time cash drains not covered by basic health insurance plans, such as installing stair-lifts or entry ramps in the home.

CRITICAL ILLNESS POLICIES PROVIDE "LIVING BENEFITS"

Advances in medical technology, and the resulting extended lives, have created a need for a new category of insurance called "critical illness" or "dread disease" coverage. While many employer health plans or individual disability-insurance plans will replace income lost in such situations, they may not provide lump-sum payments for such one-time contingencies.

This is the dilemma that prompted Marius Barnard, brother of famous South African heart transplant surgeon Christiaan Barnard, to pioneer critical illness insurance in

A PRODUCT FOR THE GROUP MARKET

Last year, Blue Cross's Ontario unit added critical condition insurance, called LifeLink, to its individual or family health and dental plans at no extra cost, and it has also introduced a similar product for the group market, which is also served by Liberty Health, a unit of Connecticut-based Liberty Mutual. LifeLink provides a $10,000 lump sum to individuals or their spouses under age 55 who suffer from any of 18 conditions. Between 55 and 64, the lump sum drops to $5,000.

Andrew Yorke, chief operating officer of Blue Cross Ontario, predicts LifeLink will "be a very popular product, especially with the baby boom generation, which is more concerned about living benefits rather than death." LifeLink does not include breast cancer but does cover Alzheimer's, Parkinson's disease, senile dementia, multiple sclerosis, blindness, deafness, paralysis (if permanent loss of two or more limbs), third degree burns covering at least 20% of the body, coma, liver or lung failure or transplant. Benefits are not paid if the prospective recipient had the condition before taking out the policy.

Critics point out that $10,000 does not go far and that Blue Cross has excluded the age group 64-plus – most likely to succumb to such conditions. "At the very age bands where the prevalence of these diseases is heightened, the coverage is much less," says Fred Holmes, senior benefits consultant with Towers Perrin Inc. "They're catering to the baby boomers aged 30 to 50 who think they may get these diseases. Some will, but they should read the fine print about how badly you must be caught by the disease for a payout."

Mike Guest, a principal at consultants Ernst & Young, agrees the conditions specified in LifeLink are "catastrophic in nature. You have to be down for the count for these to pay out." Indeed, Blue Cross emphasizes that LifeLink covers only the severe medical conditions that are outlined in the contracts. For a heart attack to qualify it would have to be the most severe category defined by the Canadian Cardiovascular Society.

Notably absent from Blue Cross coverage is HIV or full-blown AIDS, although it has been included in some policies elsewhere. Consultants say such policies don't cover situations in which there's an element of human choice – even though, as the Red Cross tainted blood scare demonstrated, AIDS can be involuntarily contracted. Nor does the Blue Cross literature mention Ebola or other deadly diseases of the 1990s.

South Africa in 1983. He found that while many heart transplant patients were able to prolong their lives, they did so at tremendous financial expense. Unlike life insurance, which only pays beneficiaries after a policyholder dies, critical illness insurance is a "living benefit," providing a one-time, tax-free payment. And while the number of life insurance policies sold worldwide is dropping – and disability insurance sales are flattening – since 1993 the critical illness insurance business has been booming.

Since its adoption in South Africa, critical illness coverage has spread to Australia, Britain, Japan, some U.S. states and now Canada. Half a million policies were sold in the first six months in Japan alone, says Marius Barnard, who was in Canada last summer to promote Canada Life's new LifeAdvance critical illness policy. Early policies covered the "big five" events of heart, coronary bypass, cancer, stroke and renal failure. This soon expanded to what one consultant calls a "big gruesome list" of 20 or 30 conditions, as new insurers sought to differentiate themselves. Still, the lion's share of claims in 1995 were for female cancer, mostly of the breast. Half of all benefits paid out worldwide are for cancer, heart attack or stroke.

INCREASE IN CRITICAL ILLNESS POLICIES IS FUELLED BY A TWO-TIERED MEDICAL SYSTEM

While it costs more to buy a policy as you age, the average age for critical illness claims is just 41. Sixty per cent of recipients use the money to clear debts (primarily house mortgages), 20% invest it for income, 10% take a vacation and 8% buy new vehicles. Toronto insurance broker Sean Long adds that the rise of critical illness insurance is being fuelled by the emergence of a two-tiered medical system in Canada: the increasingly strapped provincial health care system that entails long waits for care and a system for those who can afford to pay for immediate attention. Long divides all the available policies into two groups: a B list of policies that he regards as lacking in some element of coverage and an A list of just two policies, Canada Life's LifeAdvance and Commercial Union's LifeCheque (see accompanying table).

LONG-TERM INSURANCE MAY NOT PROVIDE FOR ONE-TIME COSTS

Long notes that group insurance covers some drugs but not many of the new experimental drugs required to combat cancer. Long-term disability coverage replaces two-thirds of an individual's salary but does not cover the massive one-time costs associated with surviving a critical illness. The Canadian Cancer Society estimates 67% of cancer treatment costs are indirect expenses not covered by provincial plans. In its coverage, Canada Life lists three types of expenses: lifestyle adaptation costs, such as wheelchairs and walkers; transportation expenses; and home conversion expenses. For example, a lift for a circular stairway costs $13,000 while a home elevator runs between $15,000 and $25,000. A porch lift costs $4,500. Wheelchairs are $4,000 to $6,000, and as much as $10,000 for motorized models. It can take more than $12,000 to convert a minivan for wheelchair compatibility. Home-care companions are paid about $100 an eight-hour shift, and a nurse $240 a shift.

The market for critical illness coverage includes self-employed professionals, stress-susceptible executives, single mothers and, generally, baby boomers worried about an illness striking them or their aging parents. You can buy critical illness insurance that pays out as much as $1 million, but most benefits run between $24,000 and $125,000, paid out within 30 days, according to Canada Life.

IF YOU CLAIM A TAX DEDUCTION ON PREMIUMS, THE BENEFITS WILL BE TAXABLE

Like life insurance, the younger someone is when he or she starts paying premiums, the lower the payments. Coverage lasts until age 75, or more expensive coverage can run to age 100. Smokers pay twice as much and some people, such as cocaine users, may be refused coverage altogether, according to Long. If you die before age 75 without making a claim, 100% of the premiums will be refunded to a beneficiary. The cost of coverage can be comparable with that of insuring a car. For a fit 45-year-old male non-smoker, the LifeAdvance premium is $7.11 for each $1,000 of benefit, or $711 a year for a $100,000 policy. Most people do not claim a tax deduction as a medical expense for the premiums paid, since it would make the benefits taxable. The odds of having a critical illness rise with age. Over 50, the odds for a woman getting breast cancer or a male getting prostate cancer are nine to one, according to Commercial Union Life Assurance of Toronto.

THERE ARE FINE POINTS IN YOUR HOME POLICY

Six years ago, I was nursing my new daughter in a warm cocoon of blankets when I heard a resounding crash. With the baby howling wildly, I leapt out of bed and tried frantically (and sleepily) to insert my contact lenses, dropping one in the process. Finally, I groped my way to the kitchen on the main floor to find water and great chunks of sodden plaster everywhere, and a gaping hole where the ceiling had been. Turns out, a steadily dripping pipe on the second floor was behind all the damage. But when I called the insurance adjuster, I discovered that water damage from a drip wasn't covered under our policy.

If the pipe had burst, we'd have been OK. While the repairs to our ceiling weren't that costly – we did them ourselves – the incident brought home for me the importance of choosing a homeowners policy carefully. All that fine print can have a major impact when the time comes to make a claim. The first thing you need to know when you're choosing a homeowners policy is that they come in two basic types: the "all-risk" (also called comprehensive) or the cheaper "named-perils" (standard or basic) policy. According to Insurance Bureau of Canada consultant John Mitchell, both cover damage caused by a range of things, from storms to fires and theft. A named-perils policy, however, lists all the events that will be covered, and if they're not specifically named in the policy, you can't collect.

Your best bet, and by far the most popular, is the all-risk policy, which basically says you're covered for everything unless it's specifically excluded. This means that if by some fluke the roots of your neighbor's tree, which was previously cut down, burst through the asphalt in your driveway, you're going to be covered unless your policy specifically states otherwise. "That's an example of something you couldn't possibly put in a named-perils policy because you never would have thought of it," Mitchell says.

READ YOUR POLICY CAREFULLY TO UNDERSTAND EXACTLY WHAT IS COVERED

The good news is an all-risk policy doesn't cost too much more. You might pay $670 for a named-perils policy that would give you $200,000 coverage on your home and an additional $120,000 on the contents. But for just $40 more, you can get an all-risk policy that covers you for the same amount, according to Iby Moran, an insurance broker with Toronto-based Consolidated Insurance Brokers Ltd. But don't be lulled into a false sense of security just because you've opted for the all-risk policy. That's what we had, and it still didn't cover that collapsed ceiling.

Which brings me to a key point: look closely at the list of exclusions. Some are standard. You can't get flood insurance in Canada, for example, because floods, unlike hail or lightning, are often predictable. Neither is damage covered if it's caused by mud or snow slides, avalanches, insects and vermin, war, nuclear damage or, as we found out, "continuous or repeated seepage" (as from our leaky pipe or a worn roof). "The principle generally is that, as a homeowner, you're expected to take care of your home's maintenance and look for things like that before the situation becomes critical," says Alan Wood, vice-president of IBC's regional office in Edmonton.

COVERAGE VARIES GREATLY FROM POLICY TO POLICY

Beyond those exclusions, you'll find policies vary widely, says Ontario's insurance ombudsman Lea Algar. Some policies won't cover you for damage caused by smashing into your garage with your own car or power surges or outages that result in losses of some kind. Other policies will.

Although they all cover storm damage, you might not be covered for damage caused by snow or ice melting on your roof. And while some include sewer backup insurance as a matter of course, others require you to pay a fee of $10 to $50 a year or don't offer it at all. Earthquake-shock insurance is always extra, but how much more depends on a number of factors, including whether your house is made of brick or wood and where you live; in Toronto, you might pay $170 on a $200,000 home, compared with $600 to $800 if you live in southwestern British Columbia or the St. Lawrence Valley.

When deciding on a policy, try to anticipate your needs and situation. Be aware that some companies refuse to insure homes with wiring, plumbing and a roof that are too old. Indeed, if you own an older home, you'd be well advised to pay the extra $10 or so for "bylaw insurance," which allows you to rebuild in accordance with current building codes (a home built in 1920 on wooden pilings, for example, might have to be rebuilt on a concrete foundation at considerable cost to the owner). You'll also want a replacement-cost rider with automatic inflation adjustment. Basically, it says you're covered for the replacement cost of the home and its contents, not just the original cost or the depreciated value.

IF YOU HAVE EXPENSIVE ITEMS IN YOUR HOME, YOU CAN OBTAIN EXTRA COVERAGE

Insurance companies generally divide your belongings into categories and cap the payments for each. Amounts vary, but there might be a $2,000 limit on furs and jewelry, $5,000 to $10,000 for silverware and $5,000 for software. "If you have expensive items – whether golf clubs or home-office equipment – sit down with your insurance broker and ask specifically whether they're covered," suggests Lenore Davis, senior partner with Dixon Davis & Co. Chartered Financial Planners in Victoria. If they're not, you can pay for extra protection through a "personal articles floater." In terms of liability coverage, your insurer may automatically offer $500,000 coverage, but you're better off opting for the $1 million coverage; at just about $10 extra per year, it's easily affordable. And if you have a housekeeper, a nanny or any other kind of domestic help, make sure they're covered, too.

If you want to save yourself some money, don't skimp on the coverage; opt instead for a higher deductible (the amount of the claim you have to pay). Deductibles can range from $100 to $1,000. By accepting a $500 deductible instead of $250, you might shave 10% to 20% off the cost of your home insurance policy. Keep in mind, too, that homeowner insurance isn't like car insurance – your premium doesn't go up every time you make a claim. That said, many property insurers offer a discount in the range of 5% to 15% if you remain claims-free for a specified period of time, while others offer a flat-rate dollar amount annually. You'll lose the discount, of course, if you have to make a claim.

On the other hand, if your house is subject to repeated burglaries, the insurance company can opt not to cover you. But more likely it will ask you to install an alarm system.

When it comes to collecting after a loss, your biggest problem is going to be remembering what you had. Try to keep documentation for big purchases and consider doing an inventory of your property room by room. Davis suggests videotaping the contents of your home, so that even if everything is completely destroyed, "you've got a visual record." You should probably have any property worth more than $5,000 appraised. And send a copy to your agent, so if an appraisal goes up in flames when your house burns down, the agent has it on file.

NOTIFY YOUR INSURANCE BROKER IMMEDIATELY, AND KEEP RECEIPTS

To avoid running into trouble with your insurer, there are a few things you need to know. First, says Algar, many policies contain conditions, and if you don't abide by them, you can' t collect. For instance, if you're away for more than three to four days during the normal heating season, you must have the water turned off or have a neighbor check on the house daily. "Otherwise, if your pipes burst, you're not covered for the resulting damage." Similarly, if your house is vacant (for example, if you've moved and are trying to sell), you have to let your insurer know and make some arrangements to protect it, or you may not receive a cent if something happens.

You should try to "protect damaged property against any further damage," says Helena Moncrieff, a spokesperson for IBC. Cover a smashed window with a tarp, for example, rather than letting water pour in until your claims adjuster can see it. But keep receipts; there's a good chance your insurer will pay for emergency repairs or hardware needed to secure your home. If you're forced to leave your home and put up at a hotel, hold on to those receipts, too. Most policies will reimburse you for additional living expenses.

Don't launch major repairs without first at least speaking to your insurer. "If it's a sewer back-up, for instance," says Moncrieff, "the insurer will want to come and see your basement to determine whether it's flood water [which isn't covered] or sewage." And if lightning has damaged furniture or electronic equipment, don't simply throw it out. If you do, you will have no proof it ever existed.

As a rule of thumb, keep your insurance broker informed whether you're renovating, operating a home-based business or buying an expensive antique chair. "Talk to your insurance broker every two or three years on the phone, if you don't have time to meet," says Algar. "Communication is key."

CAR INSURANCE: LOGIC DOESN'T ALWAYS APPLY

True story. A driver with a particularly tarnished driving record was facing more than $4,000 to insure his car in Ontario. He found out the cost in Manitoba for the same coverage was less than $1,000. So what did he do? He claimed to live in Manitoba and applied for car insurance there. What's more, he's not the only one. This example, while not necessarily representative of all regional differences, shows the primary beef that most people have with auto insurance is price. Why do Ontario drivers get taken for a ride while people in Manitoba enjoy such discounted rates? As you might expect, the answer can't be framed in simple terms of exploited consumers and fat-cat insurance companies. Contrary to popular belief, insurers – Ontario insurers in particular – are not raking in big bucks from auto insurance.

AUTO INSURANCE RATES VARY FROM PROVINCE TO PROVINCE

From 1986 to 1995, there were only five years in which insurers in Ontario posted a marginal profit on auto insurance. In other years, the industry actually lost money. Much the same is true in other provinces. Rate increases have merely had the effect of maintaining the status quo against rising claim costs. In British Columbia, the government-run insurer posted a net loss of $135 million for 1996. So what gives? Well, for starters, the type of provincial system in place – private, public, tort or no-fault, the kind of car you drive, your driving record and the hits insurance companies take because of fraud all play roles in determining the premium you pay each year.

It's on the claims side – which is divided into two broad areas, bodily injury and vehicle damage – that costs are most sharply felt. As well, insurers are often the victims of unforeseeable events, like the severe winter storm that hit British Columbia at the end of 1997. This is all fine, to a point. But the bottom line, particularly in Ontario, where drivers seem to take the worst beating on price, is that consumers are fed up.

NO-FAULT INSURANCE APPLIES TO BODILY INJURY CLAIMS ONLY

That's why Rob Sampson, Ontario's minister responsible for privatization at the time, spearheaded new auto-insurance legislation in 1995. "We had to stop insurers from holding customers hostage with continuous rate increases and threats of being placed in the high-risk market," he said. "Consumers were afraid to make an insurance claim for fear of rising premiums." Accounting for roughly one-quarter of the general insurance market in Canada, Ontario's auto insurance system acts as a lightning rod for both consumers and politicians. But double-digit yearly increases in premiums weren't the only problem plaguing the system when Mike Harris and his Conservatives took office. A pure no-fault system of insurance – which few understood – proved unable to control costs.

Ontario has experimented with versions of no-fault insurance for eight years, with mixed results. "We never should have used the phrase no fault in the first place," says Stan Griffin of the Insurance Bureau of Canada. He acknowledges the term has caused confusion among consumers and endless frustration for insurers trying to explain it. No-fault insurance applies only to bodily injury claims in auto insurance (fault is still assigned to drivers for vehicle damage claims). Under no-fault, payment to victims of car accidents for injuries is not delayed until blame can be assigned. The tradeoff is that drivers forfeit the right to sue.

TIPS | TO SAVE YOU MONEY

1. Don't go with the first quote you get.
Shop around. The Ontario Insurance Commission publishes an annual *Guide to Rates in Ontario*, which compares premiums from different companies. There is also a telephone service for comparing rates called the *Consumers Guide to Insurance* (1-900-451-0486, toll  charges apply). Several direct telephone insurers can give you a quote in minutes. Check their rates and make sure you are comparing apples and apples.

2. If you don't have time to shop around, contact a licensed insurance broker. Brokers can be a good source of information and can get you a good price. Check with family or friends about brokers they use. Ask the broker about creative ways of saving money, higher deductibles, basic no-frills coverage and how this may affect you in the event of a claim.

3. Wait for your auto insurance policy to expire before you switch companies. Many insurers will penalize you for switching policies midstream.

4. Ask the company or broker about the policy on rate changes after a first claim. Some companies give existing clients a break, but others do not.

5. If you have a teenager who may start driving soon, ask about the insurer's treatment of new drivers. You may be in for an unpleasant surprise when your son is added as a secondary or occasional driver on your policy.

6. Inquire about discounts for joint home and auto insurance policies. Some insurance companies will give you a special rate if you combine the two.

7. Research the make, model and year of your car before purchasing. Insurers have implemented a new historical-claims tracking method for formulating premiums. Some cars, many sports-utility vehicles, for instance, have poor claims or theft records and will result in higher premiums.

8. If you have questions or problems with your policy or a claim, ask your broker for a clear explanation in plain English. Insurance companies have an ombudsman in place to deal with complaints. And the Ontario Insurance Commission recently hired its own ombudsman to act as a last resort for consumer beefs. You can also contact the Insurance Bureau of Canada's Consumer Information Centres across Canada.

9. Ask insurers about value-added programs they offer at no charge. This includes 24-hour assistance and claims reporting lines, support services in case of emergencies and discount cards for other shops and services.

10. Ask the broker or company about the level of service after a claim. Do they use recommended repair shops, for example, or do they provide substitute vehicles following an accident?

Several provinces, including Manitoba, Ontario, Quebec and Saskatchewan, have adopted some form of no-fault insurance to control claims costs. Before the implementation of no-fault insurance in Ontario in 1990, it was estimated that about 30% of claims payments for bodily injuries went to legal fees and court costs, for a total of $500 million in 1989.

No-fault insurance, however, has its own problems, in the form of high benefits and few controls on rehabilitation costs. These problems became obvious in Ontario when Bill 164 came into effect in January 1994. It was an ill-fated piece of legislation that promised generous accident benefits for drivers and tight controls on private insurers. Everyone was to receive what Griffin called Cadillac benefits, even if they were only driving Chevrolets. The system was prone to abuse, especially by private rehabilitation services, and the bottom line reflected this, with average annual premium hikes of more than 10% in 1994 and 1995.

PROVINCIAL GOVERNMENTS TRY TO KEEP AUTO INSURANCE PREMIUMS IN REIN

To counter this trend, the Ontario Tories introduced Bill 59, legislation that promised "rate stability" right in its title. In general, the government sought a balance between no-fault insurance and access to the courts for more serious cases of injury. The legislation introduced a standard level of accident benefits for drivers, with the option of topping up to pay for enhanced coverage. It got much tougher on insurance fraud, raising the fines for those driving without insurance from $500 to $5,000 for a first-time offence. In addition, insurers and health-care providers are working out proper fees and treatment plans for the rehabilitation of car-accident victims to ensure reasonable costs. Early results suggested the legislation achieved its goals, managing to turn back the tide of premium increases. Rates actually decreased by an average 5.4% in the first three months of 1997 and in some cases by as much as 12%.

Auto insurance is legislated by the provinces and there are different schemes across different regions. In British Columbia, Manitoba, Quebec and Saskatchewan, the government has a monopoly on auto insurance, although some of these provinces allow for limited competition on optional coverage and vehicle damage. As the home of medicare, it's hardly surprising that Saskatchewan was first to adopt a public insurance system back in the late 1940s. British Columbia, Manitoba and Quebec followed in the 1970s, frustrated by the inability of the private sector to rein in insurance premiums.

MANITOBA KEEPS COSTS IN CHECK WHILE BRITISH COLUMBIA SEES COSTS SPIRAL

The rest of the provinces have private auto-insurance models. Statistics on rate increases show that government insurers tend to offer lower premiums. Indeed, Manitoba has offered premium decreases to many of its drivers in recent years. Although several government-run programs are stable, others, like the Insurance Corporation of British Columbia (ICBC), are experiencing tough times in the face of rising claims. ICBC is the largest insurer of automobile coverage in Canada and had total written premiums of $2.46 billion in 1995 or about 15.4% of total auto-insurance premiums in the country at the time. The future of this Crown corporation is being reviewed by the provincial government.

The situation in B.C. is enlightening for many auto-insurance regimes across Canada. ICBC has endured steadily rising claims costs this decade. At the same time, it has faced rising expectations for what auto insurance should cover. Indeed, ICBC noted that of the 117,800 injury claims in 1995, more than 70% were from "mostly minor, temporary" cases, and the cost of settling these will be close to $800 million. If you add to this a tort system in which ICBC spent about $223 million in legal costs to resolve claims, you have a recipe for spiralling costs.

ALTHOUGH CARS ARE NOW SAFER, THEY ARE MORE COSTLY TO INSURE

Insurers and regulators across Canada are taking a long look at the high cost of an adversarial legal system on auto insurance, especially when it comes to minor injuries. It is not just the auto insurance system that can affect premiums, but also the kind of car you drive. The types of vehicles on the highways have changed over the years, from two-door cars and family sedans in the 1980s to more sports-utility vehicles and passenger vans. In fact, the number of passenger vans has increased by 37% in the past two years alone. Many of these vehicles have benefited from advances in technology, making them safer and more efficient but, because of their high price, also more costly to insure.

At the same time, insurers are moving to a new system of rating cars based on a system called Canadian Loss Experience Automobile Rating (CLEAR). This system looks closely at the actual claims and theft records of individual makes and models of cars and puts them into rate groups. To date, more than 25 insurers have adopted the CLEAR rating scheme, representing 57% of the Canadian market.

PRACTISING SAFE DRIVING HABITS CAN HELP MAINTAIN YOUR PREMIUMS

Another element that can affect premiums is the kind of driver you are – a prudent person who drives short distances to work or a lane-weaver who speeds from appointment to appointment. Insurers monitor years of driving experience, average amount of driving distance per year, infractions and at-fault accidents very closely and allocate premiums accordingly.

The private-insurance sector in Canada has generally relied on a four-point risk classification system. It weighs the seriousness of infractions, ranking everything from failing to wear a seatbelt to drunk driving. If a driver hits four points, he or she is placed in the residual market, with sharply higher premiums. Insurers are quite well versed in this classification system, but most consumers don't know when they are placed in the high-risk market. Lobby groups such as the Ottawa-based Citizens Forum Advocating Insurance Review have set out to rectify the situation.

In Ontario, the four-point risk classification system will be disbanded and a new system put in place. "This new system must be fair, open and give consumers advance notice of the reasons a driver would be placed in the high-risk market," he says. "The rules must be clear and be given to all drivers." For some drivers, the cost of insurance is simply too high and they have run the risk of doing without it. In a recent crackdown, the Ontario Provincial Police found that one out of every four drivers stopped did not have insurance. Ontario insurance companies paid $43 million in claims last year for accidents involving uninsured drivers. But this represents just one aspect of insurance fraud, a problem that costs the industry an estimated $1.3 billion a year. That is ultimately passed on to consumers in higher premiums.

Insurers have been hit even harder by an alarming increase in accident-benefits fraud rings, which have migrated from the U.S. into Ontario and B.C. These rings stage phony accidents and collect insurance money for supposed injuries.

GLOSSARY OF TERMS

ALL-OR-NONE

This prevents a broker from filling an order in bits and pieces, which can lead to higher commissions because of a minimum cost for each transaction. The transaction must be for the exact number of shares specified.

AMERICAN DEPOSITARY RECEIPT (ADR)

Shares of foreign companies that trade in the U.S. Banks hold the shares and issue certificates that give the holder a right to take possession. However, the stock of these foreign companies often is not registered for sales through a U.S. stock exchange. This arrangement can allow a multinational company to have an international shareholder base without being listed on several stock exchanges.

ANALYSTS

Brokerage firms employ researchers to follow corporate sectors and report on prospects for companies within those groups. Their reports provide the basis for buy or sell recommendations by the firm and for the advice that registered representatives provide to clients.

ANNUAL INFORMATION FORM (AIF)

This document contains information that must by law be disclosed but which is not included in company reports. Insider shareholdings and executive compensation are among the topics covered in the AIF.

ANNUAL REPORTS

This once-a-year accounting to shareholders contains the formal financial statements for the latest fiscal year and a report on operations from management.

ANY PART

The opposite of an all-or-none order.

ASK (OFFER)

The price sought by a seller for a security.

ASSET-BACKED SECURITY (ABS)

Bundled pools of assets are sold as units and these units are a security that is backed by an asset. Mortgage pools were the principal forerunners of the ABS market and this is now a multi-billion-dollar market in the U.S. More recently, banks in the U.S. and elsewhere have bundled credit card receivable and car loans as ABSs. The general theory is that safety in numbers provides a steady flow of income, usually interest income, while losses from defaults are spread across the pool.

AT-THE-MARKET

Buy or sell a specific number of shares at the best available price. If no buyer or seller is willing to move off the current bid-ask spread, these orders go through at the bid or ask price. Usually, these orders are executed quickly if a stock trades actively.

AVERAGE WORK WEEK

When companies have employees working overtime, it's a good sign for economic expansion.

BANK RATE

In practical terms, the bank rate is a signal from the Bank of Canada on what it thinks is the appropriate level for short-term interest rates. Also, it's what the central bank charges in its role as lender of last resort to the financial system. In its policy role, the Bank of Canada sets a 50-basis-point operating band for the overnight interest rate in the money market. As a backstop to banks and other big institutions, the Bank of Canada is a lender or a borrower. Banking rules require commercial banks to maintain minimum levels of reserves that can be turned into cash on demand. If a commercial bank cannot cover its obligations at the end of the business day by borrowing money from other institutions, it can turn to the Bank of Canada for a loan at the bank rate. Conversely, if a bank has surplus funds at the end of the day and cannot find anyone who wants to borrow, the Bank of Canada will take up the funds at a rate that is 50 basis points, or half a percentage point, below the bank rate. Most days, the banks can find better terms in wholesale markets than they would get from the central bank.

BANKERS' ACCEPTANCE (BA)

A form of commercial paper guaranteed by a large financial institution. Bank issuers collect a premium for backstopping both principal and interest and that guarantee means BAs have lower yields than commercial paper. Standard terms for BAs are one, two, three and six months. Futures contracts on BAs are traded on the Montreal Exchange, which provides a pricing mechanism for the money market.

BASIS POINT

The common way of stating a spread is in basis points, which is 1/100th of 1%. Thus the difference between 6% and 7% is 100 basis points.

BEARER SECURITY

A stock or bond certificate that is not registered and that is cashable or tradable by the holder.

BENCHMARKS

Pricing in fixed income markets is done in relation to benchmark securities, such as treasury bills and government bonds. The Bank of Canada defines certain government bond issues as benchmarks. A key criteria is the amount in bonds issued for each benchmark. Usually, it's a minimum of $6 billion. The goal is to have enough bonds in circulation so that there will be ample liquidity in the market and no pricing distortions because of mismatches in supply and demand. Generally, the benchmark is the security that has the best credit rating in a given market. Thus, the benchmark is the security that commands the lowest price and other securities would sell at a premium to the benchmark. For example, a corporation might pay 7% to borrow for 10 years when the federal government can get money at 6%. Government of Canada bonds are seen as safer securities because Ottawa has the ability to tax to repay its debts while a corporation is subject to market forces and can go bankrupt. The Bank of Canada now identifies benchmark bonds for terms of two, three, five, 10 and 30 years. Investment dealers will use other actively traded government issues as benchmarks for intervening years out to 10 years but the central bank's list provides the basic benchmark pricing.

BID

The price offered by a buyer for a security.

BLIND POOLS

This is a special vehicle of the Alberta Stock Exchange, which calls them junior capital pools. Essentially, they are an investment in a management or promoter group. Funds are raised by these groups, which then search out investment projects. Thus, the planned use of funds is not known when the investment is made.

BLOCK TRADE

A trade above a specified volume level (the *Financial Post* carries lists of transactions of more than 100,000 shares or a value of more than $1 million). Usually, a block trade is a transaction between institutional accounts.

BLUE CHIPS

These are the shares of large, reputable companies with a long history of profitability and regular dividend payments. The term is thought to come from poker, where blue chips are worth the most.

BOARD LOTS

This is the basic volume unit in which stocks trade on an exchange. For most stocks traded in North America it is 100 shares. But the definition may be different for shares valued under $5 and over $100.

BONDHOLDERS

Bondholders are a specific class of lender and provide part of the long-term capital of the company. Creditors such as banks and other financial institutions provide operating capital to finance inventory and day-to-day operations. Lenders often have a prior claim on assets of the company.

BOND MARKET

Most bonds have terms between two and 30 years and actively traded issues are within this range. Bonds have been issued for longer terms but generally they are not actively traded.

BOND PRICE AND PRICING

Shortly before a new issue of bonds goes on the market, the underwriter fixes the interest rate according to prevailing rates at the time. Then on the day that trading begins, the bond must be priced for sale. If market yields have moved up or down since the rate was set, the price is adjusted. That means the issuer of the bond – a corporation or a government – will get slightly more or less from investors than it would if the bond were issued at par. Take the example of a 10-year bond that pays interest at 6.125%. But market conditions have changed slightly and on the issue day market yield has to be set at 6.176% in order to attract investors. In this example the price would be 99.624 instead of par at 100.

BONDS

Holders of bonds are lenders and receive regular interest, or coupon, income. Governments, utilities and large corporations are the traditional issuers of bonds and most bonds are rated by credit rating agencies that assess the borrower's ability to repay debts. Bondholders generally stand in front of shareholders in any claim on the assets of a corporation when a company is in financial difficulty. Bonds come in many flavors. They often have provisions that make them more attractive to investors, allowing issuers to offer a lower interest rate. Bonds usually are secured by assets owned by the lender, but this is not always the situation.

BONDS WITH WARRANTS

A bond may be issued with a warrant attached. This gives the investor the right to buy a company's shares within a certain time at an attractive price.

BOUGHT DEAL

Traditional underwritings were done on a "best efforts" basis with the investment dealer acting as intermediary between the seller (the company) and investors. The underwriter would use its best efforts to sell the full amount of the issue but there were no guarantees. A bought deal means the investment dealer buys all of the new shares, thus guaranteeing the total return to the issuer. Dealers command higher fees or commissions by taking on the risk of the success of the underwriting.

BROKER

Now a general term for an investment dealer, but historically this term meant an agent who acted for the buyer or seller and collected a commission for brokering a transaction.

BUILDING PERMITS AND HOUSING STARTS

These two statistical series measure the advance stage of construction activity, so changes found in these reports are good leading indicators.

CALL LOAN RATE

This is the commercial market rate for overnight loans between large financial institutions.

CALL

An option that gives the holder the right to buy the underlying security.

CALLABLE OR REDEEMABLE

The issuer can redeem (or call in) the preferred shares. It usually pays a small premium over the initial issue price when doing so.

CAPITAL GAIN (OR LOSS)

The difference between the purchase price and the sale price of a security.

CAPITALIZATION

The share total times the current market price.

CASH FLOW

A company's net income plus non-cash transactions such as depreciation. This is a measure of funds a company has on hand to carry out day-to-day operations.

CASH MARKET

Also called the spot market. Purchase of goods for delivery on the spot. Commodities in these markets are the underlying assets for derivative markets.

CENTRAL BANK RESERVES

The Bank of Canada and other central banks have savings accounts that can be used in times of crisis to protect a country's monetary interests. This means the central bank stands ready as the buyer of last resort when others are selling the C$. Since currency value is the result of broad economic forces, central banks in large industrial countries cannot maintain an artificial exchange rate. Central banks may occasionally intervene with purchases or sales from official reserves as a way of sending a signal to markets of its view of appropriate monetary policy. But intervention mainly is done with the goal of taking volatility out of the market when there is a run on the currency. The world's reserve currency is the US$, so most holdings by central banks are in US$s. But instead of holding cash, central banks hold U.S. treasury bills or bonds. There are large liquid markets for these securities and they can easily be converted to cash. Central banks also hold Special Drawing Rights (SDRs). An SDR is essentially a central bank currency created by the International Monetary Fund. The value of an SDR is based on the exchange rates of the US$, German mark, Japanese yen, British pound and French franc and the weightings of these currencies in an SDR is proportionate to their IMF quotas.

CERTIFICATE OF DEPOSIT (CD)

Funds deposited with a financial institution for a specific term. CDs are the retail equivalent of money market paper and short-term bonds.

CLASS A OR CLASS B SHARES

Some companies have more than one class of common stock and often these are identified as class A or class B. The usual reason is that voting rights will vary among classes. The origin of this arrangement generally is that an entrepreneurial founder raised funds by selling stock but wanted to retain voting control of the company. One way of achieving this goal was to have voting and non-voting shares, also called restricted shares. Another was to have multiple voting stock, where each share had more votes than the company's standard common stock. Some of these arrangements provided certain dividend guarantees to classes of stock with reduced voting rights. Generally, the voting stock trades at a premium price in the market.

CLOSE

The last price at which a security trades during a trading period.

COLLATERAL TRUST BONDS

Secured by other securities but not property.

COMMERCIAL PAPER

Short-term notes issued by non-financial corporations. Commercial paper is a corporate equivalent of government treasury bills. An example of a commercial paper issuer would be a manufacturer of household appliances that must finance inventories.

COMMODITIES

The raw materials of commerce, such as food products, metals and fuels.

COMMON STOCK (SHARES)

A common stock is an ordinary equity stake in a company. Each share carries one vote in the affairs of the company.

CONSUMER PRICE INDEX (CPI)

This is the most widely used measure of inflation and covers a large basket of consumer goods. The Bank of Canada watches the CPI when setting monetary policy, but the bank's interest is in "core CPI," a definition that excludes energy and food. The theory is that energy and food costs are subject to unpredictable factors, mainly the weather, and price changes for these items are not a true reflection of basic cost pressures in the economy.

CONTRACT

The basic unit in derivatives trading. With stocks, a contract usually represents 100 shares of the underlying security.

CONVERTIBLE BONDS

Bonds that can be exchanged for a company's common shares. Like regular bonds, they pay a fixed rate of interest and have a specified maturity date. Conversion terms are specified at the time of the issue. Convertible bonds combine the security of bonds with the opportunity to make gains from the appreciation of common share prices.

CONVERTIBLE

Convertible preferred shares give the right to convert shares into another class of stock – usually common shares – at a set price.

CORPORATE NOTES

Unsecured promises to pay. As an obligation to pay interest and principal, a note ranks behind all other fixed-interest securities issued by a borrower.

CORPORATE PROFITS

A rise or fall in profits can affect the amount of capital available for business spending and expansion, so profitability is a closely watched indicator.

COUPON VERSUS YIELD

The coupon on a bond is literally the portion of a certificate that is clipped and presented for payment when interest is due but the coupon also is used as a term for the rate of interest a bond pays. Yield is the current return on a bond in the market. As market conditions change, yields on bonds rise or fall. If a bond is bought at par, then the yield and the coupon rate are the same. But if the yield falls, the price of the bond must rise. And rising yields mean falling prices.

COVERED OPTION WRITER

The writer of an option collects premium income and typically the option position is offset by a position in the underlying security so that any loss by the writer in the option is covered by a gain in the underlying security.

CROSS RATES

Foreign exchange values between currencies. Most Canadians think of the C$ in relation to the US$ because the U.S. is Canada's most important trading partner and its most popular tourist destination. But the globalization of commerce and of investing means that security holders must be more aware of currency values. Trading in major currencies now is a huge market and there are futures markets in all the major currencies so that financial institutions and corporate treasurers can hedge currency risk.

CUM DIVIDEND

Stocks trade cum (with) dividend between the time a dividend is declared payable and the date the payment is made.

CUMULATIVE DIVIDENDS

If a company decides not to pay dividends when due, these unpaid dividends accumulate and must be paid before common dividends or when preferred shares are redeemed. With a non-cumulative dividend, there are no arrears.

CURRENCY OPTIONS

Also known as foreign-exchange options, currency options on the C$ trade on U.S. exchanges. Options on other major currencies are traded around the world.

CURRENT ACCOUNT

The accounting of Canada's international dealings. The bottom line is a net number after accounting for exports, imports, flows of investment funds, tourist travel and certain transfers in or out of the country such as pension payments to Canadians living abroad.

CUSIP NUMBER (COMMITTEE ON UNIFORM SECURITY PROCEDURES)

Each security has a unique number, an identification tag that can be useful in identifying securities when doing research.

CYCLICALS

These are shares of companies that are particularly sensitive to changes in economic conditions, usually those changes that naturally occur in the business cycle when the economy is expanding or slowing.

DAY

An order is valid only for the day on which it is placed.

DEBENTURES

Not backed by specific assets. Debentures sometimes are issued by corporations with few tangible assets – such as service companies – or corporations whose assets have already been pledged for another purpose. Some blue chip companies may be able to successfully borrow from investors without pledging assets. A debenture partially backed by some assets is known as a secured debenture.

DERIVATIVES

Derivatives are securities that are "derived" from another security, such as an underlying financial instrument, a stock or a commodity. Also called synthetic securities. Derivatives are contracts between buyer and seller. In the case of exchange-traded derivatives, the specifications are defined by the exchange. Derivative contracts traded over the counter often are tailored to the situation and specifications may vary widely. Futures and options that trade on exchanges are a basic example and derivatives now encompass a broad array of financial products that largely trade in over-the-counter markets.

DIRECTORS

Directors are members of the board and have policy authority over the running of a company, including the power to appoint the chief executive.

DISCLOSURE DOCUMENTS

Details that must be disclosed under regulatory guidelines and rules are contained in the disclosure documents. Reports to shareholders often provide considerable detail beyond the regulated minimum because companies are competing for investor dollars and need to provide reasons why an investor should buy the securities of a particular company.

DISCOUNT BROKER

This term applies to firms that perform a traditional brokerage role as intermediary and do not provide research advice to clients. They charge lower trading fees than the full-service brokers, which include research in their range of services.

DIVIDEND INCOME

The share of a company's profits distributed to a shareholder. Generally, the policy and rate for common share dividends are set by the board of directors. Preferred share dividend rates usually are established in the terms of the issue and can only be suspended under unusual circumstances.

DIVIDEND RECORD DATE

The date on which a dividend is paid, which means the shareholder of record on that date receives the payment.

DIVIDEND YIELD

The annual dividend payment expressed as a percentage of the stock price.

THE DOW

The Dow Jones average of 30 industrials is the world's most widely followed stock index and among the oldest (begun in 1896). It has been expanded beyond the original industrials category and now includes a selection of stocks that is considered representative of the breadth and reach of big business in the U.S.

DURABLE GOODS

Orders for durable goods – products expected to last more than three years, such as business machinery and major household appliances – are a leading indicator because company orders respond to changes in demand. Retail sales of durable goods to consumers are another leading indicator. Because such purchases can be put off during bad times, any increase reflects a changing trend in consumer spending.

ECONOMIC INDICATORS

They are divided into three categories – lagging, coincident and leading. Lagging indicators arrive after the fact; coincident indicators describe current conditions; and leading indicators forecast changes in the economy. Many of these numbers are generated by Statistics Canada, the federal government's central fact-gathering agency. Investors look most closely at leading indicators because economic trends affect prices of securities. Leading indicators include hiring patterns, money supply, corporate profits, housing starts, orders for durable goods, average hours worked by salaried employees and stock market indexes.

EITHER-OR

This is an order to buy one of two or more specified securities. As soon as one order is executed, the others are cancelled.

EARNINGS PER SHARE (EPS)

Net income divided by the number of shares that a company has issued.

EURO

The name for a pan-European currency scheduled to go into circulation in 1999. If development of the euro proceeds according to plan, it will eventually replace the national currencies in Western Europe and become an alternative to the US$ as a reserve currency. The accepted capitalization of the word euro is a formal part of the agreement. It's Euro in Germany and euro everywhere else.

EURODOLLAR

Originally, a market in Europe in US$ deposit claims on U.S. banks. The practical effect of this arrangement allowed these banks to expand their operations outside the U.S. regulatory environment. The market has expanded into other currencies and has become an international financing pool run by the world's largest financial institutions. Generally, the eurocurrency market is beyond the scope of regulation in the home countries of participating banks.

EX-DIVIDEND

Stocks trade ex- (without) dividend after the record date.

EXPANSION
The business cycle has its ups and downs. The good times are called an expansion.

EXPIRY DATE
Futures and options contracts have an end date and the most active trading period usually is within 90 days of expiry. For most exchange traded securities, this date usually is on the third Friday of the month.

EXTENDIBLE AND RETRACTABLE BONDS
An extendible bond gives the holder the right to exchange the bond for a longer-term bond at the same or a higher rate of interest. A retractable bond allows the investor to redeem the bond at par earlier than the original term. For example, a 10-year bond could be redeemed in five years.

FED FUNDS RATE
The U.S. equivalent of the bank rate. The U.S. central bank is the Federal Reserve Board and this is the rate for "funds at the Fed," which are mainly used to cover deficiencies in legal reserves.

FINANCIAL INSTRUMENT
A general term for stocks, bonds, money market paper and currencies.

FINANCIAL STATEMENTS
In the annual report, these are the audited financial results for the year, including a balance sheet, a statement of profit and loss, a statement of retained earnings and a set of notes that explain any unusual items in the reports.

FISCAL YEAR
For most companies, the fiscal year is a January-to-December calendar year, but some companies have different yearends for financial accounting. Retail businesses, for example, tend to have yearends in January or February when inventory levels are lowest.

FOREIGN-PAY BONDS
Some bonds issued by Canadian institutions are denominated in foreign currencies. Foreign-pay bonds are used to raise money in international markets. For example, bonds denominated in yen will appeal to Japanese investors, and those in U.S. funds will appeal to Americans – or they may be bought by Canadian investors seeking exposure to foreign currencies.

FORWARD CONTRACT
Similar to a futures contract, except that a forward contract trades over the counter. Forward exchange rate contracts provide for delivery of a specified currency amount at a fixed exchange rate at a future date. A forward rate agreement (FRA) provides for delivery of a specified amount at a fixed interest charge at a future date. Forwards generally are used by businesses to hedge risk and common terms are up to 12 months.

FUTURES

A contract traded on a recognized exchange in which the seller agrees to deliver a specified commodity or financial instrument at a future date at a specified settlement price. A risk in the futures market is that the seller must pay the price of the underlying security on settlement date, which may be substantially greater than the price on the date on which the contract was sold. Futures are traded on a wide range of farm products, all the basic industrial metals, all the standard industrial fuels, financial market indexes and on several common interest-sensitive instruments, such as benchmark bonds, bankers acceptance notes and treasury bills.

FUTURES OPTIONS

Options on futures contracts for commodities, currencies, stock indexes and other instruments are listed on North American commodities exchanges.

GDP DEFLATER

The national accounts system produces two sets of calculations on economic output. GDP at today's prices is "nominal" GDP. Statistics Canada also calculates GDP using prices in a base year, which is defined as "real" GDP. The difference between real and nominal GDP is inflation and this measure is an implied price index called the GDP deflater.

GROSS DOMESTIC PRODUCT (GDP)

This is the most frequently used measure of Canada's overall economic performance. It's the sum of all the goods and services produced in the economy. A change in GDP represents growth or contraction of the economy. Real GDP is a calculation of national accounts that is adjusted for inflation so that it measures the volume of production, rather than the value. The total value of production is nominal GDP. Comprehensive figures are published every three months and are adjusted to smooth the effects of seasonal changes in the economy. A separate monthly series of seasonally adjusted GDP accounts provides a more frequent monitor of economic activity. At one time, gross national product (GNP) was the conventional measure of economic expansion. The major differences between the two yardsticks are that GDP does not include returns from Canadian investments abroad but does include the returns from foreign capital invested here. GNP includes goods and services produced by Canadians abroad but doesn't include returns to non-residents from Canadian investments in other countries.

GROWTH STOCKS

These are the shares of companies that are seen to have above-average growth potential in revenue so that investors can profit from a rapid rise in market value.

HIGH

The highest price at which a security trades. This usually means during a trading day unless specified otherwise.

INCOME STOCKS

These shares are bought for their dividend potential. Income stocks are of companies with solid earnings records that pay above-average returns to investors.

INDEXES

Indexes are a commonly accepted way of measuring direction of price moves in the stock market. Major indexes contain a representative collection of shares listed on a stock exchange and thus are considered indicators of market direction. Specialized indexes and subindexes of the major indexes are used as benchmarks for stock performance of particular companies within their sectors.

INDUSTRIAL PRODUCT PRICE INDEX

This index measures cost pressures at the factory level.

INSTALMENT RECEIPTS

A securities issue of stocks sold on the instalment plan. Buyers pay for the shares in two or more payments over a specified period. Certificates are issued when the shares are fully paid but they trade as instalment receipts from the time of the first payment. Pricing of instalment receipts in the secondary market will factor in the deferred payments.

INTEREST-RATE OPTIONS

Options on three-month bankers' acceptance notes and on long-term government of Canada bonds trade on the Montreal Exchange.

IPO (INITIAL PUBLIC OFFERING)

This is a new issue of securities offered to the investing public for the first time.

JUNK BONDS

Historically, bond financing has been used to finance projects with long productive lives, such as railways, roads, industrial plants, pipelines and electrical generating stations. More recently, there has been an active market for high yield bonds, colloquially known as junk bonds. These issues have been used to finance high risk activities and corporate restructurings.

LABOR FORCE SURVEY

GDP numbers take time to collect, so economists look for more recent numbers when assessing the state of the economy. The labor force survey is a good measure of changes in the pace of economic activity. Statistics Canada surveys the workforce every month to assess these changes. A few days after the end of each month, it reports on estimates of total employment and the number of people looking for jobs. There are breakdowns by region, gender, age and whether part- or full-time work is being done. The profile of hiring activity from this survey is a good coincident indicator of economic activity.

THE LANGUAGE OF BOND RATINGS

Rating agencies grade bonds on a letter scale that is designed to measure risk. Among the general principles of rating credit is the rule that the top rating goes to the sovereign credit. That means when Canada is rated double A for bonds sold in foreign markets, no province or corporation in Canada can have a higher rating. As a general rule, bonds rated triple B and higher are considered investment grade. Below triple B is non-investment-grade and the jargon term for this category is junk bonds. Investment dealers prefer the term "high-yield" for non-investment-grade, reflecting the fact that issuers of these bonds pay more to borrow because the lender is unlikely to recover much if there is a default. Each rating agency will have a unique way of stating its rating, so that triple A appears slightly differently. However, the meaning of a credit rating at each level is roughly equivalent. (For purposes of illustration, the triple A section shows different ways of stating a rating.) AAA, A++, AAA: Highest-quality bonds. These offer the highest protection for principal and interest. AA: Superior credit quality, but marginally lower than the highest-quality bonds. A: Good to medium-grade bonds, still considered a good risk with substantial protection of interest and principle. Issuers with this rate may be susceptible in an economic downturn. BBB: Medium-grade quality bonds with adequate protection. Some potential weaknesses exist or issuers in this category are at risk to changes in the economic cycle. BB: Lower-medium grade bonds. These offer uncertain protection and may be considered mildly speculative. B: These bonds are considered speculative with little investor protection, especially during times of economic weakness. CCC: Highly speculative bonds that may be in danger of default. CC: Generally, bonds in this category are in default or have other serious problems. C: In default.

LEVERAGE

The use of borrowed funds to buy securities. Otherwise, the purchase of securities, such as futures or options, that only represent a portion of the value of an underlying security. Use of leverage can be profitable even with seemingly small changes in the price of a security but losses can rise quickly when prices move in the wrong direction.

LIBOR (LONDON INTERBANK OFFERED RATE)

Benchmark rates in the eurocurrency market. These are interbank rates for short-term loans in major currencies.

LIMIT

The maximum bid price for a purchase or the minimum sell price. These transactions may take longer to complete than an at-the-market order, or may never be executed.

LIQUIDITY

Liquidity refers to the ability of a market to absorb buy or sell orders with no unusual distortion in pricing.

LOW

The lowest price at which a security trades. This usually means during a trading day unless specified otherwise.

MANAGEMENT

Under the CEO, management has control over the day-to-day operations of the company.

MANAGEMENT DISCUSSION AND ANALYSIS (MD&A)

A statement from management in the annual report that contains a detailed discussion and analysis of information in the annual information form.

MARGIN

A margin account is a loan facility where a brokerage firm acts as a banker to lend funds to a client for investment purposes. Typically, the broker holds the securities as collateral. Rules on margin lending require clients to provide additional funds if the price of a security falls below a pre-set ratio of market price to cash invested by the client.

MARKET PRICE

The most recent price at which a security traded. If there has been no transaction in a security during the trading day, the list of prices will show bid and ask prices (bid on the left, ask on the right).

MERCHANDISE TRADE

The most detailed breakdown in the current account number is for trade in goods, or merchandise trade. This set of statistics includes breakdowns by categories of goods – from autos, computers, pulp, minerals and so on. Other tables break out the numbers based on trade with each of Canada's national trading partners.

MID-CAPS

The mid-cap group are companies that have grown out of the start-up stage but are smaller than the large capitalization blue chips.

MONETARY CONDITIONS INDEX (MCI)

The Bank of Canada developed the MCI as a guide to setting monetary policy. The intent is to recognize the fact that the C$ exchange value is significant in policy setting because export and import volumes now represent a large portion of the national accounts. A decline in interest rates means an easing in monetary conditions but the impact of a drop in rates can be offset by a rise in the value of the currency. MCI combines these two and a 100 basis point change in three-month commercial paper rates is equivalent to a 3% change in trade-weighted value of the C$. The currency value in MCI is an index based on Canada's share of trade with the 10 largest industrial countries.

MONEY

Most Canadians see coins and bills as simply money, but each has a different status. Coins are a commodity sold by the Bank of Canada in its role as fiscal agent for the government. The central bank sells coins to commercial banks. The difference between the production cost and the face value is pure profit. For large denominations, such as the $2 coin, the profit is substantial. Bills, also called banknotes, are a promise to pay and are carried as a liability on the Bank of Canada's balance sheet. Canada is no longer on the gold standard and the practical effect of the central bank's obligation is to pursue policies that protect the value of the currency in international markets.

MONEY MANAGERS

This is a general term for those who oversee the investment of client funds. Fees vary depending on the type of service and the level of client involvement. A mutual fund is a common money management function and in this situation the manager has discretion on investment decisions with a pre-established set of rules and guidelines. Higher levels of individual service will involve consultation with the client but typically these managers will have minimum amounts for individual client portfolio size, often $500,000 or more.

MONEY MARKET

Securities in the money market are short term, up to a year. Generally, the most active markets are for securities with a three-month term.

MONEY SUPPLY, THE 3MS

An increase or decrease in money supply is a sign of loosening or tightening credit conditions. The money supply is the total amount of money in the economy available for investments and transactions. Currency, in the form of bills and coins, is just a small part of the money supply. The rest is held in bank deposits. There are several measures of the money supply in Canada: M1: This is the total of all the currency – banknotes and coins – in circulation outside of chartered banks, plus demand deposits at chartered banks (usually money in business chequing accounts that can be immediately spent). M2: This is M1 plus the money in personal savings deposits and most term deposits, such as guaranteed investment certificates. M2+: This is M2 plus deposits at trust and mortgage loan companies, credit unions, money-market mutual funds and life insurance company annuities. M3: This is M2 plus non-personal fixed-term deposits and foreign currency deposits of residents booked in Canada.

MONTREAL MARKET PORTFOLIO

This Montreal Exchange index is comprised of the 25 most heavily capitalized stocks listed on at least two Canadian exchanges.

MORTGAGE BONDS

Mortgage bonds are secured by mortgaged property. First mortgage bonds are a corporation's senior securities because these bondholders have first crack at the company's assets if the company is liquidated.

MUTUAL FUNDS

Holders of mutual funds are indirect investors. These are pools of money used to buy a variety of securities. A balanced fund will have a mix of basic investment vehicles and there are several types of specialized funds that direct pooled funds into more exotic markets.

NAKED OPTION WRITER

An option writer who does not have an offsetting position in the underlying security is said to be "naked."

NASDAQ COMPOSITE

The National Association of Securities Dealers Automated Quotation (Nasdaq) system is an interdealer market, as distinct from a stock exchange where trades are processed through a neutral intermediary. The Nasdaq composite index includes all shares listed on the senior listings board, which now totals almost 6,000 stocks.

NATIONAL ACCOUNTS

This is the bookkeeping for the country as a whole. The accounts have breakdowns of income and expenditures. On the income side, the broad categories include wages and salaries, corporate profits, interest, investment gains and taxes. Major spending categories include consumer purchases of goods and services, business investment and government buying. On the spending side there are adjustments for changes in inventories and a net calculation of imports minus exports.

NET CHANGE

The change in price from one period to another, usually the latest closing price compared with the previous day's close.

NET INCOME

Money left in the accounts of a business after all expenses and taxes have been paid. Dividends are paid out of net income.

ODD LOTS

Any number shares less than a board lot.

OPEN INTEREST

In options markets, the number of outstanding contracts for a particular series of options.

OPEN OUTCRY (AUCTION) TRADING

The traditional method of trading securities on a stock exchange floor. Transactions are conducted face-to-face. In Canada and the U.S., most stock, bond and currency trading now is done through computer terminals in investment house trading rooms but derivatives trades are still mainly done on trading floors.

OPEN

Also known as a good-till-cancelled order, this remains in effect until executed or cancelled. They are usually orders to buy shares at a specified price and generally a cancellation date is set in advance.

OPTIONS

A right to buy or sell a specific security at a fixed price, called the strike price or exercise price. The holder of an option has no obligation to complete the purchase or sale. Consequently, the risk in buying an option is limited to the purchase price. Options are available on many kinds of investments in Canada and in foreign markets.

ORDER MATCHING ON THE SCREEN

Stock trading systems now allow traders to complete a transaction over a computer network. Elaborate security codes and pre-authorized credit limits are part of the rules for the new digital world of securities trading.

OUT OF THE MONEY

If an option contract expires when the strike price is on the wrong side of the market price, the contract is out of the money.

OUTPUT GAP

When setting monetary policy, the Bank of Canada's goal is to align interest rates with the non-inflationary rate of economic activity. Finding the right mix involves an estimate of the optimum growth rate for the economy. The difference between the optimum rate and the estimated actual rate is the output gap.

PAR VALUE/NO PAR

If a bond or stock has a stated face value, that is the par value. This is the amount that is payable on maturity or liquidation. With bonds, it is common practice to use 100 as par and thus a premium or discount off par is readily seen as a percent. Generally, common stock has no par value while bonds and preferred stock do have par values.

PENNY STOCKS

These shares trade for less than $1, and are usually speculative. The oil and gas and mining industries have a high proportion of penny stocks. In Canada, many of these trade on the Vancouver Stock Exchange.

PLACING AN ORDER WITH A BROKER

The first step is opening an account, at which time the broker will complete a form that includes a risk profile of the investor. When buying securities, investors should be aware of the language of stock orders because sending the wrong signal can be a costly mistake.

PREFERRED STOCK (SHARES)

Holders of preferred shares sit a notch above common shareholders when it comes to payment of dividends or claims on a company's assets. Preferred shareholders are entitled to dividend payments – which can be a fixed or variable amount – before common shareholders get theirs. Like common shareholders, preferred shareholders are part owners of the company but usually are non-voting unless the company falls behind in dividend payments. If a company is dissolved, preferred shareholders are entitled to a share of the company's assets after creditors are paid and before common shareholders receive payments. Preferred shares usually have a par value, which fixes the amount a shareholder gets on redemption. For that reason, the market value of preferred shares may be pegged to changes in general interest rate levels in the economy, much like a bond.

PRICE INDEXES

Measure changes in the cost of a basket of goods over time. Current practice in index design is to use chain-weightings, which adjust for changes in consumption patterns over time.

PRIMARY MARKET

New issues of fixed income securities are simply new loans. Pricing in the primary market is based on yields in the secondary market.

PRIME RATE

At one time, prime was the rate banks charged for loans to their most creditworthy business customers. Now, business financing is much more diverse and the prime rate has become an important benchmark for consumer loans. It's still a rate that applies only to the best credits. Frequently a loan rate will be set in relation to the prime rate – for example, one percentage point above prime.

PROGRAM TRADING

Program trading can apply to any market but often is associated with derivatives. The "program" is a computer program and the existence of massive computing power allows traders to do sophisticated analyses of prices in different markets. A common use of program trading is to find price differences between different markets. An earlier term is arbitrage, which involves buying a security on one exchange and selling on another where stocks are interlisted between two exchanges. Shares of several Canadian companies are listed in Toronto and New York, so currency exchange value is a factor in arbitraging prices between the two markets. Program trading takes arbitrage a step further by trying to find a profit from pricing differences between cash and futures or options markets. Program trading also can be used to change the asset mix of a portfolio.

PROSPECTUS

A legal document that describes securities being offered for sale to the public.

PUT

An option that gives the holder the right to sell the underlying security.

QUARTERLY REPORTS

These documents contain basic financial disclosure on a quarterly schedule plus update reports from management on corporate developments during the year.

RAW MATERIALS PRICE INDEX

Measures costs at the most basic level in the economy.

REAL ESTATE INVESTMENT TRUST (REIT)

An investment trust that holds a combination of real estate assets, including mortgages and property. REITs are structured somewhat like a mutual fund. However, there is one important distinction. With a mutual fund, the potential loss to the investor is limited to the amount invested. With REITs, the issue of liability to the investor is a grey area and there may be an exposure to risk beyond the value of money invested. REITs use the basic trust structure, which provides certain tax advantages to the investors. But a REIT is unlike a standard trust, where the person providing the funds is not the beneficiary. An investor in a REIT also is a beneficiary.

REAL RETURN BONDS

The federal government issues 30-year bonds with interest rates that are adjusted to account for inflation. The base rate is 4.25% and the return is adjusted according to a formula based on the consumer price index.

RECESSION

When things get really bad, it's a recession. The most common definition is two consecutive quarters of decline in real gross domestic product. A recovery begins when the economy starts to move out of the bottom of its cycle, with increasing demand for goods and services, increasing investment and growing employment.

REDEEMABLE BONDS

Also known as callable bonds, they give the issuer the right to pay off – or call – the outstanding debt after a specified date. This allows a corporation to retire high-interest debt when rates drop and borrow elsewhere. Investors often are paid a premium when bonds are called in recognition of the fact they are being deprived of future income.

REGISTERED REPRESENTATIVE OR ACCOUNT EXECUTIVE

These are common terms for brokerage house sales agents who deal with retail clients (ordinary investors) in the buying and selling of securities.

RETRACTABLE

The shareholder can require the issuer to redeem the preferred shares on a specified date at a specified price.

REVENUE

Money taken in from the ongoing operations of a business. Extraordinary items, such as the sale of assets, are not counted as revenue.

RIGHTS

Rights allow the holder to buy more shares directly from the company. Usually, rights are issued at a discount to the prevailing market price, often a deep discount. A specified number of rights allows the holder to purchase a share, usually a common share, as a preset price. Generally, rights have a short lifespan, a few weeks or a few months. Most rights become listed securities and can be traded.

ROYALTY TRUSTS

An investment trust that gets income from royalties. The most common form of income is from owning a stake in an oil or gas well. Royalty trusts have many features in common with REITs.

SECONDARY MARKET

Trading in securities that are already in circulation, which is most of the daily activity that occurs on the Toronto Stock Exchange and other equity markets, is done in the secondary market. When the initial buyer of a security sells, the trade is done in the secondary market. Most of the trading volume in securities markets involves transactions in bonds, stocks, bills and other securities in circulation.

SECURITY CERTIFICATES

Security certificates proof of ownership of stocks or bonds when the name of the beneficial owner is registered. As a practical matter, few investors now take physical delivery of security certificates. Registries are being converted to electronic record keeping and ownership records usually are maintained through an investment dealer.

SETTLEMENT PERIOD

After a securities transaction is executed by the trader, the buyer and seller have a pre-set time limit to complete the deal with a transfer of funds. Settlement periods vary among markets but most transactions must be completed within three days.

SHAREHOLDERS

Shareholders are the owners and the equity stake in the company is represented by stock.

SHORT SALE

The sale of a stock that an investor does not own. The seller uses borrowed shares that are on loan for a fee. The intent of a short sale is to buy at a later date, when the price of a security has fallen, to return the borrowed certificates. If the price rises, the short seller has a loss. Short selling often is done on margin, so a short seller will be forced to "cover" by buying stock if the price rises.

SINKING FUND BONDS

A sinking fund is a sum of money set aside, usually annually, by the issuer of a bond or debenture to be used to repay all or part of the debt by maturity. This provides added security for investors; consequently the yields on sinking fund bonds may be lower than those for other bonds. Redeemable bonds often have sinking fund provisions.

SMALL-CAP STOCKS

These are shares of companies with low capitalization – the number of outstanding shares multiplied by the share price. Small-cap stocks are sometimes defined as having capitalization of $100 million or less.

SPECIALISTS (PROS OR MARKET-MAKERS)

Investment house traders who trade as principals in securities. These traders stand ready to buy or sell and thus ensure there is liquidity in the market.

SPREAD

The difference in interest rates, or yields, between two securities. When the federal government borrows at 6% and a company borrows for the same term at 7%, the spread is one percentage point.

STANDARD & POOR'S 500 (S&P 500)

The Standard & Poor's index of 500 stocks is a broad measure of stock market performance and includes shares of most of the large public companies in the U.S. This index is followed closely by investment professionals because a futures contract based on the index is a key indicator of market trends.

STOCK CONSOLIDATION

The opposite of a stock split. Usually this involves stock of a junior company that is out of favor. Management will consolidate the stock to reflect the reality of the market.

STOCK EXCHANGE SEAT

Canadian exchanges are structured as co-operatives and the members are the firms that make up the investment dealer community. The seatholders are the member representatives from those firms. The term "seat" stems from the days when stocks were traded by brokers sitting around a table.

STOCK INDEX OPTIONS

In major markets, the option on an index is a driving force in the momentum of the cash market. The most widely followed in North America is the option on the S&P 500 index and moves in the market for this option typically are a leading indicator for the direction of prices in the cash market for stocks in that index.

STOCK MARKET INDEXES

The direction of general stock markets reflects investor sentiment about future profits in the business sector.

STOCK OPTIONS

Exchange-traded puts and calls are available on stocks of most senior Canadian companies and some mid-sized firms. A standard equity option usually covers 100 shares, with an expiry date of three, six or nine months from the day it is introduced. A special class of options, called long-term equity anticipation securities (LEAPS), has a two-year term.

STOCK SPLIT

Literally, a subdivision of a company's shares into two or more new shares. Directors of most companies prefer to have the stock price within a reasonable range of the average trading price on the exchange where the issue is listed. If the price rises to a high level, it will be split to bring the price closer to the average trading price. Stock purchases generally are in lots of 100 shares and pricing is aimed at putting the cost of 100 shares within the budget of a typical retail investor.

STOP-LOSS

An order to sell a stock when its price falls below a specified limit, known as the stop price.

STREET NAME

A security certificate that is held in the name of an investment dealer on behalf of a client.

STRIP BONDS (SOMETIMES CALLED STRIPPED BONDS)

Created when an investment dealer literally strips the interest coupons from the bond. High-quality bonds usually are used for this purpose, often the bonds of provincial governments. Coupons and the principal amount, known as the residue, are sold separately at deep discounts. When bond residue matures, the bondholder receives the principal. Holders of the coupons receive the interest payments, but they can't be collected until maturity. That means there are no periodic interest payments to reinvest. The structure of strip bonds means that they are highly sensitive to changes in interest rates. Thus market prices for these instruments can be highly volatile. Another reason for the volatility is that the majority of strip bonds are bought by investors who hold to maturity and this lack of liquidity in many issues affects the price.

SUBORDINATED DEBENTURES

Corporations will meet their obligations to holders of more senior securities before paying their debts to holders of subordinated debentures. The latter's rights are subordinate to those of other creditors.

TERM VERSUS DURATION

The term to maturity is a simple calculation with a calendar. If a bond is issued at par with a fixed interest rate, the calculation of return to maturity is straightforward. Valuing a bond becomes more complicated if the purchase price is not par because a capital gain or loss becomes part of the equation when the bond reaches par at maturity. This involves the concept of duration, which adjusts the term according to present value of coupon and principal. These calculations involve complex formulas and require computer power to assess the relative values of different bonds at different prices.

TIME VALUE

The amount by which the current normal market value of a right, option or warrant exceeds its underlying value. Essentially, time value is the financing cost of a hedge.

TORONTO 35

An index of 35 blue chip stocks on the TSE. It includes most of the big Canadian companies across the major industry sectors.

TOTAL EQUITY CAPITAL

Total equity capital is the number of shares in circulation.

TRADERS

Persons authorized by a stock exchange to buy or sell. In Canada most traders now conduct transactions over computer trading screens in investment house trading rooms. Exchanges also authorize independent traders, called "locals." The objective in having a large pool of traders is to provide liquidity to the market.

TRADING AS PRINCIPAL

Transactions by an investment dealer for its own account. Traditional brokerage firms only acted for clients when trading stocks but banks and bond trading houses frequently traded for their own accounts in currency and fixed income transactions and now the large investment dealers trade as principal in a broad range of securities.

TRANSFER AGENT

Companies have a designated agent, usually a trust company, that maintains a list of shareholders and records all transfers of ownership in shares of the company.

TREASURY BILLS

Short-term notes issued by a government's treasury. They are short-term loans that provide the government with cash for day-to-day operations. The common terms are three, six and 12 months. T-bills are an important element in the securities market because they provide investors with a way of deploying idle cash. T-bill yields are important indicators of interest rates in commercial lending.

TRIPLE WITCHING HOUR

A slang market term for the last hour of a Friday on which quarterly contracts expire in stock futures, stock options and index options. The big volume on these contracts is on a quarterly basis with March, June, September and December expiry dates. Program traders adjust their positions on those dates and this process can cause volatility in underlying cash markets for equities. Those distortions can have a ripple effect on currency and fixed income markets.

TSE 300

An index of the shares of 300 companies listed on the Toronto Stock Exchange. They are mainly the 300 largest companies, although there are other inclusion criteria, such as length of time listed on the TSE and representation in various industry sectors.

UNITS

Securities can be bundled and sold as a unit. Common combinations are a common stock with a right or a warrant attached.

VARIABLE (FLOATING) RATE

A loan pegged to the prime rate is essentially a variable rate loan because the prime rate, and hence the loan rate, can change when monetary conditions change. Usually, the prime rate does not change frequently but there are other loan rate benchmarks that can fluctuate more frequently as conditions change in money and bond markets. For example, a loan rate may be pegged to an average of treasury bill yields over a specified period.

VOLATILITY

In its standard definition, volatility is a measure of the rate of change in the price of a security over a specified time. The usual yardstick is standard deviation from average price. Volatility also has become a sophisticated security in the over-the-counter market where investors take on the risks of volatility in a security, a process that works much like an expensive insurance policy in high-risk markets.

VOLUME

The number of security units traded during a specified period. With stocks it is the number of shares; with bonds and currencies it is the value; and with derivatives, such as futures and options, it is the number of contracts.

VSE COMPOSITE

A Vancouver Stock Exchange index that mainly includes junior companies. Vancouver listings are heavily weighted with junior mining and start-up technology companies.

WARRANTS

A warrant is similar to a right, but usually has a lifespan of a year or more. Typically, warrants are issued as part of a stock offering and the warrant is considered an inducement in the sale of the shares. Like rights, warrants will be listed securities and can be traded.

WHOLESALE FUNDS

A general term for transactions between banks, other large financial institutions and big corporations that have active financing operations (such as carmakers that have financing and leasing subsidiaries). Transaction size in the wholesale market generally is at least $100,000 and often much larger. Interest rates in the wholesale markets influence the cost of funds for small businesses and consumers.

WRITER

The creator of an option, a shorthand term for underwriter.

YIELD CURVE

A list of yields for common terms of treasury bills and government bonds that is displayed graphically. In a normal market, the cost of money rises as the term of the investment lengthens and a graph of these yields appears as a curve.

ZERO-COUPON BONDS

Issued without interest coupons. They are sold at a discount to face value, with the difference between the selling price and the face value representing the investor's return.

NOTES

NOTES

NOTES

NOTES

NOTES